COLLABORATIVE RESEARCH in ORGANIZATIONS

We dedicate this book to our sponsors—the Swedish Foundation for Knowledge and Competence Development (KK Foundation), the Swedish Institute for Working Life (NIWL), AstraZeneca, Ericsson, Telia, Volvo Car Corporation, the Institute for Management of Innovation and Technology (IMIT), Stockholm School of Economics, and Chalmers University of Technology—for sharing our vision about the importance of collaborative research in organizations.

COLLABORATIVE RESEARCH in ORGANIZATIONS

Foundations for Learning, Change, and Theoretical Development

Editors

Niclas Adler
Stockholm School of Economics

A. B. (Rami) Shani
California Polytechnic State University

Alexander Styhre
Chalmers University of Technology

SAGE Publications
International Educational and Professional Publisher
Thousand Oaks ▪ London ▪ New Delhi

For information:

Sage Publications, Inc.
2455 Teller Road
Thousand Oaks, California 91320
E-mail: order@sagepub.com

Sage Publications Ltd.
6 Bonhill Street
London EC2A 4PU
United Kingdom

Sage Publications India Pvt. Ltd.
B-42, Panchsheel Enclave
New Delhi 110 017 India

Printed in the United States of America

Library of Congress Cataloging-in-Publication Data

Adler, Niclas.
Collaborative research in organizations: Foundations for learning,
change, and theoretical development / Niclas Adler,
A. B. (Rami) Shani, Alexander Styhre.
        p. cm.
Includes bibliographical references and index.
ISBN 0-7619-2862-6 (cloth) — ISBN 0-7619-2863-4 (pbk.)
    1. Management—Research. 2. Research teams. I. Shani, Abraham B.
II. Styhre, Alexander. III. Title.
HD30.4.A34 2004
658.4′007′2—dc21   2003004708

This book is printed on acid-free paper.

03   04   05   06   10   9   8   7   6   5   4   3   2   1

Acquisitions Editor:	Al Bruckner
Editorial Assistant:	MaryAnn Vail
Copy Editor:	D. J. Peck
Production Editor:	Diane S. Foster
Typesetter:	C & M Digitals (P) Ltd.
Proofreader:	Sally M. Scott
Indexer:	Molly Hall
Cover Designer:	Janet Foulger

Contents

List of Figures

List of Tables

Foreword I: The Added Value of Collaborative Research to Management Practice

The car industry is facing the dawn of a third century. In some ways, much has changed, yet some of the core managerial issues remain. The fundamental challenges faced during the early formation of the industry in engineering, producing, and selling cars are still with us today. The ways in which managerial challenges are addressed have changed numerous times.

The car industry has, despite recent significant reductions, built up a large overcapacity. This overcapacity has created pressure on pricing, with no room for price increases and with large discounts as a standard. Small margins, together with an intensifying global competition and informed customers demanding more product content, create great challenges in a continuous search for efficiency and synergies in the construction, production, and selling of cars. The car producers are then left with two major choices: follow others in the industry or create their own paths. The first choice will lead to a pure struggle on efficiency, whereas the second choice will lead to a challenge of predictability and branding. Regardless of the choices made by individual car producers, the industry as a whole is facing a number of new and complex challenges. Many demand significantly decreased emissions, and customers are asking for larger cars with stronger engines. The growing demands on efficiency and flexibility in all company processes has led to outsourcing of large subsystems of cars as well as searching for synergies and parallel use of components and modules. At the same time, customers are looking for strong branding, product differentiation, and value for their money.

Volvo Car Corporation has taken a lead position in safety and the environment. It has been continuously launching new features since the introduction of the three-point seat belt in 1959. In 1972, Volvo's first environmental policy was articulated at the UN Environmental Conference in Stockholm, Sweden. This landmark environmental policy continues to guide industrial action worldwide.

Volvo today competes in the premium segment, where economies of scales have to be exploited despite lower potential for large volume and greater demands on differentiation as well as for high product and service quality. The necessity to understand both the targeted market and the nature of the brand becomes even more important. In the case of Volvo, the core values of safety, environment, and quality need to be imprinted into the product and its services. The challenge increases in the outsourced world when we, as a company, do not own the various contact points with the customer as retailers, service shops, and finance and insurance institutions. The product is normally in daily use, the customer has continuous contact with the result of our attempts, and it is a challenge to differentiate through our core values. The products need to be extended with design, joy of driving, and hassle-free ownership also colored by the core values. Being a part of a major car company, Ford Motor Company, has also led to new demands such as internalizing a new corporate culture, communicating in a foreign language, and adopting new management approaches. A 75-year-old company with a strong history and tradition meets a 100-year-old company with a different but strong history and tradition as well. Major challenges in leveraging collective initiatives, structures, tools, and ways of working without losing individual identities emerge.

The questions and considerations that executives deal with tend to be complex and are changing continuously. The number of stakeholders increases, and the nature and logic of their interests often collide. The art of balancing these stakeholders' interests in the long term is at the core of managing. Our strategic and operative planning is dependent on tools, models, and frameworks that support this balancing act. In our operation, we have virtual product development and virtual design. Virtual production is being explored to capture the latest approaches. In research and development (R&D) there is a deep understanding of the complex technologies that constitute the making of a car. The development of our overall management approach has not reached the same advanced level. Management is, and often has to be, guided by experience and feeling, but the opportunity to fully leverage ongoing R&D on management has not yet been fully explored. Virtual management, with the possibility to test actions and decisions before they are made, is not in our hands. Managing a major company leaves little time for the necessary reflection and daily operative questions that often take the focus away from long-term challenges and considerations. Managers are most often left to handle situations without the support of aggregated and systematic learning from colleagues, history, and/or other examples.

Organizations also tend to become more complex and more dependent on boundary-spanning interactions, deliberations, and innovations. In the competition we currently face, competitive advantage is probably just as dependent, or even more dependent, on how we handle our management technology as it is on how we handle the other technologies that we, as a company, base our business on. Our competitive position will be based not only on what products we launch but also on our ability to continuously form strong strategies, organizational designs, and leadership frameworks. To meet the challenges, all of our leaders and managers must continuously evaluate and reflect on how their managerial approaches support the purpose of our organization. Every management solution that is put into action will have its drawbacks, and being aware of these drawbacks will help us to develop and compensate for them.

It is an appealing thought, but it is a major challenge to establish a tradition and capacity for R&D on management in companies. Such R&D could be a continuous source for input into complex managerial decisions, for evaluation and redesign of solutions, and for support in governing various management consultancy endeavors. Such research and development could also be an important vehicle for the necessary support, continuous training, and reflection by all leaders and managers in the company. This volume on collaborative research in organizations opens up a promising path to develop the area of R&D on management technology. However, the challenge is great, and to develop the right research approach that will supplement other traditional orientations is likely to take time.

Since 1997, together with AstraZeneca, Ericsson, Telia, Stockholm School of Economics, and Chalmers University of Technology, we have actively engaged in the early formation of the FENIX program. The purpose of the collaboration is and has been to develop an alternative path for joint R&D on management with researchers and managers from other companies. Six executive Ph.D. candidates from our organization have been selected to be trained in how to initiate, design, and run R&D initiatives in the field of management. This volume captures some of the learning from this special partnership between industry and academy. Niclas Adler, Rami Shani, and Alexander Styhre, with contributions from many of the management researchers associated with the FENIX program, have documented the essence of collaborative research in organizations. The 18 chapters in the book provide a window into the complexity of designing and managing collaborative research efforts in organizations. Collectively, the framing (Part I), lenses and mechanisms (Part II), and nine different illustrations from specific collaborative research efforts in a variety of industrial settings (Part III) present an approach that is worth reading about, reflecting on, and exploring further. At Volvo, this collaboration has been an added value to our practice. The knowledge generated throughout the various collaborative research projects provides an opportunity to address managerial challenges. It also serves as a way in which to build on our knowledge and develop some critical managerial capabilities of reflection in action. Executive Ph.D. candidates seem to provide a promising way of strengthening the collaboration and its outcomes.

The so-called global business society raises new challenges. There is an old saying, "All business is local," and a slogan saying, "Think global, act local." The management processes of tomorrow will have to consider and be able to maximize compromises among local traditions, demands, and cultures and global trends of consumerism such as more value for the money, less loyalty, brand perceptions, and high expectations on customer satisfaction. This book presents a roadmap for gaining the managerial knowledge and competencies needed to address the emerging challenges.

Overcapacity that will trigger incentive wars in the market, coupled with cost reductions, will demand new governance. We will have to take into account that corporate citizenship will play a key role in how to manage companies in the future. Business profits and benefits will need to be balanced with social fairness and responsibility for the environment. We will also need to cope with a new future of global leadership, cultures, and trends that will compete with existing old economies and new economies such as China and India. We foresee a new world of maximized global opportunities and minimized local threats. As managers, we need the best possible prerequisites to cope with the most important challenges and to capture the most promising opportunities. This book articulates one possible path that provides insights and competencies needed to learn about management technology in the emerging global business environment.

—*Hans-Olov Olsson*
President and Chief Executive Officer
Volvo Car Corporation

Foreword II:
Some Challenges of
Collaborative Research

Contemporary writing in the natural, social, and management sciences indicates some fundamental changes in the social production of knowledge (Gibbons et al., 1994; Nowotny, Scott, & Gibbons, 2001; Pettigrew, 1997, 2001; Ziman, 1994). The changes include who is involved in the production of knowledge, the process of knowledge production and types of available knowledge, new levels of international collaboration in research, and new settings and opportunities for knowledge production, dissemination, and use. This thesis of a change in the character of knowledge production rests on a broad-ranging theoretical and empirical argument. Nowotny and colleagues (2001) characterize this as a co-evolutionary process between science and society. The elements of the change are many, but the most often detailed ones include the following:

- A more porous boundary between science and society
- A resultant loss of researcher autonomy
- A breakdown of assumptions about unitary views of science and linear notions of the scientific process
- A greater range of participants in the knowledge development process and greater pluralism of research practice
- A greater recognition of the localized (in time and space) character of research practice and outcomes
- A wider recognition of the emergent, rather than planned, views of the research process
- A recognition of the complex interactions among multiple stakeholders in the research process and a more contested landscape for evaluating the quality and relevance of research processes, outputs, and outcomes

These elements, and the forces driving them, are themselves contested. Even the advocates of a change thesis, such as Gibbons and colleagues (1994) and Ziman (1994), recognize that the process is still emergent, that the rate of change varies in different national and disciplinary communities, and that responses are predictably customized to local institutional, professional, and resource conditions (see also Whitley, 2000). There exists a lively debate about the extent of convergence and divergence of knowledge production among scientific communities in various parts of the world. The normative attraction of the divergent science position is linked to the pragmatic virtues of pluralism in social science (Morgan, 1983; Pettigrew, 2001). One of the lessons from the natural history of the development of the social sciences is that there can be no one best way in which to frame, produce, disseminate, and use knowledge.

The force of these debates about a new social production of knowledge is also penetrating the various fields of management. A recent special issue of the *British Journal of Management* (Hodgkinson, 2001) is a useful place to find the variety of perspectives that exist in the United Kingdom and the United States. The current edited collection, *Collaborative Research in Organizations,* offers an insight into Scandinavian, French, and American sets of experiences. Collaboration and partnering between those in university settings and those in nonuniversity settings is now an increasing feature of knowledge production in the management field and is frequently tied to the aspiration that management knowledge should meet the double hurdle of scholarly quality and relevance (MacLean, MacIntosh, & Grant, 2002; Pettigrew, 1997). The debates on collaboration are also multifaceted, but within them are a number of partially contested assumptions. First, there is the view that collaborative knowledge production is intrinsically superior to unrestrained competition. Second, collaboration offers greater efficiency and value for the money in the use of public and private sector research funds. Third, collaboration can add real tangible value in scholarly research. Through collaboration, we can deliver research outcomes that are not possible with solo or single-team scholarship.

These general observations on collaborative research demand the unpacking of the term *collaboration*. In Chapter 5 of this volume, collaborative research is defined as *an emergent and systematic inquiry process, embedded in a true partnership between researchers and members of a living system for the purpose of generating actionable scientific knowledge.* This is a noble ambition that taps into long-term debates in the social sciences about "knowledge for what purpose" (Lynd, 1939) as well as the humanistic desires of many social and management scientists to both engage with and intervene in the settings they study. Collaborative and interventionist forms of inquiry remain a minority taste in the social sciences. In Part IV of the book, Niclas Adler, Rami Shani, and Alexander Styhre are careful to note the epistemological, political, ethical, and efficiency critiques directed at various kinds of collaborative research. These criticisms are, of course, relative to other forms of inquiry, which themselves have their strengths and weaknesses. There is indeed no one best way in which to frame, produce, disseminate, and use knowledge.

But the word *collaboration* in the context of research activities not only needs unpacking (as this volume begins to do) but also needs theorizing and locating within the more general set of experiences captured under the phrase *collaborative working*. Recent writing on collaboration by Huxham and Vangen (2000) and Huxham and Beech (2003) may offer such a liberating opportunity. One crucial feature of research collaboration not elaborated in this volume, and yet the basis of the reported research studies that are of enormous practical significance, is the rise of international collaborative research in the natural sciences and, increasingly, the social sciences. The management of dispersed research and development collaboration is now crucial in university-, industry-, and government-based science (Boutellier, Cassman, & Von Zeowitz, 1999). Recently, there has been growth in the number of large-scale international collaboration studies in management. Notable examples on both sides of the Atlantic include the GLOBE leadership research (House, Javidan, Hawges, & Dorfman, 2002), the CRANET research on international human resource management (Brewster, Tregaskis, Hegewisch, & Mayne, 1996; Tregaskis, Mahoney, & Atterbury, 2003), and the INNFORM program of research on innovative forms of organizing and company performance (Pettigrew & Fenton, 2000; Pettigrew et al., 2003). The INNFORM program addressed two collaborative themes: scholarly collaboration between geographically dispersed teams and the co-production and co-dissemination of knowledge between those in university settings and those in nonuniversity settings. The experiments in collaborative research chronicled in this volume are timely and important. With this greater openness to research practice come greater possibilities for learning but also some real challenges. Collaborative research may well bring greater complexities and transaction costs in the research process. Will the benefits outweigh the costs? What additional intellectual, social, and political skills are demanded of everyone in these kinds of knowledge production? What are the special challenges imposed on those who coordinate or lead this kind of research, and how do we prepare future generations of scholars to be motivated and skillful in collaborative research? Finally, what kind of knowledge will emanate from collaborative research, and what reception will that knowledge have among scholars, practitioners, and policymakers? These are some of the big questions stimulated by this book. The answers to these important questions will, of course, emerge only after considerable time and extensive debate.

References

Boutellier, R., Cassman, O., & Von Zeowitz, M. (1999). *Managing global innovation*. New York: Springer.

Brewster, C., Tregaskis, O., Hegewisch, A., & Mayne, L. (1996). Comparative research in human resource management. *International Journal of Human Resource Management, 7*, 585–604.

Gibbons, M. C., Limoges, C., Nowotny, H., Schwartzman, S., Scott, P., & Trow, M. (1994). *The new production of knowledge.* London: Sage.

Hodgkinson, G. P. (Ed.). (2001). Facing the future: The nature and purpose of management research re-assessed. *British Journal of Management, 12.* (Special issue)

House, R., Javidan, M., Hawges, P., & Dorfman, P. (2002). Understanding cultures and the implicit leadership theories across the globe: An introduction to project GLOBE. *Journal of World Business, 37,* 3–10.

Huxham, C., & Beech, N. (2003). Contrary prescriptions: Recognizing good practice tensions in management. *Organization Studies, 24,* 69–93.

Huxham, C., & Vangen, S. (2000). Leadership in the shaping and implementation of collaboration agendas. *Academy of Management Journal, 43,* 1159–1177.

Lynd, R. S. (1939). *Knowledge for what? The place of social science in American culture.* Princeton, NJ: Princeton University Press.

MacLean, D., MacIntosh R., & Grant, S. (2002). Mode 2 management research. *British Journal of Management, 13,* 189–208.

Morgan, G. (Ed.). (1983). *Beyond method: Strategies for social research.* Newbury Park, CA: Sage.

Nowotny, H., Scott, A., & Gibbons, M. (2001). *Re-thinking science: Knowledge and the public in an age of uncertainty.* Cambridge, UK: Polity.

Pettigrew, A. M. (1997). The double hurdles for management research. In T. Clarke (Ed.), *Advancements in organizational behaviour: Essays in honour of D. S. Pugh* (pp. 277–296). London: Dartmouth.

Pettigrew, A. M. (2001). Management research after modernism. *British Journal of Management, 12,* 61–70. (Special issue)

Pettigrew, A. M. (Ed.). (2003). *Innovative organizations in international perspective.* London: Sage.

Pettigrew, A. M., & Fenton, E. M. (Eds.). (2000). *The innovating organization.* London: Sage.

Tregaskis, O., Mahoney, C., & Atterbury, S. (2003). International survey methodology: Experiences from the Cranfield Network. In W. Mayrhofs, C. Brewster, & M. Morley (Eds.), *Trends in human resource management in Europe.* London: Butterworth Heinemann.

Whitley, R. (2000). *The intellectual and social organization of the sciences* (2nd ed.). Oxford, UK: Oxford University Press.

Ziman, J. (1994). *Prometheus bound: Science in a dynamic steady state.* Cambridge, UK: Cambridge University Press.

—*Andrew M. Pettigrew*
Professor of Strategy and Organization
Warwick Business School, Associate Dean
Warwick University

Preface

The original idea for this book dates back to a 1-week retreat that we—the FENIX community of researchers and practitioners—held in October 2001. The purpose of the retreat was to reflect, as a community, on our learning from 5 years of participating in (and leading) a set of very ambitious and innovative collaborative research endeavors. The projects were conducted within the context of a long Scandinavian tradition of boundary-spanning collaboration between management researchers and companies. One of the major outcomes of the retreat was the realization that, as a community, we are obligated to share our learning—the result of which is this volume. At the core of the partnership, one can find 36 multidisciplinary researchers and practitioners in diverse industries and geographical locations from 10 different academic institutions and 9 companies.

This volume provides up-to-date, state-of-the-art knowledge on collaborative research in and with organizations. Management science faces a number of challenges and opportunities that are embedded in its interdependencies with management practice. The basic premise in our research is that management science discourse is likely to benefit from substantial experimentation with collaborative management research efforts. Similarly, the organization's ability to handle the increasingly complex management problems requires the development of elaborate approaches for the continuous development and re-creation of strategy formations, organizational designs, and leadership models. This book is about bridging the challenges and opportunities faced by management science and management practice through the exploration of collaborative research approaches.

Numerous books, articles, and other publications can be found that criticize academic management research for being overly theoretical and abstract without sufficiently recognizing the problems and challenges facing the acting manager. Yet there are only a few reported research initiatives that have actively sought to bridge the suggested academy-industry gap. Most of the recent literature focuses on policy-related issues. This book offers empirically based evidence of new collaborative efforts in academy-industry partnership mechanisms and analyzes their theoretical implications. Following the framing of the emerging challenges (Chapters 1 through 4) and the collaborative research approaches, lenses, and mechanisms (Chapters 5 through 9), the central part of the book (Chapters 10 through 18) presents research results from explicit academy-industry collaborative research efforts carried out by researchers in true partnership with individuals in leading corporations. Thus, the book reflects on actual experiments in collaborative methodology and their findings. The final part of the book (Part IV) integrates the findings, puts them in the context of the current state of the art, and identifies directions for the development and sustainability of collaborative research partnerships.

The volume uses, as a point of departure, the works of Kurt Lewin, William Foote Whyte, Einar Thorsrud, Fred Emery, Chris Argyris, Donald Schön, Björn Gustafsen, Jane Bartunek, Meryl Louis, David Cooperrider, Suresh Srivastva, Ed Schein, David Kolb, Tom Cummings, Edward Lawler, Jr., III, Roger Evered, David Coghlan, Frank Friedlander, Peter Reason, Bill Pasmore, and William Torbert, to mention a few researchers who have contributed to the development of collaborative research. Our goal was to advance the scientific knowledge about collaborative research in a comprehensive interdisciplinary and action-oriented approach by integrating practices in successful projects with the existing body of knowledge. As such, the empirical studies present research results from explicit academy-industry joint research efforts. The studies document both the collaborative process of the projects and the specific scientific knowledge and actionable knowledge that were generated.

Students of management and organizational studies, academics, and executives should find this volume to be a valuable resource for learning, reflection, research, and practice. The book should also be of distinct interest to scholarly practitioners in management, specialist staff professionals, managers, and unions. Individuals interested in the emerging field of academy-industry collaborative research partnerships are likely to find the book to be thought provoking. The book offers theoretical contributions to the understanding of academy-industry collaboration in the field of management as well as more empirically based findings and practical advice on how academy-industry collaborative partnerships can be organized and evaluated. The book provides some guidance on how to build and sustain boundary-spanning knowledge creation processes through new types of partnerships.

—*Niclas Adler, A. B. (Rami) Shani,*
and Alexander Styhre
Stockholm, Sweden

Acknowledgments

This volume has been made possible through the setup of and work within the FENIX research program. Hence, the book owes its existence to the founders of FENIX: AstraZeneca, Ericsson, Telia, Volvo Car Corporation, Stockholm School of Economics, Chalmers University of Technology, Institute for Management of Innovation and Technology (IMIT), Foundation for Knowledge and Competence Development (KK Foundation), National Institute of Working Life (ALI), and the Swedish Agency for New Technology Development (NUTEK). The work that is reported in the book would not have been possible without the support, funding, and close cooperation of the participating organizations—AstraZeneca, Ericsson, Volvo, TeleNordia, *Göteborgs Posten* (Gothenburg Daily), SIF (Swedish white-collar trade union), NovoNordisk, Telia, Kaiser Permanente—and the significant support and funding from the KK Foundation.

The idea of assembling this volume and taking on the task of exploring and developing frameworks, models, and approaches for collaborative research is an endeavor inspired by important work of others, and we would especially like to highlight the importance of the work at the Swedish Institute for Administrative Research (SIAR), CGS, Ecoles des Mines, Center for Strategic Studies, Warwick Business School, Orfalea College of Business, and Center for Effective Organization (CEO).

Numerous colleagues took part in exploring the collaborative research approaches, in implementing the change and learning initiatives in the companies, and in aiding our endeavors of making some kind of synthesis out of them. We have a total of 39 contributors to the writing of this volume, and we acknowledge the boundary-spanning cooperation that finally led to the book. In addition to the authors who have helped us to finish the book, many others have made major contributions to the work on which the book rests. We especially acknowledge the invaluable contributions by our colleagues engaged in the FENIX program at Stockholm School of Economics (Sven Hamrefors, Christer Karlsson, Håkan Linnarsson, Jan Löwstedt, Claes-Robert Julander, Ragnar Kling, Cassandra Marshall, Fredrik Nordin, Michael Román, Andrew Schenkel, Ylva Wallentin, Johan Westberg, Gunnar Westling, and Udo Zander); at Chalmers University of Technology (Maria Backman, Bo Bergman, Fredrik Dahlsten, Michael Eriksson, Cecilia Gustafsson, Kamilla Kohn, Mats Lundqvist, Mats Magnusson, Christina Mauléon, Sanne Ollila, Sten Setterberg, Per Svensson, Peter Ullmark, Mats Williander, and Pär Åhlström); at Ecoles des Mines

(Pascal Le Masson and Blanche Segrestin); at Halmstad Högskola (Henrik Florén, Max Lundberg, and Joakim Tell); at Jönköping Business School (Leona Achtenhagen, Mike Danilovic, Leif Melin, and Thomas Müllern); at Lund School of Economics and Management (Thomas Kalling); at University of California, San Diego (Mary Walshok); at National Institute for Working Life (Peter Docherty and other colleagues); at Harvard Business School (Michael Beer); at Trinity College (David Coghlan and Paul Coughlan); at Politechnico di Milano (Mariano Corso, Gianluca Spina, and Roberto Verganti); at Orfalea College of Business, California Polytechnic State University (Michael Stebbins, James Sena, and Ram Krishnan); at Stockholm School of Entrepreneurship (Per-Olof Berg); at Gothenberg School of Economics and Commercial Law (Anders Edström and Torbjörn Stjernberg); and at Royal Institute of Technology (Jan Forslin).

We also acknowledge the many persons from the various organizations who took an active part in pursuing these research projects, and we especially thank the FENIX board for taking an active role in building the experience: Anna Nilsson-Ehle, Lars Engwall, Arne Filipsson, Christer Karlsson, Jan Eric Sundgren, and Sten Wikander (from the former FENIX board), as well as Johan Carlsten, Peter Docherty, Hans Glise, Mats Karlsson, Kerstin Kyhlberg-Hanssen, Charlotta Källbäck, and Udo Zander (current board members).

Niclas Adler acknowledges the people at AstraZeneca, NovoNordisk, and Ericsson who have been engaged in forming the new set of collaborative research projects for inspiration to assembling this volume. He also acknowledges colleagues in the formation of a new research project on "private risk and global regulations" (Jim Foster and Ken Oye at Massachusetts Institute of Technology and Thomas Bernauer at Swiss Federal Institute for Technology) for ideas regarding this book.

Rami Shani acknowledges Dov Eden of Tel Aviv University for the ongoing challenge about scientific research methodologies, the Case Western Reserve University connection, and ongoing stimulating discussion about collaborative research in and around organizations (Frank Friedlander, David Kolb, David Brown, Marty Kaplan, and Gervase Bushe). He also acknowledges Bill Pasmore for triggering his curiosity about the merits and added value of action research and collaborative research in organizations. Special thanks go to the California Polytechnic partnerships, support, and friendship system: Rob Grant, Ram Krishnan, Mike Stebbins, Jim Sena, David Peach, Rebbeca Ellis, Bill Boynton, and Terri Swartz.

Alexander Styhre acknowledges the contributions of the people at Volvo Car Corporation, Ericsson, AstraZeneca, and a number of other companies that have been participating in joint collaborative research projects. In addition, he thanks colleagues at the FENIX research program at Chalmers University of Technology and Stockholm School of Economics for making the experience of working in the academy rewarding. Finally, he acknowledges his former colleagues at Lund University, the late Richard Sotto (his former supervisor), and Pushkala Prasad for showing that academic work can always be something different from what one tends to believe at first sight.

We also acknowledge each other and the FENIX learning community. This volume has been a synergistic effort that would not have been completed without a combination of our experiences, energy, and endurance along with that of our FENIX colleagues. Special thanks also go to our copy editor, Anita Söderberg-Carlsson at FENIX, whose ever cheerful, patient, and constructive support has lightened our work and heightened its quality despite tough time schedules; and to Elaine Elkin-Shani, who made our language understandable to people other than ourselves.

Finally, our deepest thanks go to our wives, Pernilla, Elaine, and Sara, with whom we have discovered the real meaning of collaborative partnerships.

—*Niclas Adler, A. B. (Rami) Shani,*
and Alexander Styhre
Stockholm, Sweden

PART I

Framing the Challenge

Part I of this volume is aimed at capturing and elaborating on some of the major challenges that management research and management practice face. Reviews of historical patterns and emerging characteristics of the nature and logic of the practical and theoretical discourses and approaches are used in framing the future challenge. It is suggested by various authors that collaborative research represents an old tradition in the field of organization and management studies where practical and theoretical interests are no longer seen as being in opposition. The argument advanced in this volume is that the theoretical development of the field and management practice would benefit from closer cooperation with practicing managers. Classics in the field of management and organization studies are often provided by practicing managers and policymakers such as Frederick W. Taylor, Henri Fayol, Mary Parker Follett, and Chester Barnard. For these writers, it was primarily their practical concerns that guided their theoretical contributions. In Part I, the traditions of the "theoretical manager" are referred to as one important component in collaborative research.

In Chapter 1, Hatchuel and Glise present a historical perspective on contemporary management dilemmas. They underline the current combination of a mass financial capitalism and an innovation-based capitalism. Looking to history, they recall three important developments that shaped classic management: the Italian *compania*, the manufacturer model, and the Fayol-Taylor view of the modern enterprise. The authors argue that this legacy is not adapted to the current challenges and that the current trend toward a *neo-compania* model does not fit an innovation-based competition either. So what should be the new principles of management? Following a historical perspective, the authors suggest that a new revolution in management

1

could be triggered by collaborative research efforts in which researchers and innovative firms, such as those in the pharmaceutical/biotech industry, address the challenges of the current dilemmas. Similar to textiles during the 18th century, mechanics during the 19th century, and computers during the 20th century, they could contribute to rebuild management.

In Chapter 2, Starkey and Tempest take as their starting point an influential article by Robert Hayes and William Abernathy, "Managing Our Way to Economic Decline," published in 1980 in the *Harvard Business Review*. It argues that the failure of American managers to keep their companies technologically competitive was inexorably leading to economic decline. The chapter authors adopt the position of the devil's advocate and propose that academic research has itself been a willing, if unconscious, accomplice to economic decline. They argue that far too much management research has little relevance to management practice, so that expenditure on research generates little in the way of added value. Furthermore, research has been used to inform a management curriculum that has too often been preoccupied with the short term and efficiency at the expense of innovation and entrepreneurship. Finally, the authors propose that the task of business schools might be to act as the facilitator of a genuine collaborative effort between practitioners and academics in the process of knowledge creation, sharing, and diffusion.

In Chapter 3, Stymne presents a narrative of his personal experiences from various attempts at creating new knowledge through collaborative research. The journey entails seven milestones, ranging from the shift from a company-centered perspective to a "Simonian" contextual perspective in Swedish business studies around 1960, to the role of Kurt Lewin and how his heritage of ideas for action research and participative management has been developed, to an illustration of how a new organization had to be established in the form of the autonomous research institute SIAR (Swedish Institute for Administrative Research) to make clinical organizational research possible. A fourth milestone is the attempt to change the direction of the quest for industrial democracy toward participative management. The French Grandes Ecoles of Engineering, which provided a cognitive perspective on the role of technology in the process of organizing, is followed by the chapters of IMIT (Institute for Management of Innovation and Technology) that emphasized the concurrent production of academically valid and industrially relevant knowledge. The author finishes his journey in the borderland by elaborating on the experience from FENIX, where the executive Ph.D. candidate is performing the crucial role of a link between academy and industry.

Finally, in Chapter 4, Adler and Norrgren argue that whereas historically management science was built by reflexive practicing managers, today it is carried out by a discourse dominated and driven by academic ideals embedded in theoretical and methodological rigor. They then describe how the different stakeholders prescribe a renewal by the introduction of different collaborative research approaches. This leads to two fundamental questions:

1. Can management research contribute to management practice? If so, can practicing managers become convinced that they can gain from true collaboration with organizations?

2. Can academic researchers become convinced of the added value of collaboration with practitioners?

The authors state that these questions need to be answered not only through academic debates and stakeholder statements but also through real experimentation and reflections. They then use illustrations from actual experiments and their formation and discuss and analyze how the strategic discourse and intent expressed by stakeholders are put into action from the perspective of research organizations pursuing a collaborative approach.

Taken together, the chapters in Part I frame the challenge facing academy and industry and set the stage for the exploration of collaborative management research. Part II provides alternative roadmaps of collaborative research, lenses, and mechanisms, whereas Part III captures specific illustrations in diverse companies and industries. The four chapters of Part I represent a framework from which the development of individual collaborative research projects can be examined.

1

Rebuilding Management

A Historical Perspective

Armand Hatchuel and Hans Glise

During the last third of the 20th century, a new world emerged. The whole landscape of science and engineering was changed by the combination of computation and communication techniques. In addition, the discipline of biology gave birth to new sciences and industries. During the same period, education, training, and research became central regulating processes of social and economic dynamics, an evolution now popular through the concept of "knowledge society." The advanced world is now largely urban and highly skilled, contrasting more than ever with developing countries. An increase in wealth and welfare systems (e.g., pension funds) spurred unprecedented developments of worldwide financial markets. In reaction, modern societies showed a real ability to change rapidly. In both Europe and the United States, deep cultural revolutions occurred concerning family life, customs, habits, and tastes. These countries are now far different from what they were at the end of the 1960s. Finally, the late 20th century was the first period in history to witness the joint consequences of modernity, education, capitalism, and democracy.

Such a major transformation could not leave management practices unchallenged. The persistent debates about company governance, the financial pressures of nervous stock markets, the complexity and uncertainty of industrial networks and alliances, the emergence of new demands and values from clients and consumers, the increased empowerment of employees, and the difficulties of globalization are only the visible signs of a new era of tensions about the nature and accountability of management. Indeed, businesses have never been easy to run. Yet nearly a century of teaching and research in business popularized the idea that management concepts, techniques, and principles were well established. This view is no longer unquestioned. The aim of this chapter is to show that contemporary tensions, issues, and dilemmas faced by companies and organizations require a real *aggiornamento* of existing managerial principles.

This chapter is structured as follows. First, we briefly review three of the main revolutions that made "management" as we know it: the *compania* model, the manufacturer model, and the Fayolian-Taylorian legacy. Second, we show that these three models are now challenged by a new destructive dilemma that results from the simultaneous development of a new stock market-based approach of the firm and of a competition regime based on "intensive innovation." These conflicting constraints paved the way for a "*neo-compania* model." Yet this model neglects the long-term collective learning and cooperation required by intensive innovation. Third, the pharmaceutical and bioscience industries are evoked as some of the best places where these tensions can be observed. Therefore, they may play a major role in the development of new approaches of management. Finally, the question of how we rebuild management research is raised. The concluding section of the chapter sketches some principles for such a breakthrough.

Three Revolutions That Shaped Classic Management

What is management? The shortest answer could be that management is what managers do. The problem is that the commercial companies of the Italian Renaissance were not managed like the enterprises of the 20th and 21st centuries. We could restrict the answer to contemporary managers, but what about future managers? One can argue that management is driven by some constant tasks. Like the Renaissance merchants, modern managers *buy, sell,* or *produce* certain goods or services. They *take risks* and *deal with employees and partners*. Still, such a standardized description masks the change over time of the content, processes, and competencies required by these tasks. The Renaissance merchants could hardly imagine that the entrepreneurs of the industrial revolution would be philosophers and scientists. The latter never foresaw that the bureaucratic complexity of some modern companies would be more important than the political and administrative systems of cities and states.

If one surveys the management principles and tools of a new high-tech company, a mix of old and new systems will appear. Most accounting principles are more than five centuries old, whereas the software supporting them did not exist before the 1970s. Contemporary management is the accumulation of several managerial revolutions, and any given company uses several layers of this legacy without even being conscious of doing so. Breakthroughs in management were never written on a white sheet of paper. They transformed and extended existing concepts and methods. But let us now take a look at some of the main layers that made management history.

The Italian Compania:
Profit Centers, Accounts, and Collective Ventures

Nearly all the basics of business were already established around 1500 at the end of the Italian Renaissance. During the Middle Ages, Europe witnessed the formation of a system of international commerce. From Asia to England, from Africa to the Baltic Sea, goods were transported, exchanged, and sold. Cities began to organize so as to host the merchants, to rule their activities, and to provide them with protection and litigation systems. The complexity of trade, travel, and change favored innovative forms of association, payment, and credit. The banking system co-emerged with *companias,* a specific form of collective business that flourished particularly in northern Italy during the Renaissance times (Favier, 1987; Origo, 1957). The practices of the compania constituted a "management model." It shaped and influenced all of what was later called economic and business thinking. Contrary to perceived wisdom, it is not economic and business theory that gave birth to the compania. History tells us that the reverse process occurred. It was the innovative practice of the Italian merchants that served as a reference for the emerging economic and business thinking. This can be established by looking at how the model of the compania provided answers to the two issues of "company identity" and "value creating knowledge" discussed earlier in the chapter.

The Compania's Identity: Both Individual and Collective. The word *compania* speaks for itself. The first forms of collective business established their identities on friendship or family links (*compagno* means "friend"). However, with the extension and complexity of operations, the links between members of the same compania became more formal and contractual, allowing membership to persons having no family links with the founders of the companies. In spite of these interpersonal relations, the compania was never thought of as a permanent endeavor. Companias were limited in time and scope. Moreover, inside a compania, a new commercial opportunity could lead to the formation of a different entity dedicated to the new trade. Old members could decide their share in the new business. Hence, the model of the compania combined collective and individual identities. The major companias were ruled by their founders, but each compania was a collection of related businesses where the "parent" compania was committed diversely. The parent compania could be the main partner or be represented by a commissioned member. Finally, the compania was a structured coalition of individual merchants, each one having a different commitment to the whole. In modern language, the compania appeared not only as a network but also as several clusters of "profit centers." This model determined our view of business, capital, and shareholding. However, if companias had employees, this type of relationship had, at that time, only a small part in the identity of the whole business.

Creating Knowledge in the Renaissance Compania: Mail, Accounting, and Social Geography. Companias were entirely devoted to commerce. They designed complex operations, trading goods, and credit involving several partners in highly turbulent and uncertain environments. Famous Tuscan companias shared regular mailing services (Origo, 1957). Some merchants wrote thousands of business letters during their lifetimes. New information on events, positions, goods, partners, and payments was already vital. The merchant philosophy did not separate knowledge from action. In commercial activities, knowledge determines the nature of action, and action contributes to learning both for oneself and for others. This conception of rationalized action prepared for the development of a "scientific logic" (Favier, 1987). Reliable accounting was crucial for the compania's governability. It provided a means for reflexive practice. It was also a tool for control and trust within and outside the compania. The famous interpretation by Luca Paciolo of double-entry accounting (published in 1495 inside a treatise on arithmetic) is a good indication of the sophistication reached by Venetian traders. The compania model was described as a simultaneous flow of goods (or money) and knowledge (via bookkeeping). Yet accounting was not enough to perform and extend the trade. The Italian merchants developed special schools for trade. They supported the realization of books, maps, and instruments that helped in traveling, described tastes and habits of other people, and gave access to know-how. Arithmetic, astronomy, and geography were taught in these schools. Beyond intellectual curiosity, such education had an operational value for the core activities of the merchants. What management theory and practice owes to the Italian compania cannot be overemphasized. This model settled new foundations for business and economic theory. It invented accounting, markets, and shares. It prepared for the scientific revolution of the 16th and 17th centuries. Nevertheless, it was tailored for a commercial company and not for a manufacturing one.

The Management of Manufacturers: Corporate Bodies and Technical Departments

The model of the compania came from commerce. The merchants of the Italian Renaissance had no reason to commit themselves to production. They could rely on guilds and artisans to create the goods they sold. The process that brought a generation of "entrepreneurs" to design and build manufacturers took nearly two more centuries. Establishing a manufacturer responded to different opportunities. Many of the French manufacturers of the 17th century corresponded to a public policy aiming to support new trades or to protect old ones (Ladurie, 1991). The British manufacturers of the 18th century resulted from different entrepreneurial logics. Whereas the early textile manufacturers were seeking economies of scale, this was not the case in metalworks or potteries, where process innovation and new machinery were better reasons to establish a new manufacturer. Among the British heroes of the industrial revolution, one can easily differentiate several manufacturing strategies (Berg, 1994; Schofield, 1963). The management of manufacturers had a few things in common with the old compania. For sure, the basics of accounting and commerce were still useful, even if they needed important modifications. Several problems raised by manufacturers were nearly completely new. They led a new generation of authors, such as Charles Babbage in his book *Economy of Machines and Manufactures* (Babbage, 1832), to call for a new era in management. One chapter of the book offers a method on "how to observe and evaluate a manufacturer"; obviously, bookkeeping could not capture manufacturing costs and ways of improvement. During the same years, the newborn railway companies began to expand the manufacturing rationale on a gigantic scale, introducing communication and timetable techniques as central management tools. The new manufacturing world asked for the aggiornamento of the compania model.

The Collective Identity of Manufacturing Companies. The merchant compania was a complex network often scattered among various locations. The manufacturer model was linked to a territory. Within the shops, it required new rules, discipline, and order. Also, separated trades became interdependent and coordinated through control and circulation patterns. The monetary resources that were needed to establish a manufacturer or railway company were no longer open to individuals, even the richest, and the risks were much higher. The compania was virtual and invisible, often requiring delegation and distant management. The manufacturer was concrete and visible, and it allowed direct control of operations. Its collective nature was obvious, and it gave birth to new labor unions. These unions reinforced the vision of the manufacturer as a new social world, a new model of work and collective action that rebuilt a new image of the "company." During the 19th century, the concept of "corporate body" established the manufacturing company as an institution and a legal entity. However, the old membership philosophy of the compania was not adapted to the new personnel. Workers and employees of the new manufacturers developed new forms of identities through unions. The history of what was later called industrial relations is well known. It gave birth to a new management model that displayed a new layer above the old compania model.

Creating Valuable Knowledge in the Manufacturing System. Settling a manufacturer required preexisting knowledge and tools. Yet manufacturers became learning places for both workers and employers. Experiments, tests, and comparative analysis were much easier than in the old dispersed shops. Also, a new logic of accounting became possible. The problem of balancing payments and debts among various merchants no longer existed and was now one of creating cost control and quality (Parker & Yamey, 1997). The impressive innovative power of the industrial revolution is one of the consequences of the manufacturing system. New management required more than arithmetic and geography, like in the merchant compania. Scientific management is traditionally linked to Taylorism, but history confirms that the early manufacturers had already understood the managerial use of scientific inquiry in the improvement of their trade (Schofield, 1963). Within the manufacturing model, businessmen were even more committed to complex commercial actions (suppliers and clients were vital), but they were different from their merchant ancestors. A new managerial identity emerged as new types of knowledge and skills appeared: Engineering, organization, finance, law, and philosophy were of immediate value.[1]

With the manufacturing model, management was no longer limited to flair, trickery, or inborn business talent. The new industrial leader was not viewed as a merchant purely taking advantage of supply and demand. He was perceived as an empire builder who creates new goods, new plants, and new jobs. The discourse of political economy praised the entrepreneurs because they created profits and jobs. A powerful figure could also oppress workers or creditors when his action was not counterbalanced by unions or state regulations. During the 19th century, economic knowledge became an academic discipline. Yet new management principles and tools appeared more in engineering reviews and textbooks than in economics. At the turn of the 20th century, a new revolution in management openly criticized the economic view of business. The modern enterprise was born.

The Foundations of the Modern Enterprise: The Fayolian-Taylorian Legacy

The beginning of the 20th century was an intense and creative period for management. Obviously, management was not a new phenomenon at that time. Yet it is widely accepted that from 1890 to 1920, the essential foundations of "modern management" were settled through the seminal contributions of Henri Fayol and Frederic Taylor. The "fathers of modern management" were neither great merchants nor great entrepreneurs; neither Fayol nor Taylor created new businesses.[2] They both were employed as managers by industrial companies (mining and metal making), where they became directors. Fayol was at the top management level of the company, and Taylor was at the plant level. What change did they make to the compania model or to the manufacturing model? Actually, they contributed to two major evolutions that led to our concept of the modern enterprise.

The New Identity of Companies and Managers. Fayol belonged to the first generation of engineers and reached an executive position in a great company but was not an owner. During his long career, the extension of manufacturing, the intensity of work organization, and the speed of technological change increased markedly. Fayol described management as a varied and continuous process requiring appropriate information, multiple skills, and coordination ability. This process could no longer be run by board members or owners because they had lost direct contact with the day-to-day operations. Fayol formulated a theoretical distinction between the board members and the "executive managers." However, the consequences of this distinction went far beyond a mere job description. What was the rationale of these new executive managers? What would be their goals and values? These new players became the human symbols of a new concept of business. They were the new identity and visible body of the modern corporation. This new entity takes into account several stakeholders and tries to create wealth, loyalty, welfare, or brand in an enduring way.

A New Source of Knowledge: Design and Production as a Scientific Process. Taylor's contribution aimed at a similar philosophy but through a different path. He criticized existing employee-employer relations (Taylor, 1895). In spite of a new manufacturing culture, the wage system still belonged to the compania history. Job payment was still organized as if the workers were individual merchants; they had to bargain piece rates and work assignments with the foremen. Taylor fiercely criticized such trade-offs. He rejected the idea that accurate work times could result from a bargaining process between foremen and workers, and he advocated that work rules be established through scientific studies performed by experts and specialists commissioned by the managers. This view meant that important changes should occur on the shop floor. Plant managers had to feel fully responsible for the whole operational process occurring in the factory. Consequently, the enterprise should be perceived as a well-regulated social system and not only as a set of commercial relations between employers and employees. This meant that employment was not limited to a mere purchase of a workforce. It also meant that industrial work should be perceived as a mix of individual efforts, adherence to factory rules, and willingness to learn. Workers were now supposed to receive specific training, to develop workplace relations, and to prove their capabilities and autonomy if they expected careers in the company. This new vision was consistent with the increasing social role of enterprises in modern societies. Under Taylorism, work—however simple or complex—required research, expertise, and methodology.

All this paved the way for the *white-collar worker* and scientific revolution that followed the Fayolian and Taylorian breakthroughs. In the enterprise of the late 20th century, research, design, and development became large parts of the big companies. Obviously, the doctrines of both Fayol and Taylor contributed to building a new collective identity of the company and a new perception of the learning processes it required. We still see business as a compania when we look for monetary flow, assets, and credits. We see it as a manufacturer when we approach the operational aspects of its processes. And we think of it as an enterprise when we adopt a strategic framework to look at all of the capabilities, resources, and duties that these entities develop in our societies.

This third management model favored a better integration of the enterprise with modern societies. Managers became popular professionals. Western governments became proud of their industrial champions, and advanced nations allocated important resources to the development of enterprises. When the Communist countries collapsed at the end of the 1980s, it became obvious that with the special types of capitalism, where companies can grow, where they can create wealth and jobs, and where regulations protect workers, welfare had no realistic competitor. Yet it was not the end of history for management. A new era, where management would be severely challenged, was already beginning.

The Dilemmas of Contemporary Businesses

As stated earlier, the last decades of the 20th century were characterized by a steady increase in wealth and education in the advanced societies of the West and East. In these countries, the values of democracy, autonomy, and individualism were the values not only of the "elite" but also of a large "middle class" of white-collar and highly skilled workers and employees. In most countries, the numbers of engineers, scientists, and graduates increased each year in significant proportions. Meanwhile, the emergence of powerful mass media (e.g., radio, television, the Internet) contributed to the extension of fashion and to systematically organized obsolescence and renewal of tastes, habits, and values. Sports, leisure/travel, health, quality of life, and popular art are now standard aspirations in major parts of the democratic societies. All of these changes deeply transformed "consumption" and destabilized the relationship between ownership and enterprise.

The New Logic of Consumption:
Intensive Innovation-Based Capitalism

Advanced societies hold the classic economic view that consumption, as determined by needs, revenue, and individual preferences, has limited relevance. Advertisement policies, credit systems, brands, collective cultural trends, and opinion leaders (Hatchuel, 1996) are often better descriptors of contemporary consumption than the old ones. The wealthier and the more educated people become, the more they desire self-realization through social differentiation and social innovation. These deep cultural changes contributed to new critical movements (around environmental, gender, and humanitarian issues). They are no longer determined by the classic employee-employer antagonism. It is irrelevant and oversimplistic to encompass these movements in the popular concept of *globalization*. To a large extent, these changes have been built endogenously by wealth and education. The increase of exchange among nations that occurred during the same period can be perceived not as a cause but rather as a consequence of such long-term trends. In modern terms, globalization should be viewed as "co-emerging" with the enrichment and educational trends of postwar societies.

One quick way in which to comprehend the intensity of these changes is to compare a popular car from the 1970s with one from the year 2000. Even for the nonspecialist, changes in design are obvious. Recent popular cars offer a large variety of options, add-ons, and choices. In the newer car, comfort, security, reduced noise, and practicality of use or functionality are obviously improved. Gas consumption and pollution are substantially diminished. In reality, these evolutions contributed to a new form of competition that has been labeled "intensive innovation-based competition" (Hatchuel, 1996; Hatchuel, Lemasson, & Weil, 2002). The compania, the manufacturer model, and the Fayolian-Taylorian doctrines were not prepared for this form of competition in classic financial contexts. In the new context of financial mass markets, it is not that far from making a square out of the circle.

The New Logic of Business Ownership: The Destabilizing Effects of Financial Mass Markets

Another direct consequence of increased wealth and education in welfare societies is the well-known deregulation of financial markets and the formation of powerful pension funds and financial companies. The more modern societies organized a popular capitalism, the more they organized a new major dilemma for managers. Traditionally, citizens of advanced societies had a conflict between their interest as consumers and their interest as salaried producers. Consumers seek low prices and competitive pressure on companies, whereas salaried workers expect high wages and a stable working environment. In addition to this old antagonism, "mass capitalism" added a new conflict of interest between shareholders and employees. Shareholders want quick returns, high bonuses, tight control on managers, and open financial markets. Because anyone can be a consumer, an employee, and a shareholder simultaneously, the overall pressure on companies necessarily increases as mass capitalism increases. This is obviously what happened during the past two decades or so. The image of "financial capitalism" became a new source of criticism, amplified by the fact that profitable companies could nevertheless adopt downsizing plans to improve their shareholders' value. During the same period, the development of debates concerning "corporate governance" and "business ethics" was also an important sign of the contemporary lack of legitimate rules concerning top management. In spite of its peculiarities, the Enron/Arthur Andersen affair will probably stand as a landmark case for this new history of management.

The central role of innovation in competitiveness and the emergence of mass capitalism are not the only changes that are now challenging management. One may also consider the need for globalization strategies, the necessity of developing core competences and human capital, and the network-based structuring of enterprises. But most of these popular issues can be perceived as consequences of these two basic changes. Moreover, these two evolutions settle a central dilemma between the complex collective learning that is required by innovation and the financial logic that creates strong incentives toward externalization and contractual logic.

Networks and Business Units: The Logic of the Neo-Compania Model

The most popular of these new managerial trends, both in practice and in the literature, can be placed under the same umbrella: a neo-compania model of management whose main features are now popular and can be sketched.

A Network and Contractual Logic Inside and Outside the Firm. The basic philosophy of this model is rather old and traces back to the Italian compania. In modern economic jargon, it says that a business or collective entity should be viewed as a "nexus of contracts" (Demsetz, 1988). This entity should limit itself, whenever possible, to coordinating and integrating a set of external suppliers. This structure is already common in the building trade and the movie business. One can even tell that historically a company without stable suppliers could not survive and that the machine tool industry relied heavily on suppliers since its birth. But the notion of a network company attracted more and more management discourse. This can be recognized in the huge amount of literature from various disciplines on the concept of "network company" or similar concepts.[3] The main advantages attached to this model are linked to its supposed robustness to turbulent markets and to its flexibility for introducing new and radical technologies.

Organizing by Projects and Business Units. Obviously, even a strong strategy of outsourcing will not clear up firms (Jarillo, 1993; Miles & Snow, 1992). Yet the same network philosophy is also used inside the firm. Within companies, it is widely advocated to enhance "project-based organizations" or "business units" or any form of empowered teams to which measurable goals can be assigned. The underlying logic seems to reach a generalized division of activities to emphasize and control accountability and commitment from each division. Ideally, each unit should be a "profit" center or a "quasi-firm" that may be easily supported or downsized according to its results. This scheme has obvious limitations, but it describes correctly the core philosophy of the neo-compania model.

Human Resources Flexibility. Not surprisingly, in the model of the neo-compania, each individual is viewed as an individual entrepreneur who has to choose continuously between leaving or staying in the compania. From the company's point of view, the personal development of employees can still be favored, but a planned career is no longer a realistic approach (Hall, 1996). From the employee's point of view, the only robust logic is to maintain a good level of employability that allows job mobility from one company to another.

Management Under Tight Shareholder Control. It is now widely recognized in the media that new corporate governance principles are driven by the necessity to obtain transparency and control of a manager's actions by shareholders and independent administrators.

Taken as a whole, the preceding four features seem strongly consistent. The underlying thought can be described as a return to the early ages of business and explains the label of neo-compania. The neo-compania means easier management of the firm's domain and frontiers, be it through acquisitions or downsizing. It means a strong decentralization of decision processes, increased autonomy of work units, and clear figures of profitability from each part of the company. It allows quick strategies that can send good signals to the stock market. The neo-compania model is attractive for managers, shareholders, and financial analysts. Hence, it is the management model that mirrors nearly perfectly the financial mass market requirements. Yet in spite of its alleged advantages, the neo-compania model is not adapted to the innovation processes that are required by contemporary competition. Instead of renewing the Fayolian-Taylorian legacy, it tends to abandon it.

Alternative Management Models
for Innovation-Based Competitiveness

The main weakness underlying the neo-compania model literature is its oversimplistic and noncontextual treatment, even when it seems to succeed. Moreover, research shows that effort has been made to limit its drawbacks and to foster collective learning and dynamic cooperation that are needed in a context of intensive innovation (Hatchuel, 2001).

The Debates in the Literature: Neglecting the Contemporary Context.
Network-based organizations are usually compared with integrated companies or hierarchies, as if the content and meaning of hierarchy and integration were unique and straightforward. If the latter were true, why can we observe some "hierarchies" that are innovative and others that are not? The comparison is made while looking for universal advantages or shortcomings of each model as if the form, speed, and content of competition had no influence (Park, 1996). What is at stake is not a universal comparison between two models but rather how they fit with a new form of competition, that is, "intense innovation" rivalry.

Moreover, the comparison does not take into account the financial mass market and its impact on the management of projects, business units, and suppliers.

Learning From Repeatedly Innovative Companies: Platform Strategies and New Innovation Policies. Recent research has shown clearly that intensive innovation requires (a) a different model of strategy and organization in innovative "hierarchies" and (b) a "platform" approach of the network logic.

The automobile and high-tech industries are often given as good examples of network-type industries where project-based organizations are emphasized and key developments and innovative aspects of the businesses are contracted out. Yet in both cases, one can observe that the project-based organization finds its limits when innovation stands in *horizontal* processes, creating synergies and interdependencies between business units and projects. The recent development of "platform strategies" (Gawer & Cusumano, 2002) is good evidence of the limits of the neo-compania model as it rebuilds leadership logic and requires, from the platform leader, a capacity to manage intensive collective learning both inside and outside the company.

Research on companies innovating repeatedly and successfully (Hatchuel, Lemasson, & Weil, 2001) also shows that they manage long-term learning by carefully designing "product lineages," that is, a series of product sequences that do not necessarily have in common the same components or parts but that require a common area of interrelated competencies. Program management in aircraft building and therapeutic areas in the pharmaceutical industry are examples of these product lineages. In this approach, business is primarily thought of not in terms of products, markets, and competencies but rather in a *conceptual* description of "business areas" where collective learning and long-term commitment, inside and outside the company, is actually desired, shared, rewarded, and managed. Platform management is a special case of such concepts when technical interdependencies are central in product design. In other industries, these areas are identified as "innovation fields" (Hatchuel et al., 2001), that is, concepts that are strategy generators, giving birth to several related businesses and products while maintaining the continuity that is needed for management and cooperation. In short, the more intense innovation is, the more we need to come back to the main drivers of management mentioned earlier, that is, strengthening the identity of business entities and the collective processes that nurture the production of valuable knowledge. Obviously, what is true between companies is also true within the firm. Intense innovation and corresponding collective learning lead many people in companies to be involved in variable and flexible "design-oriented groups" (Hatchuel et al., 2002), where many members are coming from inside and outside the company. This is an important challenge that is often counteracted by the evaluation systems inspired by the neo-compania model. It stresses results and accountability at each business unit level, often neglecting interdependencies and collective learning that shaped the result.

All of this highlights the central aim of new managerial concepts that limit the domain of the neo-compania and renew the Fayolian-Taylorian legacy in a world that has been drastically changed by their own impact. The success of a consortium such as Airbus seems to indicate that collective learning between partners may be ensured by long-term commitment in strategy and by stable work-sharing rules that allow continuity and loyalty between partners. But where are such models more likely to appear? The chapter concludes by suggesting that the pharmaceutical and bioscience industries are contexts in which such new concepts and models are likely to emerge. Furthermore, the features of collaborative research in management fit well with the emerging challenges and will likely facilitate the development of new management concepts and models.

Discussion and Conclusion: Collaborative Research for the Invention of New Management Models

Since the middle of the 20th century, an unprecedented amount of research has been devoted to management practice. The views of the founders have been discussed, criticized, and tempered. Companies have also adapted themselves to puzzling waves of change. Several tools and techniques have been developed and widely implemented. Yet a comprehensive alternative to the Fayolian-Taylorian heritage has not been established. Fayol's structural principles have been contextualized and critically examined, but firms are still seeing themselves as administrative processes seeking coordination, anticipation, and cooperation. Taylor's principles of scientific study have been balanced by human-oriented and empowering procedures, but modern firms maintain a central distinction between design and operations. The difference today is that design and research departments are now, in many cases, bigger than operational ones.

The contemporary dilemmas between the temptations of a neo-compania model and new management models driven by intense innovation, long-term learning, and cooperation reopen a period of fundamental change. At this stage, it is not possible to predict what will be the results of these dilemmas. The neo-compania model is praised from a stock market and financial perspective. It can be supported by Web-based communication techniques and global logistics. But today's competitiveness is not based uniquely on scale effects, cost reduction, and volume. Even in developing countries, such product strategy is controversial. The neo-compania model is weak not because it creates opportunistic behavior from the quasi-enterprises that form it (Goshal & Mohan, 1996) but rather because it has a limited capacity to respond to an innovation-based competition that was never so widely installed in the whole socioeconomic context. Moreover, the combination of the neo-compania model with shortsighted and nervous stock markets amplifies disruptive behaviors. Innovation will be neglected or developed under harsh and unrealistic pressure without any collective reflexivity and learning, thereby increasing tensions and stock market nervousness as well as, in some cases, accelerating bankruptcy. Can we invent new models? What are the companies that could be ideal for fundamental innovations in management?

The Pharmaceutical and Bioscience Industries: A Good Place for Management Renewal?

Within a management research perspective, many pharmaceutical and bioscience companies are facing very interesting challenges. Traditionally, this sector has been relatively lucrative, with a good return on investment and very steady growth. The money spent on research and development (R&D) has increased gradually over the years. In many countries, the system of a third payer has benefited the industry. The climate for innovations has been very good, and the market size has been adequate for small and local players. Until recently, no company has had a worldwide market share of more than 10%. One new invention has been enough to build a whole pharmaceutical company (e.g., SKB, Glaxo, AstraZeneca).

Recently, some changes have occurred. The cost spending on R&D in the pharmaceutical and bioscience areas has been projected to outweigh the future income potential. The output in R&D is decreasing, and so the cost per marketed drug is increasing. This means that small to medium-size companies can no longer develop these drugs alone. The demand for payback increases, and a major drug has to be a success in the United States, representing about 50% of the world market. Several mergers and takeovers have taken place among major pharmaceutical companies; thus, the first company with a worldwide market share larger than 10% has seen the day. The reason for these mergers and takeovers has been competition, that is, to acquire a pipeline of drugs to complement the existing ones. In some cases, a takeover has been explained by the need to take over one drug only. Major cost increases can be found in research technologies, genetics, molecular biology tools, high throughput screening, and so forth. The users of drugs question the need for major cost increases for minor innovations, and regulatory authorities question patent prolongations and even support the entry of generic drugs into markets.

A first wave of restructuring has already taken place by creating larger companies. Thus, the pharmaceutical industry is moving away from a neo-compania model. But the main challenges for the industry are still ahead. What will happen to innovation and long-term survival? Will the new giants be able to survive under high financial pressures? It is unlikely that they will. The pharmaceutical and bioscience sector will have to renew its way of looking at management to solve the great dilemma between financial returns and innovation long-term strategy. New models of basic discovery research and collaborations are emerging. One important aspect in pharmaceutical research is that innovations are still done by single individuals—and these may, in turn, change a whole research field. Thus, innovations do not have to follow a specific route or fit with other parts of treatment like an automobile part or a telephone. Single research efforts may change the whole environment. The players in this field will have enormous possibilities to try out new ways of collaborating and managing. Today's high stock evaluation of the pharmaceutical and bioscience companies will survive only through a high level of innovation, bringing forward new products that may change health care. One can expect that giant companies will dominate the market, while research companies and academia will produce the innovation. This could, in turn, present aspects of the neo-compania model, but the challenges coming from users, regulations, and research costs will also foster a management model based on collective learning and cooperation. How will such models combine and give birth to several contingent variants? This is the current managerial challenge in these industries. The pharmaceutical industry is a privileged case where heavy science work, long product design, and high uncertainties offer a special battlefield for alternative management models.

Finally, the pharmaceutical and bioscience industries have to generate sustainable profits by serving at the forefront of human needs in health and quality of life. They explore the most advanced areas of the biosciences and are expected to show good compliance to human and social ethics. Like textiles during the 18th century, mechanics during the 19th century, and computers during the 20th century, they could be one of the main contributors to a new mode of management.

The Need for a New Collaborative Management Research Methodology

How have management models been invented and developed? The history of management does not support the idea that management models are discovered in the academia and implemented afterward by companies. Most management techniques are first developed in practice. Furthermore, the theory-driven models do not fit with management models that concern collective action processes that have to be recognized, understood, and made actionable for concerned people. The compania model, the manufacturing model, and the Fayolian and Taylorian experiences use a variety of techniques, but a model cannot be reduced to these techniques.[4]

There is no pure laboratory strategy for management models. Research has to be congruent with action. This calls for new research methodology that overcomes the shortcomings of classic academic research. New approaches are discussed extensively in other chapters of this volume. The main idea is simple: Management research has to be organized and treated as any other form of R&D (Hatchuel, 2001). This does not mean that resources cannot be found in academia. Quite the contrary, management research in the workplace, like any other R&D, may benefit from partnerships between academics and companies. The development of such collaborative research processes inside the company deserves careful scientific and practical discussion (Hatchuel, 2001; Shani & Docherty, 2003).

Finally, the agenda for rebuilding management is now clearly in front of us. The contemporary dilemmas on management could have disruptive and destructive effects on business survival. They could even endanger the secular success of modern capitalism if they are not understood. To respond to these dilemmas, the neo-compania model appeals to many practitioners and academics. But it is not adapted to intensive innovation-based competition. It is neither a good model for creating identity and commitment nor a good model for producing valuable knowledge and innovation. The current crisis in company governance is only one symptom of its drawbacks. Many other symptoms are visible only at the operational level of companies. However, the neo-compania model is useful for highlighting what is missing: ensuring long-term collective learning and cooperation within companies and between partners.

We cannot expect that financial markets will suddenly behave differently. We cannot expect that the rhythm and scope of innovation will be tempered. Discovering new management models will be the joint task of companies and researchers willing to cooperate. This form of collective action is in itself emblematic of such new models of management. It is a sign of consistency that the form of research advocated corresponds to the type of management model we look forward to developing.

Notes

1. From 1750 to 1850, many of the famous manufacturers were also members of prestigious philosophical and scientific societies of their time (Schofield, 1963).

2. An exception was the Taylor Society, a consulting firm.

3. Frery (1997) indicates that he found more than 40 different labels for the same idea of a company made by a network of companies. Saussois (1997) remarks that this conception is embedded in the difficulties of economists and sociologists to give a substantial theory of the firm.

4. The development of management techniques often follows the development of a management model. (Planning techniques were developed decades after the birth of the manufacturer model.)

References

Babbage, C. (1832). *The economy of machinery and manufactures.* London: Charles Knight.

Berg, M. (1994). *The age of manufacturers 1700–1820.* London: Routledge.

Demsetz, H. (1988). *Ownership, control, and the firm.* Oxford, UK: Blackwell.

Favier, J. (1987). *De l'or et des épices: Naissance de l'homme d'affaires au moyen-âge.* Paris: Fayard.

Frery, F. (1997). La chaîne et le réseau. In P. Besson (Ed.), *Dedans dehors* (pp. 23–52). Paris: Vuibert Fnege.

Gawer, A., & Cusumano M. A. (2002). *Platform leadership.* Boston: Harvard Business School Press.

Goshal, S., & Mohan, P. (1996). Bad for practice: A critique of the transition cost theory. *Academy of Management Journal, 21*(1), 13–47.

Hall, D. T. (1996). *The career is dead—Long live the career: The relational approach to career.* San Francisco: Jossey-Bass.

Hatchuel, A. (1996). Coordination and control. In *International encyclopedia of business and management* (pp. 762–770). London: Thomson Business Press.

Hatchuel, A. (2001). The two pillars of new management research. *British Journal of Management, 12,* 33–39. (Special issue)

Hatchuel, A., Lemasson, P., & Weil, B. (2001). From R&D to RID: Design strategies and the management of innovation fields. In *Proceedings of the Eighth International Product Development Management Conference* (pp. 415–430). Enschede, Netherlands: EIASM.

Hatchuel, A., Lemasson, P., & Weil, B. (2002). From knowledge management to design-oriented organisations. *International Social Science Journal, 171,* 25–37.

Jarillo, J. C. (1993). *Strategic networks: Creating the borderless organization.* Oxford, UK: Butterworth-Heinemann.

Ladurie, E. L. (1991). *L'ancien Régime, tome 1–2,* Paris: Hachette Pluriel.

Miles, R. E., & Snow, C. C. (1992). Causes of failure in network organizations. *California Management Review, 28*(3), 62–73.

Origo, I. (1957). *The Merchant of Prato.* London: Jonathan Cape.

Park, S. H. (1996). Managing an interorganizational network: A framework for the institutional mechanism of network control. *Organization Studies, 17,* 795–824.

Parker, R. H., & Yamey, B. S. (1997). *Accounting history.* London: Clarendon.

Saussois, J-M. (1997). L'entreprise à l'épreuve du dehors et du dedans. In P. Besson (Ed.), *Dedans dehors* (pp. 3–23). Paris: Vuibert Fnege.

Schofield, R. E. (1963). *The Lunar Society of Birmingham*. London: Clarendon.

Shani, A. B., & Docherty, P. (2003). *Learning by design*. London: Blackwell.

Taylor, F. (1895). A piece-rate system: Towards a partial solution of the labor problem. *ASME Transactions, 16,* 883–903.

Researching Our Way to Economic Decline

Ken Starkey and Sue Tempest

This chapter takes as its starting point an article by Robert Hayes and William Abernathy, "Managing Our Way to Economic Decline," published in 1980 in the *Harvard Business Review*. It argues that the failure of American managers to keep their companies technologically competitive led to economic decline. According to Hayes and Abernathy (1980),

> By their preference for servicing existing markets rather than creating new ones and by their devotion to short-term returns and "management by numbers," many [U.S. managers and firms] have effectively forsworn long-term technological superiority as a competitive weapon. Consequently, they have abdicated their strategic responsibilities during the past two decades. American managers have increasingly relied on principles which prize analytical detachment and methodological elegance over insight, based on experience, into the subtleties and complexities of strategic decisions. As a result, maximum short-term financial returns have become the overriding criteria for many companies. (p. 70)

We adopt the position of the devil's advocate and propose that academic research has itself been a willing, if unconscious, accomplice to economic decline. Far too much management research has little relevance to management practice; thus, expenditure on research generates little in the way of added value. Research has also been used to inform a management curriculum that has too often been preoccupied with the short term and efficiency at the expense of innovation and entrepreneurship. One could plausibly argue that U.S. managers were castigated by Hayes and Abernathy (1980) for having done nothing more than acquire knowledge from the courses taught in American business schools.

The academic community has been complicit in the development of the professional manager who lives the view of strategy expounded by Hayes and Abernathy, primarily through the development, refinement, and adherence to the M.B.A. curriculum. It is also partly reinforced by and explicable in terms of the market for and the ritual of international business school ratings published by *Business Week, Financial Times,* and others (Starkey & Tempest, 2001). What has emerged because of this complicity between business and business schools was eloquently summed up by Hayes and Abernathy (1980) nearly a quarter of a century ago:

> What has developed in the business community, as in academia, is a preoccupation with a false and shallow concept of the professional manager, a "pseudo-professional" really—an individual having no special expertise in any particular industry or technology who nevertheless can step into an unfamiliar company and run it successfully through strict application of financial controls, portfolio concepts, and a market-driven strategy. (p. 74)

Ironically, Hayes and Abernathy (1980) looked to Europe, and particularly Germany, France, and the Benelux countries, as producers of world-class, technologically superior products. Since then, U.S. productivity has improved considerably, and—some would argue—so has the innovative potential of parts of the U.S. economy (e.g., Kanter, 1995; Saxenian, 1994). From the U.K. perspective, we continue to wrestle with the problem of relative decline and attempt to counter it with investment in human and social capital to build a new "knowledge economy." The United Kingdom, uncertain of how this is to be accomplished, looks to the United States for lessons. This tendency is demonstrated clearly in the recent announcement by the U.K. Department of Trade and Industry of hiring Michael Porter as a consultant to advise U.K. companies on their poor productivity performance.

There now seems to be a consensus that the future of competition at the firm, national, and regional levels will depend on the potential to master the production of knowledge. It is now widely recognized that knowledge is a key resource in organizations (Dixon, 2000; Nonaka & Takeuchi, 1995). Yet the production of management knowledge and its evolution have received little attention (Suddaby & Greenwood, 2001). A key concern for business school academics should be reflection on the significance of their research role in a world where accountability is something we cannot ignore. Perhaps the United Kingdom, with its growing emphasis on public sector accountability, provides a taste of things to come for other European countries. The U.K. business and management schools, along with all other university departments, are funded by central government grants for research and teaching. Research funding is allocated by performance in the Research Assessment Exercise, which rates departments on a scale of 1 to 5 (where *5 = the majority of research is of "international" standard*). There is also competition for research funding from a variety of research councils and other bodies.

_____What Is the Added Value of Management Research?

To understand the current situation of management research and its potential, we need to examine critically the complex relationships that govern the genesis and development of management knowledge itself and the role of the business school in knowledge creation and diffusion. We need to focus on the following:

- Changes in management practice
- Changes in academic practice
- How knowledge is codified in management texts (journal articles, academic monographs, management best-selling texts, and teaching textbooks)
- The relationship between research and the business/management school curriculum
- The relationships among this curriculum (particularly the M.B.A. and executive short-course teaching), the knowledge it embodies, and the development of management practice
- The role of the various players in the knowledge "value chain"— consultants, management writers, management gurus, professional service firms, and so forth

It is potentially useful to compare and contrast the production and development of knowledge and professional practice in the business school context with medical and pharmacy school contexts. Although differing in the dimension of professionalism, medical and pharmacy schools can be seen as comparable to business schools in a number of ways. Both have a major research role and an educational role. Medical schools educate medical and medicine-related students in their teaching hospital role. Pharmacy schools educate students for pharmacy research and for business careers in retail pharmacy. In the medical and pharmacy school contexts, we see a complicated alignment of research, teaching, and practical roles that presents a major management task for the leaders of such schools.

Business schools also span a similar range of roles but seem less concerned about interaction with the practice of management than medical and pharmacy schools seem concerned about the practices of medicine and pharmacy, even though there are influential contributions to executive education in leading business schools. Another of our initial propositions is that medical and pharmacy school staff are also more involved in the practical application of knowledge to patient care than business school staff are committed to improving the practice of management. Business school staff are more committed to generation of knowledge about management than to generation of knowledge that generates better management practice. Compared with any other professional school (e.g., medical, law, engineering), the engagement of business school faculty in Anglo-Saxon countries with the problems of practice is low.

There are extenuating factors here that partly explain the knowledge dynamics in various professional contexts. For example, the professionalism of knowledge in the medical context and the existence of clear ethical guidelines and processes of knowledge capture patenting in the development of new drugs and medical technologies that are not present in the business school context. These provide clearer pathways to knowledge production and diffusion. Innovation too seems more of a concern in the practice of those concerned with both research and practice in other contexts. Medical and pharmacy academics, for example, have research and teaching roles and are closely involved in the application of knowledge at the innovative frontiers of patient care in the research and development of new medical practices and drugs. What one also finds in the medical and pharmacy contexts are major innovations in new business developments, with spin-off companies being developed for new medical technologies and, in pharmacy in particular, biotech drug developments either as stand-alone companies or in alliance with major pharmaceutical companies (Franklin, Wright, & Lockett, 2001). Indeed, the latter is a major feature of current developments in the pharmaceutical industry.

The nearest parallel in business schools is the role of business school academics as management consultants whose major offering is in new management ideas, some of which are sometimes adopted by management consultants who at times attain "guru" status. But it is probably fair to say that the commercialization of ideas is, perhaps ironically, less of a concern in the business school than in the medical or pharmacy context. In brief, business schools, for a variety of reasons, tend to adhere to a Mode 1 "pure academic" paradigm of knowledge creation (Tranfield & Starkey, 1998). In the medical and pharmacy contexts, there is greater emphasis on the co-production of knowledge with end users (patient groups, pharmaceutical companies, and others). In the latter contexts, there seems to be a more harmonious balance of Mode 1 and Mode 2 knowledge production paradigms and the bridging of the gap between theory and practice in interdisciplinary contexts (Gibbons et al., 1994; Starkey & Madan, 2001; Starkey & Tempest, 2001; Tranfield & Starkey, 1998).

The Knowledge System of the Business School

To change this situation, we have to research and understand the extent to which it persists, and the reasons why, to enable us to better understand the dynamics of the "knowledge system" of the business school and the potential contribution of the business school to the evolving knowledge economy.

Views on this differ. A former president of the American Academy of Management argues for the business school:

> It is the rare manager or firm that creates knowledge about management, and it is even rarer for a consultant to create knowledge (although some assuredly do). Thus, [business schools'] potential value-added contribution over time may well be the creation of knowledge. As a result, effective basic and applied research may be our long-term competitive advantage. (Hitt, 1998, p. 218)

Others are less confident. Peter Drucker, reflecting on the evolution of management knowledge in which he has been a key player, concludes that so far as management education is concerned, management research is "totally unimportant," that the management school is primarily a professional school and "not a Ph.D. mill," and that in a professional school the emphasis should be on teaching (Drucker, 2001, pp. 16–17). Similarly, Kay (2001) argues that little business research has had a positive impact on management practice. He cites the Black-Scholes theorem in finance as one example of research that has had a major impact. However, the evolution of the Black-Scholes model into the practical development of the company long-term capital management (LTCM), built around the investment theories of Myron Scholes and Robert Merton (themselves Nobel Prize-winning laureates), illustrates the disasters that can occur when theory is applied too rigorously and distorts practice (Lowenstein, 2001). LTCM, Enron, and "Enronitis" eloquently demonstrate what can happen when financial theory takes management practice beyond realistic limits.

Eccles and Nohria (1992) argue that much management research is no more than old wine in new bottles. For example, Mary Parker Follett argued during the 1920s for a greater emphasis on the importance of "cross-functioning"—the replacement of "vertical authority" with "horizontal authority"—to promote the exchange of knowledge in organizations.

> The decentralization of authority is only one example of a "new" management theme that turns out to have been quite common throughout this century. Others include producing quality products, providing responsive customer service, formulating strategy in a way that takes into account distinctive internal capabilities, rewarding performance fairly, and running a socially responsible enterprise. (p. 5)

Why are managers taken in by a "hype" that obscures little new or cumulative knowledge development? To the extent that we fail to reflect on our own history and to understand the dynamics that shape it, we remain condemned to repeat it.

Suddaby and Greenwood (2001, pp. 936–937) argue that business schools serve three main functions: *due diligence,* that is, a quality control function of testing and refining extant knowledge; *research-led innovation,* which produces insights that form the basis for new managerial knowledge; and a *dissemination function* through socializing consumers to the value of particular product and service offerings. Perhaps this view represents more of an ideal type than current practice. Indicative of the growing debate about the role of the business school in management development and practice was the launch in 2002 of the *Academy of Management Learning and Education Journal.* A key contribution to this debate is provided by Pfeffer and Fong (2002) in the first edition of this journal.

Pfeffer and Fong (2002), in an article that has spawned huge debate in the United States, contend that business schools have two key outputs—career development and knowledge creation—both of which would be expected to have a positive impact on management practice. Management education is generally seen as enhancing the career outcomes of business school graduates. However, Pfeffer and Fong's findings suggest that there is no correlation between either having an M.B.A. degree or the grades obtained from courses and subsequent career success. This finding raises questions about the effectiveness of business schools as a forum for management education.

One key problem that Pfeffer and Fong (2002) suggest is the emphasis placed on business school M.B.A. programs to talk about management rather than to practice management. This is borne out by the experience of Marjorie Scardino, chief executive officer (CEO) of the global media group Pearson (owner of the *Financial Times* and *The Economist*), who earlier in her career spent some time running her own business and considered doing a course at Harvard Business School. Interestingly, she was advised by one of the deans of the school, "You are learning so much more having your own business. You would just be bored" (quoted in Vinnicombe & Bank, 2003, p. 42). Scardino retains a skeptical attitude toward the value of business education in her role as CEO at Pearson:

> We try to find people at Pearson who have had unusual careers or haven't just completed university or business school. Business schools tend to teach people conformity in the way they think, and we want just the opposite—creativity and asymmetrical ways of approaching problems. (p. 42)

This suggests a perceived lack of alignment between what business schools provide in terms of teaching and what firms require. It reinforces the case that business schools may have much to learn from other practice-based schools such as medical and pharmacy schools. Indeed, to combine the role of knowledge development and training, Pfeffer and Fong (2002) suggest, "All that is required is for business schools to model themselves more closely on their professional school counterparts and less on arts and sciences departments" (p. 93).

Pfeffer and Fong's (2002) second criticism of business schools concerns their research and knowledge generation role. If management research were effective, one would expect it to affect management practice. However, these authors argue that "there is little evidence that business school research is influential on management practice, calling into question the professional relevance of management scholarship" (p. 78). Business schools, therefore, are charged with not developing relevant knowledge. Indeed, Pfeffer and Fong's findings suggest that academics tend to be influenced by practitioners but that this influence is largely a one-way street, with practitioners themselves preferring to rely on nonacademic sources (consulting firms and various companies of relevance) for their management reading and business tools. One possible explanation for the relatively small impact of business school research on practitioners, they propose, is that academics tend to focus on theory-oriented research that can be validated and to specialize their knowledge base for their own professional status. It is problem-oriented research with a more holistic or multidiscipline stance that is often more useful to the business community (p. 88).

We need to be sensitive to the criticisms of the possible "irrelevance" of management research (Hambrick, 1994), critiques of its morally and politically contentious character, and debates about the future of management research and management schools (Starkey & Madan, 2001) while addressing the extent to which management research and business schools may have been complicit in a knowledge creation, validation, and socialization process detrimental to management practice. Management researchers, by their own admission and desire, tend to live in self-enclosed, quasi-tribal groupings. The various tribes come together during the transmigrations of conference season, but in ways that remain hermetically and hermeneutically sealed from the "outside world." In the words of an elder of management research, a former president of the U.S. Academy of Management, talking about the annual academy meeting in North America, "Each August, we come to talk with each other; during the rest of the year, we read each others' papers in our journals and write our own papers so that we may, in turn, have an audience the following August: an incestuous closed loop" (Hambrick, 1994, p. 13).

Research is often prized more for its methodological sophistication than for its substantive contributions to knowledge of the world of practice, to the extent that business schools, particularly in the United States, place most emphasis on quantitative analysis and on "objective" and "general" rather than on the "subjective" and "local." This can lead to risk aversion because information relating to new markets and innovations may be too subjective to fit into the formal models developed and taught in business schools and hence is rejected. It can also lead to obfuscation.

At a more fundamental level, some commentators have gone so far as to suggest that the research-practice gap stems from academics' and practitioners' differing assumptions and beliefs and that the different values and ideologies of these distinct communities could hinder more collaborative approaches to knowledge development and use in the management field (Shrivastava & Mitroff, 1984). This means that "perceived usefulness requires far more than simply doing research in relevant areas" (Mohrman, Gibson, & Mohrman, 2002, p. 369). It also requires a greater focus on the relationship between researchers and practitioners that enables them to appreciate their respective "thought-worlds" (p. 372). Doctoral education has been criticized in the United States as being concerned with producing a highly specialized product that nobody, except for universities themselves, wants (Dent, 2002, p. 137).

It is interesting that recent research in strategic management, arguing for a resource-based view of strategy, stresses the importance to firms of the more difficult to capture knowledge and the firm's unique and difficult to imitate competencies as a source of competitive advantage (Barney, Wright, & Ketchen, 2001). On the other hand, management practice may itself have been selective in its use and development of knowledge, failing to learn from potentially "relevant" research. These issues merit serious critical examination because they are crucial to the ongoing legitimization of management research and the role of the business school.

Toward a More Collaborative Approach to Management Research

On a more positive note, there is evidence to suggest that contextual changes are occurring that may be encouraging a more collaborative approach to management research that engages both practitioners and academics (Rynes, Bartunek, & Daft, 2001). This in itself may be a key to fostering greater cross-community understanding between the worlds of business and scholarship and a more committed engagement with the challenges of the co-production of knowledge (Gibbons et al., 1994). The challenge of global competitiveness is encouraging practitioners to be more receptive to academic ideas for organizational effectiveness. Collaborative management research involves bringing together managers and academics to actively shape the research process and the analysis of results. Such collaboration contains inherent tension but may enhance knowledge development and dissemination by raising the number of practitioner participants and/or raising response rates, improving content-coding schemes, providing alternative interpretations of findings that do not necessarily build from previous theory, and leveraging dissemination through face-to-face interaction rather than relying on documents that might not be read (Amabile et al., 2001; Rynes et al., 2001).

Amabile and colleagues (2001) contend that collaborations between academics and practitioners in the field of management are rare and distinctive in that they are cross-profession and that the existent management literature on collaborations provides little effective guidance for cross-profession collaboration. Their findings point to at least a couple of practical challenges: frustration with initial meetings as academics focused on presenting information, whereas practitioners sought to discuss issues, and disappointment in the level of involvement in the study by practitioners attributed to academics holding a top-down "principal investigator" model of research projects, in contrast to practitioners who sought more team-based approaches to collaboration.

This points to the need to explore new models of management research that build on genuine practitioner-academic collaboration. There is evidence to suggest that such innovative models of business school and management research are emerging. The United Kingdom is uniquely placed as the nexus between Continental Europe and the United States to harness and integrate the best from both continents. However, the emerging model of "best-in-class" research and of the world-class business school in the United Kingdom is very much "Americanized." We suggest that the United Kingdom has much to learn from Continental European—in particular, Swedish and French—models of research development and interaction between academe and business as examples of the effective involvement of researchers in the co-production of effective management knowledge to improve design innovation (Hatchuel, Lemasson, & Weil, 2001) and in innovation in new modes of research and management development, for example, the FENIX research and executive Ph.D. program.

Conclusion: The Role of the Business School in a Changing University

There are broader issues that affect the role of management research and its pursuit in the business school context. First, we raise a number of fundamental questions. Then, we conclude by addressing the role of the business school in today's university.

We need to theorize the potential role of management research in terms of the arguments of Michael Gibbons and colleagues that we need to rethink social science (Nowotny, Scott, & Gibbons, 2001). We attempt to answer the vexed question of what exactly the knowledge generated by management research has contributed to management practice and what it might contribute in the future. A number of key questions suggest themselves. The following are major but not necessarily exclusive:

- What theories of knowledge development are most relevant to the business school context?
- What is the genealogy of knowledge within this sector of higher education? What are the key factors and dynamics in the history of

business schools that have led to current approaches to knowledge production in management research?

- How have the roles of business school academics changed and developed, and how should they develop, particularly their research practices?
- How does management research affect the practice of management, and how should it, if at all?
- What is the optimal link between research and teaching?
- What are the various national models of business school and management research? In particular, how relevant is the U.S. model to other national and regional contexts?
- What alternative scenarios exist for the future of business schools, and what are their relative merits and dangers?
- Where do business schools sit in the current tensions facing the university system?
- What are the relationships between business/management schools and other players in the production of management knowledge and the market for management research (e.g., business and public sector organizations, consulting firms, management gurus, training organizations, corporate universities)?

Management research is a relatively young discipline. Indeed, some would argue that it is not a discipline at all. For example, opponents of Oxford University's establishment of a business school saw this development as the very antithesis of what a university should stand for. Management research still has much to do to establish its legitimacy. If it fails in this task, the best it can hope for is marginalization. Management academics seem to us to demonstrate a dangerous tendency to isolationism. In part, this reflects the situation of a young discipline—if management is indeed a discipline—struggling for legitimacy among its older colleagues. It also reflects the pride of an academic group that has created a business whose market potential is considerable and currently far outstrips most of its university compatriots, for example, in the demand for its degrees.

But there are dangers in isolationism and in the current vogue for business-related courses. The business school is not its own master and will need to situate itself in the broader context of a more complex and socially distributed space for knowledge production and dissemination if it is to play a significant role in the future. Debates and experiments that are aimed at producing researchers who are more attuned to the problems of practice and of educating "scholarly practitioners" are now under way. In both cases, while providing a solid grounding in research skills, methodology, and so forth, the focus of such an initiative (e.g., executive Ph.D. programs) needs to confront challenging ontological issues that might not fit well with the traditional orthodoxies of scientific research.

"Doctoral students in management need to be prepared for a turbulent environment in which senior people undertake new initiatives without roadmaps that could be drawn from prior experience" (Dent, 2002, p. 141). The traditional Ph.D. has been highly discipline specific and specialized. Notwithstanding the strengths of specialization and discipline focus, these are unlikely on their own to cope with the complexities of the contemporary management landscape. Therefore, we need more emphasis on interdisciplinary and transdisciplinary research design and practice as well as more team-based projects than has been the norm (Tranfield & Starkey, 1998). We also need to reflect seriously on our criteria for evaluating doctoral work that engages more with practice (Winter, Griffith, & Green, 2000).

There are broader issues here as well. There is an increasing debate in Europe about the gap between research and practice, a debate that also resonates with debates about relevance in the United States (e.g., Hambrick, 1994). The issues raised in these debates go far beyond the confines of management and business schools. In essence, they are debates about the future of the university and its role in economic growth and social development (Wolf, 2002). Since the Enlightenment and until recently, the university existed as a privileged space for knowledge creation. Its claim on this space and the rationale for society to cultivate such a space is now under increasing attack (Delanty, 2001). Gibbons and colleagues (1994) hypothesize a new knowledge space, far more public and far more contested in terms of a growing dissonance of parties with their own knowledge claims. A key new problem has emerged in this space: a new form of knowledge production with many knowledge producers seeking to develop knowledge that is quintessentially problem specific. In this new space, researchers and knowledge users engage in a variety of innovative modes of knowledge co-production.

Some, primarily the postmodernists, argue that the traditional idea of the university is now bankrupt both morally and practically (Lyotard, 1984; Readings, 1996). They claim that the university has

> reached its end, and with the closure of modernity it has collapsed into a bureaucratic enterprise bereft of moral purpose. Its founding cognitive ideas—the universality of knowledge, the quest for truth, the unity of culture—are becoming irrelevant, and the social and economic reality has instrumentalized the university to a point that has made its autonomy neither possible nor desirable. If the university is not to degenerate into technocratic consumerism by which students become mere consumers of knowledge, and the university [becomes] a trans-national bureaucratic corporation legitimating itself by the technocratic discourse of "excellence," it will have to discover another role. (Delanty, 2001, pp. 5–6)

What the future role of the university will be is unclear. However, we agree with Delanty's vision, which we think is particularly relevant to the business school and its educational mission that encompasses both research and teaching roles.

> One of the unexplored tasks of the university is to be able to be a site of interconnectivity, between the diverse forms of knowledge that are now being produced. The university is the key institution in society that is capable of mediating between the mode of knowledge, the articulation of cultural models, and institutional innovation. (pp. 8–9)

The unexplored task for the business school is to act as the nexus for knowledge creation, sharing, and diffusion. The business school is to develop itself as the chosen site for new ways of doing business that adapts to the broad needs of business, potential stakeholders, and society.

References

Amabile, T. M., Patterson, C., Mueller, J., Wojcik, T., Odomirok, P. W., Marsh, M., & Kramer, S. J. (2001). Academic-Practitioner collaboration in management research: A case of cross-professional collaboration. *Academy of Management Journal, 44*(2), 418–431.

Barney, J., Wright, M., & Ketchen, D. (2001). The resource-based view of the firm: Ten years after 1991. *Journal of Management, 27,* 625–642.

Delanty, G. (2001). *Challenging knowledge: The university in the knowledge society.* Milton Keynes, UK: Open University Press.

Dent, E. B. (2002). Developing scholarly practitioners: Doctoral management education in the 21st century. In C. Wankel & R. DeFillippi (Eds.), *Rethinking management education for the 21st century.* Greenwich, CT: Information Age Publishing.

Dixon, N. (2000). *Common knowledge.* Boston: Harvard Business School Press.

Drucker, P. (2001, November–December). Taking stock. *BizEd,* pp. 12–17.

Eccles, R. G., & Nohria, N. (1992). *Beyond the hype: Rediscovering the essence of management.* Boston: Harvard Business School Press.

Franklin, S., Wright, M., & Lockett, A. (2001). Academic and surrogate entrepreneurs in university spinout companies. *Journal of Technology Transfer, 26,* 127–141.

Gibbons, M., Limoges, L., Nowotny, H., Schwartman, S., Scott, P., & Trow, M. (1994). *The new production of knowledge.* London: Sage.

Hambrick, D. A. (1994). Presidential address: What if the academy actually mattered? *Academy of Management Review, 19,* 11–16.

Hatchuel, A., Lemasson, P., & Weil, B. (2001). From R&D to RID: Design strategies and the management of innovation fields. In *Proceedings of the Eighth*

International Product Development Management Conference (pp. 415–430). Enschede, Netherlands: EIASM.

Hayes, R. H., & Abernathy, W. J. (1980, July–August). Managing our way to economic decline. *Harvard Business Review*, pp. 67–77.

Hitt, M. (1998). Twenty-first century organizations: Business firms, business schools, and the academy. *Academy of Management Review, 23*, 218–224.

Kanter, R. M. (1995). *World class: Thriving locally in the global economy.* New York: Simon & Schuster.

Kay, J. (2001, February). Management research or management consultancy? In *Do we need a separate Research Council for management research?* (report of a seminar at the Department of Trade and Industry). London: Council for Excellence in Management and Leadership.

Lowenstein, R. (2001). *When genius failed: The rise and fall of long-term capital management.* London: Fourth Estate.

Lyotard, J-F. (1984). *The postmodern condition: A report on knowledge.* Manchester, UK: Manchester University Press.

Mohrman, S. A., Gibson, C. B., & Mohrman, A. M. (2002). Doing research that is useful to practice: A model and empirical exploration. *Academy of Management Journal, 44*(2), 357–375.

Nonaka, I., & Takeuchi, H. (1995). *The knowledge-creating company.* Oxford, UK: Oxford University Press.

Nowotny, H., Scott, P., & Gibbons, M. (2001). *Rethinking science: Knowledge and the public in an age of uncertainty.* Cambridge, UK: Polity.

Pfeffer, J., & Fong, C. T. (2002). The end of business schools? Less success than meets the eye. *Academy of Management Learning and Education, 1*(1), 78–95.

Readings, B. (1996). *The university in ruins.* Cambridge, MA: Harvard University Press.

Rynes, S. L., Bartunek, J. M., & Daft, R. L. (2001). Across the Great Divide: Knowledge creation and transfer between practitioners and academics. *Academy of Management Journal, 44*(2), 340–355.

Saxenian, A. (1994). *Regional advantage: Culture and competition in Silicon Valley and Route 128.* Cambridge, MA: Harvard University Press.

Shrivastava, P., & Mitroff, I. I. (1984). Enhancing organizational research: The role of decision makers' assumptions. *Academy of Management Review, 9*, 18–26.

Starkey, K., & Madan, P. (2001). Bridging the relevance gap: Aligning stakeholders in the future of management research. *British Journal of Management, 12*, 3–26. (Special issue)

Starkey, K., & Tempest, S. (2001). *The world-class business school: A U.K. perspective.* London: Council for Excellence in Management and Leadership.

Suddaby, R., & Greenwood, R. (2001). Colonizing knowledge: Commodification as a dynamic of jurisdictional expansion in professional service firms. *Human Relations, 54*, 933–953.

Tranfield, D., & Starkey, K. (1998). The nature, social organisation, and promotion of management research: Towards policy. *British Journal of Management, 9*, 341–353.

Vinnicombe, S., & Bank, J. (2003). *Women with attitude: Lessons for career management.* London: Routledge.

Winter, R., Griffith, M., & Green, K. (2000). The "academic" qualities of practice: What are the criteria for a practice-based Ph.D.? *Studies in Higher Education, 25,* 25–37.

Wolf, A. (2002). *Does education matter? Myths about education and economic growth.* London: Penguin.

3 Travels in the Borderland of Academy and Industry

Bengt Stymne

The port town of Gävle, which during the years following the end of World War II had once been assigned staple privileges for the northern part of Sweden, epitomizes the meeting between the academy and industry. Of course, at that time, the imposing caserns at Kungsbäck, on the western fringe of the town, had not yet been transformed into a regional university but rather still housed the 14th infantry regiment. My academy was the "Public Higher Institution of Learning." The school building had a flight of curved steps leading down to the "Rådhus esplanade" (town hall esplanade) that stretched down from the theater built in a classical style in the north to the well-proportioned magistrates building by the river in the south. Not that we were allowed to enter the school by the main entrance at that time; we had to use the back doors from the schoolyard. However, after 8 years of study, the main door would open for the pupils who had passed the scrutiny of the censors so that they could descend the steps, shining white caps on their heads (as a token of having passed the "student exam"), to family and friends who awaited them in the crowd assembled among the abundance of spring flowers by the esplanade's sparkling fountains. For some, the wait was somewhat anxious because a few of the pupils, even on that joyous day, would have to leave bare-headed by the back door.

I liked that world of learning. I also liked to walk down to the bustling harbor with its row after row of storehouses, many of which contained plants for roasting coffee that filled the streets with a tempting aroma. I enjoyed walking over to the other side of the river, where streets named "First Long Street" and "First Cross Street" (and so forth) contained foundries, engineering workshops, and factories making technical products and candy. From afar, one could hear the intense hammering from the shipyard. Especially during rainy days, one could sense the characteristic smell from the plants for making cellulose and paper situated still farther out along the shoreline of the bay.

One weekend when my siblings and I were quite young, we found our father sitting on a stool in the garden vigorously stirring a curious mixture of chemicals. He explained that he was trying to make floating soap, an undertaking that we children immediately approved of because we faced the constant problem of chasing the soap in the bubble bath. Later, I followed father to the small laboratory in the soap factory where he worked. A man in a white coat dropped liquid into test tubes and watched them change color. I was fascinated by these acts of investigation and creation. I think it occurred to me already then that I would like to investigate how things worked to be able to find new things that people would like to buy.

Growing up, my perspective changed. One after the other, the plants for coffee roasting disappeared until only one large grim-looking plant of *Gevalia* remained. The hammers of the shipyard became silent. The soap factory suffered economic troubles and was taken over by a multinational corporation, the British-Dutch Unilever.

I discovered, at 11 years of age, that the world was not to remain the same. Gävle was no longer the center of the world. The soap factory could no longer provide a living and a position in society for our family, and we had to move to another town. I wondered why all of this had to happen to us. That enigma may be part of the explanation of why I became a researcher and an economist. I wanted to understand the economic forces that so influenced our lives. I especially needed to understand why the floating soap never left the laboratory to be the smashing success I had fantasized about. The rest of this chapter is the story about how I continued to travel in the borderland between industrial reality and economic theory in attempting to solve that riddle.

Handbook of Engineering, 1959–1961

My journey continues at the end of the 1950s at the Stockholm School of Economics. General management was taught under the heading of "administration," and we learned about organizing from the *Handbook of Engineering* (Ingenjörshandboken 7, 1951). In the attic of the school, small offices were arranged to house an expanding number of doctoral candidates. These candidates were not to be confined only to the attic; they were expected to spend a year at an American university as well. When they came back, they brought home with them a different perspective on management (Danielsson, 1976).

The new perspective involved looking at the firm from the outside in and seeing it as an open system. According to the dominating perspective of seeing the firm from inside out, goals were set by the top layer of the firm, and it was the task of management to see to it that the goals were reached.

From the new perspective of looking at the firm as a part of the environment, the goals are not set by the top management. Instead, goals are a product of the exchange process among the various stakeholders that make up the firm. What one stakeholder contributes will serve as a reward for another. Through mutual adjustments, an unstable balance between contributions and rewards is temporarily created. Like a drunk on his way from the pub, the firm is stumbling along to regain the balance it is constantly on the verge of losing. The goal of the firm that could be imputed from this perspective, if any, is not one set by management or the owners but rather is *to obtain an unstable balance so as to survive.*

Management in a Changing World, 1961–1964

After graduation, I was asked to join the "Society in the Attic," as the Economic Research Institute at the school sometimes was called with reference to Kreuder's (1946) book. One of the other doctoral candidates in the attic was Eric Rhenman. He was 7 years my senior, educated as a chemical engineer in addition to having his master's degree in management and economics. He had already gained some practical experience and had a position as administrative director of the Atomic Energy Corporation that the government had entrusted with the task of finding peaceful ways in which to use nuclear energy in Sweden. He invited me to make a discovery trip with him by writing a book based on the ideas emerging in the field of management. The outcome of our joint effort was a book titled *Företagsledning i en föränderlig Värld* (Management in a Changing World) (Rhenman & Stymne, 1965). The book was our attempt to formulate the theoretical consequences of the change in perspective. We tried to present Simon's inducement-contribution model (March & Simon, 1958) in a way that made its consequences for management understandable. In the book, we also ventured to make a connection between existing management practice and the new ideas about management. We sympathized with Fayol, who had suggested that assembling the experiences of a number of successful business leaders would result in useful knowledge for handling management problems. However, we sided with Simon in believing that all the experience and ideas of experienced managers were not necessarily useful; they would have to be tested and elaborated by systematic and scientific study of management problems in practice.

During the beginning of the 1960s, computers started to become a hot topic. As part of my research for a licentiate degree, I conducted a study of the impact of "electronic data processing" (Stymne, 1966). At that time, a heated discussion was going on among practitioners and academics as to whether computers would result in a centralization of information and decision making at the top of the organizational pyramid or whether information would be distributed to more people further down the hierarchy and thereby pave the way for more decentralization. Therefore, I set out to observe the information flow in the car insurance department of an insurance company. The analysis of the information flow did not, however, make full sense of the processes I saw evolving.

Up until then, I had perceived the task of management as a process of decision making. I think I then saw the organizational dimension of management for the first time. It is not the trends in the environment that bring about change in a firm. Changes in the environment may, on an abstract level, be said to make adaptation of the organization necessary, but they do not change the company or act as agents of change. The necessary energy for change in the company that I studied seemed to be generated by an internal power struggle. External events, such as the arrival of computers, become arguments in the quest for power and control.

ISR and the Center for Group Dynamics, 1964–1965

After having finished the work for the licentiate thesis, it was my turn to go to the United States for a year of study. My thesis supervisor in Stockholm, Gunnar Westerlund, had carried out an experiment influenced by research at the University of Michigan (Westerlund, 1952). By his mediation, I was invited to stay at the Institute for Social Research (ISR), where I even got a job as a research assistant in its Center for Group Dynamics. The center had been started by Kurt Lewin and had been moved from the Massachusetts Institute of Technology to Michigan after Lewin's death. Lewin, a Jewish refugee from Hitler's Germany, had been impressed by how children in American families were treated as equals and how they were consulted on important family matters.

Lewin used experiments to show that this kind of participative management also worked in other settings (Lewin, Lippitt, & White, 1939). Lewin's ideas of participative management were also tried out in what he called *action research* (Chein, Cook, & Harding, 1948). These ideas were taken up by ISR, where various forms of cooperation between industry and the university were developed. The ideas of participative management that became a theoretical mainstay for research at the institute are presented by Likert (1961) in the influential book *New Patterns of Management* (see also Marrow, Bowers, & Seashore, 1967), which gives an account of an industry-academy collaboration in bringing about participative management.

The open intellectual climate at the University of Michigan was strikingly different from what I had experienced in Sweden. The library that occupied a central place on the Ann Arbor campus was the heart providing oxygen to academic life and debate. It was open day and night. It was not reserved for the librarians, as was often the case in Sweden. You were free to roam over the stacks, which had desks interspersed where you could work, and the staff would help you to make the photocopies you wanted. The openness of the academic climate was also evident in the habit of scholars to issue invitations to anybody interested to come to their offices for "brown bag" luncheons and to hear about the latest research findings. ISR invited academics from other departments and universities as well as managers to their weekly staff luncheons.

The close contacts between ISR and industry produced a great amount of interesting research. It was not confined to action research on participative management. Cooperation between General Motors and Austrian economist George Katona had resulted in the recurrent surveys of consumer confidence that are still playing such an important role for investment plans of firms and actors on the global financial markets to this day.

SIAR, 1966–1970

While I spent my time as an academic journeyman in America, Eric Rhenman (see Stymne, 1995) continued to realize his ideas about conducting research in close cooperation with management practice. During his own study period in the United States, he was impressed with consulting companies such as Arthur D. Little, Batell, RAND, and Stanford Research that based their work on systematic research and scientific knowledge. Therefore, Rhenman wanted to combine consulting and research. He suggested to IVA (the Royal Academy of Engineering Research) that it would be the appropriate host to such an outfit on the borderline between industry and academy. IVA, however, declined to lend its support to the idea. Disappointed, Rhenman accepted an offer to move to Africa as the administrative director of LAMCO, a company set up by the Grängesberg mining company to exploit a mine of iron ore in Liberia.

At this stage, Paulson Frenckner, a professor at the Stockholm School of Economics, together with Rolf Lahnhagen, director of the Council of Personnel Administration, a research organization supported by both the unions and employers, intervened and helped Rhenman to establish a research group of his own at the school's Economic Research Institute that would permit him to pursue his idea of research in close connection with industry. Tensions soon surfaced. The institute wanted to keep a clear line of demarcation between academic research and consultation. Because Rhenman's ambitions were too high to be contained an established structure, he decided to set up an interdependent organization for this new type of research. He asked me and three other young researchers to establish a foundation that would be the legal form of a new institute that we called the Swedish Institute for Administrative Research (SIAR).

Gaining Academic Credibility

The new institute began its life in the basement of a block of flats in the outskirts of Stockholm. The first years of operation, from 1966 to 1970, were used for work on a number of different projects (SIAR, 1972). An intensive interchange with social scientists from other countries took place. The list of guests who influenced our thinking included William Buckley, Fred Emery, Larry Greiner, Jay Lorsch, and Alvin Zander. Some of them stayed with us for up to a year.

To gain academic respectability, it was stipulated that all project leaders in SIAR should have Ph.D. or licentiate degrees. This requirement led to frenzied report writing that was backed up with incessant seminar activities. Clients were also invited. Some chief executive officers probably felt some astonishment when they descended the narrow stairway leading to the basement that housed SIAR to participate in the seminar with the researchers that was regarded as necessary preparation for a project.

In the beginning, most income came from a few building and construction companies and from associations of firms from that industry. Generous grants from the Bank of Sweden's Three-Centenary Fund and the Social Science Research Council, among others, contributed substantially to improving the economic situation and to making it possible to carry out academically oriented research. The pioneer spirit among the very young co-workers helped to improve the institute's economy as well.

Clinical Organization Research

A methodological idea was to carry out *clinical organization research*. This term denotes research aimed at simultaneously solving organizational problems and acquiring increased knowledge about the way in which organizations function. An adviser or researcher could practice clinical organization research and, at the same time, systematically record observations so as to give an account of his or her experiences later on (Stymne, 1970, pp. 25, 306). One reason for carrying out clinical research is that it is a way in which researchers can follow processes that would otherwise be difficult to gain access to, for example, how top management deals with strategic questions.

The projects had the form or consultations paid for by the investigated organizations. The clients were aware that the material gathered during projects was going to be used for academic research and publication. The projects involved a high degree of interaction between the researchers and the clients. A group consisting of the top management team and researchers met regularly over extended periods of time to analyze the organization's situation and action alternatives.

We soon concluded that one major obstacle in the management's decision processes was lack of knowledge about the industry and the environment in which the firm worked. Therefore, *hearings* were arranged with key representatives of various sectors of the firm's context. Another weakness was the shortcomings of group dynamics of the management team. Therefore, the question of how the group functioned was raised. Psychologists and psychiatrists took part in these discussions, and special sessions were held that dealt with the group dynamics among the researchers of the institute.

Special investigations of key issues in the client organizations were undertaken. The technique most commonly used was interviewing, as the SIAR co-workers developed a certain mastery in being able to extract much information in a short time as well as to generate explanations and hypotheses in the dialogue with the interviewees. Survey instruments for assessing various aspects of organizational functioning were developed. A main theoretical tool for making sense of the information gathered was the analyses of mechanisms that produced vicious and virtuous circles or chains of behaviors in the organization (see, e.g., Buckley & Sandkull, 1971; Normann, 1972).

The Impossibility of Long-Range Planning

What SIAR soon found out from its clinical research was that long-range planning was impossible as a paradigm for adaptation to a changing environment. We found that this impossibility was well expressed in Ashby's (1956/1969) law of requisite variety (Rhenman, 1973). Survival depends on a match between the organization's capabilities and the various states that the environment could assume. Because there is always a number of possible states that the environment can assume, the main problem for an organization is not to forecast what will occur but rather to develop the capability to respond adequately to whatever will happen. With this in mind, SIAR concentrated on developing an understanding of how organizations could attain the requisite variety to survive in a partly unpredictable environment. In this effort, we were guided by a systems theory borrowed from biology and by Selznick's (1957) theory of distinctive competence.

Selznick's theory of distinctive competence led us to understand a firm's competence as a system consisting of two components: a value system and a number of value-supporting systems. The values are what the collaborators consider to be the meaning of both their own activities and the activities of the organization as a whole. The value-supporting systems are the artifacts that make the realization of values possible and that symbolize and remind people what the values are. An example of a value is *customer orientation*. A system supporting this value could be a routine for catching and acting on customer complaints. To achieve a distinctive competence, the values of a firm, as well as its value-supporting systems, have to match the needs of the firm's environment. When there is a good match, the firm has found a niche characterized by distinctive competence. In such a favorable case, the development of the firm and the environment will be linked, as Sommerhof (1969) suggested, by directive correlations.

To denote such a situation of a system of mutually supporting elements, the concept of a *business idea* was developed (Normann, 1975). To secure a parallel development of the organization and the environment, *organizational learning* becomes essential. SIAR found that *divisionalization* could be used as a tool for organizational learning if each division was designed around a business idea (Edgren, Rhenman, & Skärvad, 1983).

Stepping Over the Borderline, 1970–1997

Up to the beginning of the 1970s, SIAR's activities had been a period of learning and theoretical development. The clients had been involved in the process of discovery, but it is uncertain how much customer value the projects created. Rhenman believed that the time had come for commercial exploitation of the results. A certain strain developed between the more consultancy oriented collaborators and the more academically oriented ones, resulting in a few leaving the institute. As described in what follows, I left to lead a project on action research.

During the years that followed, SIAR developed into a more clear-cut consultancy firm. Offices were established in the United States in Cambridge, Massachusetts, as well as in Helsinki, London, Manila, Milan, Paris, and Tokyo. When the Soviet state broke down, SIAR saw an opportunity to establish activities in the Baltic area, and offices were opened in Tallinn, Riga, Vilnius, and St. Petersburg. Rhenman also believed that the creation of the European Union with a new common market made it necessary for SIAR to have a substantial presence on the European mainland as well. Therefore, in 1991 SIAR merged with the French firm Bossard. When Rhenman suddenly died of a heart attack in the beginning of 1993, SIAR-Bossard could no longer maintain its unique competence, and in 1997 Groupe Bossard was bought by Cap Gemini. SIAR-Bossard ceased to exist as a firm with its own distinct identity in 1997, when it was integrated into Ernst & Young after that company had also been acquired by Cap Gemini.

SIAR attempted to combine consultation and research. The period from its start to the beginning of the 1970s was very rich in new ideas and publications. Some already had an influence on management thinking, especially through the writings of Richard Normann. SIAR represented a resource-based view of business strategy. Finally, this view of strategy was more commonly accepted in the management field during the 1990s. The acceptance was not, however, due to SIAR's contributions; rather, it was based on the writings of others.

For SIAR's practice, the role of values for the success of business activities was even more important than the role we ascribed to resources and structures. Theories that ascribe a central role to values are still not widely accepted in the management field. The rich literature around corporate culture deals with values, of course, but does not really relate them to strategy. The emerging research on how organizations are socially constructed is more akin to our ideas about values but lacks the action-oriented perspective for which SIAR strived (Carlsson, 2000).

Three researchers from Uppsala University (Engwall, Furusten, & Wallerstedt, 1993) compare Rhenman to Oscar Sillén, another foreground figure in Swedish management thinking. They suggest that establishing oneself like Sillén, as an academic authority rather as a practitioner in the field, makes it easier both to publish and to study practice because one then gets consulted as an expert in various interesting and problematic situations.

URAF, 1970–1980

The next stop on my journey is URAF in 1970. Sweden had been governed by a Social Democratic government since 1932 (with the exception of a short interlude in 1936). The establishment of *industrial democracy* had always been on the agenda of the party. However, the Social Democratic government had followed a very pragmatic policy for labor market questions that, following the celebrated "Saltsjöbaden Agreement" on industrial peace in 1938, were delegated to the Employers Confederation (SAF) and the Confederation of Workers Unions (LO).

By the end of the 1960s, the heyday of what has been called "the Swedish model" had come to an end. After the events of 1968 and some conspicuous strikes in Sweden during the years that followed, industrial democracy was again put on the political agenda. Following the tradition to resolve labor market problems by negotiation, the employers and unions had set up a national bipartisan body called the Development Council. URAF (Development Council's Task Force for Research) was organized to coordinate a research program to provide input into the process. Experiments were going to be carried out in various industries to find ways in which to organize work in a more democratic way. The Stockholm School of Economics was approached about being responsible for research focusing on white-collar workers, and the school asked me to head a project in that area.

The actual experiment took place in the Skandia Insurance Company. A research program called PMO (People and Organization) was established with five researchers. The research design built on the sociotechnical theory stemming from research on the introduction of modern production methods in the coal mining industry by the Tavistock Institute of Human Relations in London (Trist & Bamforth, 1951).

The British industry had shown limited interest in adopting the ideas of Tavistock, and researchers from there turned instead to Norway, where Einar Thorsrud was trying to get the industry committed to the sociotechnical perspective. Thorsrud published a couple of books together with Fred

Emery, a Tavistock researcher who became interested in Norway (Emery & Thorsrud, 1969; Thorsud & Emery, 1969). They argued that legislation about board representation for workers would not give them any more influence where such mattered, that is, at their place of work and over their daily tasks. As an alternative, they suggested that the sociotechnical ideas could be used for designing an organization of work that de facto would mean more participation for the individual worker.

The experiment in Skandia took place in the Department for Business Insurance in Göteborg, Sweden. A project group that included researchers, the department's management, and personnel representatives was responsible for the process of change. The group analyzed the department's organization and worked out a new design. The old way of organizing consisted of several specialized work groups. Work, according to the new design, was carried out in integrated groups that performed all tasks for a certain group of clients. The task of managing the department was made more participative by being entrusted to a team that, in addition to the department manager, included representatives from the integrated work groups as well.

The researchers of PMO performed a variety of roles in the project (Docherty, 1976). We provided conceptual input to the discussions in the project group by explaining the ideas of sociotechnical theory. We interviewed and carried out a questionnaire survey with the personnel about their work and how they experienced their situation, and we fed the results back to the project group. We also tried, in various ways, to facilitate the design work and decision making in the project group.

The outcome of the experiment in Skandia was a reasonably well-functioning new way in which to organize work in the insurance department. The new way of organizing work was radically different from the traditional way and was experienced as satisfactory by the people working in the department. The experiment also demonstrated that it was possible to manage a department with an extended leadership function that involved representatives of the personnel. As researchers, we learned that a participative process of change is possible and that it could bring about a broad commitment among the personnel. From the repeated interviews with personnel that were undertaken, it became evident that each individual experienced a unique change process. The custom to depict organizational change with the help of repeated questionnaire studies as a smooth curve hides these individual change processes (Stjernberg, 1977, p. 243).

The forces that wanted to use political power to advance the position of labor became too strong for the political system to even consider a better way of organizing daily work as an alternative to granting the unions more power. The research aimed at producing demonstration projects failed to diffuse widely in the Swedish industry. They did not even diffuse within the companies where the experiments had been carried out despite quite a good deal of attention from outside Sweden, especially for Volvo's Kalmar factory (Gyllenhammar, 1977). However, the ideas that came out of the research projects about instituting teamwork, using flexible and multiskilled groups, and assigning more control over the workflow to the workers have survived. These ideas have become integrated in the standard way of thinking about organizing, although under labels other than sociotechnical theory, for example, *business processes* and, more recently, *sustainable work systems* (Docherty, Forslin, & Shani, 2002).

Technology and les Grandes Ecoles in Paris, 1980–1987

In the URAF projects, we had observed that changes related to information technology (IT) were even more influential than actual change projects in triggering organizational change. That insight led the continued work of the PMO research program to concentrate on the relationship between IT and organization of work. One conclusion drawn from these studies was that it was not fruitful to regard the IT as an external force that had certain effects on the organization, for example, to cause deskilling. It was more fruitful to regard the new technology as a tool to be used. To use IT efficiently, new ways in which to organize work had to be invented, and new skills had to be acquired by the personnel (Löwstedt, 1989).

The studies of IT and organization made me want to get more insight into the role of technology in organizing. I thought that I could gain such insight in France because I had the impression that both the state and French companies pursued policies that favored technological development and innovation. During 1985 and 1986, I had the opportunity to stay at Ecole Centrale, the group CRG (Centre de Recherche de Gestion) at Ecole Polytechnique, and the group CGS (Centre de Gestion Scientific) at Ecole des Mines de Paris. Both CRG and CGS had been formed by engineers who were interested in the application of operation analysis to industrial practice. However, their focus had successively changed, and they had become deeply involved in the problem of managing technology. They studied this problem by completing projects in close interaction with firms such as Renault and public agencies such as RATP, which run the "Metro" (Paris's public system of underground transport).

One form of interaction between the researchers and the practitioners was "reflection groups." Researchers and practitioners would meet to carry out a thorough discussion of the problem at hand. After the meeting, the researchers would spend considerable time, perhaps several weeks, on writing the minutes from the meetings and analyzing the substance of the discussion. Emphasis was put on understanding the logic of the discussion and on uncovering the assumptions on which it was built. CGS tried to understand how the involved actors felt. This approach was different from the one used by ISR and Tavistock that was most interested in how people felt and the social dynamics of the groups.

The analyses made by CGS indicated which assumptions were critical for solving the problem at hand. Therefore, careful studies were undertaken to find out about the validity of these critical assumptions. The results of the empirical observations would be fed back to the reflection group, and a new discussion that incorporated the new findings could ensue. This discussion could, in turn, produce new critical assumptions. In this way, an interchange between researchers and practitioners, interspersed with empirical observations, could go on iteratively for several years (Moisdon, 1992).

IMIT, 1988–1997

In 1988, the Stockholm School of Economics wanted to insert a semester of studies that would integrate the first 2 years of basic studies and to prepare the students for the more specialized studies during the final part of the 4-year master's program. I was responsible for organizing a course that was based on dynamic theories of economic development as a contrast to the more traditional equilibrium models. The course emphasized the role of industrial markets, technological development, and the management of technology. The ideas of economist Eric Dahmén were important for the design of the course (Dahmén, 1988). Much of the input for the new course could be drawn from the research done at the Institute for Management of Innovation and Technology (IMIT), of which I became the head on my return from France.

IMIT's research is based on cooperation between researchers from the schools of engineering in Göteborg (Chalmers), Lund, and Stockholm and the Stockholm School of Economics. More important, the research is carried out on problems of practical relevance and in close contact with industry. IMIT should not provide consultancy but rather should offer industry contract research that would result in reports of interest to the industrial sponsor as well as in scholarly publication. Examples of research carried out within the frame of IMIT are organization of work in production units of SKF and Volvo. IMIT also participated in the international project of the Future of the Automobile that resulted in the book *The Machine That Changed the World* (Womack, 1997). The IMIT projects have resulted in a number of doctoral theses. In addition, IMIT has been able to provide a number of opportunities for senior researchers to stay in the university and continue their research in the area of innovation and management.

The IMIT experience proved to me that it is possible to carry out research in close contact with industry, which is fully or partly industry financed, without assuming the role of a consultant. Not being a consultant may even be an advantage given that it is easier to get an understanding from the sponsors that research must take time and that the expectation for immediate results should not be too high.

_____**FENIX, 1997–**

FENIX is the latest leg on my voyage in the borderland between academy and industry. My experiences in France, the course on industrial development, and the research of IMIT had convinced me that the research and development aiming at product development to create value for customers is a key issue for the international competitiveness of Swedish industry.

Questions related to the organizing of product development during the 1990s were treated in meetings with colleagues in the IMIT network and with researchers from Ecole des Mines. Three of the participants in these discussions—Niclas Adler, Horst Hart, and Flemming Norrgren—had been involved in research on the organization of product development in Ericsson and Volvo, among others. The results were seen as successful by the people from the companies, and they decided to support a larger joint endeavor. An application for a grant for the co-founding together with industry of what was going to be FENIX was submitted to the "Foundation for Knowledge and Competence." The foundation had invited applications for Ph.D. programs aiming at research of relevance for industry and in close collaboration with industry. The grant was obtained after a long period of negotiations. A decisive factor for the success of the grant probably was the backing from the industry.

The name FENIX was chosen for the new program as a metaphor depicting a new and beautiful bird that would rise from the ashes of the old system. For me, FENIX meant that much of what I had learned from the various milestones in my journey could be put into practice and combined with the ideas and experiences of others. The program also had the quality that James (1910/1911) had called "the moral equivalent of war," that is, an exciting adventure where new paths had to be made in the academic landscape, resistance had to be overcome, and innovative solutions had to be found for the problems encountered.

One main idea of FENIX is to bridge the gap between the academy and industry. The bridge is personalized by the executive Ph.D. candidate[1] who continues to work in his or her company in parallel with the doctoral studies and research. The intention is that the research topic should be a question that has a high degree of relevance for the firm. The formulation of the problem, from the perspective of practice, would be taken from the candidate's own experience, from company history, and from discussions with other people in the company. The candidate would then bring the problem over to the academic side, where fellow candidates, supervisors, and academics in FENIX's network of contacts would take part in the process of reformulating the problem into a researchable project out of what is already known and not known, suitable theories, and available research methods. The process ideally should be iterative, with the executive Ph.D. candidate carrying a successively sharpened and information-rich project between the firm and the university.

Above the Borderland

The FENIX bird is still up in the air and moving along with high-flying plans for the future. Therefore, the time has not yet come for me to reflect over the FENIX experience. What I can do at this stage is summarize some of the things I have learned from my 60 years of travel in the borderland between academy and industry that can be of relevance for FENIX's future activities in that borderland.

I put two basic questions in my luggage when my journey started. Why did floating soap not become a success? Why did the bustling industry in my hometown disappear (and why did my family have to move)?

The answer to the first question about floating soap is quite clear. Technical invention is not enough to guarantee success. A new product must fulfill a market need. Getting to know the market's needs may require even more work and inventiveness than does developing a product. Even a combination of product knowledge and market knowledge may be a necessary but not sufficient requirement for success. In addition, customers may have to be made aware of both their need and the possibility of getting it fulfilled. To fulfill all of these requirements for commercial success, different kinds of knowledge have to be mobilized and made to interact. Still, many Swedish firms are technology driven. Their problem is to find ways in which to organize so that the knowledge spheres of technology, market, and sales become mutually reinforcing. In other words, the motto of FENIX, *business creation through knowledge creation,* is still valid as a program for future research.

The answer to the second question about why the soap factory and other industries in Gävle did not survive is a bit more complicated. Why do structures that we have come to regard as established turn out to be ephemeral? One reason is that most firms go out of business sooner or later. No one can expect to recognize the industrial landscape of his or her childhood. However, a few firms survive, albeit in a different shape. Even in Gävle, some survived. The profits from Korsnäs paper and pulp industries were used by its owner, Jan Stenbeck, to build a media empire. The radio producer that moved into the old tobacco factory became a part of Ericsson Radio that is a key to Ericsson's success in systems for mobile telephony. The second question could, therefore, be reformulated in a more meaningful way: Will a firm that acquires and applies research-based management knowledge stand a better chance than other companies of becoming one of the few survivors? Still, I am not sure of the answer to that question. Therefore, I think it merits more research.

Firms that become involved in the FENIX research and executive Ph.D. program are, in fact, engaged in acquiring and applying research-based management knowledge. If the FENIX projects result in knowledge that can be deemed relevant for understanding the central problems of management, the research has made a potential contribution to that second reformulated question. If the research can also result in action that helps the firm to handle its situation in a better way, an even stronger indication of the potential of collaborative management research has been achieved. This volume provides support for these assertions.

Why Boundary-Spanning Research?

Innovations and new knowledge in the area of management tend to emanate from practice rather than from academic research. Academic research has hitherto been relegated to document developments and knowledge that have been created elsewhere.

Business firms are *socially constructed*. They are influenced by laws and rules and by the more or less implicit theories of managers, personnel, and other actors of how reality hangs together. For management science to contribute to improved practice, it must influence these implicit theories and perhaps also make them more explicit. Valid knowledge about what influences what cannot be gained from rigorous observation of reality in a positivist spirit. The reason is that the action, to a large extent, is determined by the actors' implicit theories that can vary considerably independent of observable empirical facts.

The implication is that the management researcher, who has an ambition to contribute to the competence of managers, has to produce theories that are not necessarily fully based on empirical facts. Instead, they should be suggestions to practitioners about suitable ways of reasoning on which to base their actions.

If the theories produced by management scientists are not demanded by practitioners, and if they cannot be conveyed to them, management research risks being looked on as academic exercises in the production of models not anchored in the reality of business. Theory production, therefore, has to be made in close cooperation with practitioners. In this way, practitioners will be able to relate the models to the reality they themselves experience. They can also contribute by suggesting such changes in their own models that can lead to theoretical innovations. Reality has to be co-produced by management scientists and practitioners.

Note

1. The ideas behind and experiences from the executive Ph.D. program are described in Chapter 6 of this volume.

References

Ashby, W. R. (1969). Self-regulation and requisite variety. In F. E. Emery (Ed.), *Systems thinking* (pp. 105–124). Harmondsworth, UK: Penguin. (Original work published 1956)

Buckley, W., & Sandkull, B. (1971). *A systems study of regional inequality: Norrbotten a fourth of Sweden* (SIAR Research Paper 22). Stockholm: Swedish Institute for Administrative Research.

Carlsson, R. (2000). *Strategier för att tjäna pengar: Om affärsidén och andra SIAR-begrepp* (Strategies for making money: About the business idea and other SIAR concepts). Stockholm, Sweden: Ekerlids.

Chein, I., Cook, S., & Harding, J. (1948). The field of action research. *American Psychologist, 3*, 43–50.

Dahmén, E. (1988). "Development blocks" in industrial economics. *Scandinavian Economic History Review, 1*, 3–14.

Danielsson, A. (1976). *Företagsekonomi, begreppsbildnihg, och terminologi* (Business administration, concept formation, and terminology). Lund, Sweden: Studentlitteratur.

Docherty, P. (1976). *Forskarroller i ett aktionsforskningsprojekt* (The role of researchers in an action research project). Stockholm, Sweden: URAF.

Docherty, P., Forslin, J., & Shani, A. B. (Rami). (2002). *Creating sustainable work systems*. London: Routledge.

Edgren, J., Rhenman, R., & Skärvad, P-H. (1983). *Divisionalisering och därefter* (Divisionalization and after). Stockholm, Sweden: Management Media.

Emery, F. E., & Thorsrud, E. (1969). *Form and content in industrial democracy*. London: Tavistock.

Engwall, L., Furusten, S., & Wallerstedt, E. (1993). *Bridge over troubled waters.* Working Paper No. 4, Department of Management, Uppsala University, Sweden.

Gyllenhammar, P. G. (1977). *People at work*. Reading, MA: Addison-Wesley.

Ingenjörshandboken 7. (1951). *Organisation och ekonomi* (Handbook of engineering, Vol. 7: Organization and finance). Stockholm, Sweden: Nordisk Rotogravyr.

James, W. (1911). The moral equivalent of war. In W. James, *Memories and studies*. New York: Longmans, Green. (Original work published 1910)

Kreuder, E. (1946). *Gesellschaft vom Dachboden* (The society in the attic). Stuttgart-Hamburg, Germany: Rowohlt.

Lewin, K., Lippitt, R., & White, R. (1939). Patterns of aggressive behavior in experimentally created social climates. *Journal of Social Psychology, 10*, 271–299.

Likert, R. (1961). *New patterns of management*. New York: McGraw-Hill.

Löwstedt, J. (Ed.). (1989). *Organisation och teknikförändring* (Organization and technological change). Lund, Sweden: Studentlitteratur.

March, J. G., & Simon, H. A. (1958). *Organizations*. New York: John Wiley.

Marrow, A. J., Bowers, D. G., & Seashore, S. E. (1967). *Management by participation*. New York: Harper & Row.

Moisdon, J. C. (1992). *Report on research at the Centre de Gestion Scientific (CGS): Current developments and future prospects*. Paris: Ecole des Mines.

Normann, R. (1972). *Effektiv samhällsplanering eller kontrollerad slumpprocess? En systemstudie av bostadskvoteringen* (Effective social planning or a controlled random process: A systems study of the regulation of the housing market). Lund, Sweden: Studentlitteratur.

Normann, R. (1975). *Management for growth*. Chichester, UK: Wiley.

Rhenman, E. (1973). *Organisation theory for long-range planning*. Chichester, UK: Wiley.

Rhenman, E., & Stymne, B. (1965). *Företagsledning i en föränderlig värld* (Management in a changing world). Stockholm, Sweden: Aldus.

Selznick, P. (1957). *Leadership in administration.* Evanston, IL: Row, Petersen.

Sommerhof, G. (1969). The abstract characteristics of living systems. In F. E. Emery (Ed.), *Systems thinking.* Harmondsworth, UK: Penguin.

Stjernberg, T. (1977). *Organisational change and quality of life: Individual and organizational perspectives on democratisation of work in an insurance company.* Stockholm, Sweden: Stockholm School of Economics, Economic Research Institute.

Stymne, B. (1966). EDP and organisational structure: A case study of an insurance company. *Swedish Journal of Economics, 68*(2), 89–116.

Stymne, B. (1970). *Values and processes: A systems study of effectiveness in three organisations.* Lund: Studentlitteratur.

Stymne, B. (1995). Eric Rhenman: Nydanare inom svensk företagsekonomi (Eric Rhenman: Regenerator of Swedish business economics). In L. Engwall (Ed.), *Föregångare inom företagsekonomin* (Forerunners in business economics) (pp. 369–394). Stockholm, Sweden: Center for Business and Policy Studies.

Swedish Institute for Administrative Research. (1972). *Stora organisationers problem i en strukturellt föränderlig miljö* (The problems of large organizations in a structurally changing environment). Stockholm: Author.

Thorsrud, E., & Emery, F. E. (1969). *Mot en ny bedriftsorganisation* (Toward a new way to organize industrial activities). Oslo, Norway: Tanum.

Trist, E. L., & Bamforth, K. W. (1951). Some social and psychological consequences of the longwall method of coal-getting. *Human Relations, 4*(1), 3–38.

Westerlund, G. (1952). *Group leadership: A field study.* Stockholm, Sweden: Nordisk Rotogravyr.

Womack, J. P. (1997). *The machine that changed the world.* New York: Rawson Associates.

4

Collaborative Research

Strategic Intents and Actual Practices

Niclas Adler and Flemming Norrgren

Management science, founded by reflexive practicing managers, is defined today by a discourse dominated and driven by academics' ideals on theoretical and methodological rigor. However, various stakeholders call for a renewal by the introduction of different collaborative research approaches. Besides questions on ontology, epistemology, and rigor, two fundamental questions still lack a convincing answer:

1. Can management research contribute to management practice? If so, can practicing managers be convinced of the added value of management research?

2. Can management research gain from true collaboration with organizations? If so, can academic researchers be convinced of the added value of the true collaboration in management research?

These questions need to be answered not only through academic debates and stakeholder statements but also through real experimentation and reflection based on the results of the collaborations. This chapter uses a series of experiments with collaborative and interdisciplinary management research that have been performed since 1988 at a group of Swedish universities involving Swedish companies and organizations.

By using illustrations from the experiments and their formation, the chapter discusses and analyzes how the strategic discourse and intent expressed by stakeholders are put into action from the perspective of a research organization pursuing a collaborative approach.

The Debate on Collaborative Research

Future opportunities for management science are often captured in discussions on how managers and management researchers, research programs, and companies can best join forces in the quest for knowledge creation (Starkey & Madan, 2001). Today, leaders of business schools emphasize the importance of leveraging the opportunities by developing their schools' competence in managing the boundaries and providing support and attractive partnerships for different kinds of companies. Departments of education and research both underline the economic value of academic-industry partnerships and initiate discussions and formal programs with the purpose of meeting the challenge. The discourse within management science has followed the prescriptions of methodological and epistemological renewal introduced by Gibbons and colleagues (1994), among others, launching the notion of Mode 2 research. Mode 2 research has been advanced as a boundary-spanning research approach where traditional disciplines merge in search of practical solutions. Mode 2 research is said to be transdisciplinary and takes place in a global scientific arena with many players, where universities constitute only one player—but still a very important player.

The quality of research is measured not only by intellectual interest but also in terms of social, political, and economic usefulness (Ernö-Kjölhede, 2001). The most attractive knowledge producers are those with a great capacity for transforming academic knowledge into applications for resolving problems and making problems the basis for the theoretical discourse. The primary intellectual stimuli do not necessarily come from the researchers' own disciplines or even the academic environment; rather, they come from the group of practitioners who formulate problems and when knowledge is not transferred from one domain to another but instead is co-created in a collaborative process. For management science, this has been described as a necessity to change both the academic mind-set and how managers and firms get involved in the research process by revisiting both epistemology and methodology.

In a recent special issue of the *British Journal of Management*, Starkey and Madan (2001) address the challenge of bridging the relevance gap and aligning stakeholders in the future of management research. They conclude that in order to meet this challenge, academic institutions need to be restructured; new forums, associations, and journals need to be created; new roles and incentives need to be developed; new measures of academic impact need to be implemented; and new timely research approaches need to be developed. Hatchuel (2001) adds to the case that Starkey and Madan (2001) make by formulating a vital question on the nature of management science. Hatchuel (2001) concludes that management science is a design science geared to the investigation of collective action.

Pettigrew (2001) continues with a statement that the management research community has a long way to go to realize its potential and raises the issues of capacity, capability, and delivery for the future of management science. Pettigrew, who concludes that research without scholarly quality will satisfy no one and will certainly disable researchers' capacity to meet the double hurdle of scholarly quality and relevance, proposes a more active approach. Huff and Huff (2001) introduce the need for Mode 3 management research, not only moving from Mode 1 to Mode 2—or the co-existence of both—but also addressing the broader issues of relevance. This discussion is representative of a growing discourse where earlier debates, held mainly within groups of action and intervention researchers, have been expanded into a broader group of management researchers. The discourse is reflected in special issues of management research journals such as *Organization, Administrative Science Quarterly, British Journal of Management, Academy of Management Journal, Academy of Management Review,* and *Academy of Management Executive* as well as at major conferences.

The contemporary scholarly debate can be captured by two major perspectives. The first focuses on emerging opportunities motivating an exploratory approach where management researchers need to explore new ways in which to leverage the empirical settings to extend and innovate managerial models and theories so as to avoid the risk of letting the discourse be dominated by what Hodgkinson, Herriot, and Anderson (2001) call pedantic research. Pedantic research, defined by Hodgkinson and colleagues as research that is perceived as being qualified in terms of both theoretical and methodological rigor, nevertheless lacks the necessary practical relevance. Two quotes can illustrate the point made: "If the duty of the intellectuals in society is to make a difference, the management research community has a long way to go to realize its potential" (Pettigrew, 2001, p. 61) and "Changes currently underway in their external environment will require that business schools engage in a fundamental rethinking of existing structures and process" (Starkey & Madan, 2001, p. 23).

The second perspective focuses on emerging risks, motivating methodologically and theoretically rigorous approaches, where management researchers stay independent and take control over the process while safeguarding that the discourse is not being influenced by what Hodgkinson and colleagues (2001) call *populistic research*. Populistic research is defined by Hodgkinson and colleagues as research that is perceived as practical and relevant but that lacks theoretical and methodological rigor, hence launching the thesis that the mere complexities of knowledge production inhibit collaborative approaches. Collaborative research approaches by definition focus on short-run rather than deep-seated processes and will not be able to carry a true scientific discourse over time. The following two quotes illustrate this point: "To ask practitioners to play major roles in setting research agenda is to risk condemning business school research to a permanent triviality" (Kilduff & Kelemen, 2001, p. 56) and "Attempts to adopt collaborative research approaches will leave business schools with no defensible social role" (Grey, 2001, p. 27). However, the two perspectives agree that management science has to find productive ways in which to manage the increasing demands from various stakeholders through more collaborative approaches despite the differences in strategies and structures they propose.

New Challenges for Research Funding

Competition for governmental funding in university-based research has been steadily increasing during recent years—not least in Sweden, where management research is clearly following the trend. However, much of the current research policy is geared toward integrating public research with stakeholders. Hence, applied research and research initiatives—preferably co-funded by industry—have experienced a number of new opportunities following the introduction of new governmental or other initiatives. Universities are in line with the dominant political trends, highlighting their mission as an actor in socioeconomical development. Many initiatives aim at putting pressure on business schools to increase their interaction with relevant companies and executives. The notion of a "triple helix" of science policy—that is, developing and leveraging relationships and boundary-spanning cooperation among universities, industry, and governmental agencies (elaborated on by Leydesdorff & Etzkowitz, 1997)—is strongly promoted by policymakers. The idea is to capture the expanding role of the knowledge sector that, in turn, is supposed to give priority to research initiatives and research programs that bridge boundaries. Like the Mode 2 approach, the triple helix model of innovation is nonlinear and is not seen as being based on either a science push or a market pull model (Ernö-Kjölhede, 2001). This agenda sets a stage where success in getting funding for research lies in the ability to leverage the research part of the initiative. The objectives have been to enhance knowledge transfer between sectors and to raise competence levels within society. By strengthening networks and competence in setting up and running boundary-spanning initiatives, economic growth is postulated. The tools used to promote this development include joint funding from various sectors, cross-disciplinary research, boundary-spanning ambitions, and new areas for research with a large potential (Schild & Hanberger, 2000).

In parallel with this development, large companies extend their focus on building a capacity to meet the increasing demands on continuous development within highly knowledge-intensive fields. Chief executives highlight the necessity to promote, build, and leverage new organizational strategies and structures supporting the continuous creation, dissemination, and use of knowledge. Corporate knowledge and knowledge provisioning as a main vehicle in the strategy processes has been elaborated on by numerous management researchers during the past decade (see, e.g., Nonaka, 1994) and is actually mirrored in recent organizational innovations such as corporate universities—with an integrated responsibility for long-term competence focus. In addition, we have seen the emerging roles of chief knowledge officers and knowledge centers in some leading companies. For management science and management researchers, this development provides opportunities based on a continuous reflexivity on managerial strategies, structures, and processes that can support future innovations in management research and also compensate for decreased governmental funding for research.

Fifteen Years of Collaborative Research: The Emergence of FENIX

The foundation for FENIX was established during a 10-year period by the setup of two previous research centers: AVK (Arbetsvetenskapliga kollegiet [Swedish]), the Gothenburg Center for Work Science (1988–1994), and its successor CORE (Center for Research on Organizational Renewal) (1994–2000). In a way, the three research centers—AVK, CORE, and FENIX—represent 15 years of experience in changing the way in which management research is organized, is funded, and relates to stakeholders outside of the research community. The three centers represent three generations of development toward a collaborative research mode. The formation of the three centers also mirrors a change process taking place within university-based management research. The story is told through two lenses: (a) basic assumptions governing stakeholder decisions and (b) actions and character of stakeholder collaboration. Examples and illustrations are given from the early phase (AVK, 1988–1994), the maturing phase (CORE, 1994–1997), and the expansion phase (FENIX, 1997–present).

Principles Governing the Programs

In the early discussions around AVK during the late 1980s, various stakeholders, such as managers from large Swedish companies and organizations, union representatives, research foundations, and university management, expressed serious concerns about the competitive situation for management research in relation to the strong needs in companies and the growing demand for high-quality undergraduate, graduate, and executive education. To meet this growing need, it was decided to invest in a special program that would give favorable conditions for associate professors, Ph.D.'s, and Ph.D. students in the field on the condition that the initiative could (a) cut the lead times for the Ph.D. programs, (b) decrease the dropout rate from the Ph.D. programs, and (c) conduct multidisciplinary research. Behind the initiative were those in the labor market who wanted to promote the area and who were especially eager to support the development of multidisciplinary research to better capture some of the complex phenomena in contemporary work organizations. The assumptions behind the support for the initiative were that by providing attractive platforms for young management researchers, they will stay in the field; by supporting multi-disciplinary research, young management researchers will renew the field; and by focusing on efficiency in Ph.D. programs, long-term resource needs will be secured.

The first center, AVK, was set up in 1988 in Göteborg as collaboration among researchers from various departments at two universities. It was funded mainly by a research foundation governed by the parties of the labor market and was limited in time to 6 years. The expectations of the center were met to a large extent. All but 2 of the 20 Ph.D. students finished their degrees, the lead times for the students were reduced by 40%, and the center rated well in terms of scientific publications despite having a faculty from four different disciplines. However, the two universities that were involved never embraced the initiative or provided the necessary support in terms of allocating senior faculty to the research program, research seminars, or Ph.D. student supervision. Instead, the center became detached from the two universities and established its own faculty by providing short-term employment for Ph.D.'s and associate professors. The rationale for this detached position, formulated by the university representatives, was fear of the drain of resources from the ordinary programs. The rationale of the senior faculty at the universities centered on the idea that the multidisciplinary research center was thought to generate less interesting research and lower quality in the Ph.D. program. The assumption behind the critique was that the scientific discourse would be less elaborate and that meeting the demands of defending a Ph.D. thesis necessitates a longer time period than the expected 4 years. The consequence for the center and its work was higher risk, low incentives for young researchers, and an integration problem for the Ph.D. students who worked in the center but were supposed to graduate in a department at one of the two universities.

Following the experiences and results from AVK, the research foundation decided to launch a new national initiative funding three new centers selected from a national competition. The external stakeholders formulated four new goals for the coming centers, namely, that (a) research should strive to work cross-disciplinary and not just have a multidisciplinary faculty, (b) action research should be given priority, (c) relevance for industry should be made more explicit through choice of topics, and (d) the centers should be affiliated with universities rather than being managed as an independent and separated institution as during the early phases of AVK. The basic assumption was that by integrating the new initiatives into universities, they may become vehicles for changing the way in which universities worked. One of the three proposals that won the competition came from one of the research groups at AVK, and that proposal led to the formation of CORE in 1994.

Already after a few years, CORE showed clear results, meeting three of the initial four expectations. Cross-functional groups involving psychology, sociology, business administration, economics, and engineering were running different research projects with co-authored journal publications in the various disciplines as a result. The research projects were set up in collaboration with managers and specialists. The center was jointly governed by academics, university representatives, and company representatives, with the chairman of the board coming from a company. One university was formally accepted to make the center part of its structure but still failed to allocate necessary support in terms of senior faculty and infrastructure and did not pay any attention to the experiences that emerged from the large project. The center expanded the cooperation with Swedish companies. For example, it conducted 10 different research projects funded or co-funded by, and in close collaboration with, Ericsson during the period from 1994 to 1997, involving large numbers of managers and specialists from Ericsson. The projects resulted in interesting experiences and actual experiments in the company as well as in many publications and a Ph.D. thesis. The center also held early discussions on the nature of collaborative research approaches. However, the center did not pursue the action research path in an elaborate way and did not succeed in convincing the host university that there was interesting learning coming from the center. The rationale of the university representatives and senior faculty was again centered on the idea that populistic research produced little or no academic value if based on a set of projects jointly defined together with companies. In addition, the university representatives expressed their reluctance to take part in research pursuing action research methodologies, based on the basic assumptions that building truly joint collaboration with companies will take substantial time and energy and is likely to yield questionable results at best.

Built on the response from Swedish companies and the experiences from joint research projects, a new initiative was born in 1997 when one of the research groups at CORE spun out to establish a new initiative in the boundary between universities and companies. The initiative secured active support from top management in four major Swedish companies, and a new governmental foundation for research and development funded the initiative. In late 1997, 14 million Euros were invested by an initial group of stakeholders (the four major companies, the research foundation, and two additional funding agencies) for a 6-year program to be executed on a national level involving two universities, two colleges, an international visiting faculty, and a substantial number of company employees mainly from AstraZeneca, Ericsson, Telia, and Volvo. The new initiative was named FENIX to underscore the necessary renewal in becoming a research organization in the boundary between universities and companies. The initial stakeholders agreed on six goals for FENIX: (a) to move from working cross-functionally in research projects toward building a transdisciplinary, co-located research program in management; (b) to intensify collaboration with managers and specialists during all phases of the research process; (c) to enable theoretical contributions to the field as a result of developing closer collaboration between practice and theory while developing new research methods; (d) to develop new methodologies that leverage the strength of the close collaboration of the various stakeholders in the research process; (e) to deliver scientific training for persons from companies; and (f) to continuously reflect, analyze, and document the experiment and its outcomes so as to influence management research approaches at the participating universities.

The expansion phase of FENIX has so far resulted in the formation of a boundary-spanning research organization involving more than 100 senior researchers, Ph.D. students, and managers and specialists from participating companies in the actual research projects. A total of 20 leaders from the four major companies have been recruited to pursue an executive Ph.D. program (examined in Chapter 6), 3 have graduated before the expected time, and most of the others are progressing according to the original plans despite working only parttime at their respective companies. Another 13 traditional academic Ph.D. students have graduated as a result of the joint research endeavors. A faculty of 12 senior researchers at the two universities constitutes the core of the research organization, and another 5 senior researchers from France and the United States are an integral part of the research program. An additional 24 senior researchers are engaged in the various research projects or in the supervision of Ph.D. students. Fully 35 research projects have been jointly designed by academics and practitioners, and more than 100 managers and specialists in the companies have actually been working on the research projects. The original budget for the 6-year period has been exceeded by 65% after 5 years due to new external funding for research projects. Three of the original founding companies have decided to further support the expansion of the initiative, one new company has joined the program, and discussions are being held with two more possible new corporate partners. The number of publications has been rising steadily, exceeding 250 over the past 5 years. FENIX has joined forces with North American, French, and British researchers and research groups in launching experiences of new methodological development in management research. Currently, discussions to expand the experiment are taking place with two European universities. However, the sixth initial goal—to actively influence university work processes—has continued to be the most difficult one to achieve. Only incremental changes can be noted, such as educational and pedagogical methods in Ph.D. programs, and the launch of derivative products such as new master's programs for managers.

Collaborative Research With Various Stakeholders

Since 1988, each phase in the experiment has faced growing interest and engagement from the corporate partners. More time is being spent by managers and specialists from the companies in the research projects and other emerging joint activities. During the first phase—the Gothenburg Center for Work Science—the experiment was managed and controlled by the researchers. It was funded mainly by the government but increasingly engaged managers and specialists from the companies and organizations that were studied in the research and governance of the experiment. The Ph.D. program was successful in finalizing theses in four different disciplines.

During the second phase—the Center for Research on Organizational Renewal—managers and specialists were invited to take an active part in the management and control of the experiment. A group of companies was funding and co-funding separate research projects, and the amount of time that executives spent in the projects increased over the years. The senior researchers significantly improved their productivity in publication during the period.

During the third phase—FENIX—executives were invited to take an active role not only in defining areas for research and governance of the experiment but also in actually designing and working in the research projects. The results from the Ph.D. program and the executive Ph.D. program, as well as the productivity of senior researchers, have steadily increased over the years.

During the early phase of AVK, stakeholders did not take an active role in the formation of the center other than their substantial funding and agreeing on its three main goals. The original initiative to start a collaborative center was the result of a top-down/bottom-up approach. In addition to the rationale and assumptions accounted for previously, board members were concerned about the lack of work science-oriented researchers that could take on the roles of the pioneering professors who would soon be retiring. Individual researchers in two of the universities dominating this area got involved early in developing a response to the funding organization. The other stakeholders were university management and some of the pioneering professors in various departments.

During the maturing phase—the formation of CORE—both university representatives and corporate representatives took part in the overall governance through the board, and the chairman was recruited from industry. The various stakeholders also jointly agreed on the four main goals for the center. Companies were engaged as co-sponsors for some of the projects. Managers and specialists from various companies were also active in the formulation of research topics in the three different research groups and in the formation of new research projects. However, the academic researchers conducted the research, and Ph.D. students and the various stakeholders were invited to research seminars where findings were presented and discussed.

The third-generation center, FENIX, originated through extending the stakeholder involvement in the collaborative research programs. From the outset, the principle was set that at least 50% of the funding should be invested by companies. The new research foundation decided that industry would have board representation that was just as strong as the academic institutions had, with the chairman of the board being recruited from industry. It was also required that the majority of Ph.D. candidates would be managers from the companies and that the center should develop new ways for cooperation based on more systematic collaboration between academics and practitioners. Half of the funding was placed in the university system and half in an independent research foundation, but detailed contracts between the stakeholders regulated how the program should be managed as one integrated center with one management and one board.

The new center became productive in terms of academic output as well as in attracting practitioners into the actual research processes. There were 20 applicants for each position to the executive Ph.D. program, and new company-financed projects were added. Research groups in other universities wanted to join, as did more companies. The board and the management of the center called an extra board meeting and invited the management of the two universities to participate in a discussion on how to expand the center. The board of the center suggested a more permanent structure to be owned jointly by industry and universities. The meeting quickly turned into a debate between university management, on the one side, and industry board members and management of the center, on the other. The university representatives doubted and questioned the given account of the initial success and did not want to support a co-owned new structure that would "compete" with the existing departments. Despite the fact that 2 years earlier the university representatives had voiced their opinion that the center would risk becoming a disguised consultancy activity with poor research, they expressed deep concerns that too much emphasis had been given to scientific productivity and too little attention had been given to the relevant criteria. The discussion yielded no decisions.

The initial two questions can be recapitulated as follows:

1. What learning can be drawn from the experiments and three phases of development in a collaborative research organization, and can management research contribute to management practice? If this is the case, can practicing managers become convinced of it?

2. Can management research actually gain from true collaboration with organizations and their actors? If so, can academic researchers become convinced of it?

Despite the challenges, the companies gradually became more involved in the actual research. A significant gap still remained for management research to contribute to management practice. Three quotes from vice presidents at two of the participating companies and another major Swedish company illustrate the remaining challenge:

You provide a great description of the important problems and challenges, but we here at the headquarters already have a number of solutions and plans and now only foresee some implementation problems in fixing it. (vice president, participating company)

What you show has a high face validity, but now we do not need more analysis—we need action. (vice president, participating company)

I don't see what we possibly could learn from such a cooperation, and we do not have the time to teach you or the other companies how to best manage R&D [research and development]. (vice president, non-participating company)

The real challenge is that managers probably first have to be convinced that management research can contribute to dealing with everyday problems. Management research probably cannot gain from true collaborations until academic researchers become convinced that they may benefit from it and invest the necessary time and effort into developing new research approaches that leverage the true collaboration. Three quotes from senior researchers and university management at the participating universities serve as illustrations of this parallel challenge:

The conception of executive Ph.D. is problematic from the start and does not make sense. By definition, a manager and a researcher are at the opposite ends of a continuum. (senior researcher)

From my many years of experience in the field, I know that action and reflection must be separated in time and space and most often also in person. (senior researcher)

Do you really need to build a separate organization for this? Is it not better to have a small program office that supports ongoing research in the area at the different departments? (senior university administrator)

Despite the challenges, unproven answers, and lack of convincing argumentation and results, corporate support has increased over time, while the participating universities have remained skeptical and disinterested despite growing international interest. The rationale for the growing corporate interest can best be explained by the necessity for corporations to enhance their reflective capability on management issues. The rationale for the university stakeholder actions can best be explained by considering collaborative research approaches as a major learning challenge that necessitates double-loop learning.

Industry Interests in Collaborative Research

Earlier work has shown that, with growing knowledge intensity and complexity of managerial challenges, the nature of the relationships have changed from pure sponsorships to different forms of partnerships (for a review and an argument, see Jacob, Hellström, Adler, & Norrgren, 2000). Despite all attention and expressed intention to meet the challenge and to bridge boundaries and gaps, collaborative research approaches still generate continuous conflicts within the university system. Such efforts do not fit with the dominating incentive system. Furthermore, relatively few examples of successful collaborative joint ventures between universities and corporate partners can be found in the literature.

Earlier work (Jacob et al., 2000) suggests that changing the role of industry from being sponsors of particular research projects or initiatives to becoming partners in setting them up and supporting their execution will reduce the risk of developing *populistic science* (Hodgkinson et al., 2001). However, the problem of continuous development of theoretical and methodological rigor that can leverage the close cooperation with the empirical settings remains. By going one step further and building strong reciprocal relationships, and by developing structures and processes where the responsibilities are shared by academics and practitioners, new innovations in methodological and theoretical rigor may emerge.

Moving from *partnership* to *collective action* necessitates that the carriers of the endeavor are able to make an effective argument that every participant is likely to gain significantly from the collective action. Not having the examples or illustrations of successful experiments or the shared experience makes such a task very difficult.

Our interpretation of the results obtained during the experiment is that it is not the increasing scientifically "canned" knowledge (e.g., dissertations, publications) that has led participating companies to develop their commitment from partnership to collective action. The increased funding of research is matched by increased interaction between researchers and practitioners. During the latter stages of the third phase of the experiment, these interactions also started to result in field experiments (see, e.g., Roth, 2002) where academics and practitioners manifested collective actions. Hence, we would suggest that the combination of tacit and explicit knowledge in collaborative teams (developing a shared knowledge and language) and the possibilities to experiment with actions are what attract interest. One senior executive in the participating companies argued,

> If you can convince us that management research actually could be a vehicle for reflexive change and development within our company and [could] enhance our own capacity—we really have an interesting future ahead of us. (vice president of research, participating company)

Academic performance also plays an important role in terms of legitimacy. Key executives in the participating companies strongly believe in the necessity of continuous reflexivity around strategies and structures. However, pure reflexivity is not legitimate to prioritize in ongoing corporate operations. Collaborative research approaches have the potential to legitimate necessary reflexivity and to introduce frameworks and models explaining and illustrating the role of reflexivity in the development and formation of strategies and structures. As pointed out in Chapter 1 of this volume, R&D on management has the potential to become a natural and functional process in companies.

Collaborative Research and the Lack of Organizational Learning

Despite the various contributions of the three collaborative research projects, academic researchers remain doubtful whether the experiences are sustainable. This suggests a lack of organizational learning. In our view, there is evidence of what Argyris and Schön (1978) call *double-loop learning* among the industry partners yet relatively little within the universities. One of the major reasons why learning is limited is that there seems to be a larger gap between what Argyris and Schön call *espoused theory* (theories and behaviors that are adhered to officially) and theories in use (theories and behaviors that are actually employed) among university stakeholders than among industry representatives. Even if university representatives formally declare their interest in developing more collaboration among disciplines and between academia and practice, they do not act in accordance with their espoused theory. The lack of learning for the university part of the collaborative approaches can also be seen as a result of the type of issues that are at stake. Collaborative research centers are attempting to radically change a core activity of the university. Recruiting Ph.D. students from managerial ranks and supporting them as cohorts so as to complete their Ph.D. studies on a part-time basis while maintaining the same cycle time is a radical change from the individualistic situation of in-house recruited Ph.D. students. It also represents one of the "holy cows" of academic training: The academic approach with continuous questioning may be regarded as being threatened by the involvement of practicing managers in the research process. The combination of radical change and core activities is an example of an area where political behavior would be probable, thereby inhibiting learning and promoting defensive behavior. For the corporate stakeholders, although the involvement in the research programs is important enough for them to increase the investment, it represents not a core activity but rather a possible enhancement.

One other reason for lack of at least double-loop learning on behalf of the academic stakeholders may be that it involves persons acting within the same power structure. The management of the collaborative research center cannot ignore the partner university administration. It must at least be accepted as a legitimate partner to be able to hire Ph.D. students. The university management is well aware that it has the formal power to block some initiatives or ideas. The dependency can be seen as one source of blocking learning because it can prevent the willingness to exchange open and valid information that is a prerequisite for double-loop learning. The same relation is not present in the cooperation between the collaborative research center and the corporate stakeholders. The center has not faced the same unilateral control that can be formally wielded by the partner university.

This takes us to a situation where the path dependence of relationships develops into different routes for the collaborative approaches. The relationships with universities gradually become more detached. Universities invest less money, time, and interest save for episodic interventions to stay in control over some important issues and to avoid changing their basic routines and rules. In essence, the stability of their theories in use and their development in espoused theories in favor of collaborative research widen the gap between what they say (espoused theories) and what they do (theories in use). On the other hand, industry has invested more effort, time, and money over the period while remaining positive about the collaborative approaches that then reduce the gap between espoused theories and theories in use. The commitment to collaborative research—manifested in actual decisions and activities rather than in formal statements—is perhaps best illustrated by the investment in prolonging and expanding the partnership during a difficult economic time for most of the corporate partners. The sustainability of the experiment today is dependent on corporate support, and the diffusion of the experiences appears to be limited to actors working within the environment.

It continues to be an open question whether undertakings such as FENIX and its predecessors have a future within the established university structures. An example from an ongoing FENIX research project reveals that it is not only universities that have a problem in introducing external collaboration. A study of a very ambitious market orientation change program involving several hundred of the most prominent managers revealed that, out of more than 100 change initiatives, only 30% involved market or sales functions, 15% had contacts with end users and customers, and 6% resulted in changes that would directly affect customers. The remaining actions dealt mainly with policymaking and administrative issues, that is, internal company actions. Thus, making our espoused theories about "market orientation" and our theories in use on this matter converge is not just a problem facing universities exclusively; it is a problem facing industry as well. The future of collaborative research activities puts some demands on our ability to develop arenas for learning and reflexivity.

References

Argyris, C., & Schön, D. (1978). *Organizational learning: A theory of action perspective.* Reading, MA: Addison-Wesley.

Ernö-Kjölhede, E. (2001). *Managing collaborative research: Unveiling the micro dynamics of the European triple helix.* Copenhagen, Denmark: Copenhagen Business School Press.

Gibbons, M., Limoges, C., Nowotny, H., Schwartzman, S., Scott, P., & Trow, M. (1994). *The new production of knowledge.* London: Sage.

Grey, C. (2001). Re-imaging relevance: A response to Starkey and Madan. *British Journal of Management, 12,* 27–32. (Special issue)

Hatchuel, A. (2001). Management pillars. *British Journal of Management, 12,* 33–39. (Special issue)

Hodgkinson, G. P., Herriot, P., & Anderson, N. (2001). Re-aligning the stakeholders in management research: Lessons from industrial, work, and organizational psychology. *British Journal of Management, 12,* 41–48. (Special issue)

Huff, A. S., & Huff, J. O. (2001). Re-focusing the business school agenda. *British Journal of Management, 12,* 49–54. (Special issue)

Jacob, M., Hellström, T., Adler, N., & Norrgren, F. (2000). From sponsorship to partnership in academy-industry relationships. *R&D Management, 30,* 3.

Kilduff, M., & Kelemen, M. (2001). The consolations of organization theory. *British Journal of Management, 12,* 55–59. (Special issue)

Leydesdorff, L., & Etzkowitz, H. (1997). A triple helix of university-industry-government relations. In H. Etzkowitz & L. Leydesdorff (Eds.), *Universities and the global knowledge economy: A triple helix of university-industry-government relations.* London: Pinter.

Nonaka, I. (1994). A dynamic theory of organizational knowledge creation. *Organization Science, 5,* 14–37.

Pettigrew, A. M. (2001). Management research after modernism. *British Journal of Management, 12,* 61–70. (Special issue)

Roth, J. (2002). *Knowledge unplugged.* Ph.D. dissertation, Chalmers University of Technology, Göteborg, Sweden.

Schild, I., & Hanberger, A. (2000). *Industrial research schools: A real-time evaluation of the Swedish Knowledge Foundation's research school programme.* Evaluation Report No. 6, Umeå Center for Evaluation Research, Umeå University, Sweden.

Starkey, K., & Madan, P. (2001). Bridging the relevance gap: Aligning stakeholders in the future of management research. *British Journal of Management, 12,* 3–26. (Special issue)

Academic
Commentary on Part I

David Knights

*Department of Management,
University of Keele, United Kingdom*

I am extremely pleased to be contributing in a small way to this volume because I have always seen myself as an academic who seeks to collaborate with, rather than stand aloof from, management as a practice. As is clear from the four chapters that constitute this first part of the volume, however, there are only a handful of industry-university collaborations and even fewer that have survived beyond a fairly limited period. Of course, this section of the volume is intended largely to provide a framework for the rest of the book, where I presume more practical examples of academic-industry partnerships can be found. The first two chapters in this section offer broad solutions to the problems in suggesting the medical, pharmaceutical, and bioscience collaborations as a model, and the final two chapters document in some detail the contradictions and tensions of academic-industry collaboration. While supporting these broad solutions, I suggest that an ethical/critical approach is the most appropriate way in which to avoid some of the tensions that accompany university-industry collaborations.

Hatchuel and Glise (Chapter 1) provide a strong justification for pursuing academic-industry collaborative research, arguing that many management ideas throughout history, and especially those having the greatest impact (e.g., those of Fayol and Taylor), were a result of some form of theory-practitioner collaboration. However, once having placed ideas about management and the contexts in which it is practiced into historical perspective, the authors conclude that the current situation demands a form of collaboration that might better be based on the research and development (R&D) model as practiced by the pharmaceutical and bioscience industries. Here, contemporary large corporations, often formed out of major mergers and acquisitions, collaborate closely with academics in their programs of scientific discovery to develop new products designed to improve the health and well-being of populations. In the light of recent problems surrounding Enron and WorldCom, perhaps the R&D model of industry-academic research collaboration is appropriate for developing innovative forms of corporate governance.

Starkey and Tempest (Chapter 2) follow a similar line of argument about the need for new thinking within social science and the production of management knowledge. Subscribing to a similar notion of the co-production of knowledge, their suggestion is that we compare the production of management knowledge with knowledge produced by pharmaceutical and medical schools to explore possibilities of improving the relationship between management theory and practice. In the absence of a more engaged role with practitioners, business schools will have no alternative way in which to secure their legitimacy other than through a technocratic discourse of "excellence." The league table form of elitism does not appear to have been successful with practitioners in the United States. Despite this, it seems to be the model that the United Kingdom is seeking to emulate. The authors suggest an alternative in that given the proliferation and complexity of knowledge in contemporary society, academia could fill an important gap in acting as a nexus for communicating, disseminating, and creating knowledge that is of value to, and relevant for, business and society.

Whereas these first two chapters look to the future of academic-industry collaboration without actually examining current concrete examples, the authors of the final two chapters in this section reflect historically on their personal experiences with academic-industry collaboration largely in Sweden. The authors of both report comparatively successful industry-academic collaborations that nonetheless suffer a number of tensions and difficulties.

Stymne (Chapter 3) describes a lifetime of practical experience of seeking to work as an academic researcher with industry. In so doing, he makes it clear how frequently industry-university collaborations or partnerships experience difficulties. In a truncated academic autobiography, Stymne not only provides a historical review of the changes that affected his intellectual development in respect to the vexed question of the relationship between the theory and practice of management but he also records a number of industry-university collaborations in which he has been involved. Perhaps one of the most successful was the Swedish Institute for Administrative Research (SIAR), established in 1966. But as Stymne points out, tensions appeared early in SIAR's development, particularly around maintaining a demarcation between research and consultancy. Because of this, its founder, Eric Rhenman, pulled SIAR away from the Stockholm School of Economics, where it had been based, and began pursuing what became known as clinical organization research. Here, the researchers would seek to solve organizational problems while, at the same time, recording their observations for purposes of academic research. Stymne describes how after a period of only 4 years since SIAR's formation, although clients had participated in the process of research, there was uncertainty as to whether practitioners benefited much from the projects. The tension between the values of academia and those of commercial life reemerged, with the result that SIAR became a commercial consultancy to eventually merge with the French consultants Bossard.

Adler and Norrgren (Chapter 4) provide an account of the early developments leading to the current FENIX program, which is probably the most advanced form of industry-academic collaboration in Europe and perhaps in the world. I am not sure that the program was called "FENIX" because it was seen to be rising from the ashes of past failures, but that would be partly appropriate given the difficulties that nearly every previous program had experienced. Nonetheless, the authors see the earlier phases[1] as important in preparing the ground for FENIX to emerge in 1997 with joint funding of 14 million Euros from a group of industry, university, government, and other agencies. Although highly successful in terms of levels of funding, volumes of research, and practitioner involvement as well as in the launching of an executive Ph.D. program, a major problem is that industrial leaders often see the activity as failing to have an impact on their practice. In addition, the activity continues to create major conflicts within the universities. Although espousing in theory the importance of industry-academic collaboration, university practice often contradicts this ideal. Furthermore, the traditional university structure, its career and incentive system, and its values rarely are conducive to the development and expansion of industry-academic collaboration. This may often result in pushing activists in this field to move outside of this structure, but the experience of doing so (e.g., SIAR) is a hostage to fortune in terms of shifting the work in the direction of outright commercial modes of management consultancy.

Both of these final two chapters report on experiences that reflect many of my own in attempting to forge closer links with industry. Indeed, the opposition to the industry-academic partnerships that I was forging around 1997–1998 resulted in massive conflicts. These led to my transferring part of the activity to Nottingham University, where it continues to thrive but at a much-reduced level of activity compared with the level that had been proposed earlier.

It may be argued that the conflicts and tensions experienced by the experiments recorded here are not dissimilar to those experienced by a number of U.K. attempts at closer relations between industry and academia. Many of the industry-academic collaborations in the United Kingdom that existed during the 1990s have now been abandoned due partly to pressure from practitioners for them to offer consultancy services at a price lower than can be found in the commercial marketplace. A partnership with human resource management practitioners and academics was organized by David Guest from Brunel University but collapsed after a few years due to conflicts between academic and business interests. One of a similar nature, organized from the London Business School and then from the Cranfield

School of Management, has recently been run down because its director, Veronica Edwards, sees it as conflicting with her career interests to publish through academic channels. It is interesting to note here how even the highly successful Tavistock Institute of Human Relations in the United Kingdom declined during the 1980s partly because it had difficulty in securing practitioner interest in its research outputs. Some of the Tavistock researchers turned their attention to Scandinavia, where their ideas secured a more favorable reception due to the more established interests in industrial democracy and worker participation.

Only three U.K. university-industry collaborations focused on management or business schools appear to be continuing currently. First, Roger Undy at Oxford University runs a Personnel Director's Forum exclusively from the private sector with high fees. Second, under the leadership of John Purcell, the Bath Business School runs a Human Resources Directors Forum that is active but more as a way of exchanging ideas on topics of mutual interest to academics and industry rather than as a vehicle for original research. With approximately 50 participants, including academics as well as public sector and private sector senior managers, the latter two groups contribute $600 (U.S.) per annum for the meetings, dinners, and a small contribution to the school's research activities. Third, I continue to organize with colleagues (including Ken Starkey) a Financial Services Research Forum that I originally established in 1994 at the University of Manchester Institute of Science and Technology. This now is run from the Nottingham University Business School, and despite the demise of the stock market and its negative effect on financial service companies, the forum has retained a membership of 26 organizations that funds research at approximately $225,000 (U.S.) per annum. One reason for its continuity, I would argue, has been the refusal to allow the activity to slip down the road of consultancy. This is not to argue that those tensions do not exist, but if industry-university collaboration is to survive, it has to be distinctive from both consultancy and conventional academic work. One aspect of that distinctiveness is to retain a critical edge on issues that are discussed or researched, and throughout the forum's existence much of the research has refused to pull any punches and has sought to challenge the practitioners to reflect critically on their practices. It may be argued that we have been helped, rather than hindered, by the "bad press" that the U.K. financial services have suffered since new regulations at the point of sale were introduced during the late 1980s. With a greater dose of moral or ethical self-reflection generated by the collaboration with academics, perhaps the forum members could avoid some of the scandals and mistrust that the industry currently suffers.

In conclusion, I think that industry-academic collaboration has to develop a distinctive approach that I am not sure is reflected entirely in these introductory chapters. There is, for example, a danger reflected somewhat in the final two chapters of simply acceding to, rather than seeking to constitute, the increasing demands of the different stakeholders in any collaboration. Also, there is always the danger that closer relations between academia and industry will result in a lack of realism, on the one side, and in a collapse into managerialism, on the other. A lack of realism can result in practitioners withdrawing or placing enormous pressure on the academics to be more relevant. The response, as in some of the examples in these chapters, may be to become managerialist in the sense of allowing practicing managers to define the problems and then to focus research directly on seeking solutions to them. In extremis, as in the case of SIAR, the academics turn toward commercial consultancy.

Although these responses are recorded in some detail in the final two chapters of this section, the concern is primarily with the tensions that surround industry-academic collaboration. Despite the rhetoric of support from the universities, these tensions derive from both sides of the industry-academic divide. The solution offered by the first two chapters in the section is one of following the R&D model, or some variant of it, evident in pharmacy, medicine, and bioscience, but this solution is not entirely convincing because the parallels between these spheres and other businesses would appear to be limited on the surface. This is because there is much more of a consensus regarding the importance of developing new drugs and medical knowledge than there is regarding the concerns of many of the sectors in which management is involved more generally. Few would challenge the search for improvements in medical health and well-being, but in terms of our own case of financial services there is not the same consensus around the products that they offer. However, on closer reflection, the gap between the two might not be so great, for it is less the products themselves than the methods of production and distribution that are contentious, not just in financial services but also in relation to health products. In particular, it is the fact that they are produced and distributed primarily for private profit and that medical and/or financial health/security is simply a means to an end. Is our health, whether in relation to bodily or financial well-being, safe in the hands of major drug or financial corporations? There are clearly significant ethical issues surrounding both of these sectors that perhaps industry-academic collaboration should focus on. None of the chapters in this section discusses these concerns, and yet these concerns could represent the most crucial point whereby public academics and private managers can come together for both mutual and social benefits. Academic-industry collaboration should not seek to directly emulate mainstream research, on the one hand, or consultancy, on the other, because such collaboration will probably always fall short of the standards of either. Instead, it should be assertive about its own distinctive contribution. My view is that to remain relevant without being subservient and to retain its academic credibility and independent integrity, an ethical/critical approach to research is the most appropriate contribution academics can make to industry.

Note

1. The early phase was the Gothenburg Center for Work Science between 1988 and 1994. Its successor, the Center for Research on Organizational Renewal (1994–1997), is seen as the maturing phase leading to the expansion phase of FENIX.

Executive Commentary on Part I

Mikael Dohlsten

Professor, Global Vice President,
AstraZeneca R&D, Mölndal, Sweden

The pharmaceutical/biotech industry is characterized by strong emphases on scientific excellence and medical or technological breakthroughs as a strategic foundation. This has been fueled by large research and development (R&D) investments, the employment of highly skilled scientists, and the establishment of exclusive R&D facilities often co-located near leading universities and hospitals. The pharmaceutical/biotech industry has endured very long product cycles; for example, the time from project idea to drug release on the market takes 10 to 15 years. Most pharmaceutical/biotech companies have experienced a large attrition of projects; for example, only 1% of early discovery projects end up as products. Pharmaceutical/biotech companies have consequently been exposed to high business risks. However, sustained growth of the industry has been secured by the launch of patent-protected innovative products that have fulfilled medical needs in the health community. These blockbusters have delivered large financial returns of investment, and with billions of U.S. dollars, annual sales have supported continuous reinvestments in expanding R&D endeavors. Recently, pharmaceutical/biotech companies have faced growing costs for R&D's newly launched products, higher rates of competing projects, shorter periods of market exclusivity, and increased price pressure on new products. Most of the current leading pharmaceutical/biotech companies fail to increase R&D output, as measured in product numbers, and are heavily dependent on the success of single products.

The management of pharmaceutical/biotech companies faces five imperative and interdependent challenges: (a) to formulate a vision and a clear long-term strategy aimed at delivering innovative products; (b) to develop tactics to sustain an efficient R&D operation and a leading quality pipeline; (c) to define annual challenging goals that focus on short-term delivery; (d) to develop leadership values to manage creativity, commitment, and control; and (e) to reduce the risk by renewing and developing a valuable product pipeline. Collaborative management research projects in more mature and established industrial sectors can provide vital knowledge and learning. The four chapters in Part I discuss how symbioses can be obtained in an interactive dialogue and true cooperation among management researchers, executives, and specialists facing large and complex managerial challenges. Contemporary management principles can be understood and developed by studying a historical perspective, as discussed in Chapter 1 by Hatchuel and Glise, or in real-time analyses exemplified by the Swedish Institute for Administrative Research (SIAR), Institute for Management of Innovation and Technology (IMIT), and FENIX, as described in the chapters by Stymne (Chapter 3) and Adler and Norrgren (Chapter 4). It is possible that new and future managerial models and approaches can be developed jointly through extensive experimentation and rigorous analysis.

In science-based corporations facing highly complex managerial challenges, we foresee that the traditional development initiatives seem to be dependent on and carried out by leading management consultancy firms such as McKinsey, Arthur D. Little, and Andersen Consulting. This dependency has some major limitations that can be augmented and strengthened by the development of an internal capacity and tradition to handle managerial challenges as elaborated in this section of the volume. Collaborative management research, providing the analytical toolboxes, frameworks, and process control rather than providing predefined solutions, may foster a climate of self-reflection and organizational learning that contributes to a competitive advantage in both medical science and management science. Hence, there is a great potential for collaborative research. As Starkey and Tempest conclude in Chapter 2, "The unexplored task for the business school is to act as the nexus for knowledge creation, sharing, and diffusion . . . that adapts to the broad needs of business," given that the format for the cooperation is perceived as valuable for both groups of actors on a long-term basis as well as on a short-term basis.

At AstraZeneca, as well as at other major pharmaceutical/biotech companies, we have been challenged with the fact that the outcome of R&D projects may often be highly unpredictable but, at the same time, may constitute the foundation for our company. The R&D strategy is there to outline the research focus and to integrate an analysis of the medical opportunity, technical feasibility, and capabilities. In many companies, the strategy is supplemented by studies on future change scenarios in health care, technology, and patient demands. This serves as an opportunity to assess priorities to changes in the external environment. Today, pharmaceutical/biotech R&D interacts mainly with internal customers such as marketing companies, representatives from medical and regulatory organizations, and representatives from health-providing and health-managing organizations. In the future, increased business focus may be directed at patients as end customers given that we can foresee a shift in power balance from health providers to end customers. It is possible that financial providers, acting on behalf of end customers, health insurance companies, or a national social security system, will also be a stronger target for R&D strategies. Given the uncertainty in predicting trends in medical opportunity, technology breakthroughs, and scientific innovation during a 5- to 10-year perspective, combined with the current 10-year product cycles, it is conceivable to balance emphasis on a long-term strategy with strong pragmatic decision making based on tactical progress in internal projects. Thus, the strategy may, in an extreme setting, be crucial for guiding 3-year investments in infrastructure, heavy equipment, key technology/science platforms, and recruitment of new capabilities, while the actual business area focus may be induced by real-time adjustments to internal tactical progress in a few R&D projects. The pragmatic integration of a midterm-focused strategy and short-term tactical decision making has led us to elaborate on a *"stractical" approach* that guides the management of our R&D. The stractical approach is driven strongly by our own R&D capabilities and uses market analyses to set a highly competitive commercial end product profile with the potential to deliver a unique and successful product. The stractical approach is based on cautious changes in business focus when medical opportunities and technical breakthroughs open new avenues. Stractical changes in direction will be characterized as "drift and shift," involving gradual internal entrance into neighboring but not remote technology areas, and use of a strong external alliance network to bridge vulnerable periods of gaps in internal capabilities. The drift and shift strategy limits the ability to capture suddenly appearing large distal business opportunities versus more "hit-and-run," purely tactical strategies. On the other hand, it limits misinterpretations or misjudgments in areas with limited internal experience seen during hit-and-run periods. The stractical approach will favor a gradual internal adaptation period and avoid premature entrance into a new, technically complex, but strategically promising area. The stractical approach helps in achieving the balance between risk and innovation, and it emphasizes the long-term core areas when entering into new emerging business areas.

In large, experienced, and profitable pharmaceutical/biotech corporations, there is a need for gradual improvements to continuously enhance the value of the R&D pipeline and sustain a competitive business. The internal development of new managerial models and approaches as the stractical approach is necessary and made possible by boundary-spanning cooperation. Management research can provide the necessary rigor and can guide experimentation, analysis, and reflections to launch new models or approaches. Collaborative management research also has the potential to catalyze the internal thought processes and revitalize actual management practices by creating an inquisitive collaborative research climate that engages different executives and specialists in the corporation. To secure the evolution of competitive R&D, reflexive executives and specialists can leverage from collaborative research with management researchers and others struggling with similar challenges to capture tacit and explicit knowledge in collaborative teams, as discussed in Chapter 4 by Adler and Norrgren. We at AstraZeneca look forward to continued joint elaboration on managerial challenges to secure the development of leading-edge managerial approaches and sustainable competitive advantage.

PART II

Collaborative Research

Some Lenses and Mechanisms

Part II of this volume is aimed at presenting an overview of the different schools of collaborative research and providing some lenses and mechanisms that can facilitate collaborative research activities. Whereas the first part of the volume explored some of the historical traits of management research and some of the challenges facing the fields of management practice and management research, Part II seeks to outline some of the schools, roles, arenas, and mechanisms of collaborative research activities. It may be possible here, drawing on new institutional theory, to talk about the *morphology* of collaborative research and the different forms of interaction in collaborative research settings.

After traveling with Hatchuel and Glise (Chapter 1) through the history of and possible future for management practice and research, with Starkey and Tempest (Chapter 2) on the rocky management research discourse road, in the borderland together with Stymne (Chapter 3), and now as a passenger in the formation of the FENIX experiment, a number of questions have been raised. Part II of the volume, which focuses on lenses and mechanisms for collaborative research, bridges part of the gap between possible opportunities and feasible approaches. It elaborates on different lenses and mechanisms and their rationales, and it opens the door to the third section of the volume, where actual cases and illustrations on collaborative research endeavors are described.

In Chapter 5, Shani, David, and Willson review and discuss the essence of eight different schools or traditions of collaborative research. Applying two different models for analysis, Habermas's knowledge interests model and Hatchuel's management science model, the authors show that there are shared trajectories and knowledge interests in these different collaborative research orientations at the same time as there are significant differences among them. Collaborative research is not a single unified perspective on management research; rather, it is characterized by some shared elements and a number of divergent views that constitute a broad range of methodological tools to leverage a true partnership with the companies that are being studied.

In Chapter 6, Hart, Kylén, Norrgren, and Stymne present the rationale behind and experiences from the FENIX executive Ph.D. program. They analyze its role in building and leading collaborative research settings. According to the authors, collaborative research needs a long-term commitment from both researchers and participating companies. An executive Ph.D. program is one way in which to establish a shared arena for collaborative efforts. The authors investigate a number of practical topics related to the management of an executive Ph.D. program and show how seemingly small decisions may have significant implications for the program. The chapter provides a number of valuable experience-based learnings from collaborations in the Ph.D. program setting.

In Chapter 7, Roth, Sandberg, and Svensson explore the complex role of the collaborative researcher who is a member of the organization under study. The authors present three mini-case studies from their own collaborative research efforts in AstraZeneca (pharmaceuticals), Telia Promotor (telecommunications), and Ericsson (telecommunications). Referring to their own roles as the boundary-spanning researchers within and between the academy and the business world as *insider action researchers* (IARs), the authors show how the IAR role is inherently dynamic and needs to be situation and context dependent. They argue that the dynamic nature of the IAR role and its context requires continuous reflection, examination, balancing, and nurturing throughout the collaborative research process.

In Chapter 8, Börjesson and Fredberg discuss how they have been using a collaborative research mechanism labeled "jam sessions" in their collaborative research activities in the digital media industry. In the authors' account, the jam session is both a methodology aimed at data collection and joint data analysis with the participants of the jam session and an arena for open communication about shared concerns and interests. The jam session mechanism, highly influenced by recent writings in management research about self-organizing processes, is proposed as a useful mechanism in collaborative research activities.

Finally, in Chapter 9, Stebbins and Valenzuela present the structural learning mechanism as an arena in which collaborative research can be housed, nurtured, and led. Building on earlier notions of parallel learning structures, action research systems, and clinical inquiry methodologies, the authors present a case study of a health care organization that spans more than 26 years of collaborative research. While illustrating the nature of the structural learning mechanism, the case documents successful collaboration between researchers and company members in the ongoing investigation of problematic areas as well as in the pursuit of practical actions and, at the same time, contributions to the scientific body of knowledge. The structural learning mechanism is proposed as a useful mechanism that forms and institutionalizes partnerships that are critical for collaborative research.

Thus, the aim of Part II is to offer some mechanisms and analytical framework that can guide academic researchers and practitioners to set up, design, and organize collaborative research endeavors. In Part III of the volume, nine empirical cases of collaborative research projects in a variety of organizations and industries in different geographical locations are presented. The different orientations, lenses, and mechanisms presented in Part II are integrated into the discussions of the chapters in Part III.

5

Collaborative Research

Alternative Roadmaps

A. B. (Rami) Shani,
Albert David, and Cory Willson

Historically, management research is embedded in the study of organizational and management issues for the purpose of generating scientific knowledge. As of late, we have witnessed an emergent critique that management research does not seem to be of high relevance to managerial practice. Some label this discrepancy as "the relevancy gap in management research" (Starkey & Madan, 2001). At the same time, a relatively recent phenomenon is the pressure to produce knowledge for the consumption of managers and organizations—and not necessarily for science (Beer & Nohria, 1999).

In parallel with the ongoing development of "the traditional management research" approaches, we have witnessed the development of more "participative management research" approaches that attempt to generate knowledge that simultaneously satisfies the needs of both the scientific community and organizational members. The origin of the collaborative management research approaches can be traced to the works of John Collier and Kurt Lewin during the late 1940s and early 1950s that, independently of each other, coined the *action research* approach (Pasmore, 2001).

Collaborative management research, at the most basic level, brings about the challenge of balance and interdependence between actors, between academic research and actual applications, between knowledge creation and problem solving, between "inquiry from the inside" and "inquiry from the outside," between potentially competing goals and visions, between information and technology exchange. In the context of this volume, collaborative management research is viewed as *an emergent and systematic inquiry process, embedded in a true partnership between researchers and members of a living system for the purpose of generating actionable scientific knowledge.*

Thus, at the center of collaborative management research, we find a few key elements that require preliminary attention. *True partnership* refers to the dynamics of equality and integration—based on values, actions, processes, and consequences—around a shared goal or vision for the purpose of creating something (scientific and actionable knowledge) by two or more entities. *Emergent and systematic inquiry process* refers to the notion that although many things critical to the research process emerge, the inquiry process is managed in a systematic and reflective way. In the case of most other strategies of research, the specifics and details of the research processes are predetermined and planned in advance of the actual study by the researcher who is detached from the living system. In collaborative management research, the dynamic nature of the relationship between the actors, as well as the synergies that evolve during formal and informal interactions, frames and influences the inquiry process and its outcomes. For example, as the relationships between the actors mature, so does the degree of sharing tacit and explicit knowledge; thus, the data collection process and the data collected are affected. *Actionable scientific knowledge* refers to the knowledge creation process that meets the criteria and needs of both the scientific community and the organization. Knowledge resides within the minds of individuals who are part of micro-communities and communities-of-practice. These are small groups whose members share knowledge as well as common values and goals (Brown & Duguid, 1991). The ultimate success of knowledge creation depends on how these groups and other organizational members relate throughout the knowledge creation process (Adler & Shani, 2001; von Krogh, Ichijo, & Nonaka, 2000). Collaborative management research is viewed as an enabler of knowledge creation because it provides the methods, mechanisms, and processes for the interaction between the microcommunities and other relevant individuals inside and outside the organization for the purpose of creating new knowledge that can be acted on around critical themes and issues.

This chapter provides an initial comparative overview of eight collaborative management research approaches at the foundation of which varied forms of partnerships between researchers and organizational members can be found. The next section reviews and briefly examines action research, action science, appreciative inquiry, clinical field research, developmental action inquiry, intervention research, participative inquiry, and table tennis research. A comparative-based discussion concludes the chapter.

Collaborative Management Research Orientations: A Brief Overview

Inherent in each scientific inquiry approach are basic values, assumptions, and beliefs about the nature of reality and what constitutes valid knowledge. In a landmark piece, Evered and Louis (1981) contrast two predominant scientific approaches they call "inquiry from the outside" and "inquiry from the inside." They argue that most organizational research seems to be guided by one of these paradigms or the other. At the most basic level, inquiry from the outside calls for detachment and neutrality on the part of the researcher, who typically gathers data according to a priori theory-driven research questions with operationalized variables. The data are factual and context free, and the inquiry aims at uncovering knowledge that is universal and generalizable. Inquiry from the inside calls for firsthand involvement and immersion of the researcher. A priori analytical categories emerge through the social system interactivity. The data are contextually embedded and jointly interpreted, and the inquiry aim is to uncover situationally relevant knowledge that can guide action in the immediate situation and provide input in developing hypotheses to guide further inquiry. The work by Evered and Louis (1981) and others (e.g., Bartunek & Louis, 1992, 1996; Lawler & Drexler, 1982; Pasmore & Friedlander, 1982) served as a catalyst by triggering the development of various aspects of collaborative management research as an emerging orientation to management research.

In the context of this volume, we go beyond analyzing and criticizing the epistemological deficiencies of the various knowledge production and scientific methods. Following Hatchuel's (2001) call for the development of clear scientific identity of management research, differentiating it from social and economic studies, our goal is to advance collaborative management research as a paradigm that revisits and combines the rigor and standardization of the inquiry from the outside orientation with emergent discovery, reflexivity, and action qualities of the inquiry from the inside orientation.

At the outset, it is important to note that all of the emerging collaborative management research orientations attempted, in one way or another, to combine some of the features from both the inquiry from the outside and the inquiry from the inside orientations. They seem to share in common the value that knowledge production and action processes are not set apart as two different processes and that some type of a research team composed of individuals from within and outside the organization is created to lead the research effort. This section briefly reviews eight different collaborative management research orientations. Although an account of the development and comprehensive nature of each of the eight schools of thought is beyond the scope of this chapter, the following provides a brief overview of their essence. Table 5.1 provides a comparative synopsis of the various schools based on their theoretical foundation, lead contributors, and basic definition.

Action Research

The credit for coining the term *action research* seems to have been given to Lewin (1946) and Collier (1945), who independently suggested a strategy for collaboratively studying and simultaneously changing (or developing) social systems. Lewin's attempts to solve social problems using systematic

Table 5.1 Collaborative Research: A Snapshot Review

	Action Science	Appreciative Inquiry	Clinical Inquiry/Field Research	Developmental Action Inquiry	Intervention Research	Participative Inquiry/Action Research	Table Tennis Research	Action Research
Theoretical Roots	Cognitive theory Communication theory Human development Organizational psychology	Humanism Human system development Communication theory	Clinical psychology Applied sociology and anthropology	Human development Clinical and organizational psychology	Engineering science Organization theory Collective action theory	Social and political economy theory A hybrid of action research, cooperative inquiry, action science, and developmental action inquiry	A hybrid of action research, intervention research, participative inquiry, and action science	Experimental social psychology Cultural anthropology Sociotechnical systems
Contributors	Torbert Argyris Schön Dewey	Cooperrider	Schein	Tobert	Hatchuel David	Reason Whyte Tandon	Adler Shani	Lewin Collier Passmore
Basic Definition	Social practice that integrates production and use of knowledge to promote learning with and among individuals and systems whose work is characterized by uniqueness, uncertainty, and instability	A systematic discovery process that is aimed at helping human systems to accomplish tasks, generate new learning, and produce knowledge	An inquiry process in which the researcher acts as a "helper" (or a human system developer) to practitioners seeking assistance in gathering data in clinical settings created by the client who seek help	An emergent inquiry process, embedded in first-, second-, and third-person research practices that combines inquiry with productivity to enhance the organization's efficiency and effectiveness	A comprehensive methodology for producing knowledge and change that is both contextualized and formalized	Emergent inquiry process that fosters creative thinking and action by maintaining total equality among all research participants	Collaborative interdisciplinary inquiry of practitioners and researchers for the purpose of understanding organizational phenomena through intense dialogue, action, and reflection	Emergent inquiry process embedded in partnership between researchers and practitioners to address an organizational issue and produce scientific knowledge

data collection, feedback, reflection, and action were pioneering and are at the foundation of the learning process (Pasmore, 2001). Collier, a commissioner of American Indian Affairs from 1933 to 1945, developed his notions of collaborative action research in which representatives of the various parties participated in understanding and improving race relations (Collier, 1945). During the past 50 years, action research has developed as a major field of research that involves a cyclical process composed of a variety of activities and phases that integrate research and action in living systems (Coghlan & Brannick, 2001; Reason & Bradbury, 2001).

Action research is viewed as an emergent inquiry process embedded in partnership between researchers and organizational members for the purpose of addressing an organizational issue (or problem) and simultaneously generating scientific knowledge (Levin & Greenwood, 2001; Shani & Pasmore, 1985; Susman & Evered, 1978). Action research is a philosophical view that encompasses the need for the generation of new knowledge in organizational settings and the desire for ongoing organizational renewal (Coghlan, 2001; Margulies & Raia, 1978). It is ideology that assumes common interests in solving problems by analyses of individuals, groups, and organizational issues (Brown & Tandon, 1983). It seeks to improve the organization's ability to understand itself and develop self-help competencies (Friedlander & Brown, 1974). It is context bound (Levin & Greenwood, 2001). It is embedded in an inquiry cycle with a set of phases such as self-reflection, historical and situational analysis, interpretation of meaning, construction of models, development of propositions, empirical hypothesis testing, generation of shared meaning, scientific experimental implementation, and diffusion of knowledge (Pasmore & Friedlander, 1982; Shani & Bushe, 1987; Susman & Evered, 1978). It is based on collaborative relationships between actors within and outside the system (Reason, 1988). It is about the management of four emergent processes in the discovery journey: the socio-task system, the co-inquiry process, the integration process, and the experimentation process (Levin & Greenwood, 2001; Shani & Bushe, 1987).

Action research seems to evolve into a family of approaches that aims at discovery and human dialogue and around issues that are at the very center of human life (Greenwood & Levin, 1998). Action research, since its inception, has become the springboard for the development of inquiry approaches (Reason, 1994). At some level, it has become a generic term that is used to refer to a bewildering array of activities and methods. It includes a large variety of inquiry streams within which are multiple paradigms or methodologies with their own distinct emphasis (Chisholm & Elden, 1993; Coghlan & Brannick, 2001; Greenwood & Levin, 1998).

Action Science

The term *action science* was initially coined by Torbert (1976) and was further developed by Argyris (1980); Argyris, Putman, and Smith (1985); and

Argyris and Schön (1989). All were concerned with the self-development process of the individual before he or she becomes capable of valid action and the spontaneous tacit "theories-in-use" that participants bring to practice and research. At the core of action science is the focus on the cognitive processes of individuals' theories-in-use, which are described in terms of Model 1 (strategies of control, self-protection, defensiveness, and covering up embarrassment) and Model 2 (strategies eliciting valid information, free choice, and commitment).

According to Friedman (2001), action science is viewed as a form of social practice that integrates the production and use of knowledge for the purpose of promoting learning with and among individuals and systems whose work is characterized by uniqueness, uncertainty, and instability (p. 159). Action science is about creating conditions of collaborative inquiry in which people in organizations function as co-researchers rather than as participants (Argyris & Schön, 1989). It is an inquiry into a living system (Torbert, 1976), an intervention into a system for the purpose of promoting learning and contributing to general knowledge (Argyris et al., 1985). Action science is a scientific process that aims at generating knowledge that is useful, valid, descriptive of the world, and informative of how we might change it (Argyris et al., 1985). Furthermore, it is one of the most popular "action technologies" in use today (Raelin, 1997).

Action science is viewed as a social practice that integrates the production and use of knowledge to promote learning among individuals and systems that function in environments of uncertainty and instability. To produce knowledge that serves action, action science focuses on blind spots, dilemmas, and constraints present in systems that are undetected by those involved, with the hope of freeing them to act in a more informed manner. David (2001a, 2001b, 2002) argues that by constructing and testing theories in practice, action science researchers are able to learn about actors' behavior and reasoning and can use this knowledge to transform the system from within.

Action science involves three primary activities: *descriptive explanation* of a phenomenon implying how it might be changed, *proposed alternative* that transforms the phenomenon (to a desirable result), and *development of a plan* to get to this desired end (Argyris, 1999). Theories are constructed and tested in practice by examining the actors' behavior and reasoning. Consequently, action science produces alternatives to the status quo and shapes change efforts around the freely chosen values of social actors (Friedman, 2001) on a specific relational mode focused on group dynamics (David, 2001a).

Developmental Action Inquiry

Torbert (1999), in his critique of the evolving definition of action science (as was developed by Argyris), argues, "The term has come to sound too much like already knowing how to act and interpret action and not enough like continual, existential, relational searching for how to act and interpret and envision action" (p. 191). Accordingly, Torbert renamed the research/ practice process as *developmental action inquiry* in contrast to the related action science, action inquiry, and cooperative ecological inquiry paradigms.

Developmental action inquiry combines inquiry with productivity to enhance the organization's efficiency and effectiveness. Philosophically, developmental action inquiry research is based on the idea that, from the standpoint of researchers, all actions are inquiries and all inquiries are actions no matter how objective those actions may be (Fisher & Torbert, 1995). Consequently, researchers focus both on individuals and on the organization as a whole, seeking the transformation at all levels of organizational life. Torbert advocates the linkage between the ability to engage in the rigor of action inquiry and the stages of ego development. Thus, individuals can engage effectively in collaborative inquiry only during the latter stages of ego development. As individuals reflect on their behavior-in-action, their behavior toward others is such that it invites them to do likewise. Torbert introduces three pathways to carry out action inquiry: first-person, second-person, and third-person research/practice developmental concepts.

First-person research/practice skills and methods address the ability of the researcher to foster an inquiring approach to his or her life, to act with awareness and choose carefully, and to assess effects in the outside world while acting. Second-person research/practice addresses the researcher's ability to inquire face-to-face with others into issues of mutual concern. Third-person research/practice skills and methods address the ability of the researcher to extend these relatively small-scale projects into a community of inquiry around a shared concern or issue involving persons who cannot be known to each other face-to-face (Torbert, 1998).

At a generic level, the process of developmental action inquiry involves the following: testing the appropriateness of purposes and strategies, correcting errors to increase the immediate effectiveness of outcomes, testing the organizations' strategy, generating long-term effectiveness of outcomes, evaluating individual purposes and visions, developing a shared vision, and redefining strategies that are out of line with this vision. The intended outcomes are increasing the awareness of a shared mission; enhancing commitment among all practitioners; establishing dialogue on the lack of alignment of individual, group, and corporate objectives and actions; and facilitating better alignment of individual and organizational mission and operations (Torbert, 2001).

Participative Inquiry/Action Research

Participative inquiry or *participative action research* is a hybrid of action research, cooperative inquiry, action science, and developmental action inquiry principles as well as anthropology research techniques. Participative action research is associated with the work of Whyte (Whyte, Greenwood, & Lazes, 1989), Brown (1993), and Tandon (1989). Some argue that it is probably the most widely used practice because it emphasizes the political aspects of knowledge production (Reason, 1988). At a basic level, participative action research is primarily an egalitarian participation by a community to transform some aspects of its situation or structure (Coghlan & Brannick, 2001; Whyte et al., 1989). Furthermore, it implies "an effort on the part of people to understand the role of knowledge as a significant instrument of power and control" (Fals-Borda & Rahman, 1991).

The functional philosophy of participative inquiry is captured in the words of Kabir: "If you have not lived through something, it is not true" (quoted in Reason, 1988). In light of this, participative inquiry facilitates experience through creative thinking and action. Maintaining total equality among all research participants is essential, so no distinction is made between researchers and practitioners. Furthermore, some argue that participative action research explicitly requires client participation "in the control of the entire process" and defines all participants as "researchers" (Brown & Tandon, 1983).

The process of participative inquiry involves three phases: problem identification, solution seeking, and solution implementation. Researchers employ formal and informal interviews to help facilitate discovery, communication, and education. *Emancipation* and *education* are the intended outcomes of researchers as they work to establish dialogue among all participants who are affected by a specific problem (Reason, 1988).

Clinical Inquiry/Field Research

The distinguishing character of *clinical field research* or *clinical inquiry* is embedded in the setting of the activity. Unlike most other collaborative research approaches, in which the researcher creates the situation where learning takes place, with clinical inquiry the learning opportunities arise in situations where the setting is created by the "client" who seeks help (Schein, 2001). "Clinical" refers to those trained helpers who work with human system development. The helpers act as organizational clinicians in that they emphasize in-depth observation of current practice, build theory and empirical knowledge through developing concepts that capture the real dynamics of the system, emphasize the exploration of the potential effects of the inquiry, and operate from models of what it is to function as a healthy system and focus on pathologies, puzzles, and anomalies that illustrate deviations from healthy system functioning (Coghlan & Brannick, 2001; Schein, 1987).

In its broadest sense, the principles of clinical field research (as a theoretical framework) seek to inform all forms of research on humans (Schein, 1987). Hence, clinical field research attempts to influence both the philosophy of research and the methodology. In practice, clinical field research involves gathering data in clinical settings created by people seeking help on specific problems, inquiring about organizational and human behaviors based on the clinician's theory of health, validating data through predated responses to interventions, and analyzing data at case conferences with other professionals (Schein, 2001). At the most basic level, research outcomes are aimed at aiding clients who are seeking help and gaining a deeper understanding of the inner workings and power centers of organizations so as to inform theoretical models of organizational life.

Intervention Research

Intervention research has emerged out of the school of thought that has centered on the research-oriented partnership led by Armand Hatchuel and Albert David at Ecole des Mines in Paris. At the core of the approach is the aim of advancing a methodology that is built on more universal principles than is the classic action research (Hatchuel, 2001). Managing the contextualization and formalization of change in organizations is at the heart of what Hatchuel (1986) calls intervention research. More than any other intervention, intervention research attempts to enumerate the dynamics of contextualizing and formalizing change and to provide a methodology for the creation of that change.

Intervention research attempts to design and implement management models, tools, and procedures in the field of more or less well-defined transformation projects, producing knowledge that serves action and builds management science theories (Hatchuel, Masson, & Weil, 2002). This complex and difficult task of producing dual-natured change consists of the contextualization and formalization of change progressively and simultaneously throughout the process of the intervention. Reality is both shaped and interpreted in real time by those involved. Consequently, the researcher is not simply an observer but also an intervener who has access and gives access to the heart of management (David, 2001a).

Intervention research methodology is founded on five principles: increased rationality, open-endedness, scientific nature, isonomy, and two levels of interaction (Hatchuel, 1994, as cited in David, 2001a). Some of these principles are found in part in other research methodologies. The unique contribution of intervention research is that it seeks to establish itself as a comprehensive methodology for producing knowledge and change that is contextualized and formalized, thereby contributing to management theory and practice.

Interviews, documentary analysis, and observation of the actors at work will produce a first set of knowledge on the system studied and help to elaborate a first series of hypotheses on its possible trajectories. However, on a second level, the transformation process sparked off by formalizing and contextualizing changes (e.g., a new decision-aiding tool, a new organization of innovation processes) will, in turn, produce very wide-ranging scientific knowledge: (a) about what is changed (e.g., a new management technique, a new organization of innovation), (b) on the implications of change on relational and knowledge systems within the organization, and (c) on change and steering change (e.g., the intervention process as a change-steering process).

Appreciative Inquiry

The term *appreciative inquiry* was coined at Case Western University by David Cooperrider and his colleagues to capture early notions that deeper level dialogue—as opposed to problem solving—is instrumental in helping human systems to accomplish tasks, generate new learning, and produce knowledge (Cooperrider, 1986). During the past 15 years, appreciative inquiry has been advanced beyond an ideological and philosophical orientation to a theory and method for systems learning and development. In its broadest focus, "appreciative inquiry involves a systematic discovery of what gives life to a living system when it is most alive, most effective, and most constructively capable in economic, ecological, and human terms" (Cooperrider & Whitney, 2001). Thus, "appreciative inquiry involves the art and practice of asking questions that strengthen a system's capacity to apprehend, anticipate, and heighten positive potential" (Cooperrider & Srivastva, 1987).

Appreciative inquiry is viewed as a cyclical spiral composed of four basic elements: *discovery* (what gives life), or the best of what is—appreciating; *dream* (what might be), or what the world is calling for—envisioning results; *design* (what should be), or the ideal—co-constructing; and *destiny* (how to empower, learn, and adjust/improvise)—sustaining. Appreciative inquiry is an approach that attempts to create new theories/ideas/images that aid in system development (Cooperrider & Srivastva, 1987). The most fundamental innovations of appreciative inquiry are the learning-by-design orientation, the systematic collection of stories, and the dialogue around them (Barrett, 1995; Bushe, 2001). Thus, in the context of learning by design, appreciative inquiry seeks to fundamentally build a constructive ongoing dialogue among people in an organization about past and present learning capacities, processes, outcomes, achievements, strengths, innovations, opportunities, unexplored potentials, strategic competencies, visions of values, and possible futures. Taking all of these together, appreciative inquiry, in a deliberate fashion, seeks to facilitate a positive change orientation that will unleash untapped system learning capability.

Table Tennis Research

Table tennis research emerged as a collaborative inquiry methodology at the FENIX program in Sweden (Adler, 1999; Adler & Shani, 2001; Hatchuel, 2001). The approach was labeled table tennis research to capture the intense dialogue among the various actors as well as the nature and character of the relationships between researchers and organizational members in the discovery process. At the center of the approach are a few guiding principles: The effort is conducted in real time and focuses on "red and hot" issues. To be red and hot, the research issue must be perceived by the key actors as being of vital strategic importance for the company. Table tennis research is driven by intermediate theories created and developed in continuous jam sessions. It is based on emergent and iterative research designs, has boundary-spanning ambitions and beliefs, and consists of a research team composed of both practitioners and researchers from various disciplines. In addition, research is viewed as a model for action (Adler & Shani, 2001).

Intense interaction among skilled players is the imagery that is suggested by table tennis research. The approach explicitly seeks to establish a multidisciplinary team of researchers and practitioners for the purpose of identifying, studying, and solving problems in organizational life. Through intense dialogue, action, reflection, analysis, and implementation, researchers work side by side with practitioners to gain a deeper understanding of organizational dynamics (Adler & Shani, 2001). The transdisciplinary orientation brings together a set of complementary skills, perspectives, and knowledge bases for the purpose of gaining a more comprehensive and holistic appreciation of organizational phenomena being studied.

Table tennis research involves identifying red and hot issues that exist in the natural work setting; generating intermediate theories in the intense dialogue, reflection, and action of numerous jam sessions; and researchers developing local theories of action and publishing their reflections in scientific journals (Adler & Shani, 2001). The outcomes of table tennis research are designed to establish mutual learning systems for researchers and practitioners, thereby producing actionable knowledge, challenging traditional notions of quality and validity, and generating new insights into organizational systems and the research process itself.

Collaborative Management Research Orientations: Initial Comparative Discussion

An in-depth comparative investigation of the various collaborative management research schools of thought is beyond the scope of this chapter. Our attempt here is to provide an initial comparative perspective as a foundation for ongoing exploration of the various collaborative research projects that are reported in Chapters 10 through 18 of this volume. A snapshot summary of the essence of each of these approaches is provided in Table 5.1. As can be seen, the various schools of thought are rooted in a wide range of theoretical foundations, including engineering science, cognitive theory, communication theory, organization theory, economic theory of the firm, human and organization development theory, organizational

Table 5.2   Comparative Investigation Using Habermas's Criteria of Knowledge

	Technical	**Practical**	**Emancipatory**
Habermas's view of the three cognitive interests	Information that expands our power of technical control	Interpretations that make possible the orientation of action within common traditions	Analyses that free consciousness from its dependence on hypostatized power
Collaborative research schools of thought	Manipulation and control of the environment (both natural and social)	The understanding of meaning in a specific situation so that a decision can be made and an action can be taken	Generating knowledge that furthers human autonomy and responsibility
Action research	To a limited extent	To a moderate extent	To a major extent
Action science	To a limited extent	To a moderate extent	To a major extent
Appreciative inquiry	To a limited extent	To a moderate extent	To a major extent
Clinical inquiry/field research	To a moderate extent	To a limited extent	To a major extent
Developmental action inquiry	To a limited extent	To a moderate extent	To a major extent
Intervention research	To a moderate extent	To a moderate extent	To a major extent
Participative inquiry/action research	To a limited extent	To a moderate extent	To a major extent
Table tennis research	To a moderate extent	To a major extent	To a major extent

psychology, collective action theory, clinical psychology, social psychology, sociology, anthropology, and sociotechnical system theory.

A first glance at the basic definitions reveals that each school of thought seems to have a somewhat different methodological orientation, ranging from specific research design methodologies to experimental designs, to quasi-experimental designs, to emergent research process, to a systematic discovery process. The aims of the orientations seem to vary from generating scientific knowledge to solving problems, to helping grassroots social recovery, to helping an organization/client system that seeks help, to integrating production and use of knowledge, to creating a learning organization, to combining inquiry with productivity to enhance organizational efficiency and effectiveness, to producing knowledge and change that is both contextualized and formalized, to fostering creative thinking and action in systems.

A deeper level of investigation into the nature of and lineages among the various collaborative research schools of thought is likely to shed important light on their respective characteristics and overlapping assumptions. For that purpose, we use two sets of lenses: Habermas's (1981) typology of knowledge (Table 5.2) and Hatchuel's (2001) criteria of management science methodologies (Table 5.3). Habermas concludes that there are

Table 5.3 Comparative Investigation Using Hatchuel's Principles of Management Science Methodologies

	Increased Rationality	Scientific Nature	Isonomy	Open-Endedness	Two Levels of Interaction
Hatchuel's criteria of management science methodologies	The research favors a better balance between the knowledge of the facts and the relations that they enable between the actors	The researchers' search for the ideal truth. The researchers must have a critical attitude toward the facts	The research effort of understanding must be applied equally to all of the actors involved	The emergent quality of human interactions in the discovery process makes it impossible to specify in advance the path of the research and the results that will be obtained	The nature of the research emphasizes working at two levels of interactions that have an impact on one another: the research mechanism and the search for knowledge
Collaborative research schools of thought Action research					
Action science	To a moderate extent	To a major extent	To a major extent	To a major extent	To a major extent
Appreciative inquiry	To a moderate extent	To a moderate extent	To a major extent	To a major extent	To a moderate extent
Clinical inquiry/field research	To a moderate extent	To a limited extent	To a major extent	To a major extent	To a moderate extent
Developmental action inquiry	To a limited extent	To a moderate extent	To a moderate extent	To a major extent	To a moderate extent
Intervention research	To a moderate extent	To a major extent	To a major extent	To a major extent	To a major extent
Participative inquiry/action research	To a major extent	To a major extent	To a major extent	To a major extent	To a major extent
Table tennis research	To a moderate extent	To a moderate extent	To a major extent	To a major extent	To a moderate extent
	To a major extent	To a major extent	To a major extent	To a major extent	To a major extent

essentially three human or cognitive interests that are directed toward three types of knowledge: technical ("orientation toward technical control"), practical ("orientation toward mutual understanding in the control of life"), and emancipatory ("orientation toward emancipation from seemingly 'natural' constraint"). At the most basic level, what separates collaborative management research from the many other traditional research approaches is the attempt to pursue all three interests simultaneously.

Examining the various collaborative research schools of thoughts while using Habermas's typology reveals some additional insights about their nature, similarities, and differences. For example, whereas all of the collaborative research orientations pursue the emancipatory interests to a major extent, most of them (with the exceptions of intervention research and clinical inquiry) pursue the technical interests to a limited extent. They seem to vary from a limited, to a moderate, to a major extent on pursuing the practical interests. Furthermore, whereas both intervention research and table tennis research pursue the technical interests to a moderate extent and the practical and emancipatory interests to a major extent, action research, participatory inquiry, developmental action inquiry, action science, and appreciative inquiry pursue the technical interests to a limited extent, the practical interests to a moderate extent, and the emancipatory interests to a major extent. Thus, at a deeper level, Habermas's typology provides a way in which to explore some of the subtleties among the various schools of thought.

Some Additional Observations

Collaborative research in management sciences is designed to produce knowledge that is scientific and actionable. As we have seen by using Habermas's view on human interest and knowledge creation, each of the collaborative management research orientations seems to have a set of distinct features. Hatchuel (2001) advances a set of five criteria or principles to examine the merit of research in management science. From a methodological perspective, the arrival of a new actor(s) in the collective action process affects the system's status quo. The collaborative research models are, therefore, more complex (and some would argue more sophisticated) than classical research approaches; the clear distinction between the researcher and the system being observed becomes more complex in collaborative research. On the one hand, the researcher participates in the action in a concrete manner; on the other hand, the actors are led to reflect on their own system of action. There is two-way learning (Hatchuel, 1994) between the "intervener-researcher" and the "reflective practitioner" (Schön, 1983). The intervener-researcher and the actors with whom he or she is working form a group of actors collectively involved in a learning process. One of the consequences is that the researcher will have to be able to analyze himself or herself in the process of acting. The researcher's action is one of the events subjected to analysis. From a scientific standpoint, it is of vital importance to be able to find out how, with what legitimacy, and up to what point the researcher should design and prescribe the transformations of an organized system as well as under what conditions the knowledge stemming from the intervention may be considered scientific.

Hatchuel's criteria provide additional insight into the nature of the various schools of thought: the principle of increased rationality (research favors a better balance between the knowledge of the facts and the relations they enable between the actors), the principle of scientific nature (the researcher must constantly have a critical attitude toward the facts), the principle of isonomy (the effort of understanding must be applied equally to all of the actors involved), the principle of open-endedness (it is not possible to specify in advance the path that the collaborative research project will take and what results will be obtained from it), and the principle of two levels of interaction (collaborative research implies both a search for knowledge and an intervention mechanism). Table 5.3 provides a synthesis of the comparative investigation along the lines of Hatchuel's criteria.

As can be seen in Table 5.3, using Hatchuel's criteria reveals the following common characteristics. Scientific knowledge is produced through in-depth interaction with the "field," but the field here is not a field as in classical sociology or ethnology but rather an empirical co-design space. Consequently, the interaction with the field is not just a dialogue between existing theories and what can be inferred from empirical data, as viewed by the classical research approaches. A closer examination of the table reveals the following. All of the orientations meet at least four of Hatchuel's five principles to a moderate or major extent (David, 2001a; Hatchuel, 1994), and intervention research and table tennis research meet all of Hatchuel's criteria to a major extent. The criteria of increased rationality are evident to a moderate or major extent in all but clinical inquiry, the criteria of scientific nature are evident to a moderate or major extent in all but appreciative inquiry, the criteria of isonomy are evident to a major extent in all but clinical inquiry, the criteria of open-endedness are evident to a major extent in all but action science, and the criteria of two-level interaction are evident to a moderate or major extent in all of the schools of thought.

Conclusion

Collaborative management research is not a way in which to produce knowledge for action but rather a process of action by itself. Consequently, it represents one theory among various theories of the social role of management research. In other words, it does not replace other empirical approaches but rather includes them; it represents a generalization that explicitly takes into account the fact that "no theory of collective action can be made without a theory of design" (Hatchuel, 2001, p. 38). Yet researchers shoulder the responsibilities of exploring the various collaborative research options and making choices of best fit. Considering the variety of schools in collaborative research, researchers may sometimes be looking for the meaning of their social mission. But collaborative research gives to scientific knowledge in management a status that makes it compatible with a theory of collective action that explicitly considers management research as a grounded engineering activity that includes the researchers as social actors. The final section of the volume, comprising Chapters 10 through 18, provides specific illustrations of collaborative research projects, each of which seems to have followed a distinct collaborative research orientation of a pure or hybrid nature.

References

Adler, N. (1999). *Managing complex product development*. Ph.D. dissertation, Economic Research Institute, Stockholm School of Economics, Stockholm, Sweden.

Adler, N., & Shani, A. B. (Rami). (2001). In search of an alternative framework for the creation of actionable knowledge: Table-tennis research at Ericsson. In W. A. Pasmore & R. W. Woodman (Eds.), *Research in organizational change and development* (Vol. 13, pp. 43–79). Amsterdam: Elsevier Science.

Argyris, C. (1980). *Inner contradictions of rigorous research*. New York: Academic Press.

Argyris, C. (1999). *On organizational learning*. Oxford, UK: Blackwell.

Argyris, C., Putnam, R., & Smith, D. (1985). *Action science: Concepts, methods, and skills for research and intervention*. San Francisco: Jossey-Bass.

Argyris, C., & Schön, D. A. (1989). Participatory action research and action science compared. *American Behavioral Scientist, 32*, 612–623.

Barrett, F. (1995). Creating appreciative learning cultures. *Organizational Dynamics, 24*(1), 36–49.

Bartunek, J. M., & Louis, M. R. (1992). Insider/Outsider research teams: Collaboration across diverse perspectives. *Journal of Management Inquiry, 1*, 101–110.

Bartunek, J. M., & Louis, M. R. (1996). *Insider/Outsider team research*. Thousand Oaks, CA: Sage.

Beer, M., & Nohria, N. (1999). *Breaking the code of change*. Boston: Harvard Business School Press.

Brown, J. S., & Duguid, P. (1991). Organizational learning and communities of practice: Towards a unified view of working, learning, and innovation. *Organization Science, 2*, 40–57.

Brown, L. D. (1993). Participative action research for social change. *Human Relations, 46*, 249–273.

Brown, L. D., & Tandon, R. (1983). Ideology and political economy in inquiry: Action research and participatory research. *Journal of Applied Behavioral Science, 19*, 277–294.

Bushe, G. (2001). Five theories of change in appreciative inquiry. In D. L. Cooperrider, P. F. Sorensen, Jr., T. F. Yaeger, & D. Whitney (Eds.), *Appreciative inquiry: An emerging direction for organization development* (pp. 117–128). Champaign, IL: Stipes Publishing.

Chisholm, R. F., & Elden, M. (1993). Features of emerging action research. *Human Relations, 46*, 275–289.

Coghlan, D. (2001). Insider action research projects: Implications for practicing managers. *Management Learning, 32*(1), 49–60.

Coghlan, D., & Brannick, T. (2001). *Doing action research in your own organization*. London: Sage.

Collier, J. (1945). United States Indian Administration as a laboratory of ethnic relations. *Social Research, 12*, 275–286.

Cooperrider, D. L. (1986). *Appreciative inquiry: Towards a methodology for understanding and enhancing organizational innovation*. Unpublished doctoral dissertation, Case Western Reserve University.

Cooperrider, D. L., & Srivastva, S. (1987). Appreciative inquiry in organizational life. In W. A. Pasmore & R. Woodman (Eds.), *Research in organizational change and development* (Vol. 1, pp. 129–169). Greenwich, CT: JAI.

Cooperrider, D. L., & Whitney, D. (2001). A positive revolution in change: Appreciative inquiry. In D. L. Cooperrider, P. F. Sorensen, Jr., T. F. Yaeger, & D. Whitney (Eds.), *Appreciative inquiry: An emerging direction for organization development* (pp. 5–29). Champaign, IL: Stipes Publishing.

David, A. (2001a). Intervention research as a general framework for management research. In A. David, A. Hatchuel, & R. Laufer (Eds.), *The new foundations of management sciences* (pp. 193–213). Paris: Vuibert/FNEGE. (English translation)

David, A. (2001b). Model implementation: A state of the art. *European Journal of Operational Research, 134,* 459–480.

David, A. (2002). Intervention methodologies in management research. In *Conference proceedings, European Academy of Management* (pp. 8–11). Stockholm, Sweden: European Academy of Management.

Evered, R., & Louis, M. R. (1981). Alternative perspective in the organizational sciences: "Inquiry from the inside" and "inquiry from the outside." *Academy of Management Review, 6,* 385–395.

Fals-Borda, O., & Rahman, M. A. (Eds.). (1991). *Action and knowledge: Breaking the monopoly with participative action research.* New York: Intermediate Technology/Apex.

Fisher, D., & Torbert, W. (1995). *Personal and organizational transformation: The true challenge of continual quality improvement.* New York: McGraw-Hill.

Friedlander, F., & Brown, L. D. (1974). Organization development. *Annual Review of Psychology, 25,* 313–341.

Friedman, V. J. (2001). Action science: Creating communities of inquiry in communities of practice. In P. Reason & H. Bradbury (Eds.), *Handbook of action research: Participative inquiry and practice* (pp. 159–170). London: Sage.

Greenwood, L. E., & Levin, M. (1998). *Introduction to action research.* Thousand Oaks, CA: Sage.

Habermas, J. (1981). *Knowledge and human interests.* Boston: MIT Press.

Hatchuel, A. (1986). Rational modeling in understanding and aiding human decision making. *European Journal of Operational Research, 24,* 178–186.

Hatchuel, A. (1994). Les savoirs de l'intervention en entreprise (The knowledge and skills of the intervening researcher in companies). *Entreprise et Histoire* (French Journal of Enterprise and History), 7, 59–75.

Hatchuel, A. (2001). The two pillars of new management research. *British Journal of Management, 12,* 33–40. (Special issue)

Hatchuel, A., Masson, P. L., & Weil, B. (2002). From knowledge management to design-oriented organizations. *International Social Science Journal, 171,* 25–37.

Lawler, E. E., III, & Drexler, J. A. (1982). Participative research: The subject as co-researcher. In E. E. Lawler, III, D. A. Nadler, & C. Cammann (Eds.), *Organizational assessment: Perspectives on the measurement of organizational behavior and the quality of working life* (pp. 535–547). New York: John Wiley.

Levin, M., & Greenwood, D. (2001). Pragmatic action research and the struggle to transform universities into learning communities. In P. Reason & H. Bradbury (Eds.), *Handbook of action research: Participative inquiry and practice* (pp. 103–113). London: Sage.

Lewin, K. (1946). Action research and minority problems. *Journal of Social Issues, 2,* 34–36.

Margulies, N., & Raia, A. D. (1978). *Conceptual foundations of organization development.* New York: McGraw-Hill.

Pasmore, W. A. (2001). Action research in the workplace: The socio-technical perspective. In P. Reason & H. Bradbury (Eds.), *Handbook of action research: Participative inquiry and practice* (pp. 39–47). London: Sage.

Pasmore, W. A., & Friedlander, F. (1982). An action research program for increasing employee involvement in problem solving. *Administrative Science Quarterly, 27*, 343–362.

Raelin, J. A. (1997). Action learning and action science: Are they different? *Organizational Dynamics, 26*(1), 21–34.

Reason, P. (1988). *Human inquiry in action.* London: Sage.

Reason, P. (1994). Three approaches to participative inquiry. In N. Denzin & Y. Lincoln (Eds.), *Handbook of qualitative research* (pp. 324–339). Thousand Oaks, CA: Sage.

Reason, P., & Bradbury, H. (2001). *Handbook of action research: Participative inquiry and practice.* London: Sage.

Schein, E. (1987). *The clinical perspective in fieldwork.* Newbury Park, CA: Sage.

Schein, E. H. (2001). Clinical inquiry/research. In P. Reason & H. Bradbury (Eds.), *Handbook of action research.* (pp. 228–237). London: Sage.

Schön, D. (1983). *Educating the reflective practitioner.* San Francisco: Jossey-Bass.

Shani, A. B. (Rami), & Bushe, G. R. (1987). Visionary action research: A consultation process perspective. *Consultation, 6*(1), 3–19.

Shani, A. B. (Rami), & Pasmore, W. A. (1985). Organization inquiry: Towards a new model of the action research process. In D. Warrick (Ed.), *Contemporary organization development* (pp. 438–448). Glenview, IL: Scott, Foresman.

Starkey, M., & Madan, P. (2001). Bridging the relevance gap: Aligning stakeholders in the future of management research. *British Journal of Management, 12*, 3–26. (Special issue)

Susman, G. I., & Evered, R. D. (1978). An assessment of the scientific merit of action research. *Administrative Science Quarterly, 23*, 583–603.

Tandon, R. (1989). Participatory action research and social transformation. *Convergence, 21*(2/3), 5–15.

Torbert, W. (1976). *Creating a community of inquiry: Conflict, collaboration, transformation.* London: Wiley.

Torbert, W. (1998). Developing wisdom and courage in organizing and sciencing. In S. Srivastva & D. Cooperrider (Eds.), *Organizational wisdom and executive courage* (pp. 222–253). San Francisco: New Lexington Press.

Torbert, W. (1999). The distinctive questions developmental action inquiry asks. *Management Learning, 30*(2), 189–206.

Torbert, W. (2001). The practice of action inquiry. In P. Reason & H. Bradbury (Eds.), *Handbook of action research: Participative inquiry and practice* (pp. 250–260). London: Sage.

von Krogh, G., Ichijo, K., & Nonaka, I. (2000). *Enabling knowledge creation.* New York: Oxford University Press.

Whyte, W. F., Greenwood, D., & Lazes, P. (1989). Participatory action research. *American Behavioral Scientist, 32*, 513–551.

6

Collaborative Research Through an Executive Ph.D. Program

Horst Hart, Sven F. Kylén,
Flemming Norrgren, and Bengt Stymne

A *manager* is an actor who acts to control and influence the actions of others to obtain certain ends. Managers are assumed to base their actions on their often implicit conceptions of how their world hangs together and about information regarding the situation in which they are acting.

A *management scientist* or *researcher* is an actor who produces explicit theories and models explaining how the world of managers hangs together. To be valid, scientific models have to be justifiable in terms of known facts. Therefore, an important part of the actions of management researchers is to make investigations to find empirical evidence.

We hold that managers can develop the capability to act more effectively by using explicit models of how things hang together as a basis for their actions. For an explicit model to be a basis for action, it has to be internalized, understood, and accepted by the manager. Models that are explicit, internalized, understood, and accepted by the manager we call *actionable knowledge* in this chapter (Babüroglo & Ravn, 1992).

Collaborative management research can take many forms (as described in Chapter 5 of this volume), and it happens when managers and management scientists cooperate in the production of explicit models, in the creation of management action, and in the gathering of information about the immediate

AUTHORS' NOTE: The authors thank the Swedish Knowledge Foundation as well as AstraZeneca, Ericsson, Volvo, and Telia for their long-term commitment and financing that made the FENIX executive Ph.D. program development possible. In addition to the authors of this chapter, the core faculty of the executive Ph.D. program that took part in the development of the initial program included Niclas Adler, Sofia Börjesson, Armand Hatchuel, Mats Lundqvist, Mats Magnusson, and Rami Shani.

situation as well as about the more general context in which management action is to be taken. We claim that actionable knowledge is better co-produced in interaction between the manager and the researcher than if a model is just handed over from the researcher to the manager, for example, in the form of a lecture or a book. By interacting and dialoguing with the manager, the management researcher gets a possibility to influence the implicit models of the manager. One could even say that the researcher becomes a partner in the ever-ongoing social construction of the manager's world.

Management science sides with Max Weber in believing that organizations that seek to make use of rational models as the basis for planning and action are more effective than organizations that use other prime criteria (Weber, 1947), for example, family solidarity. Rationality means that action should contribute to goal fulfillment. We think that the degree of rationality of management action can be increased if it is based on explicit rather than implicit theories. The reason is that explicit theories are possible to discuss and criticize, whereas implicit theories are hidden. To be able to reflect on his or her actions, the manager has to construct or adopt an explicit theory that can function as a tool for the reflective process. One important function of collaborative research between managers and researchers, therefore, is to make the models on which management action is based more explicit.

Like all good theories, actionable knowledge should be based on verified evidence. Collaborative research has an important role to play in the verification process because the knowledge on which managers base their actions is most often neither explicit nor verified. The research of Brunsson (1985) shows that the knowledge on which managers base their actions is not just unverified but also often in contradiction to the evidence. In other words, implicit management knowledge is often plainly wrong. The effects of management action based on such knowledge, therefore, are often disastrous. There is a whole school of thought called "new institutionalism" that devotes itself to showing how such unsubstantiated knowledge is diffused. To put it briefly, new institutional theory (e.g., DiMaggio & Powell, 1991; Meyer & Rowan, 1991) shows that managers imitate each other just to look modern or progressive. They adopt fashionable management models just as they buy the type of cars in vogue among successful people. According to this view, the consultant industry is seen as the hawkers of management fashion (Collins, 2000).

Even if managers have access to actionable knowledge in the form of an explicit and verified model, they must have correct information about the current situation to act in a rational manner. The researchers in collaborative research could fulfill an important role in gathering and interpreting such information using the skills learned in a Ph.D. education.

Management science aims at producing theories that explain how and why managers act as they do. It should also produce more normative research, that is, models that show the various action alternatives that are available and what consequences they have. Collaborative research provides academic researchers with great opportunities to observe how managers act and to build an understanding of the contextual factors that could explain their actions.

An ultimate goal for research in management is to make the art of management action better informed. We argue that collaborative management research will contribute to that goal. This does not mean that the art of management can become fully rational. Management action is based on models, information, and values. The values also include aspects that can never be made fully explicit and that are of a political or an ethical character and are related to the managers' own personal strivings. Collaborative research will help to make management action more rational as well as to make the models of management science better. The responsibility of action will ultimately remain with managers and can never be fully explained or made completely rational with the help of management research. However, making managers aware of the moral dimension of leadership in addition to providing them with actionable knowledge may help them to take action that is not just rational but also morally justifiable.

The FENIX executive Ph.D. program is aimed at educating persons who can act both as management researchers and as practicing managers. They must be viewed by their companies as good leaders with high potential for future top management careers. Ideally, they should serve as a bridge between management science and management practice. Executive Ph.D. candidates should, together with other managers, be able to take action based on actionable knowledge. They should also, together with other management researchers, be able to help managers to establish knowledge on which they can base their actions.

_____Navigating Between Scylla and Charybdis

Over the years, there have been several attempts to start research groups with collaborative management research as the main vehicle for knowledge creation. Such adventures have to cross troubled water (Engwall et al., 1995), and most have been sucked in by either the Scylla of consulting on starboard or the Charybdis of pure academic research on port. In Chapter 3 of this volume, we learned how the Swedish Institute for Administrative Research (SIAR), gearing starboard from having been based on collaborative research, became a consultant firm. The Building Research Group at the Stockholm School of Economics was originally set up to do research of value for the Swedish building industry during the 1960s. However, it headed more port and was eventually absorbed by what is now the Center for Management and Organization, which has been given a decidedly academic profile under the leadership of Sven-Erik Sjöstrand (Engwall et al., 1995). It is obvious that these "small islands" of such alternative practices often have had a hard time surviving.

During the 1990s, the government instructed the Swedish university system to take on a *third mission* by being useful to the surrounding society. During the 1990s, the FENIX executive Ph.D. program became one of many initiatives of national authorities and funding agencies. To improve cooperation between academia and industry, *research schools* were created. Most of the research schools were designed as 6-year programs educating Ph.D. candidates doing research in science and technology of immediate relevance for Swedish industry. The executive Ph.D. program was one of a few examples within social science.

The Ph.D. program was named an *executive* Ph.D. program to capture the profile and background of the Ph.D. candidates who were targeted for the program. They were supposed to come from the participating companies with significant leadership experience, were expected to continue to work in their companies in parallel with the studies, and were expected to remain in leadership positions after having earned their degrees. The rationales for this choice were as follows:

- On the completion of the program, participants will be prepared to function as leaders for complex and innovative business, particularly within research and development (R&D).
- Executive Ph.D. candidates are intended to become a link between the academic and industrial worlds through understanding and coping with the logic of both systems.
- The results achieved through research in the program should influence renewal processes in partner companies and in participating academic environments.

The FENIX executive Ph.D. program was, at the time of this writing, approaching the completion of its initial program funding of 6 years. However, the board and the management group of FENIX have decided to continue to operate and develop the executive Ph.D. program. Also, partners from industry have decided to take a larger responsibility for financing the program. However, many questions remain to be resolved if the executive Ph.D. program is to become a sustainable system for collaborative management research.

Points of Departure

The FENIX executive Ph.D. program is not standing alone but rather is the educational part of a larger research program with the mission of enhancing knowledge creation that is of relevance for practitioners as well as for academic researchers. The reason is that the Ph.D. candidate should be part of a community of colleagues from the company and from the academy that are bound together by a shared interest in solving more overarching questions to which the individual Ph.D. thesis can provide only partial answers. The Ph.D. candidate's membership in the community transcends both the period of thesis writing and the results of the thesis. By linking the thesis research to broader interests, the probabilities of a sustainable program were expected to increase.

The executive Ph.D. program recruited high-potential candidates from AstraZeneca, Ericsson, Telia, and Volvo. The goal was to educate experienced leaders of tomorrow such as future executives, knowledge brokers, and network operators. These four companies all had distinguished histories of being innovative and of being good at integrating technological and scientific advancements in their products. Therefore, they were seen as partners with a genuine interest in building a sustainable community for learning more about business creation through knowledge creation.

There was some discussion as to whether the course work and theses of the executive Ph.D. candidates should fulfill the same rigorous academic requirements that the Stockholm School of Economics and the Chalmers University of Technology have for their traditional academic Ph.D. candidates or whether they should be more practically oriented or narrow in their focus as on a doctorate degree. The choice was that high academic standards should be achieved, supported by the participating universities and the initial FENIX faculty but also by the participating companies. Otherwise, it would not have been possible for the executive Ph.D. candidates to obtain the legitimacy required to be accepted as legitimate researchers by academic colleagues, and the companies indicated that they wanted to get "real Ph.D.'s." However, it was seen as equally important that the candidates gain legitimacy in their managerial roles. Therefore, the curriculum included the development of managerial and leadership skills of the participants. In addition to contributing to academic knowledge, their theses should be relevant to practice both during the research process (through various interventions and interactions with the companies) and in terms of focus actionable knowledge in the end result (the theses). Thus, the executive Ph.D. candidates have to integrate local (implicit) practitioner theories with general (externalized knowledge) scientifically based theories for the purpose of producing new and generalizable knowledge for action.

Expectations of the Participants

When designing the program, the faculty of the executive Ph.D. program wanted to avoid some pitfalls of previous attempts to increase cooperation through industrially oriented research schools. One such pitfall is the possible marginalization of Ph.D. candidates, becoming accepted by neither the companies nor the university. Hence, it was decided that candidates should keep on working in their companies for 50% of their time and should spend 50% of their time doing research. Still, they were supposed to complete their studies within the same time frame as full-time Ph.D. candidates. Of course, academic Ph.D. candidates also spend a good deal of their time involved in other activities beyond their studies and research, for example, serving as research assistants and teaching. But living in two quite different worlds put especially tough demands on the executive Ph.D. candidates. To meet these demands, a supportive structural mechanism had to be designed (Shani & Docherty, 2003). Also, it was essential that the candidates be highly motivated and have considerable personal capacity. Therefore, candidates were chosen among applicants who were considered by their employers to have a high potential for managerial positions. In addition, candidates were screened with the help of tests and interviews to ensure their capacity and motivation.

The companies subscribed to this approach. Before recruiting the candidates, an extensive internal promotion of the program was done in the companies. It resulted in 15 applications per available seat and made possible the implementation of a selection procedure with tough criteria to be met for candidates to become accepted. The screening process involved numerous aptitude and personality tests, recommendations and reference checks, special writing ability tests, and interviews done by psychologists and faculty.

The Training Process

When building up the executive Ph.D. program, a set of principles was emphasized from the beginning, as described in what follows.

Teamwork. In contrast to a traditional Ph.D. education, the executive Ph.D. program is built on teamwork right from the start. In each of the years 1998 and 2000, a cohort of 10 new executive Ph.D. candidates were recruited. All members of a cohort started at the same time and were kept together as a class. They took courses and formed a learning community where candidates from the various companies lent each other mutual support. Every candidate was assigned to a "research team" consisting of two or three faculty members, two or three other executive Ph.D. students, and some traditional academic Ph.D. students. The first research papers are frequently co-authored with a faculty member or a more senior Ph.D. candidate to ensure skills training in terms of a "master apprenticeship."

Emphasis on Structured Writing Skills. Candidates were encouraged to start writing scientific papers right from the beginning. By the end of the first year, they were expected to deliver their first conference papers. They were then supposed to continue the writing process by turning their papers into articles for scientific journals.

The Ph.D. thesis is a compilation thesis. That is, it consists of four or five articles, all of which should be "publishable," that is, having a desirable academic quality that would enable them to be published in double-blind, peer-reviewed journals. At least two papers must be accepted for publication by refereed journals before the thesis may be defended. The thesis also has to include an extensive introductory kappa or synopsis that provides a frame for the dissertation and integrates the results reported in each of the papers in a coherent way.

Twice-a-year special workshops have been designed for improving writing skills. They include intensive feedback sessions with individual faculty members as well as simulated scientific conferences with participation of all candidates and faculty as well as invited guests. In addition, candidates are required to present papers at international scientific conferences once a year and to get feedback from the international research community.

Continuous Workshops. A 3-day workshop is held every month where Ph.D. courses are given and candidates can meet to discuss and work on research projects. These workshops alternate between the two major university hubs (the Chalmers University of Technology in Gothenburg and the Stockholm School of Economics in Stockholm), and this makes the candidates travel together and spend time socializing outside of their normal settings. Every semester, a 2-week internship is held with an especially intense workshop (both content-wise and socially), and family members are welcome to join during the final day and a half. Every year, there is a prolonged workshop during the summer to go abroad and take courses at a demanding foreign university.

Close Supervision. Every candidate has a tutor and a supervisor, both of whom are given resources to work closely with the candidate and to spend more time with him or her than is normally allocated in Ph.D. programs. In addition, a third supervisor is assigned during the final year and a half to support the final stages of the thesis work. At workshops and writing training sessions, international faculty provide extra feedback and supervision to the candidates who require special attention or who desire more supervision. Supervisors are expected to work in close collaboration with their candidates in jointly designed research projects to increase collaborative research activity beyond that which has to do with manuscript production.

Boundary-Spanning Exercises. Students and faculty jointly run seminaries at universities as well as "jam sessions" normally held at companies (see Chapter 8 of this volume). The ambition is to bring in somewhat larger groups (15 to 20 persons) from both companies and universities to share know-how and experiences and/or to start new knowledge-creating projects. Research projects are designed jointly by the candidates, FENIX faculty, and other managers from companies, and progress report meetings are held continually at the companies to discuss emerging results, focus, and upcoming studies within the research projects, helping to maintain interest in and contributions to the candidates' research projects.

Teaching, Learning Environment, and Action Patterns

The FENIX executive Ph.D. program is part of a learning environment where the candidates spend time with faculty, building up a joint foundation for learning. Teaching in the format of traditional lectures takes place to only a limited extent. The main emphasis is on discussions of ongoing research projects and studies, findings from various companies, literature seminars, and assignments aimed at personal reflection and development. A key aspect of all the elements is that the program is aimed not only at the acquisition of theoretical knowledge and methodological expertise but also at putting leadership skills into practice. Therefore, the candidates' own presentations and argumentations are important. As a consequence, there is much emphasis on the participants' improving their pedagogical expertise and acquiring the capacity to express themselves and the rationale behind their theses both orally and in writing.

The discussions within the FENIX research program also demonstrate a number of particular features, as described in what follows.

Perspective Breaking and Pluralism. The aim is to provide scope for different, and preferably contradictory, perspectives and approaches. For certain parts of the courses, researchers with differing views and opinions are invited to take part in constructive debates on what is being conveyed in the courses.

A Tolerant and Constructively Critical Approach. The adoption of such an approach would result in careful examination of the content of the course literature, and opposing colleagues' written documents would emerge as particularly important activities. There is much emphasis on reflecting on the information conveyed and related personal experience.

A Clear Link to Practical Action. This link between theory and action takes place through the practical and skills-training elements of the program. This could, for example, lead to the candidates' research tasks being linked to practical problems, field experiments being performed at companies, and leadership development increasing the capacity to deal with candidates' own situations.

Collective learning is not only aimed for by teamwork arrangements. Every Thursday, all candidates and faculty are expected to spend the full day working at the FENIX premises in Gothenburg or Stockholm, and a 90-minute seminar is scheduled. The rest of the time is to be used in more informal ways according to the needs of the candidates, faculty, and/or research projects. Open office landscape is used when applicable to encourage spontaneous meetings and discussions.

Interest in learning across borders has gradually increased by bringing in more international faculty. This reflects the need for mirroring the fact that research is founded in an international community and also reflects the expectations from partner companies. When the FENIX executive Ph.D. program started in 1998, the corporate partners were content with the program being a "national" program (the program had only two core faculty members from outside Sweden). Five years later, the corporate partners are demanding that the future program be built around international faculty.

Course and Thesis Work

During the program, each participant pursues scientific research, which is documented in a thesis that carries a total of 80 credits (80 weeks). The scientific work leading to a Ph.D. should fall within the framework established for research within the FENIX research program, that is, business creation through knowledge creation. The work should satisfy both the scientific and practical relevance stipulations. The actual writing of the thesis should be done throughout the whole program. The executive Ph.D. candidates' researching problem areas through literature studies as well as practical problems or concerns through their company role facilitates this process. By formulating their thoughts in working papers presented for and discussed with research colleagues, candidates eventually produce scientific articles.

The compilation format for the thesis was chosen for process control purposes and so that the emerging results could be integrated in shorter cycles. Despite the limitations of the compilation format, so far as space to elaborate on empirical depth and format for capturing a large and integrated study are concerned, the strengths given the purpose to deliver continuous output from the research process, keep track of progress with a short total time for pursuing the program, and socialize the candidates into the world of academic research as soon as possible were considered greater. On a more detailed level, there are certain elements that the thesis should contain.

- A general synopsis—a kappa—containing a summary of the articles in the thesis, a positioning of the research and the pursued research studies and methodologies, and an integration and synthesis of the different results to an overall message constructing the thesis should be included.
- Four to five publishable articles, of which at least two have already been published and one already has been accepted for publication in a good journal, should be included. One of the contributions should be a reflective article on leadership based on the participants' own experience of leadership on the practical level. This article should

make use of research within the field as well as literature and arts subject sources. At least one of the four or five articles should be written by the executive Ph.D. candidate on his or her own.

The examiner and supervisory committee could, for example, increase the requirements regarding the number of articles if this is necessary for the thesis to qualify as an academic Ph.D. thesis. In the final analysis, it is the examiner/supervisor who makes that decision. Finally, the scientific work should be defended at a public defense.

The six courses in the research methodology area are given priority during the first year to provide the candidates with a scientific perspective and a toolbox for participating in the research projects. The courses range from theory of science to more practical orientations such as how to design a collaborative management research project or how to choose among available qualitative and quantitative methods for various research purposes. Special attention is given to action research so as to promote the candidates' ability to introduce field research that is perceived as valuable to the participating companies. Through these courses, the executive Ph.D. candidates learn, for instance, how to arrange their theses and/or how to organize research projects involving several participants and find out which techniques are available to create new knowledge. At the same time, they acquire the capacity to use some of these techniques in their own work.

An early emphasis on methodology is important not only to socialize managers to the world of research but also to advance the collective learning given that candidates have different backgrounds. Even though engineers and M.B.A.'s are the most well represented among the participants, there are also behavioral scientists, biologists, and architects among the candidates. Furthermore, the increased rigor in judging how knowledge is created and interpreted gives the candidates preparation for managing knowledge after the completion of the program. It also gives them a special position in their companies as "experts" in evaluating the foundations of change programs, consultancy reports, and advice or prevalent managerial techniques.

The 30 credit points in management and business development can be designed individually to some extent because of the special interests and thesis work of the candidates. Normally, three courses are compulsory and three are electives, chosen in cooperation with the participant's tutor and supervisor. The electives are dependent on the thesis work and the work situation of the individual executive Ph.D. candidate. The profile of these courses makes up the "expertise" of the executive Ph.D. candidates and thereby adds to their perceived value to the companies. Some will specialize in project management, whereas others will specialize in change or knowledge management.

Because the candidates have leadership experience prior to entering the FENIX executive Ph.D. program, they already have attended leadership courses during their careers. However, the Ph.D. courses in this area are different from these past courses in that they are based on both skills training and the theoretical underpinning of a specific area of leadership development. The courses require active reflection of trying out leadership skills as well as examining the theoretical bases of the skills training. The courses range from political leadership to organizational learning or coaching, and one course is elective.

The Embeddedness of the Executive Ph.D. Program

From our perspective, an executive research and training program provides advantages over conventional academic research and training. Such advantages include accessibility to existing research topics and detailed information as well as options to discuss and continually evaluate findings together with practicing managers at the participating companies that share an interest in particular topics. But an executive research and training program must also organize its activities in relation to a more complex situation where the collaborative management research approach involves more active stakeholders. Such a program needs to meet the conventional academic standards as well as the relevance demands and must do so with short lead times for the candidates. The executive Ph.D. program needs to develop a support system including relations other than the pure candidate-teacher/supervisor relations.

From the candidates' perspective, it is also easy to understand that there would arise some variation in the rate of success. The current situation is that most of the 10 candidates from the first group will present Ph.D. theses that are likely to be accepted by the two involved universities within the time frame of 5 academic years. They would, by definition, vary in quality and time. From the description of the program, we can conclude that investment in guidance and supervision is substantial. Setting aside the differences in personality, the important question is whether there are factors in the way of organizing the program that influence differences in candidates' success. In other words, given the fact that investment in teaching and coaching is roughly equally distributed among the Ph.D. candidates, is it possible to trace differences back to the organizational context surrounding each of the candidates?

We have identified three types of relations that need to be managed:

- Relations between the executive Ph.D. candidates and their supervisors
- Relations between the executive Ph.D. program and the companies
- Relations between the companies and their executive Ph.D. candidates

Candidate-Supervisor Relations. From a historical perspective, the traditional relations between a Ph.D. candidate and his or her institution is that of a near absence of active mentoring and supervision. A traditional Ph.D. candidate had the exclusive right to spend much time, effort, and energy on his or her own thesis work. This system was efficient so long as academically trained people controlled the labor market. They had to wait for academic positions, and the waiting time could just as well be spent on thesis writing. Beginning in the 1970s, an expansion of the academic system, as well as— for some disciplines—an emerging labor market outside of the universities, started a reform period during which Ph.D. studies became more controlled and faculty became responsible for the progress of Ph.D. candidates. Ph.D. studies became related to the economic situation in the form of stipends, cheap loans, and assistant positions within the departments. With the emergence of the external labor market, firms and public administration claimed faster progress.

The FENIX executive Ph.D. program has made significant investments in mentoring and in the development of new supervision processes. Important elements of the supervision process include the following:

- Close and frequent dialogues between the candidate and his or her supervisor to prevent delays and dead ends in reading or writing
- Adjusting formal education to the specific situation for the candidate, for example, having teaching concentrated in long (3 days) and frequent workshops
- Cooperation between senior researchers and the candidate with the ambition to reformulate topics that combine interest, curiosity, and urgency among practitioners with relevant research designed to adjust to the Ph.D. thesis format
- Recognizing quality assurance procedures and using scientific international journals to validate quality and relevance
- Providing Ph.D. candidates with emotional and social support to compensate for tough workloads
- A collective learning approach where the cohort of candidates is brought forward through a group climate of openness, helpfulness, and thought support

In addition, program management had recurrent meetings with supervisors and tutors. Progress was discussed and, in cases where it was obvious that something needed to be done, extra capacity was added to the existing mentoring relations. It is obvious that an early change in the malfunctioning tutor-candidate relations saves a lot of time and energy. The supervisor committee and the candidate have to function as a team to make sure that the research and writing process will run smoothly enough. This does not work out well in every case, not even when extra support is added. The hard thing for program management is to realize that the situation cannot be expected to become better. To have the courage to exchange supervisors and tutors early in the process has saved significant time and candidate motivation.

The FENIX executive Ph.D. program needed to find postdoctoral students quite close to the associate professor qualification to be able to support the Ph.D. candidates. Such postdoctoral students had to demonstrate an interest and skills in collaborative research and had to be willing to develop a collaborative partnership around learning and inquiry with the candidates to enhance the learning process. Recruiting postdoctoral candidates with the right skills, motivation, and interests has been a perennial challenge for the program.

Executive Ph.D. Program-Participating Company Relations. The FENIX program, in relation to companies, has made several attempts to organize research projects along thematic lines, organizing project themes around more general research themes (e.g., knowledge management, business creation, project management, leadership). Activities that enable closer cooperation with companies include the following:

- Ph.D. thesis themes contributing to complex research projects/ programs
- Establishing sustainable relations between the program and companies
- Negotiating financial resources with companies and funding organizations
- Organizing and executing knowledge transfer activities
- Project management
- Establishing specific roles (functions) in the company, with the assignment to manage some of the relations to FENIX research projects (e.g., sponsors, contact persons, managers, Ph.D. candidate coaches)

The relations between the FENIX program and the participating companies have unfolded in very different ways. At the one extreme, where some Ph.D. thesis work has contributed to "fill knowledge gaps," the thesis work has become embedded in larger research projects. Thus, the candidates have become important participants in these projects and key actors in the strategic knowledge development of their companies. In other cases, the FENIX program has been less successful in creating larger and prioritized projects achieving the critical attention in cooperation with companies. As a result, the candidates have been rather left on their own with their individual and specific thesis interests and without sufficient relations to practical contexts. Some candidates have had the feeling that the companies simply wanted to be a part of FENIX, thereby just appearing to be progressive firms, rather than actually developing good personnel policies for the candidates.

In the beginning, the FENIX faculty were not aware of the impact on the progress of the candidates and did not focus on the program-company relations to the same extent as they focused on researcher-candidate relations. There was a need to have faculty present at the company sites together with the candidates to help them in building their company role.

In principle, the FENIX faculty have been aware of the importance of developing long-term relations with the partner companies. Several initiatives have been made to establish large research programs and to involve them on a broader base. From earlier experiences, the faculty had a pretty good idea what was required to build the program-company relations. The company-candidate relations were almost a white spot and have definitely been troublesome to develop.

Executive Ph.D. Candidate-Participating Company Relations. All candidates live in a complicated situation. They need to combine the role of regular employees and leaders in organizations with the role of Ph.D. candidates. The candidates need to define and develop a socially and organizationally accepted role that gives sufficient time and economic resources for their research purposes. The candidates are employed in companies where a Ph.D. in management is something quite unknown. Being perceived as absent during significant time periods due to obligations to the FENIX program creates problems for their colleagues. More important, a Ph.D. role is not defined in advance. Many of the candidates witness that they have to struggle to get their academic role accepted. It is rarely recognized, even if they seemingly look detached while employed part-time, that in reality they often have to work harder than their colleagues. From the academic side, they also are a little different. The role of an executive Ph.D. candidate is not easily defined. Compared with "regular" Ph.D. candidates, they spend less time in the academic environment. When their fellow students are spending plenty of time discussing academic matters in the coffee room or in seminars, they are rushing back to work. As a consequence, the candidates face difficulties in defining the role with regard to two social systems because their role in the companies has changed and the academic system is unfamiliar with executive Ph.D. candidates.

We have seen three different reactions to these conflicting forces. One solution is to stay close to the familiar employee role and behave as if nothing has happened. In such cases, participation in the FENIX program is rarely discussed; studies, reading, and seminar attendance are organized to minimize disturbances within the company. A second possibility is to temporarily withdraw from the company environment and maximize the academic role. Then the candidate favors a role that is alienated from the employment setting. The candidate evades engagement in work matters and tries to become even more academic than the ordinary academics. A third possibility is to balance the two roles with a focus on the development of insider action research competencies (see Chapter 7 of this volume). We have seen that with significant support from both the faculty and the company, it is possible to develop the role of an insider action researcher and to get such a role accepted.

FENIX still needs to improve the coaching of the executive Ph.D. candidates to find acceptance for the academic role while also finding a sustainable company role. The reversed mentoring was supposed to be a tool that would help candidates to find a role in the management system, but it looks as though many candidates need coaching to be able to get these activities going.

Conclusion

In many respects, the FENIX executive Ph.D. program presented in this chapter has been successful so far. The candidates have, for the most part, been able to meet academic expectations and complete the program, despite encountering strained relationships at times. Companies have decided to reinvest in the FENIX program, to take over the former governmental seed money, and to link continued research to issues of high strategic importance. Those candidates who graduated from the program in the shortest amount of time got new employment contracts that allow them to continue with research for 20% of their working time, with many of them being connected to the FENIX research program. Despite this, there are reasons to be concerned about the sustainability and diffusion of the collaborative partnerships. The experiences from the formation of FENIX (see Chapter 4 of this volume) show that recruitment of faculty is cumbersome because the incentive structure of the university system does not emphasize collaborative work. In addition, academic researchers need to further develop their ability to formulate research questions on the basis of practitioners' concerns and interests and to forge long-term relationships with practicing managers. Researchers conducting collaborative research also need to experiment with new ways of integrating practitioners throughout the research process. Finally, we believe that it is of great importance that collaborative researchers be capable of establishing international communities of practice, sharing a commitment to and an interest in collaborative research.

References

Babüroglo, O. N., & Ravn, I. (1992). Normative action research. *Organization Studies, 13*(1), 19–34.

Brunsson, N. (1985). *The irrational organization: Irrationality as a basis for organizational action and change.* New York: John Wiley.

Collins, D. (2000). *Management fads and buzzwords: Critical-practical perspectives.* London: Routledge.

DiMaggio, P. J., & Powell, W. W. (1991). *The new institutionalism in organizational analysis.* Chicago: University of Chicago Press.

Engwall, L. (Ed.). (1995). *Föregångare inom företagsekonomin* (Pioneers in business administration). Stockholm, Sweden: SNS (Studieförbundet Näringsliv och Samhälle).

Meyer, J. W., & Rowan, B. (1991). Institutionalized organizations: Formal structure as myth and ceremony. In P. J. DiMaggio & W. W. Powell (Eds.), *The new institutionalism in organization analysis* (pp. 41–62). Chicago: University of Chicago Press.

Shani, A. B. (Rami), & Docherty, P. (2003). *Learning by design: Building sustainable organizations.* London: Blackwell.

Weber, M. (1947). *The theory of social and economic organization.* New York: Free Press.

7

The Dual Role of the Insider Action Researcher

Jonas Roth, Robert Sandberg,
and Charlotta Svensson

Traditional management research tends to produce university-based knowledge that fails to be of practical value to industry (see Chapters 1 and 2 of this volume). Alternatively, different forms of academy-industry collaborations have emerged that serve as important sources of scientific knowledge creation and economic value (Adler & Shani, 2001; Lawler, Mohrman, Mohrman, Ledford, & Cummings, 1999; Rynes, Bartunek, & Daft, 2001). A variety of collaborative research schools of thought are reviewed in Chapter 5 of this volume. At the essence of such collaborative orientations, one finds researchers and organizational members working together in search of solutions to practical problems and theory development. Consequently, a capacity for transforming academic knowledge into applications for resolving practitioners' problems and/or using practitioners' problems and knowledge as a basis for theorizing becomes essential.

The shift in the relationships between the researcher and the researched is one of the more profound differences between traditional and collaborative research (Lincoln, 2001). As the boundaries between the researcher and the researched are becoming blurry and the division of power and control is dissolved, new quality of relationships emerge. In this context, the process of creating actionable knowledge must take into account that the posture of detachment ("objectivity") has taken on a new shape and meaning and so needs to be addressed.

An emerging phenomenon in collaborative research is the dual role of the insider researcher. The purpose of this chapter is to explore how an individual, acting in the dual role of practitioner *and* researcher, can contribute to knowledge production in both the organizational setting and the academy as an action researcher. For this purpose, the particularities of the dual role of the *insider action researcher* (IAR) are elaborated on. An IAR is defined as a person conducting action research in an organization where he or she is also a permanent member. To illustrate the dual-role complexity and challenges, we describe three mini-cases in which we have acted as IARs at the companies where we are employed. The aim is not to suggest a new model of action research or collaborative research. Rather, the emphasis is on roles and the possible benefits and challenges introduced by the dual role of the IAR.

Action Research and the Role of the Researcher

As we see in Chapter 5 of this volume, collaborative research methodologies fulfill simultaneously the dual purpose of generating knowledge for academy and generating knowledge for industry. Following Torbert (1999), action research was identified and discussed as one of the collaborative methodologies in which participation is a critical component. The view of the role of the researcher and the researched has gradually changed and varies with the different action research approaches. The role of the researched varies from subject to co-researcher, whereas the role of the researcher varies from being in charge of the research process to acting in collaboration with the practitioners (Chisholm & Elden, 1993; Shani & Pasmore, 1985). Lewin attributes to the researcher a central role in the process as the person with the initiative and precedence for interpreting data (cited in Westlander, 1999). The Swedish Institute for Administrative Research (SIAR) school (Stymne, 1970; see also Chapter 3 of this volume) used an analogy with medical practice and suggested the term "clinical organization research" for an adviser assisting the organization while systematically recording observations. The clinical perspective of field research emphasizes that the initiative lies with the client, where the researcher is asked to come in as a professional helper and expects the mutual extensive involvement of the researcher and the client (Schein, 1987, 2001). Bartunek and Louis (1996) describe a research process that involves a team of collaborating practitioners (insiders) and researchers (outsiders). Thus, the boundary between the role of the researcher and the researched has become blurred in collaborative research approaches (Lincoln, 2001).

Recently recognized approaches to inquiring into one's own organizational setting have been presented as self-ethnography (Alvesson, 1999) and action research from within (Coghlan, 2001; Coghlan & Brannick, 2001). The level of involvement with the studied organization is a common distinction between action research and ethnography. Gold (1958) describes various levels of participation within ethnography using the complete observer, the observer-as-participant, the participant-as-observer, and the complete participant as the ideal forms. The researcher is supposed to *participate* in the actions but often strives for marginal roles in the field settings (Freilich, 1970) to avoid "going native."

Adler and Adler (1987) propose an additional category of involvement: *the membership role*. The advantage of this role is that the organizational members recognize the researcher as a fellow member participating in everyday practices. This forces the researcher to take on the same obligations and liabilities and to change behavior accordingly. Through the researcher's membership role, his or her role repertoire expands, laying the foundation for richer experiences. The membership role can be peripheral, active, or complete. As a complete member, the researchers fully immerse himself or herself as a "native." Simultaneously, the researcher has to sustain a research perspective and objectivity, implying "the ultimate existential dual role" (p. 73).

A role can be described as a building block of a social system whose purpose is to inform the individual members about the requirements of the system (Katz & Kahn, 1978). Ashforth, Kreiner, and Fugate (2000) argue that a role is associated with specific goals, values, beliefs, norms, interaction styles, and time frames. Consequently, a socially constructed *role-based identity* (Stryker, 1980) is attached to a given role. Individuals often have several partly overlapping roles associated with multiple memberships to social systems. Individuals treat such multiple social domains as "slices of reality" with cognitively held *role boundaries* (Ashforth et al., 2000).

Ashforth and colleagues (2000) propose that role duality can be characterized on a continuum, ranging from *role segmentation* (high contrast in role-based identities and inflexible and impermeable role boundaries) to *role integration* (low contrast in role-based identities and flexible and permeable role boundaries). Within the at-work domain, role integration is common, for example, the middle manager's dual role as both leader and follower. However, segmented role duality also appears within the at-work domain, for example, boundary spanners who interact with various parties with divergent and possibly conflicting goals (Adams, 1976). The IARs are viewed as such boundary spanners because they also act in the academic domain, which is partly intertwined with their work domain as well as partly separated.

An IAR is a complete participant (Gold, 1958) with a complete membership role (Adler & Adler, 1987) expected to last permanently. IARs conduct research in the setting where they act as practitioners, applying frames of reference from the setting where they act as researchers. Coghlan (2001) argues that although this role duality is one of the key elements in insider action research, it presents many challenges for the individual IAR. In the remainder of this chapter, we further explore the characteristics of this role duality and its effect on knowledge creation for theory and practice as well as associated challenges for the IAR. In this regard, we use the role segmentation, role integration continuum (Ashforth et al., 2000) for the analysis.

Three Empirical Cases Illustrating the Dual Role of the IAR

The following three cases are examples of action research projects involving IARs. The participating companies are research and development (R&D) units of larger international groups. They operate in fast-moving industrial environments and are characterized by a high academic level in their employees. The IARs were employed by the companies involved in the research projects while doing Ph.D. studies in parallel and being connected to a research institute with senior tutors. In all three cases, the IARs had previous experience within the companies in managerial positions but had, since joining the research program, taken on more independent roles working with organizational development. Before the initiation of the research projects, the IARs prepared for and emerged into the researcher role through courses in research methodology and practical exercises.

Method

To describe the various cases, events and encounters are recollected based on the respective researchers' notes, intermediate evaluations, and research database. These notes are in the form of meeting minutes, progress reports, presentation charts, reflective commentaries by the IARs on specific events, and diaries. The cases are compared using a cross-case analysis approach (Eisenhardt, 1989), and a matrix format is used to find and compare the main characteristics of the cases. The analyses are developed in iterations with the help of external researchers, not only "outsiders" within the respective action research projects but also researchers who have not been directly involved in the projects.

Case 1: Enabling Knowledge Creation and Dissemination

People don't ask when they experience problems. They try to solve it on their own instead of asking for help.

We don't have the time to share what we know. Anyway, I doubt that anybody is interested in what we know.

These were common statements concerning knowledge creation and transfer at one of AstraZeneca's R&D sites in Sweden. AstraZeneca is a vertically integrated international pharmaceuticals company. At the clinical R&D unit, which has more than 450 employees, many initiatives have previously been undertaken to disseminate experiences from "best practice" clinical projects. Despite these efforts, the ability to create knowledge differs considerably from project to project. An action research project was started to identify problems and gain knowledge leading to the initiation of relevant initiatives for change.

Research Question and Process. In this case, the IAR's interest in knowledge creation and knowledge sharing stems from frustration experienced as a project manager. Experience was not captured or used at any place other than where it originated. The action research project sought answers to two major questions. First, can AstraZeneca make use of its potential learning capabilities to enhance the creation, development, and dissemination of actionable knowledge throughout the organization? Second, can a truly participative action research process lead to alternative initiatives for change and organizational experiments that will advance AstraZeneca's learning capabilities?

The action research project crossed established theoretical boundaries, where researchers from various disciplines jointly created new "temporary" disciplines. For instance, the outsiders consisted of people with a background in psychology, economics, and biology, whereas the insiders consisted of project managers, medical specialists, project assistants, and line managers. The action research project was based on the continuous involvement of practitioners and researchers, from formulating the problem to making changes and writing manuscripts. Data were collected from interviews, written documents, and participative observations of day-to-day activities.

The Dual Role of the IAR. The IAR was the project manager of the action research project, facilitating the workshops where data collection methods, data sharing, and data interpretation were discussed. The workshops were used primarily to share and validate the results with players from both the company and the academy as well as to refine the results and obtain input on how to alter the research design or the initiatives for change. In addition, the level of analysis, as well as where to focus and initiate the action, emerged through this interactive research design.

The role of the IAR was changing throughout the research process, alternating between the role of a researcher and that of a project manager. The insider/outsider team approach (Bartunek & Louis, 1996) helped all project members to reflect on the process and knowledge gained. Balancing within the dual role was an emergent skill that the IAR became more proficient in doing as the project developed. In the beginning, the IAR was uncertain of his colleagues' expectations of him and his level of contribution to both the insider and outsider teams. One episode early in the research process illustrates this uncertainty. The IAR was asked at a management team meeting to present the conclusions drawn so far in the research process. The IAR felt the need to come up with something even though the data had not been fully reflected on. In so doing, the IAR tried to legitimize the researcher role before it was mature in that setting, giving the opposite result.

Outcomes. The results of the research project produced a number of organizational experiments that have been initiated and are currently being led by action learning teams within the R&D unit at AstraZeneca. For example, one initiative is sharing clinical project knowledge, where appointed individuals within the organization function as knowledge brokers, facilitating knowledge transfer between clinical projects. This experiment adds value to the company by making knowledge explicit for project members as well as by making knowledge shareable between projects. In addition, the experiment adds to the knowledge of assessment techniques regarding knowledge creation over organizational boundaries (Roth & Berg, 2001) as well as factors affecting knowledge creation in professional teams (Styhre, Roth, & Ingelgård, 2002).

The action research project changed a few basic assumptions at the company. For example, knowledge transfer should start at the most basic level (i.e., the education of junior members) rather than at the more complex organizational level of transferring best practice. Another example was finding time for knowledge creation. The primary focus should be on finding time for collective reflection rather than on designing sophisticated knowledge-creating arenas. This led to experimentation centered on a comprehensive educational program with the aim of bridging knowledge from senior organizational members to junior ones using only internal personnel as a faculty in interactive learning seminars. One spin-off is networking and the setting up of meetings after the scheduled educational seminar where the need to gain more knowledge around one specific issue builds temporary microcommunities (von Krogh, Icijo, & Nonaka, 2000).

The interactive educational program has added to the knowledge of organizational learning capabilities. Organizational learning capabilities must be dynamic in their character and, as such, provide the firm with competitive advantage (Ingelgård, Roth, Shani, & Styhre, 2002). In addition, the research effort at AstraZeneca has provided insights into the literature on knowledge management, where much literature is either over- or undersocialized in its view of knowledge. We argue that knowledge creation is a nonlinear process occurring in complex multifaceted activities where a caring climate enables a sharing culture (Styhre, Roth, & Ingelgård, 2000, 2002).

Case 2: The Multiple Identity of Corporate Consulting

Who are we?

What is our mission?

These were typical questions asked at corporate consulting unit Telia Promotor, a subsidiary of Swedish telecommunications operator Telia, at the beginning of 2000. The consulting unit, with 300 employees, was having an identity crisis due to an unclear mission and a failed merger attempt with Telia's Norwegian counterpart Telenor. The identity of this consulting business was also blurred by the parent's identity, based on a product-oriented business. At this time, a new chief executive officer (CEO) was appointed at Telia Promotor, and he initiated a program of change led by advisers from an international management consulting firm.

Research Question and Process. The IAR involved in this case had a research interest in the phenomenon of corporate consulting, that is, consulting services from nontraditional consulting organizations (Kubr, 1996). In his previous role as marketing director of Telia Promotor, the IAR had experienced leveraging of the intense knowledge creation in the consulting business to the parent organization as a problematic but strategically important area. The IAR was now asked to participate in the program of change as an organizational member.

The IAR became the project manager of a subproject focusing on the organizational identity (Albert & Whetten, 1985) of the corporate consulting unit. This subproject was initiated as a result of the analysis made by the advisers in which they had described the organizational culture and identity as unclear and problematic. It was also initiated as a result of the IAR's research interest, where a previous study had ascertained identity as an important factor in knowledge extension to the parent organization (Sandberg & Werr, 2000).

The Dual Role of the IAR. At the beginning of the change program, the IAR was primarily acting as a self-ethnographer (Alvesson, 1999). When the analysis of the advisers was presented and the organization became more actively involved, the role of the IAR shifted to include more interventions as the identity project identified requirements for change and initiated the necessary actions.

The IAR found the dual role to be challenging. He had a lot of knowledge and many ideas to share in discussions related to his research topic. On these occasions, he became deeply involved in his practitioner role, and this made it hard to simultaneously enact the role of a detached researcher. On the other hand, the practitioner role as subproject manager and the simultaneous role as active action researcher were, to a great extent, overlapping. Therefore, field research was often divided between "online" interventions and "offline" tasks such as taking notes and adding personal reflections. The IAR entered all of the empirical data, such as interventions, observations, interviews, documents, and questionnaires, into a database. This was also used for the administration of the study and helped the IAR to manage the process in a rigorous manner.

In addition to the specific identity project, the IAR intervened in other ways that could be explained by his dual role. One episode illustrating this was when Telia Promotor decided on its new organizational structure.

Here, the IAR drew on relevant theories with regard to organizing (Lawrence & Lorsch, 1967), knowledge-intensive firms (Blackler, 1995; Starbuck, 1992), and empirical examples from similar consulting firms (Alvesson, 1995; Werr, Bryskhe, & Norén, 2000). Consequently, the need for a tight coupling between the salespeople and the developers and consultants involved with the assignments was highlighted by the IAR and affected the chosen organization principle.

Outcomes. In the identity project, the IAR contributed to the establishment of a new head office, to the formulation of the organization's preferred values, and to the planning of the new marketing strategy. The study also adds to the organization in terms of a deeper understanding of the multiple identities of the business, explaining much of the ambiguity at Telia Promotor.

The dual role of the IAR was a vehicle for creating new knowledge. The theoretical contribution so far is manifested in two papers. The first (Sandberg & Werr, 2001) addresses the blurring of firm boundaries and focuses on identity formation and identification within complex boundary-spanning organizations. Telia Promotor is used in this regard as an empirical example. The company's clients reside both inside and outside the parent organization, leading to multiple organizational identities (Albert & Whetten, 1985)—a staff identity and an external consultant identity. It is concluded that these multiple identities represent an unstable arrangement striving toward a clear identity. Therefore, they have to be actively managed to sustain the multiple mission of the unit.

The second paper (Sandberg, 2001) gives a detailed empirical account of how the new CEO managed the emerged identity crisis. The paper shows that the CEO's rhetoric focused on creating an identity hierarchy (Pratt & Foreman, 2000, p. 32), highlighting the external consultant identity using the information technology consulting industry as a prototype for the unit's self-categorization (cf. Hogg & Terry, 2000). The rhetoric is effective in bringing the organization's identity crisis to an end. There are, however, long-term risks with such a strategy because the boundary-spanning ability may be reduced if there is too little rhetorical support for the (secondary) staff identity.

Case 3: Toward a Multiproject Management Model

We have to prioritize Project X!

But that indicates that—at least in part—Project Y is prioritized as well since Project X is dependent on the results of Project Y. And Project Y is dependent on the results of Project Z.

The third case is a description of an action research project at one product development unit within Ericsson. The unit, consisting of 1,050 employees in

R&D, is responsible for developing products within the telecommunications system—a complex product system (Hobday, 2000) with highly integrated components and subsystems.

Research Question and Process. The IAR was working within a large-scale improvement program assisted by external management consultants. There was growing concern that this improvement program was not bringing the expected results while it was being perceived as not addressing the issues of importance to this unit. To investigate this, the IAR ran a series of workshops during the spring of 1999 involving functional managers, project managers, and process developers. The critical area of improvement was identified as related to the management of the overall project portfolio.

In parallel, the IAR was assigned a tutor in the research program. In cooperation with him, the research interest was defined and the concept of multiproject management was introduced. The IAR started discussing this concept at the company. The resulting research question was as follows: How is the cluster of simultaneously and successively executed projects to be managed within the organizational unit?

The action research project was organized as an initiative for change involving the implementation of a new project planning and multiproject management methodology. This local initiative was legitimized as part of the large-scale improvement program. A pilot phase was started in October 1999. In March 2000, the management team decided to fully implement the new methodology. Implementation was divided into three phases, each with a different focus: (a) methods and tools for planning and following up single projects, (b) behavioral aspects within the multiproject management methodology, and (c) multiproject planning and control. These steps were continuously evaluated in interviews, informal discussions, questionnaires, and meetings.

The Dual Role of the IAR. The role of the IAR changed during the process. Initially, the IAR was the implementation leader of a small change team consisting of one organizational member and three external consultants. After the decision to go for full implementation, the IAR stepped out of her leader role and became a member of the increased change team. Parallel to the process of change, the IAR analyzed the origins of the methodology and its theoretical assumptions. Gradually, the roles of the practitioner and the researcher became more integrated.

Together with her tutor, the IAR tested the internally developed conclusions, and a distanced perspective was introduced into the analysis. Also, in formal seminars, paper evaluations, and other more informal occasions, various parts of the change process were discussed, tested, and reflected on with external researchers. Through this, the IAR was well prepared to question and revise the propositions provided by the external consultants involved.

The expectations of the company regarding the role duality of the IAR changed during the action research project. One example of this is an episode during a meeting among project office managers. The organization of product development assignments into a portfolio of projects was discussed. The IAR pointed to the power balance between the functional organization and the project organization as an important aspect to consider (see, e.g., Clark & Wheelwright, 1992; Larson & Gobeli, 1987). After the meeting, one of the participants commented that this had been possible for the IAR only due to the expectations placed on her dual role, whereas introducing this political subject would be more sensitive for the other participants.

Outcomes. The organizational unit has adapted the new project planning methodology used in every new product development project since May 2000. Instructions, methods, and tools have been developed and refined. The immediate value introduced by this is the use of a common and structured method for planning and follow-up on all projects. The action research project is currently in an overlap of the second and third phases described previously.

The third phase has led to a reformulation of the research question: How is a preferred product portfolio to be realized through a project portfolio (cf. Wheelwright & Clark, 1992), with the objective of reducing complex interactions (cf. Thompson, 1967) among projects? The importance of managing input-output dependencies (De Maio, Verganti, & Corso, 1994) among projects was accentuated by applying the new project planning methodology. By following this action research project, it has been possible to gain deep empirical insights and capture the complex nature of multi-project settings (Svensson & Engwall, 2001a).

One contribution within the field of project management is the thorough evaluation of the new project planning methodology in theory and practice. The main benefit of the new methodology has been identified as the management and visualization of uncertainty within projects (Svensson & Engwall, 2001b).

During the action research project, a phenomenon was observed regarding how organizations in turbulent environments manage the paradox between structured planning and the simultaneous need to deal with uncertainty. This phenomenon was studied and analyzed as a subproject, thereby adding to the theoretical and practical understanding of how project planning implicitly assumes that the unplanned will be possible to manage on an ad hoc basis (Engwall & Svensson, 2000, 2001).

A Summary of the Cases

The three cases are summarized in Table 7.1. In all three cases, it has been illustrated how the presence of the IAR in both domains—industry and academy—was of importance in connecting the research areas with the

Table 7.1   A Summary of the Three Projects

	Project 1: AstraZeneca	Project 2: Telia Promotor	Project 3: Ericsson
Characteristics of the action research projects	• A research and development unit of an international pharmaceuticals company • Knowledge creation and dissemination identified as important success factors • A sponsor for the research project found within the company	• A corporate consulting unit of a large Nordic telecommunications operator • A failed merger attempt in the parent organization • An identity crisis • A program of change initiated by a new chief executive officer	• A product development unit at an international telecommunications equipment supplier • The multiproject environment identified as a critical improvement area • The opportunity to involve the insider action researcher recognized
The research question and process	• How to enhance knowledge creation and dissemination • Integrated insider/outsider team • Research team members involved as equals in all parts of the process of change • Action research project initiated by the insider/outsider team	• How the organizational identity is constructed and managed • Segmented insider and outsider teams • An action research study as part of a larger program of change • Initially observing participation	• How multiple development projects are managed • Segmented insider and outsider teams • An action research study as part of a larger program of change • Identification of important issues for improvement • The change team members involved as equals in all parts of the process of change
Outcomes of the action research effort	• Mutual learning • New concepts introduced • Creation of an insider action researcher role that became accepted both in academy and in industry • Actions for change for knowledge creation and sharing • Building on the theory of dynamic learning capabilities and the affects of care in professional teams	• Mutual learning • New concepts introduced • A deeper understanding of multiple organizational identities • Problematic corporate communication identified • Contribution to the new marketing strategy • A rich empirical description	• Mutual learning • New concepts introduced • Routines developed for planning and monitoring the progress of projects • Structuring development efforts into projects with respect to interdependencies • Evaluation of a project planning methodology • Assumption of the unplanned within project management

organizational issues. By being present, the opportunity was available for joint problem identification, joint knowledge creation, and joint action. For the IARs, this emerged as a dual role of practitioner and researcher. In what follows, we analyze how this role duality was handled and how it affected the outcome of the action research effort.

Building a Bridge Between Industry and Academy

In the cases described, the IARs were the architects of bridges established between the companies and the academy. However, the design of these bridges differed in each of the three cases. The action research project at AstraZeneca was planned as a true insider/outsider team (Bartunek & Louis, 1996) in which the research team, consisting of organizational members as well as academic researchers, was involved in every stage of the collaborative research process. The AstraZeneca IAR facilitated the interaction between the insiders and the outsiders.

In the Telia Promotor and Ericsson cases, the insider and outsider teams worked more as separate teams, with the IAR operating in both teams. The insider team concentrated on action, evaluation of the situation, and the change of actions, whereas the outsider team was more concerned with analyzing data and the generalizability of the outcome. The outsider team consisted of researchers with research interests similar to those of the IAR. In this context, the IAR was a relative insider (cf. Bartunek & Louis, 1996) with a parallel practitioner role, whereas the other academics were outsiders. In the insider team, the IAR was a relative outsider using the parallel researcher role.

Broadening the Bridge

In a recent study (Schild & Hanberger, 2000), 12 Swedish alternative research schools are evaluated regarding knowledge transfer between industry and academy. One of the two sets of conclusions from the study relates to the industrial doctoral candidates' roles. The report concludes that the doctoral candidates embody the knowledge transfer and thereby constitute an important link between industry and academy.

However, things are not optimal if knowledge creation is dependent on one specific individual. The challenge is to broaden the bridge for joint knowledge creation, exemplified in the cases with collaborative insider/outsider teams. The IAR played an important role in this joint team and knowledge development. Considering the knowledge created—aiming for Mode 2 knowledge production (Gibbons et al., 1994)—the people inhabiting the bridge became even more essential. In Mode 2 knowledge production, knowledge creation is highly dependent on everyone involved, but primarily on those spanning the boundaries between different organizations and environments, for example, industry and academy. However, not all researchers within the team should aim for the IAR's role duality given that objectivity and reflexivity might be endangered. Our argument is that an IAR contributes extensively to bridging the gap between academy and industry and can facilitate the joint knowledge creation necessary for both settings.

Stabilizing the Bridge
Through a Symmetrical Relationship

One of the features of the IAR's dual role is that it contributes to a symmetrical relationship between industry and academy, whereas the more traditional research is characterized by an asymmetrical relationship between the researcher and the studied context (see, e.g., Gibbons et al., 1994; Tranfield & Starkey, 1998). The IAR facilitates a relationship that is more characterized by true collaboration (cf. Amabile et al., 2001; Gibbons et al., 1994), thereby enabling Mode 2 knowledge production (Gibbons et al., 1994). In agreement with other scholars (Mohrman, Gibson, & Mohrman, 2001; Rynes et al., 2001), we believe that good social relations, mutual empathy, and common foundations are prerequisites for achieving substantial outcomes in cross-boundary knowledge creation. Therefore, creating a symmetrical relationship is fundamental to joint knowledge creation and, with that, to the creation of a stable bridge between academy and industry. This symmetry was facilitated by the IAR's dual role, with extensive knowledge of the company being studied and the research process.

_____The Balancing Act and Periodic Disengaging

Because of the iterative nature of the projects, the research process of entering, experiencing, and disengaging from a membership, as described by Adler and Adler (1987), was not linear or discretely divided. Instead, the role duality periodically changed character between high segmentation and integration as the research projects progressed. During phases of high role segmentation, the IARs could step back and apply an outsider perspective (Figure 7.1).

The IARs described in the three projects were already real natives and needed to periodically step back and apply an outsider perspective. Detachment involved increasing the contrast of the role duality rather than alternating between two roles. Even if they constantly experienced role transitions (Ashforth et al., 2000) between the roles of practitioner and researcher, it was during phases of high role segmentation that this was done consciously and reflectively.

One way in which to strengthen the outsider perspective was to temporarily disengage from the primary action. At times, it was possible for the

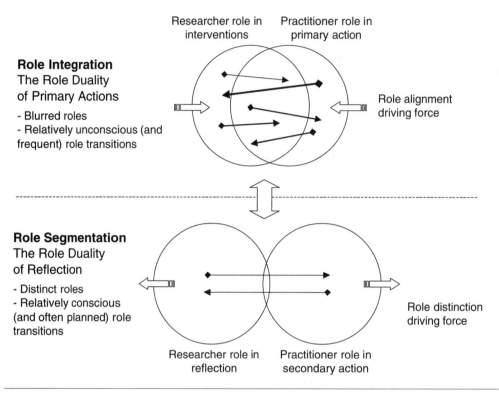

Researcher role in interventions   Practitioner role in primary action

Role Integration
The Role Duality
of Primary Actions

- Blurred roles
- Relatively unconscious (and frequent) role transitions

Role alignment driving force

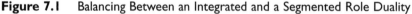

Role Segmentation
The Role Duality
of Reflection

- Distinct roles
- Relatively conscious (and often planned) role transitions

Role distinction driving force

Researcher role in reflection   Practitioner role in secondary action

Figure 7.1   Balancing Between an Integrated and a Segmented Role Duality

SOURCE: Modified and adapted from Ashforth, Kreiner, and Fugate (2000).

IARs to disengage and adopt a more distant, reflecting researcher role. Role duality was segmented by dividing up the week physically between work at the company and work at the university. In this way, the IARs could focus more on reflecting, analyzing, and writing up their research.

Thus, the role of the IAR is complex and can be viewed on multiple dimensions of complexity—from the researcher role to the researched role, from the primary role as a researcher to the primary role as a practitioner, from the blurred role to the distinct role, from the reflective role to the action role. The role duality is not easy to manage and at times can be viewed as a "near schizophrenic state" (Adler & Adler, 1987). Yet managing the role duality is likely to have a major impact on the creation of the new and relevant knowledge.

Conclusion

This chapter has focused on the exploration of the IAR as a critical role in collaborative research. The nature of the IAR role and its complexity, duality, and merit were highlighted. Three mini-cases in which the dual role of an IAR exemplifies a bridge for joint knowledge creation were described and examined. The IARs were strategically important to their companies, as well as to the academy, in that they contributed to Mode 2 knowledge production (Gibbons et al., 1994). What this meant in terms of outcomes differed among the three cases because different research issues were in focus. The AstraZeneca case focused on knowledge creation and dissemination, the Telia Promotor case dealt with organizational identity, and the Ericsson case studied multiproject management. In each of the three case descriptions, important results originating from the collaborative research projects were identified and discussed in terms of relevance to both practice and theory.

One of the main advantages of the IAR's dual role—the intention of remaining a full-fledged member in the researched setting—is also one of its major challenges. Implicitly, we have presented in our discussion the hypothesis that the duality experienced by the IAR is harder to manage than the duality often involved in roles that operate mainly within *one* domain, that is, academy *or* industry. Establishing the support mechanisms that allow the IAR to work through and manage the "near schizophrenic state" of the role is likely to be the key to sustaining true collaborative research in organizations. Beyond the lenses advanced in this chapter, the next two chapters of the volume advance "jam sessions" and "structural learning mechanisms" that can enhance the ability of the IAR to sustain the needed balance.

References

Adams, J. S. (1976). The structure and dynamics of behavior in organizational boundary roles. In M. D. Dunnette (Ed.), *Handbook of industrial and organizational psychology.* Chicago: Rand McNally.

Adler, N., & Shani, A. B. (Rami). (2001). In search of an alternative framework for the creation of actionable knowledge: Table-tennis research at Ericsson. In W. A. Pasmore & R. W. Woodman (Eds.), *Research in organizational change and development* (Vol. 13, pp. 43–79). Amsterdam: Elsevier Science.

Adler, P. A., & Adler, P. (1987). *Membership roles in field research.* Newbury Park, CA: Sage.

Albert, S., & Whetten, D. (1985). Organizational identity. In L. L. Cummings & B. Staw (Eds.), *Research in organizational behavior* (Vol. 7). Greenwich, CT: JAI Press.

Alvesson, M. (1995). *Management of knowledge-intensive companies.* Berlin: Walter de Gruyter.

Alvesson, M. (1999). *Methodology for close up studies: Struggling with closeness and closure.* Lund, Sweden: Lund University, School of Economics and Management.

Amabile, T. M., Patterson, C., Mueller, J., Wojcik, T., Odomirok, P., Marsh, M., & Kramer, S. J. (2001). Academic-practitioner collaboration in management research: A case of cross-profession collaboration. *Academy of Management Journal, 44,* 418–431.

Ashforth, B. E., Kreiner, G. E., & Fugate, M. (2000). All in a day's work: Boundaries and micro role transitions. *Academy of Management Review, 25,* 472–491.

Bartunek, J. M., & Louis, M. R. (1996). *Insider/Outsider team research.* Thousand Oaks, CA: Sage.

Blackler, F. (1995). Knowledge, knowledge work, and organizations: An overview and interpretation. *Organization Studies, 16,* 1021–1046.

Chisholm, R. F., & Elden, M. (1993). Features of emerging action research. *Human Relations, 46,* 275–289.

Clark, K., & Wheelwright, S. (1992). Organizing and leading "heavyweight" development teams. *California Management Review, 34*(3), 9–28.

Coghlan, D. (2001). Insider action research projects: Implications for practicing managers. *Management Learning, 32*(1), 49–60.

Coghlan, D., & Brannick, T. (2001). *Doing action research in your own organization.* London: Sage.

De Maio, A., Verganti, R., & Corso, M. (1994). A multi-project management framework for new product development. *European Journal of Operations Research, 78*(2), 178–191.

Eisenhardt, K. M. (1989). Building theories from case study research. *Academy of Management Review, 14,* 532–550.

Engwall, M., & Svensson, C. (2000, August). *How cheetahs run: Cheetah teams in product development projects: The most extreme form of temporary organizations?* Paper presented at the annual meeting of the Academy of Management, Toronto.

Engwall, M., & Svensson, C. (2001). Cheetah teams. *Harvard Business Review, 79*(2), 20–21.

Freilich, M. (1970). Toward a formalization of fieldwork. In M. Freilich (Ed.), *Marginal natives* (pp. 485–585). New York: Harper & Row.

Gibbons, M., Limoges, H., Nowotny, H., Schwartzman, S., Scott, P., & Trow, M. (1994). *The new production of knowledge: The dynamics of science and research in contemporary societies.* London: Sage.

Gold, R. L. (1958). Roles in sociological field observations. *Social Forces, 36,* 217–223.

Hobday, M. (2000). The project-based organization: An ideal form for managing complex products and systems? *Research Policy, 29,* 871–893.

Hogg, M. A., & Terry, D. J. (2000). Social identity and self-categorization processes in organizational contexts. *Academy of Management Review, 25,* 121–140.

Ingelgård, A., Roth, J., Shani, A. B. (Rami), & Styhre, A. (2002). Dynamic learning capability and actionable knowledge creation: Clinical R&D in a pharmaceutical company. *The Learning Organization, 9*(2), 65–77.

Katz, D., & Kahn, R. L. (1978). *The social psychology of organizations.* New York: John Wiley.

Kubr, M. (Ed.). (1996). *Management consulting: A guide to the profession* (3rd ed., rev.). Geneva, Switzerland: International Labour Office.

Larson, E. W., & Gobeli, D. H. (1987). Matrix management: Contradictions and insights. *California Management Review, 29*(4), 126–138.

Lawler, E. E., III, Mohrman, A. M., Jr., Mohrman, S. A., Ledford, G. E., Jr., & Cummings, T. G. (1999). *Doing research that is useful for theory and practice* (2nd ed.). Lexington, MA: Lexington Books.

Lawrence, P., & Lorsch, J. (1967). *Organization and environment.* Boston: Harvard Business School Press.

Lincoln, Y. S. (2001). Engaging sympathies: Relationships between action research and social constructivism. In P. Reason & H. Bradbury (Eds.), *Handbook of action research* (pp. 124–132). London: Sage.

Mohrman, S. A., Gibson, C. B., & Mohrman, A. M., Jr. (2001). Doing research that is useful to practice: A model and empirical exploration. *Academy of Management Journal, 44,* 357–375.

Pratt, M., & Foreman, P. (2000). Classifying managerial responses to multiple organizational identities. *Academy of Management Review, 25,* 18–42.

Roth, J., & Berg, L. (2001, July). *Enable knowledge creation across project boundaries: A case from the pharmaceutical company AstraZeneca.* Paper presented at the European Group of Organisation Studies Conference, Lyon, France.

Rynes, S. L., Bartunek, J. M., & Daft, R. L. (2001). Across the great divide: Knowledge creation and transfer between practitioners and academics. *Academy of Management Journal, 44,* 340–355.

Sandberg, R. (2001, July). *Rhetoric and symbolism in the reshaping of multiple identities: A study of a change program in a corporate consulting unit.* Paper presented at the European Group of Organisation Studies Conference, Lyon, France.

Sandberg, R., & Werr, A. (2000, August). *Corporate consulting: A wellspring of knowledge?* Paper presented at the annual meeting of the Academy of Management, Toronto.

Sandberg, R., & Werr, A. (2001, July). *Handling multiple identities in boundary spanning: A study of identity construction in a corporate consulting unit.* Paper presented at the European Group of Organization Studies Conference, Lyon, France.

Schein, E. (1987). *The clinical perspective in fieldwork.* Newbury Park, CA: Sage.

Schein, E. H. (2001). Clinical inquiry/research. In P. Reason & H. Bradbury (Eds.), *Handbook of action research* (pp. 228–237). London: Sage.

Schild, I., & Hanberger, A. (2000). *Industrial research schools: A real-time evaluation of the Swedish knowledge foundation's research school programme.* Umeå, Sweden: Umeå Center for Evaluation Research.

Shani, A. B. (Rami), & Pasmore. W. A. (1985). Organization inquiry: Towards a new model of action research. In D. Warrick (Ed.), *Contemporary organization development* (pp. 438–448). Glenview, IL: Scott, Foresman.

Starbuck, W. H. (1992). Learning by knowledge-intensive firms. *Journal of Management Studies, 26,* 713–740.

Stryker, S. (1980), *Symbolic interactionism: A social structural version.* Menlo Park, CA: Benjamin/Cummings.

Styhre, A., Roth, J., & Ingelgård, A. (2000). Time, time, time: Time compression, knowledge, and competitive advantage. *Journal of Global Competitiveness, 8*(1), 28–43.

Styhre, A., Roth, J., & Ingelgård, A. (2002). Care of the other: Knowledge creation through care in professional teams. *Scandinavian Journal of Management, 18,* 503–520.

Stymne, B. (1970). *Values and processes. A systems study of effectiveness in three organizations.* Lund, Sweden: Studentlitteratur.

Svensson, C., & Engwall, M. (2001a, July). *Managing boundaries, dependencies, and time: Human resource allocation in multi-project settings.* Paper presented at the European Group of Organization Studies Conference, Lyon, France.

Svensson, C., & Engwall, M. (2001b, June). *Multi-project management methods applied in new product development: An in-depth study of the application of critical chain.* Paper presented at the European Institute for Advanced Studies in Management Eighth International Product Development Management Conference, Enschede, Netherlands.

Thompson, J. D. (1967). *Organizations in action.* New York: McGraw-Hill.

Torbert, W. (1999). The distinctive questions developmental action inquiry asks. *Management Learning, 30*(2), 189–206.

Tranfield, D., & Starkey, K. (1998). The nature, social organisation, and promotion of management research: Towards policy. *British Journal of Management, 9,* 341–353.

von Krogh, G., Icijo, K., & Nonaka, I. (2000). *Enabling knowledge creation.* New York: Oxford University Press.

Wheelwright, S. C., & Clark, K. B. (1992, March–April). Creating project plans to focus product development. *Harvard Business Review, 70,* 70–82

Werr, A., Bryskhe, H., & Norén, M. (2000). *The baby elephant walk.* Stockholm, Sweden: Stockholm School of Economics, FENIX.

Westlander, G. (1999). *Aktionsforskningens framväxt och utveckling: En metodorientering* (The development of action research: A method analysis). Gothenburg, Sweden: IACTH (Arbetslivets bebyggelse-Byggnadsklimat-Arkitektur-Chalmers Tekniska Högskola).

8 Jam Sessions for Collaborative Management Research

Sofia Börjesson and Tobias Fredberg

The concept of a jam session is generally associated with playing jazz music—improvising, adding on, team playing, testing, challenging and provoking the other players, and experimenting with new expressions. In a research context, it means the very same, albeit a jam session is the vehicle for finding as well as creating new knowledge jointly by business representatives and researchers.

Jazz is sometimes used as a metaphor for organizing. Management researchers who describe organizing as jazz (e.g., Barrett, 1998; Berniker, 1998; Hatch, 1998) are fascinated by the silent self-organization that takes place in a momentarily created jazz band. It is implicitly assumed that the good music is created from the suddenly arisen harmonic organization. Although writers such as Barrett (1998), Berniker (1998), and Hatch (1998) have made important contributions to the understanding of self-organizing activities, very few have made use of the jam session metaphor in a collaborative research setting. Thus, in this chapter, a method for collaborative research that has been developed out of the jazz metaphor, the jam session, is examined. The principles for the operational method were influenced extensively by how a jam session should be constructed to create harmony but still adjusted to suit research purposes. And perhaps contrary to what is usually assumed, the disharmony is just as important as the harmony in the process.

AUTHORS' NOTE: The authors express their sincere gratitude to all those participating in the project, especially Jonas Fernström, Patric Miesenberger, and Hans Karlsson at Telenordia (BT Ignite); Bengt Uggla and Pontus Schulz at Vision (FinansVision); and Gunnar Springfeldt at Göteborgs-Posten.

Features of Collaborative Research _____

A need for renewal in management science has been suggested frequently during recent years (for an overview, see Adler & Norrgren, 2002; see also Chapter 5 of this volume), and in the context of the knowledge society, the relations between academy and industry are being altered to pace the new prerequisites encountered. The principles for renewal in management science were introduced during the middle of the 1990s by Gibbons and colleagues (1994), and that contribution was followed up recently by an even stronger work (Nowotny, Scott, & Gibbons, 2001) emphasizing the emergence of open systems in knowledge production. New principles for knowledge production have led to a shift in the relations between academy and industry from *sponsorship* to *partnership* (Jacob, Hellström, Adler, & Norrgren, 2000). The partnership, in turn, affects the prerequisites for research in a number of ways as the collaborative aspects can be recognized in all parts of the practical research (e.g., research setup, team forming, financing, identification of research problems, data collection, deliverables). Knowledge and experiences regarding joint collaborative partnerships are being developed and documented continuously. The approach described here—the jam session—is one such attempt to collaborate in academy-industry partnerships.

Most of the literature in the area treats the more *principal* aspects of collaborative networks and programes (e.g., the benefit derived from them, their advantages and disadvantages, their relevance, what issues are appropriate) collaborative research, or it covers the design of networks and programs or characteristics of joint formulation of research problems (Adler & Shani, 2001; Börjesson & Norrgren, 2002). Only recently has literature that addresses the *operational* features of collaborative research been published. Examples of this body of texts include Adler and Shani (2001) discussing the "table tennis research" approach as well as a number of insider action research projects (Roth, 2002; see also Chapter 7 of this volume). All are examples of researchers and practitioners working together in continuous dialogue. Jacob and colleagues (2000) elaborate on this continuous dialogue and discuss it as an outcome of a shift to a new approach to research in which academy and industry jointly reflect on research issues. This research approach is contrasted against a traditional view wherein research assignments are primarily defined by academic researchers themselves. Recently, there has appeared literature that draws on the theoretical denominators and similarities among field approaches within social sciences (e.g., grounded theory methodology, cooperative inquiry, action science) and their matches in management science (David, 2002; see also Chapter 5 of this volume). David (2002) refers to some of these approaches as *intervention research* in management science:

> Intervention research consists of helping to design and implement
> appropriate management models, tools, and procedures in the field,

on the basis of a more or less well-defined transformation project, with the aim to produce knowledge that serves action and management science theories of a more or less general nature. (p. 17)

The operational research methodologies used for data collection within collaborative research thus consist of a mixture of methods used in social sciences (e.g., experiments, dialogue interviews, participatory observation). There exists no clear-cut toolbox of operational methods specifically deigned for collaborative research.

An interactive research forum called *jam sessions* was developed within the FENIX research program. In this chapter, we introduce and discuss an in-depth description of the use of jam sessions. The reporting comes from the field phase of researching in a collaborative research project, "Strategizing in the Digital Media Sector." The overall objective of the project was to create knowledge and understand already existing knowledge in cooperation with three participating organizations.

In short, for the three companies, the approach in working with jam sessions proved to be beneficial both directly and as a suggestion for how to undertake future knowledge creation exercises. The companies' original motives for participating in a research setup such as ours were that they were curious and open-minded and wanted to try an alternative approach for their own development of strategic knowledge. Afterward, they expressed the following main gains:

- The open climate devoted to discussing relevant issues for them
- The language creation and conceptual development in the sessions (when the persons involved had created a common language for problematic issues, it became a tool for them to continue addressing similar questions when coming back and working with general operations in their companies)
- The opportunity to get away from the daily routines and to view issues from a different perspective in a new setting

Jam sessions could be used for both intra- and cross-organizational learning. In this project, we investigated the participating companies' strategic processes and strategic thinking, and for that reason we used only intra-organizational setups. In this chapter, we present and explore how jam sessions could serve as an interactive meeting forum, and we discuss potential benefits and pitfalls of the method.

The Jam Session Method

The three companies involved in the collaborative research project all were trying to enter what was then the emerging digital media market (the project started in 2000 and was finalized during the early spring of 2002). The market developed rapidly, with actors entering from various business areas and potential actors—both established and newcomers—all believing that they had to act, that is, strategize into the unknown with high speed and uncertainty. It was anticipated that new products and services, as well as new business models, would be requested in the near future. Therefore, the required knowledge for the development of successful digital media services was complex, and the companies assumed that already existing approaches would not do, yet they were stuck in mental models of their business. In addition, the participants thought that the time pressure was intense. These preconditions made the collaborative research design suitable. As discussed by Coughlan, Dromgoole, Duff, and Harbison (2000), two typical interactive components for a successful collaborative approach are that (a) the problem is a complex organizational problem and that (b) a reflective and questioning process around the issue is possible. The jam session, as an operational collaborative arena for knowledge development for the companies' strategic concerns, was actually never put into question by the participants; quite the opposite, it was regarded as a prerequisite for the overall collaboration. The common value and starting point was that business development was very much the same as product development. Our arena for co-creation of knowledge, therefore, became the companies' respective strategic business and product development teams.

Besides the jam sessions method, the three companies described here were studied by in-depth analyses based on mainly participatory observation. Two of these additional studies were conducted during two different 3-month studies for each company. The third study was based on an interview approach. One company was a medium-sized Swedish telecommunications operator in which the development division was the object of study. The second company was a major Swedish morning newspaper, and the study focused on one of the digital media development projects. The third company was a minor magazine, specializing in the business of the television industry, in which the additional study (an interview study) concerned a major part of the newsroom and the advertisement department.

These studies were followed by a series of jam sessions to explore the rules and logic that applied to the companies' situations. The research objective was to investigate how images of the future are incorporated in the companies' strategic work, that is, how companies construct and relate to a future market that does not yet exist. The simultaneous objective for the companies was to formulate new knowledge to undertake their strategizing (and business development) when entering the new market. The underlying question was the following: What actions can be taken?

This chapter explores the most central notions of jam sessions as we used them in this particular collaborative research project. It is worth mentioning that the jam session methodology, which emerged with and was developed by FENIX researchers, has been used within FENIX for three different purposes: (a) as a method for identifying relevant research areas; (b) as a method for communicating results, often in cross-organizational settings; and (c) as a method for creating knowledge, that is, as a method for collecting data that simultaneously creates knowledge. Adler and Shani (2001) provide some background to the work with jam sessions. They describe jam sessions as "boundary-spanning workshops where the actual research takes place. Data is collected, analyzed, and interpreted, conclusions are drawn, ideas for action are tested, and redefinition of research issues occurs" (p. 52). The co-creative FENIX principle of both the research setup and the way in which the knowledge is developed and communicated allows iterations of new knowledge to emerge and is a shared responsibility. In other words, the academic researchers are not seen as deliverers of the results; delivering is and was a collective task.

The description here is based on our own experiences from the organized jam sessions. The reflection-in-action process during the jam sessions enabled us to develop the narrative of what we did as well as the method as such, that is, a sort of self-ethnographic method (Alvesson, 1999; Alvesson & Sköldberg, 1994); we tried to study ourselves as well as the participants during the sessions. The bias risk here lies in being too optimistic of the learning dimension of the participants during the jam sessions; no quantitative data on that kind of output were collected.

Perhaps the most typical characteristics of the approach used within FENIX are the joint research problem identification and definition. Not only for co-creation purposes of knowledge but also for ensuring the alignment and commitment, a joint design of research questions and research process with the underlying intention of "win-win" is used. It is important to note that the joint approach ensures relevance and safeguards that the knowledge created is actionable; that is, it can serve as a point of departure for practical undertakings.

Working With Jam Sessions

In essence, a jam session is a method for trying to formulate what has remained unformulated. This is achieved by changing perspectives on the issues that are subject to discussion. Therefore, the outcome from a jam session series can be examined on several levels. To formulate the unformulated, the participants in the jam sessions have to put words on intangible phenomena. Thus, the jointly established and shared language is a result in itself. Analogically, jam sessions are also productive for creating taxonomies for various phenomena. During a jam session, arguments are written on a whiteboard (similar to a blackboard but with a white surface), and in many cases participants argue that certain things are more important than others, and so the list is rearranged. The creation of such lists is a good exercise because it spurs discussions. The most important research results are the insights to understanding various aspects of development work that the researchers get from the sessions. To further explore this, new jam sessions may be organized, or the method can be successfully combined with other research methods. The results from surveys or participatory studies can be used for testing during new jam sessions.

In our collaborative research, we have used jam sessions as an approach to establish a continuous dialogue in the interaction between the academy and companies. Here, we point out a number of rules that guide the work with jam sessions. Even though a jam session can be used for various purposes in the research, its characteristics remain the same. People communicate on an equal level around issues that concern them. The discussions are allowed to run freely. However, the aim of the jam session is defined from the start because the jam session might lose its focus and become nothing more than a nice chat. To avoid this, an agenda is needed for both a practical and a research point of view. As is discussed later in the chapter, the balancing of the agenda is crucial for the outcome in various stages of the research process.

Sequence

To make the jam session methodology work as a research method, one single jam session is not enough for all purposes. For example, one jam session might be satisfying when it comes to defining a research question. When using a jam session as a vehicle for knowledge creation, a series of sessions is probably required (Adler & Shani, 2001). When discussing a difficult problem, or when trying to find the problem of a product development methodology that does not work, the participants are often prevented from articulating what they are doing in their everyday work. Therefore, it is up to the researchers to interpret and elaborate with what could be called "intermediate provocations." This means pushing back into the group during the coming jam session a provocation that the participants react to and develop further. This is very difficult to do in one session because the interpretation demands timely distance to the subject.

In the research program on digital media, we used jam sessions for three purposes: (a) to articulate the focus of the research, (b) to collect data, and (c) to validate the output.

Joint Articulation of Research Questions. The discussions with the three companies in the digital media project were very open as researchers and practitioners jointly tried to narrow down the issues that the three companies found to be of central importance when addressing questions of the future in their field. We started by just asking what they thought were the major questions in their business during the next 10-year period. With this question as a starting point, we let the participants discuss the issue and arrive at a conclusion as to what they saw as the most critical questions.

In most cases, questions of all kinds can arise during a jam session, and many of them may lie outside the research focus. Representatives of one of the companies stated after a heated discussion that what they really needed to know is what their customers wanted to consume in the future. It is the responsibility of the researchers and the participating representatives of the companies to jointly discuss the applicability of the questions for a research project. (Obviously, the suggestion from the company in question had to be elaborated further.)

Data Collection. As a data collection method, jam sessions proved to be a powerful tool. It was found that an effective way of working is to let the participants discuss freely as a researcher takes open notes on a whiteboard (or something similar) and asks for inconsistencies in the arguments and comments. Many times, such inconsistencies can reveal different mind-sets and may show why development is blocked in the collaboration, for example, between departments. The establishment of a common language to describe strategic changes is also valuable for practitioners taking part in the jam sessions. From the researchers' point of view, these discussions can be very interesting because they reveal many of the strategic discussions and positions taken in the companies. During the research project, we tape-recorded all of the jam sessions and used the transcriptions as reminders of what the jam sessions had revealed. But no doubt it was primarily the subtle knowledge rather than the hard data from the tapes that constituted our research findings.

The researchers could use a variety of techniques to start discussions. In the digital media program, scenarios were used to put the focus on future issues. This approach was needed as the participants constantly fell back to discussing incremental improvements in their daily work when confronted with big difficult issues. One scenario technique used was to describe two dimensions of a future situation and to let the participants describe the main characteristics of each quadrant in the diagram that the two dimensions created. The characteristics of the quadrants were then combined to describe common characteristics of the whole diagram. This was done to promote thinking about the future that was obviously less connected to the current work situation. The next step was to make the participants describe trends today that could lead to a situation influenced by the common characteristics in the diagram. The final step was to have them conduct a discrepancy analysis of what they thought would be important and the resources they had to tackle this.

Another useful approach is to take notes during the whole session on a whiteboard. Recording the arguments for the participants to see serves to further reinforce the discussion. In this way, the discussions reach a higher level that, in turn, enhances the quality of the research results. For the same reason, widely used methods with post-it notes are also good for group work in jam sessions. The group is divided, and during a part of the jam session the various subgroups get to work separately to generate new bases for the discussions.

It is also important to remember that the participants will not agree most of the time. This disharmony can be very productive because the clash of perspectives can create new insights for the researchers and participants. A diplomatic tuning can, however, enable the discussion to proceed and avoid conflicts.

Output Validation. The data collection from a jam session needs to be validated in some way or another. In addition to being included in the articulation of the research questions, our jam session participants were available for validation of the research output. These "feedback" sessions were important for testing results of the data collection as well as for furthering data collection as the participants became acquainted with the language used or with the taxonomies developed and could help take them a step further.

The structure of the jam session emerges as the jam session goes on. It is hard to address it at first, but as the jam session unfolds it is possible to recognize the structure. Therefore, during an output validation session, the interpreted results of the data collection session can first be verified or questioned. The timely distance between the sessions seems to clear people's minds of what had occurred during the previous session. Most likely, they have also given the jam sessions some thought and have arrived at insights that take the discussion a bit further. Seeing the results from the first jam session (we presented the results from the data collection phase) in a more concentrated form also gives participants the opportunity to criticize and to think anew about the issues in question. The jam sessions for output validation often prove to be more productive with respect to knowledge creation than do their data collection counterparts (Börjesson & Johansson, 2002). The output validation sessions also provide an opportunity to study the behavior of participants of the companies on a higher level. Some conclusions from the data collection might be very uncomfortable for the participants as the researchers present them.

Researcher Participation

Jam sessions are not experiments in the sense that the participants get any question to discuss while the researchers watch the development in the sessions. The technique is much more hands-on than that. The researchers participate in the sessions, even though they are not chairing them. The role of the researcher is more of the *juris diaboli*—the devil's advocate—that puts into question the arguments formulated by the participants.

Even though the jam session metaphor suggests that jazz music is based on free composition, it is not completely improvised. There is always a script that is followed. It begins with a harmonic structure, a melody, and maybe also a rhythm (Hatch, 1998). Jam sessions are built up in a similar way. Here, the harmonic structure and the basics of the melody correspond to the agenda for the jam session. During a research project, the importance and risks of having an agenda shift. If one imagines that the research project runs in a series of loops containing formulation of questions, data collection, and output validation, the rigidity of an agenda changes during the phases. The formulation phase is—and was in our jam sessions—very open, with limited participation from the researchers' side.

During the data collection phase, the participation of the researchers increases. However, the researchers need to find the right balance between intervention and aloofness. It is easy to create closure by being too strict in the beginning of a session. The experience from the digital media project was that too rigid an agenda is counterproductive in that the creative abilities of the participants are severely hampered. Both a limited agenda and an agenda that is difficult to understand create an unclear discussion. When addressing difficult issues—and "red and hot" issues in companies often are difficult—it is easy for the participants to get stuck in discussions on incremental issues in their daily routines. The participants need to be helped in unchaining themselves from the everyday work.

During the output validation phase, the agenda setting is extensive and so the researchers are very active. It must be noted, however, that the researchers should take care to monitor what happens during the validation phase. It might be that the results are flawed or misunderstood by the researchers. Often, a new round of discussions to narrow down the essential issue takes place. It can be devastating if the process does not allow such openness for these possible changes in direction. This is especially true if the results of one round of jam sessions are used as the basis for a second round and even a third round. In this context, the recorded tapes proved to be valuable.

Pitfalls

A jam session, as in all kind of methodologies, could easily be ruined. The major possible pitfalls are (a) not balancing the agenda properly, (b) engaging the wrong participants, and (c) losing the participants to internal power struggles or to, for example, the problems discussed in the lunchroom that particular day.

Not Finding the Right Balance for the Agenda. If the researchers set the agenda too strictly, the discussion is hampered. The opposite scenario—a very open agenda—is not good either; someone has to strike the first chord in a jam session. The right agenda balance is also dependent on the group of participants. As time goes on, participants tend to loosen up and become increasingly outspoken.

In the beginning of our jam session series, we made the mistake of describing too thoroughly the topic and goal of the discussions. As a consequence, we did not obtain the results we wanted. On reflection, we realized that we had narrowed the discussions through our active agenda setting. During later jam sessions, we did have an agenda but never brought it up. The agenda was not followed, but the method proved to work out much better than our initial attempts to control the discussion.

Having the Wrong People Participating. A jam session is dependent on people being knowledgeable about the topics of discussion (Adler & Shani, 2001). However, even more important is that the participants should have approximately the same level of expertise in a field of interest. Too large a variance is undesirable. The less knowledgeable tend to take fewer initiatives and so become sidestepped during the discussions. This problem was evident during a jam session with a telecommunications operator in which a project leader took part. All of the other group members belonged to the development management team and made decisions on what products should be developed (mostly stage gate decisions). Because the project leader did not have the same broad picture of the project portfolio of the company, he brought down questions to a lower level, thereby hampering the discussions among the other participants. They appeared to think that the project leader had a personal agenda because his projects were among the projects in the portfolio.

Losing the Participants to Internal Politics. Many of the questions that can be interesting to address in a jam session are delicate ones from the viewpoint of at least some participants. The participants might have come into conflict before and might be eager to conduct a political game during the jam session. This is one more reason why the researchers should focus on trying to take people's minds off their daily duties and the discussions they have had in previous meetings. The telecommunications operator also can serve well as an example in this respect. In the beginning of our jam session series, we wanted to discuss possible strategic paths for the company. We created a scenario by extrapolating a number of graphs and describing the situation that could be the result of the extrapolation. Next, we asked what the company could do to cope with this situation. What we did not know was that the company was in the middle of its budgeting activities for the coming year. The various participants had obviously taken different positions with concern to how much money should be spent on a certain process improvement. The next 20 minutes were focused solely on budget issues. When we finally managed to break the trend, we encountered great difficulties in redirecting the discussion.

Discussion

Jam Sessions Versus Other Research Techniques

Jam sessions are, of course, not the only technique applicable in collaborative group research. Along the continuum from single-structured interviews to multidirectional exploration sessions, there are a number of different techniques for multiple interviewing. Perhaps the most well known among these

Table 8.1   Characteristics of Three Group Techniques

	Participants	**Structure**	**Purpose**
Think tanks	Experts	Arbitrary	Policymaking/Lobbying
Focus groups	Customers	Yes	Customer research
Jam sessions	Knowledgeable persons	Increasingly through the series	Research/Consultancy

techniques are think tanks and focus groups. Even though the jam session is also an open group research method, it differs from these two techniques in both scope and direction. An overview of the various group techniques is presented in Table 8.1.

Think tanks (Murray, 1996; Sherrington, 2000) are used mostly for policymaking. A vast number of articles in the academic literature (mostly in political science) discuss the impact and various uses of think tanks. The term is used both as a general one for advisory boards and as a method for group work. The method seems to be limited to the formulation of problems or the clarification of complex issues. The participants in think tanks—typically policy experts or political commentators—are knowledgeable about issues that are covered during the sessions. *Focus groups* (Parent, Gallupe, Salisbury, & Handelman, 2000; Stewart & Shamdasani, 1990), on the other hand, imply a potential buyer-seller relationship between the participants and the group moderator (the moderator may also be a contracted partner of the seller). Therefore, it is no wonder that the main use of focus groups is in marketing and health care. The purpose of focus groups is to define the main problems in an area or to reveal customer priorities in a group of people. During recent years, increasing interest has been given to the question of how to conduct focus group research on the Internet (e.g., Chase & Alvarez, 2000; Finch, 1999). An overview of the various uses of think tanks, focus groups, and jam sessions, in relation to their various uses in the research process, is presented in Table 8.2.

As suggested in Table 8.2, a jam session could be used for various purposes in research. Its characteristics remain the same—people at equal levels of knowledge meeting to openly discuss issues that concern them. The discussions are allowed to run freely. The results of the jam session are, however, defined from the start, in contrast to the results of a brainstorming session.

The most frequently used jazz metaphor is the one of improvisation that takes place on stage. Improvisation is also central for the jam session metaphor. In this respect, a jam session has similarities with both a think tank and a brainstorming session. All three encourage all kinds of initiatives. Neither self-fulfilling criticism nor negative thinking is desirable, although criticism helps to enhance a creative climate in the group. However, whereas a brainstorming session does not necessarily include a continuous flow that heads in a certain direction, a jam session has a direction, even though it is not given in advance.

Table 8.2   The Use of Three Group Techniques in Various Parts of the Research Process

	Problem Formulation	Data Collection	Validation
Think tanks	Covered	Not covered	Not covered
Focus groups	Not covered	Covered	Not covered
Jam sessions	Covered	Covered	Covered

A Collaborative Research
Method Put Into Operational Features

One general problem that is prevalent in all kinds of collaborative research—the continuous interaction reduces the time available for reflection—is also prevalent in jam sessions. Yet we believe that the design of the process with jam sessions (i.e., periods for reflection between sessions) compensates for the possible shortage of reflection in action during the sessions. Here, the recorded tapes and transcripts of the jam sessions were supportive. Another important notion is diversity in thinking. Used as a research method, the key benefit of jam sessions is that knowledge is continuously created through changing between harmony and disharmony. Various perspectives are put together, not only to be contrasted and/or compromised but also to create a joint development. The disharmonic structure does evolve into a harmonic one, either when the participants add to each other's perspectives (tune together) or when they take counterpositions during the discussions.

We believe that the jam session, as an operational arena for interaction in the knowledge creation and researching process, is an excellent vehicle for boundary-spanning groups working together. The weak point of the jam session, however, might be validity. How can research resulting from a jam session be validated? How can the intermediate theories that result from a jam session be validated as research and not just be useful as actionable knowledge for the companies?

Having conducted research with the jam session approach in the digital media program, we believe that there is good potential for solving this problem, even though it will not be easy. Analogous to what was one of the main characteristics of the program—uncertainty—research *is* uncertainty (Latour, 1998). The jam session methodology allowed us to enter these uncertain fields to explore the bases for decision making in the organizations. It allowed us to see how they pictured and valued the attainable and not-yet-attainable alternatives. Our belief is that this would have been difficult to accomplish with a more traditional research methodology. The company representatives at very high levels in the various organizations (development executives at two companies and the top management team at the third company) chose to spend time in the jam sessions and said afterward that they found them to be valuable in creating a common language and discussion forum for issues that were seldom covered due to the obvious pressure from daily business operations.

Conclusion

Working with strategic issues in a business environment, characterized by speed and uncertainty, calls for thinking about things that do not yet exist. What makes this work even harder, besides the intellectual obstacle of detaching oneself from today's concerns, is that there might not be words and concepts yet available to capture the future; one is stuck in describing something that is already known, using already known words. Here, a major benefit of a jam session is obvious. To be "deceived" by other people's perspectives but still invited to "hang on," participants are "tricked" into expressing themselves in another way. Thus, this can be viewed as a kind of experimental learning. The underlying intention of working in arenas such as jam sessions is to free minds from current thinking and current patterns of call and response behavior. If a scenario is used for setting the scene, the jam session's function is to transport minds away from today's dominant thinking, irrespective of what the scenario looks like. The relevant aspect is to find ways in which to think freely of the future.

References

Adler, N., & Norrgren, F. (2002, May). *Future paths for management science.* Paper presented at the meeting of the European Academy of Management (Euram Conference), Stockholm, Sweden. Retrieved November 8, 2002, from www.sses.se/public/events/euram/complete_tracks/collaborative_management_research/adler_norrgren.pdf

Adler, N., & Shani, A. B. (Rami). (2001). In search of an alternative framework for the creation of actionable knowledge: Table-tennis research at Ericsson. In R. W. Woodman & W. A. Pasmore (Eds.), *Research in organizational change and development* (Vol. 13, pp. 43–79). Amsterdam: Elsevier Science.

Alvesson, M. (1999). *Methodology for close up studies: Struggling with closeness and closure.* Lund, Sweden: Lund University, School of Economics and Management.

Alvesson, M., & Sköldberg, K. (1994). *Tolkning och reflektion: Vetenskapsfilosofi och kvalitativ metod* (Interpretation and reflection: Philosophy of science and qualitative method). Lund, Sweden: Studentlitteratur.

Barrett, F. J. (1998). Creativity and improvisation in jazz and organizations: Implications for organizational learning. *Organization Science, 9,* 605–622.

Berniker, E. (1998). Working the jazz metaphor: Musing driving down I-5 past midnight. *Organization Science, 9,* 583–585.

Börjesson, S., & Johansson, T. (2002, May). *Jam sessions for knowledge production.* Paper presented at the meeting of the European Academy of Management (Euram Conference), Stockholm, Sweden. Retrieved November 8, 2002, from

www.sses.se/public/events/euram/complete_tracks/collaborative_management_
research/borjesson_johansson.pdf

Börjesson, S., & Norrgren, F. (2002, May). *Yellow fields: Set up for innovative fields in management R&D*. Paper presented at the meeting of the European Academy of Management (Euram Conference), Stockholm, Sweden. Retrieved November 8, 2002, from www.sses.se/public/events/euram/complete_tracks/collaborative_management_research/borjesson_norrgren.pdf

Chase, L., & Alvarez, J. (2000). Internet research: The role of the focus group. *Library & Information Science Research, 22,* 357–369.

Coughlan, P., Dromgoole, T., Duff, D., & Harbison, A. (2000). Continuous improvement through collaborative action learning. *International Journal of Technology Management, 22,* 285–302.

David, A. (2002, May). *Intervention methodologies in management research.* Paper presented at the meeting of the European Academy of Management (Euram Conference), Stockholm, Sweden. Retrieved November 8, 2002, from www.sses.se/public/events/euram/complete_tracks/collaborative_management_research/david.pdf

Finch, B. J. (1999). Internet discussions as a source for consumer product customer involvement and quality information: An exploratory study. *Journal of Operations Management, 17,* 535–556.

Gibbons, M., Limoges, C., Nowotny, H., Schwartzman, S., Scott, P., & Trow, M. (1994). *The new production of knowledge.* London: Sage.

Hatch, M. J. (1998). Jazz as a metaphor for organizations. *Organization Science, 9,* 556–568.

Jacob, M., Hellström, T., Adler, N., & Norrgren, F. (2000). From sponsorship to partnership in academy-industry relations. *R&D Management, 30,* 255–262.

Latour, B. (1998). From the world of science to the world of research? *Science, 280,* 208–209.

Murray, G. (1996). The intellectual dynamics of the new capitalism: A review article. *Social Alternatives, 15*(1), 61–64.

Nowotny, H., Scott, P., & Gibbons, M. (2001). *Re-thinking science: Knowledge and the public in an age of uncertainty.* Cambridge, UK: Polity.

Parent, M., Gallupe, R. B., Salisbury, W. D., & Handelman, J. M. (2000). Knowledge creation in focus groups: Can group technologies help? *Information & Management, 38,* 47–58.

Roth, J. (2002). *Knowledge unplugged: An action research approach to enhancing knowing in R&D organizations.* Unpublished doctoral thesis, Department of Project Management, Chalmers University of Technology, Gothenburg, Sweden.

Sherrington, P. (2000). British think tanks: Advancing the intellectual debate? *British Journal of Politics and International Relations, 2,* 256–263.

Stewart, D. W., & Shamdasani, P. N. (1990). *Focus groups: Theory and practice.* Newbury Park, CA: Sage.

9

Structural Learning Mechanisms in Collaborative Research

Michael Stebbins and Judy L. Valenzuela

B y their very nature, collaborative research endeavors tend to require the development of mechanisms that facilitate the research and learning process. Yet regardless of the critical role that such mechanisms play, relatively little can be found in the literature about them. The purpose of this chapter is to explore the nature of structural learning mechanisms (SLMs) and illustrate their role in one collaborative research project in the health care industry over a 26-year period.

During the past few decades, there has been pressure worldwide to contain costs in health care organizations and respond to the changing needs of increasingly educated customers. This pressure transcends country boundaries and exists in public, nonprofit, and for-profit health care settings. People have more information about their medical conditions, are aware of technology advances and new treatment modalities, and seek the best care available. As with many other economic sectors, customers want to receive quality services in a timely manner, are reluctant to pay more for services, and expect health care organizations to contribute to visions of improved quality of life. It is widely observed that new public expectations, combined with demographic changes, the inability of governments to fund care, and skyrocketing health care costs, have produced a global crisis in health care.

The emerging crisis has caused health care organizations to consider collaborative research programs. For some time, the health care sector has been a fertile field for holistic change interventions (Shani & Mitki, 1996) such as sociotechnical systems redesign, reengineering, comprehensive benchmarking, total quality management, and organizational learning. Holistic programs attempt to address all aspects of the organization simultaneously, recognizing that change in one subsystem has an impact on other subsystems. Consider the potential controversies created by the following systems that rely on new information and communications technology: call centers, company interactive Web sites, and automated clinical record systems.

The sensitive nature of system changes produces a need within companies to support collaborative research that stimulates, guides, enhances, and leads changes. Toward this end, some organizations go beyond the existing formal organization to create SLMs that support and lead the research and action initiatives (Bushe & Shani, 1990; Zand, 1974). That is, the SLM sponsors, initiates, orchestrates, communicates about, and monitors research and action. It also makes adjustments in keeping with subsystem and stakeholder impacts, discouraging suboptimization.

The case in this chapter is about an SLM within Kaiser Permanente's Pharmacy Operations division (Pharmacy organization). The case documents successful collaboration between researchers and company members in pursuing investigations of "red and hot" topics or problems and exploring alternative actions while, at the same time, contributing to the scientific community. Because the case spans some 26 years, it might also be of general interest to those who are exploring the designing of sustainable collaborative research (Stebbins & Shani, 2002) and to those who value the clinical inquiry approach. Specifically, the focus of this chapter is on long-term clinical inquiry/research (Schein, 2001) in the design of learning structures, using educational interventions, facilitation, process consultation, and clinical inquiry to address real health care system needs. The goals are to promote a better understanding of clinical inquiry methodology in SLM efforts, discuss the changing roles of the researcher and the client over time, and contribute to theory on both SLMs and collaborative management research.

Collaborative Research and Learning Mechanisms

The case described in this chapter is an outgrowth of an ambitious action research program initiated during the mid-1970s called TACT (Today's Action Creates Tomorrow). The TACT program was a partnership involving outside academic researchers, consultants, internal action researchers, and mainly nonmanagerial personnel within the Kaiser Pharmacy organization. This was a first-time experience for the organization under highly unusual, poststrike conditions. The research design called for intensive training in individual interviewing and group sensing methods for 40 "opinion leaders" drawn broadly from the Pharmacy organization. These opinion leaders then designed and implemented the methods on a peer basis, eventually reaching more than 90% of the organization's employees (Stebbins, Hawley, & Rose, 1982).

Following data collection, the entire management team met with the expanded research team in a weekend meeting that, in many ways, resembled a search conference (Emery & Purser, 1996). The raw data (strengths, issues, observations, and reflections) were set into categories. All participants had the opportunity to silently review the data by category and then to write problem statements. Task forces were formed to draft action plans and implement changes. Task forces were composed of supervisors from various locations, subject matter experts from the organization, and members of the original sensing group. The TACT task forces completed their work over a 6-month period, generated waves of change, and set the stage for more focused action research programs (Stebbins & Shani, 1988). One of the direct offshoots of TACT was the creation of an SLM called the communication forum (CF).

TACT and the CF are intimately tied together. That is, older members of the organization, many of whom are now in leadership positions, *know why the CF exists.* Due largely to TACT, people within Kaiser believe that relationships between management and employees, as well as communications in general, always need work. Long-term action research positions the organization for continuing cycles of innovation and change, with close partnerships between academic researcher/consultants and organizational leaders (Block, 2000; Stebbins et al., 1982; Stebbins & Snow, 1982). The approach has roots in the field approach (Lewin, 1953) relating to habits and the conditions that must be changed.

The elaborate theoretical framework for the CF described in the case to follow is a combination of workplace democracy, SLM, and clinical inquiry/research. It is workplace democracy in the sense that most members are elected to serve limited terms as representatives of local operating units and other employee groups. Members are to be assertive in identifying issues and innovations that might be shared across the organization. The framework is an SLM in the sense that it involves members in resolving ill-defined complex problems and building adaptability into bureaucratic organizations (Bushe & Shani, 1991; Zand, 1974). SLMs provide members with a complementary setting in which to address problems, identify issues to be studied, carry out the studies, and propose innovative solutions free from the formal organization structure and culture. As such, SLMs are viewed as a formal configuration—structures, processes, procedures, rules, tools, methods—created within the organization for the purpose of developing, enhancing, and sustaining collaborative research and learning (Shani & Docherty, 2003).

Finally, the framework is clinical inquiry/research in that the principal academic researcher/consultant has been invited to help the organization work on problems that the formal organization has not solved (Schein, 2001; Zand, 1974). The researcher is called in because of his or her helping skills, and the subject matter is defined more by the client than by the researcher's agenda (Schein, 2001). The subject matter comes from issues in the work environment as the organization seeks to solve problems connected with its growth and survival. In clinical inquiry, researcher involvement is in the form of educational interventions and facilitation of the

Researcher/Consultant Initiates the Project

Subject/Client Involvement	Low	High
Low researcher involvement	1. Demography	2. Experiments and surveys
High researcher involvement	3. Participant observation and ethnography	4. Action research

Subject/Client Initiates the Project

Subject/Client Involvement	Low	High
Low researcher involvement	6. Internship	7. Educational interventions and facilitation
High researcher involvement	5. Contract research and expert consulting	8. Process consulting and clinical inquiry

Figure 9.1   Project Initiation and Degree of Involvement

collaborative research process and/or process consulting and clinical inquiry. Schein's (2001) summary of the full range of options under conditions where the researcher initiates projects, as well as where the client initiates projects, is presented in Figure 9.1.

In the case illustrated in this chapter, the first author has been an action researcher with the Kaiser Pharmacy organization for 30 years (6 years as an internal action researcher and then 24 years as an outside action researcher). His role during all phases of work has been to help design the CF SLM, expand the CF idea within the organization, facilitate a variety of collaborative research initiatives, facilitate a wide variety of meetings ranging from the CF kickoff to day-long quarterly meetings of the SLM body, and design exercises and training modules that would help CF members to diagnose and act on issues uncovered from within the organization. In line with Schein's (2001) thinking (Figure 9.1), educational interventions and facilitation produce new data, reflection on the data, and insights both on the part of clients and on the part of the clinician. Examples of insights on the part of the client are included within the case. Examples of theory building and theory application from the SLM experience have been widely disseminated (e.g., Bushe & Shani, 1991; Stebbins & Shani, 1988; Stebbins, Shani, Moon, & Bowles, 1998).

In Cell 8 of Figure 9.1, we find the consultant and the client fully involved in the problem-solving process. The search for relevant data is a joint quest. Just as clients have the opportunity to uncover data beyond the formal chosen methods, the consultant has fairly open access to observe behavior in the organization and attend meetings related to SLM activities. Thus, the action researcher is exposed to data gathered by other parties within the organization (Schein, 2001). This is second-person research/ practice in the form of speaking and listening with others (Torbert, 2001). Researchers and clients have the opportunity to publicly test whether they have really heard each other's words and whether inferences and assumptions are in line with speaker intent (Torbert, 2001). More is said about the roles of clients and researchers under clinical inquiry later in the discussion section of this chapter.

The Kaiser Permanente SLM

Kaiser Permanente is one of the oldest and largest health maintenance organizations (HMOs) in the United States. The Pharmacy organization in Southern California dispenses 20 million prescriptions a year, and the inpatient pharmacies perform wide-ranging functions that support hospitalized patients. Pharmacists, technicians, pharmacy assistants (clerks and cashiers), and central support staff personnel work in diverse medical office, hospital, and division facilities throughout California. Pharmacy operations mirror Kaiser Permanente medical facilities; there are big inpatient and outpatient pharmacies at all major medical centers along with numerous smaller pharmacies within medical center locations and satellite outpatient clinics. A typical geographic medical area has more than 15 separate pharmacies.

During recent years, the Kaiser Pharmacy organization has emphasized creation of technology-intensive facilities as an answer to rapid increases in demand for drugs and pharmacy services. For example, it has built centralized refill pharmacies (CRPs) that are far more efficient than the clinic pharmacies. Patients can order refills through automated telephone, computer, and local clinic systems without any human contact. At the CRPs, pharmacist involvement in filling prescriptions is often limited to a 40-second check of refill accuracy and later brief contacts when the patient picks up the medication at his or her local pharmacy. The central factory manager recently reported that the factory had passed the 30 million mark in prescriptions filled, saving enormous time for local pharmacies. Extensive reengineering of the refill and filling process has freed up pharmacy employee time to communicate with medical providers, provide face-to-face patient counseling, and respond to new prescription requests. However, this picture of 21st-century work life is a far cry from conditions that existed in the Pharmacy organization at the outset of our case.

The Labor-Management Crisis of 1975

In 1975, Kaiser Permanente management and the labor union were involved in very tough contract negotiations. There was a stalemate, and the union called for a systemwide strike. Prolonged negotiations and the strike left employees on the picket lines through both the Thanksgiving and Christmas holidays. Management staffed the pharmacies with nonunion employees from northern California and other locations. Essential services were maintained through the battle. Finally, union strike funds were exhausted and the union leadership capitulated. Employees returned to work with bitter feelings about the whole process and Kaiser's tough stance during negotiations. Employees had lost significant income and gained nothing in the process, and morale suffered. During the immediate months after the strike, relations spiraled downward. Disturbed about the tension and upset with their company negotiators, members of the Pharmacy organization leadership team decided to act. They met with internal and external researchers and consultants to consider long-term strike-healing options. The response took the form of a broad-based vertical linking program aimed at improving management-employee relationships as well as customer contact. The program was called TACT—an elaborate listening and action-taking effort that reached every employee.

TACT was highly successful in addressing strike-related emotions and work environment issues. One of the TACT outcomes was a mechanism to institutionalize the new management-employee dialogue. The mechanism was an SLM called the regional communication forum, and it had the following purposes:

- Discuss and investigate ways and means by which employees may better serve the needs of customers.
- Keep informal and candid lines of communication among all personnel (across levels, pharmacies, and other organizational boundaries).
- Serve as a forum for the expression of opinions in all matters affecting pharmacy operations.
- Propose ways and means by which the effectiveness and morale of the Pharmacy organization can be maintained and improved.

Tables 9.1 and 9.2 provide a snapshot of the regional communication forum (CF) over time. It started with considerable momentum and pressure from the TACT steering body. Both the steering body and the initial CF body were initially composed of union activists and managers with reputations as change leaders. These "key players" wanted to turn the page on what had been a dismal chapter in the company's history.

The meetings' climate during the early years featured confrontation, the clash of perspectives, and a spirit of problem-solving and research initiatives. The employee representatives were also active in the union, and most were used to win-lose bargaining rather than collaboration. During the early years, the meetings were chaired by elected CF officers, and the researcher served as a facilitator/recorder. The elected CF officers met with the researcher to set the agenda and discuss processes, and the officers kept

Table 9.1   Abstract of Communication Forum Phases

Phase	Topics	Meeting Climate	Activities	Outcomes
Start-up (1977–1981)	Regional CF constitution	Clash of perspectives	Mission and goal setting	Opened new communication channels
	Problem identification	Management versus employees	Sensing of issues	Conflicts resolved
	Educational and social programs	Frustrations and stress	Investigation of issues	New division incentives program
	Computers in the pharmacies	Spirit of problem solving and urgency for action	Brainstorming	Sponsorship of education programs
	Productivity/Quality of work life		Setting annual CF objectives	Local CFs established
Area CF focus (1982–1996)	Support for area forums	Listening and mutual respect	Visits to area forums	Local changes
	Quality of patient services	Optimism about local progress	Dialogue with top management	Support to local improvement programs
	Pharmacy innovations	Lateral communication	Showcasing area improvements	Implementation of social and community service programs
	Division staff office reports	Sharing information	Previews of divisionwide change initiatives	
California division focus (1997–2002)	Economic crisis for Kaiser Permanente	Sense of urgency/chaos	Meetings emphasize communication of top-down change	Dissemination of division change program information
	Creation of California division	Uncertainty/ Competition	Question-and-answer sessions	
	Statewide restructuring	Dramatic changes proposed	Listen to progress reports on major division programs	Understanding of the division perspective
	Call centers	Frustrations about workloads		
	Drug use and drug costs	Cooperation through PIP to achieve stability	Culture and work climate surveys	Upward communication of change program impacts
	Central refill pharmacy			

(Continued)

Table 9.1 Continued

Phase	Topics	Meeting Climate	Activities	Outcomes
	Over-the-counter sales		Communicating employees' view of program impacts	Area social and community service programs
	Reengineering program/PIP Incentive program changes			

NOTE: CF = communication forum; PIP = performance improvement program.

a scorecard of issues and progress (what was won and lost). Meetings were raucous due to the hot issues being addressed. The "authorization slips incident" provides a sample of the conflict.

In early 1978, forum members confronted management about a new written policy handed down from the top that came out just before the forum meeting. The language of the policy was rather terse, and employees affected by the policy were angry. The policy directed that clerks handling cash would sign authorization slips and that "failure to comply will result in termination." Employees believed that the issue was already covered by language in the union contract, they did not understand what signing the slips meant, and they objected to the strong language of the policy directive. Management representatives on the forum were mystified by the new document and the angry display of emotions. They immediately huddled and then called the responsible parties. By the next forum meeting, a revised policy and explanation had been communicated throughout the organization, and the matter was put to rest.

The Evolving Collaboration Process

During the period from 1976 to 1980, the researcher/consultant met ahead of the formal meetings with CF officers to discuss issues and set the agenda. The CF officers at this time all were nonmanagement personnel, usually union activists. The division president's top-ranking manager also attended forum meetings, so the stage was set for a negotiations climate. The researcher/consultant's role was to ensure that all issues were on the table and to facilitate collection of relevant data between meetings so that discussions would be information based. During meetings, the researcher/consultant actively facilitated discussion, often using intergroup conflict interventions to polarize the group and highlight differences in perspectives. Meetings were usually held off-site to promote a sense of equality.

Table 9.2   Regional CF and Local CF Profiles

The Regional Body
This is a learning structure that operates parallel to the regular hierarchy and organization
It does not replace the formal structure but instead promotes communication, improved services to
  Kaiser Permanente members, and innovation.
The norms of the regional CF are different from those in the formal Kaiser Permanente organization.
The goal is to create open nonhierarchical communications and relationships and a spirit of
  management-employee problem solving.
An outside facilitator is present to help plan, run, and record the meeting dialogue.

Goals:
Promote a healthy communications climate in the organization.
Provide two-way dialogue on important issues.
Link various Kaiser Permanente locations and organizational levels.
Share innovations across Kaiser Permanente unit boundaries.
Propose change and educational programs.
Improve services to Kaiser Permanente members.

The structure:
All levels of management and employees are represented in the meetings.
All major locations (areas) and units are represented.
The meetings are chaired by a member of Pharmacy Operations division top management team.
The meetings are supported by top location managers.
Representatives are elected by their peers.
Southern California regional meetings are quarterly and last all day.
The structure has changed little over 25-year time period.

Payoffs documented by outside evaluation:
Employees view the regional CF as a joint management-employee effort.
It opens up frequent and direct contact across four levels of management and employees.
It provides quick answers to issues of concern to local employees.
It provides a place for dialogue on Kaiser Permanente goals, policies, and work practices.
It provides early warning on impending problems and helps to crystallize issues through collective
  discussion.
It provides a sounding board for division staff groups as they conduct training programs, implement
  computer system changes, and provide drug information.
It has conducted specific programs such as customer relations improvement and continuing education.
Issues identified have led to numerous divisionwide change initiatives and policy/practice changes.
It provides communication support to the division's change initiatives such as reengineering.
It provides support and ideas for local CF programs and activities.

Problems associated with regional CF in the past:
Issues have been raised that embarrassed local management or proved to lack management
  perspective/information.
Information has, at times, been given to CF representatives before the management team has been
  informed.
The regional CF has moved away from designing and conducting improvement programs toward
  communications support.
Certain local managers have not supported the local or regional CF bodies.
Some CF representatives have very limited contact with other employees at locations they are
  supposed to represent.

(Continued)

Table 9.2 Continued

The Local Bodies

Local forums were envisioned at the outset, and most were formed 2 to 3 years after the 1977 regional start-up.

Local forums patterned their constitutions after the regional CF document, seeking broad employee representation.

Some forums operate with strong local management involvement, whereas others operate as separate employee bodies.

Outside evaluations of the local forums produced the following:

Opinions are expressed freely in local CF meetings.

At most facilities, local CF goals are clear.

The meetings are seen as a joint management/employee effort and are worthwhile.

The meetings result in greater awareness of employee needs and problems.

Some locations have highly ambitious patient, community, and employee service programs.

Some locations report that their forums have a sound problem identification and problem-solving process.

On the downside, however, employees report the following:

Few employees outside the CF membership know much about the local forums.

Some forums do little to directly improve employee morale or management-employee relations.

The forums directly promote improved service to patients and employee development/education to only a limited extent.

A few forums seldom meet and/or have limited support from local management.

NOTE: CF = communication forum.

Roles of the Client and the Researcher: The Early Years

During the early years, the division president regularly attended meetings and played a strong role in shaping the CF purpose, goals, and guidelines. Following is a sample of the CF member dialogue with the president:

Representative: Are we a problem-solving group?

President: Yes. The SLM should make recommendations to management.

Representative: Do we have visibility upward?

President: Yes. My representative on the SLM—a senior line manager—will attend all meetings and will be an advocate for the group's work.

Representative: Can we sponsor professional development, educational, and social programs?

President: Yes. [That is] a very appropriate role for the SLM.

Creation of Local Forums

As shown in Table 9.1, with time and regular contact with division leaders, the meetings' climate became more respectful and emphasized listening and learning. SLM members also began to see that it was rather unrealistic to have the SLM tackle many of the problems bubbling up from the various locations. It was believed that greater progress could be achieved through the creation of eight *local* forums that would address and study the unique needs of each facility. Local management could then do something about the problems. If the local forums functioned as planned, the regional SLM body could address and conduct inquiry on a systemwide initiative such as quality of patient services, facilities planning, installation of computers in the pharmacies, and related programs. However, distinguishing between local and regional issues was not always easy or helpful. The company had a practice of testing innovations scientifically at one or two locations before rolling out changes to the rest of the organization. Often, the regional SLM representatives were able to preview them and provide feedback on the proposed changes and how they might be received locally. The "computers incident" provides an example.

Anticipating major time savings through elimination of menial duties as well as accurate tracking of prescriptions, the company initiated a pilot study at one medical center location. Reaction to the experiment at the location was generally positive, but fears and rumors spread quickly through the Pharmacy organization.

At the quarterly SLM meeting, the representatives reported impending doom. Jobs would be lost, positions would be downgraded, and the pharmacist's role would replaced by a machine. Quietly, a representative of a local forum from the test location offered an opportunity: "Why not visit our pharmacy and get a firsthand look—talk to employees about their feelings?" The invitation was immediately accepted, and the regional SLM members traveled to the test site for the next meeting. Local forum members led the tour and answered questions. As the months rolled on, additional locations joined the computer network. To communicate progress, the start-up training teams visited regional and local forums. This helped to pave the way for new installations and provided a mechanism for early identification of problems. Within a year, the questions at regional forum meetings had surprisingly changed to, for example, "Who will be allowed to get the computer next?"

The Middle Years

Like many large organizations, the Kaiser Permanente organization has experienced waves of centralization and decentralization sentiment over the past 25 years. During periods of economic crisis and revenue decline, the company has looked to systemic solutions and top-down change. During periods of stability, local decision making has been emphasized.

During the period from 1982 to 1996, support for local innovation and initiatives was very popular, and area medical centers began to create pilot programs and showcase their innovations. Regional SLM meetings were held regularly at field locations to focus on local facilities, new work processes, experimentations, and service programs. Topics at regional meetings stressed quality of service and innovations that might be transferred across locations. This was also a renaissance period for local SLMs in uniting inpatient and outpatient pharmacies behind social, educational, and sports programs. Community programs, such as drug education for seniors, shelters, and meals programs, were started; various medical centers became known for their distinctive community service programs. The local SLMs also continued their record of upward reporting to the regional SLM regarding local needs and problems.

Modified Helping Roles During the Middle Years

During the 1980s and early 1990s, the researcher/consultant and key client roles and activities changed in several ways. At the local level, the researcher/consultant worked with the division president's representative to get additional forums established in all of the geographic areas. Because some of the local leaders did not see the value, both the researcher/consultant and the client worked hard to get some form of dialogue going between management and employees on a regular basis. Active intervention by the researcher/consultant and the president's representative helped local leaders to see how forums could build relationships and, at the same time, meet managerial needs. At the regional level, the researcher/consultant began to facilitate surveys of forum effectiveness and lead critiques at the end of every meeting. The idea was to begin to train SLM leaders in effective meeting processes and to encourage healthy confrontation and feedback to all concerned. Combined with independent audits of SLM effectiveness, all actors began to see how the SLM intervention might be extended and improved. By the early 1990s, the researcher/consultant contribution was mainly to provide educational interventions and encourage participation of new levels of management being added due to company growth. The client role was to help build the agenda and line up subject matter experts for brief presentations and updates on matters of special concern. The idea of having elected officers for the SLM was abandoned, and the main client began to actively chair the meetings. Both the researcher/consultant and the client periodically met with the top management team to assess the value of the CF as an SLM.

Crisis in the Marketplace

By 1996, the Kaiser Permanente HMO began to experience severe competitive pressures as other HMOs began to take away market share. At the same time, costs in the industry were escalating, plunging the organization into crisis. The HMO began to consider radical options such as divestiture of hospitals, alliances with competitors, restructuring, and aggressive cost cutting. On advice from McKinsey management consultants, Kaiser consolidated its northern and southern California regions and began to downsize. The spotlight was on the Pharmacy organization because drug use by patients was on the rise, pushing up drug costs for the entire HMO. Outside management consultants pressed the division toward reengineering of outpatient pharmacy processes through a systemwide performance improvement program (PIP). The PIP best practices program was sequentially installed at every pharmacy in California. Not surprisingly, discussions about PIP and other cost reduction programs, such as drug use control, dominated regional SLM meetings. The division was in the grip of revolutionary change. In the early part of this work, SLM representatives reported local chaos, increased workloads due to reduced staffing, and considerable stress in the workplace. Managerial changes, technology changes, work process changes, and high turnover combined to rock the entire Pharmacy organization.

Through PIP efforts during the period from 1998 to 2001 and through management emphasis on customer service, customer service ratings rose, waiting times declined, and the financial picture improved. The pharmacies began to function in more standardized ways consistent with PIP best practices. They also began to rely more heavily on central services such as the automated refill facilities. Divisionwide initiatives, such as over-the-counter (OTC) drug sales, formulary changes to reduce drug costs, drug use/drug substitution programs, and automated cash registers, dominated local attention. Regional SLM meetings focused on these ambitious programs, local involvement in the programs, and dialogue about anticipated and unanticipated outcomes. Glowing accounts of progress presented by division staff and managers who were responsible for the programs were balanced by healthy debate about the change initiatives, the change processes, and perceived impacts. The September 2000 forum review of PIP serves as an example.

The management view of PIP was that it had been an unqualified success. The productivity, cost, and satisfaction data all were impressive, leaving the impression that PIP was without flaws. In an effort to assist with PIP follow-up, the SLM surveyed employees about the program and perceived work environment impacts. Survey data indicated increased stress and job pressure, inability to manage the workload at the new volume levels, and the opinion that relationships with management were strained. Employees believed that although PIP benefited customers, it did not benefit employees. Employees perceived that cost cutting had led to inadequate staffing, higher turnover, and new recruitment and placement issues. Moreover, employees did not view the PIP gains as sustainable.

The management response at the meetings was to listen to feelings that were behind the survey numbers and to gather concrete examples. There was considerable pressure to push for staffing improvements. At the next meeting, the division president's representative reported that labor budgets for 2001 would increase, in contrast to past reductions, and that additional time would be built in for implementation of the various drug cost reduction programs. Management had recognized the workload issue and was also concerned about the inability to recruit enough pharmacists to fill open positions. The combination of internal and external forces and impacts on staffing continued to be debated at the regional forum meetings throughout 2001 and 2002.

Current Roles

Research initiatives, educational interventions, and facilitation continued to be the consultant/researcher's preoccupation during the period from 1996 to 2002, and the burden of planning and chairing meetings shifted, in large part, to the main client. This was natural in that the crisis stemming from marketplace changes called for assertive leadership and greater top-down orchestration of company improvement efforts and day-to-day processes. The main client was on the spot to supply immediate answers to questions about reengineering, drug benefit changes, and drug cost controls. To help with the dialogue on these matters, the client communicated issues to other pharmacy leaders who, in turn, visited the forum to update everyone on progress and future actions. Both the client and the researcher played important roles in highlighting intended and unintended consequences of the initiatives, triggering further problem solving. A dramatic example of the SLM in action is a recent incident related to OTC drug sales.

During 2001, the Pharmacy organization began to rely more on OTC (nonprescription) drugs as a source of revenues. At one meeting, the regional coordinator of OTC sales announced that an allergy season promotion was just under way and that lower prices for selected OTC drugs would appear that day. A quick poll by the facilitator revealed that few of the representatives knew of the promotion and that none of the stock clerk representatives was ready to meet the demand. The client immediately contacted the relevant parties (warehouse supply, other stock clerks in the field, and clinic supervisors) and verified the information. Because pricing was centralized, a decision was made on the spot to abort the promotion, and prices were changed back barely hours after the initial change. Because employees had just begun the day, no damage was done. The incident highlighted the "early warning" advantage from the SLM.

Discussion and Implications _____

The Kaiser SLM story continues to be that of a representative body (microcosm of the organization) charged with identifying, studying, and acting on big and small problems that the formal organization is not capable to address or has not yet discovered. At present, the emphasis is on improving dialogue and reflection within the organization about matters related to survival, company strategy, changed policies and procedures, and the implications for employees and customers. Reflecting on the case within this chapter, there are implications regarding the SLM as a learning mechanism, about clinical inquiry/research under conditions not created by the researcher, and about the quality of academy-industry partnerships in general.

The SLM

There are both strengths and weaknesses connected with regional and local forums. On the positive side, surveys indicate that both managers and employees believe that the main benefits are maintaining open channels of communication, sharing ideas/innovations across boundaries, conducting programmatic research and systematic reflections, and providing input on policies, procedures, and change initiatives. Although change initiatives typically have their own communications components, managers believe that the forums provide additional reinforcement and reflection on change processes and outcomes. On the negative side, top managers are concerned about the quality of forum deliberations at some of the local forums, lack of representation and communications upward from a few locations, and employee time away from the workplace in an increasingly pressured work environment.

On reflection, the Kaiser SLM has changed markedly since 1976. The CF abandoned negotiation-style meetings and conflict resolution methods and instead began to focus on listening, learning, and sharing perspectives. As agendas have moved closer to managerial preoccupations by addressing red and hot topics, the forum has developed some characteristics of an integrated learning mechanism (Shani & Docherty, 2003; Shani & Stjernberg, 1995) with critical input from various players in the regular hierarchy. That is, standing topics require the presence of specific leaders responsible for staff support and line departments. The main client (division president's representative) was a co-facilitator of the research process and served as the spokesperson for the company's position on important matters. The character of the meeting has changed greatly with the presence of so many of the company leaders. Forum officers are elected locally, but the regional body is chaired by the client. This has solidified the SLM as "institutionalized" rather than being seen as a grand experiment in workplace democracy. Gradually, the regional SLM abandoned the idea of taking on its own change programs and began supporting the organization's priorities and initiatives. This suggests characteristics of an integrated learning mechanism (Stebbins et al., 1998).

Clinical Inquiry

The consultant/researcher in long-term clinical inquiry engagements observes dynamic processes and has multiple roles to play. In the Kaiser Permanente case, the first author acted as the outsider researcher and the second author acted as the insider researcher (Bartunek & Louis, 1996). As members of an insider/outsider team, they were viewed as the champions of and for the SLM and were, at times, highly involved in making it work. On the other hand, they facilitated the conduct of regular audits of the health of regional and local forums, and they channeled this data back to management and to the forum members for reflection, problem identification, and new action. Recognizing the potential drawbacks of this approach, they periodically called in other outside scientists to evaluate SLM performance. In a climate of mutual trust and respect, the researcher/consultant has leeway in trying various interventions at the individual, group (forum), and organizational levels. This freedom allows for the testing of hypotheses about what is going on (Schein, 2001), and debriefings with the client after meetings establish whether the client sees the same phenomena and whether visitors and/or outside observers see the same things. This freedom also allows the researcher/consultant to benchmark the organization's processes against other learning organizations. Periodic exposure of SLM members to innovative structures and processes in other organizations sparks new conversations about what might be. This refutes Schein's (2001) observation that clinical inquiry has the disadvantage of preventing the researcher from broadening the subject to consider topics that the client has not established. In a situation of long-term clinical inquiry, the consultant/researcher has the opportunity to shape the research agenda.

Our goal in the Kaiser SLM was that every person attending would leave with new knowledge, insights, and/or skills. Educational interventions are the obvious way in which to meet this goal, and most regional SLM meetings build on this capability. This inevitably involves modeling, using research skills, disclosing information, mutual listening, and confronting the differences that emerge. Given the great diversity of people within the forum (e.g., ethnic, type of job, demographics), it is not hard to find topics that address personal and relational issues. To the extent that leaders within the forum are open to inquiry and learning and model the way through examples of personal transformation and sharing of influence, much can be done to create enlightenment (Torbert, 2001). It is often through educational interventions that enlightenment—where theory and practice meet—actually occurs (Habermas, 1984).

On the Quality of Academy-Industry Partnership

Gustavsen's (2001) work in establishing democratic dialogue criteria is highly relevant in reviewing the quality of academy-industry partnerships in general and the SLM in particular. Following are a few of the criteria:

- Dialogue is based on a principle of give-and-take, not one-way communication.
- All participants have the same status in the dialogue arenas.

- Work experience is the point of departure for participation.
- It must be possible for all participants to gain an understanding of topics under discussion.
- The dialogue should be able to integrate a growing degree of disagreement.
- The dialogue should continuously generate decisions that provide a platform for action.

In this vein, it is easy to see that the Kaiser Permanente SLM has been socially engineered to promote discourse and cover the ground between theory and practical action. Along the way, both theory and action are advanced through the testing of ideas, greater awareness of complexities and associations, and commitment to innovation and improvement.

Conclusion

Because of the global crisis in health care, medical organizations are moving beyond incremental changes to also consider holistic collaborative research options. The Kaiser Pharmacy organization is a leader in forming partnerships with employees to facilitate inquiry and change and to remain competitive in the marketplace. At the same time, the Kaiser organization has been able to address the intended and unintended consequences of change. The Kaiser SLM continues to promote inquiry and conversation about planned changes and has the unique capability of addressing both local and systemwide needs. As the organization has grown, the SLM shifted from being a union-oriented driver of change toward seeking more of an equal partnership that is aligned closer to the organization's formal structure. Both the researcher/consultant and the client roles have changed markedly with this transition. The new roles create a fertile field for clinical inquiry and intervention research (Hatchuel, 2001), and both the client and the researcher/consultant were highly involved in shaping agendas for conversation, inquiry, reflection, and course correction. The quality of the relationship that evolved addresses the ground between theory and practical action while contributing to the academy-industry partnership.

References

Bartunek, J. M., & Louis, M. R. (1996). *Insider/Outsider team research*. Thousand Oaks, CA: Sage.

Block, P. (2000). *Flawless consulting: A guide to getting your expertise used*. San Francisco: Jossey-Bass.

Bushe, G., & Shani, A. B. (Rami). (1990). Parallel learning structure interventions in bureaucratic organizations. In W. Pasmore & R. Woodman (Eds.), *Research in organization change and development* (Vol. 4, pp. 167–194). Greenwich, CT: JAI.

Bushe, G., & Shani, A. B. (Rami). (1991). *Parallel learning structures: Increasing innovation in bureaucracies.* Reading, MA: Addison-Wesley.

Emery, M., & Purser, R. (1996). *The search conference.* San Francisco: Jossey-Bass.

Gustavsen, B. (2001). Theory and practice: The mediating discourse. In P. Reason & H. Bradbury (Eds.), *Handbook of action research* (pp. 17–26). London: Sage.

Habermas, J. (1984). *The theory of communicative action* (Vols. 1–2). London: Polity.

Hatchuel, A. (2001). The two pillars of new management research. *British Journal of Management, 12,* 33–40. (Special issue)

Lewin, K. (1953). *Field theory in social science.* New York: Harper & Row.

Schein, E. H. (2001). Clinical inquiry/research. In P. Reason & H. Bradbury (Eds.), *Handbook of action research* (pp. 228–237). London: Sage.

Shani, A. B. (Rami), & Docherty, P. (2003). *Learning by design.* London: Blackwell.

Shani, A. B. (Rami), & Mitki, Y. (1996). Reengineering, TQM, and sociotechnical systems approaches to organizational change. *Journal of Quality Management, 1,* 131–145.

Shani, A. B. (Rami), & Stjernberg, T. (1995). The integration of change in organizations: Alternative learning and transformation mechanisms. In W. A. Pasmore & R. W. Woodman (Eds.), *Research in organizational change and development* (Vol. 8, pp. 77–121). Greenwich, CT: JAI.

Stebbins, M. W., Hawley, J., & Rose, A. (1982). Long term action research: The most effective way to improve complex health care organizations. In N. Margulies & J. Adams (Eds.), *Organization development in health care organizations* (pp. 105–136). Reading, MA: Addison-Wesley.

Stebbins, M. W., & Shani, A. B. (Rami). (1988). Communication forum interventions: A longitudinal case study. *Leadership and Organizational Development Journal, 9*(5), 3–10.

Stebbins, M. W., & Shani, A. B. (Rami). (2002). Eclectic design for change. In P. Docherty, J. Forslin, & A. B. (Rami) Shani (Eds.), *Creating sustainable work systems* (pp. 201–212). London: Routledge.

Stebbins, M. W., Shani, A. B. (Rami), Moon, W., & Bowles, D. (1998). Business process reengineering at Blue Shield of California: The integration of multiple change initiatives. *Journal of Organizational Change Management, 11,* 216–232.

Stebbins, M. W., & Snow, C. C. (1982). Processes and payoffs of programmatic action research. *Journal of Applied Behavioral Sciences, 18,* 69–86.

Torbert, W. R. (2001). The practice of action inquiry. In P. Reason & H. Bradbury (Eds.), *Handbook of action research* (pp. 250–260). London: Sage.

Zand, D. (1974). Collateral organization: A new change strategy. *Journal of Applied Behavioral Science, 10,* 63–89.

Academic Commentary on Part II

William A. Pasmore

Mercer Delta Consulting, New York

In Part II of this volume, we learn that industry-academic partnerships in research are not all the same. In fact, we are introduced to no fewer than 10 approaches to developing such partnerships, ranging from more traditional action research methods to more innovative "table tennis" and "jam session" models. What is common across these various approaches is the clear intention of creating a balanced partnership in the service of acquiring and applying knowledge to issues of both theoretical and practical interest. What varies are the roles each party plays, the methods used to collect data, the level of rigor in the inquiry, the flexibility of the approach, the intended consequences, the locus of control over design decisions, the intensity of the engagement, the sustainability of the partnership, and the values underlying the exploration.

The fact that we have moved beyond action research as a single approach to forming learning partnerships between academic and industry representatives is in itself a very positive step. Despite its power, action research could not encompass the full range of approaches, views, interests, and perspectives represented in the chapters in Part II. As is clear from these chapters, the best method for creating effective partnerships between academia and industry is one that takes into account the contextual variables inherent in each situation. A "one size fits all" approach, no matter how good that one approach might be, could never create as strong a mutual bond as one that emerges from the unconstrained efforts of academic and industry partners working together to design a unique methodology that is right for their company and problem context. Rather than presenting us with the best hammer to pound all kinds of nails, what we get from Part II is the idea that different nails require different hammers. Armed with this insight, we see the beginning of "duetero learning" about academic-research partnerships. That is, we have begun to learn how to learn about what does and does not work in various research partnerships and why.

Once we have begun to learn how to learn, the door opens to the application of greater creativity in our approaches to partnerships and less concern with dogma. We begin to ask important questions such as "What does success really mean?" and "From whose vantage point are we making critical observations of what works and what doesn't?" As academics, are we to be trapped in our historical concerns about reliability and validity, or can we seek much-needed new definitions of the usefulness and value of our work to others? As businesspeople, can we set aside our concern with short-term cost justification to explore ideas and opportunities that have the potential to change the way in which we think about our business models, strategies, and/or leadership contributions? No matter how we eventually decide to design our partnerships, it seems clear from what is written in these chapters that all parties must suspend prior notions of "the right way" in which to approach learning and must be willing instead to co-create a methodology that, although initially somewhat uncomfortable, holds the promise of being much better than anything they knew before.

What is exciting about all of this is that the partnerships described in these chapters are deeper and more consequential than their predecessors. Consultants have assisted organizations in gathering data and learning for many years, but consulting relationships have been limited by the lengths of projects or the inability to justify extended funding for consulting services. In any event, the consulting relationship is a fiduciary exchange rather than a committed equal partnership, despite rhetoric to the contrary. Academics have long drawn data samples from organizations, but with little or no interest in their findings on behalf of data providers. Occasionally, academically trained internal researchers have done self-diagnoses, only to find themselves trapped in a political web of power and relationships that interferes with insights being applied. The industry-academic partnerships described in Part II are qualitatively different and so hold much greater promise for both the advancement of science and the improvement of operations.

What is new and important about these relationships is that they begin with a more solid foundation of mutual commitment to shared outcomes. Neither party is entering the relationship lightly, out of courtesy, or with an eye toward only one's own interests. Both parties are committed to finding an approach to their collaboration that produces outcomes of significance for the other. Moreover, their institutions are more deeply committed to the work of the partnership and to increasing its visibility, its importance, and (ultimately) its value. Second, the parties themselves are better prepared to live and work at the intersection of science and action. The "academics" are not pure theoreticians or experimentalists, and the businesspeople are not untrained in scientific methodologies. Either could, albeit with some effort, cross over into the world of the other. This intersection of competencies and interests enriches the interaction between the two and enhances the products of their collaboration. Rather than simply wishing for a partnership to be balanced, the groundwork is laid well in advance to make it so. Finally, what distinguishes these partnerships from earlier efforts is that both parties expect to learn more about how to partner as they work together. There is not a preset model that must be agreed to and followed before the collaboration begins. Instead, there is an evolving approach that emerges from the interaction among the partners and others who are participating in the inquiry. The partners hold places in two corners of a triangle; the "subjects," to use an outdated and inappropriate term, hold the other corner. All three parties have influence in deciding the goals, methods, values, scope, tools, approaches, applications, insights, and sharing of knowledge that grow out of their work together. This triangle of relationships is at the heart of the new and more powerful approach to collaboration that we read about here. When all three parties are truly satisfied with their efforts together, a sustainable system of inquiry, insight, and application is created.

Whether we begin with one of the frameworks provided by Börjesson and Fredberg (jam sessions: Chapter 8), Stebbins and Valenzuela (structural learning mechanisms: Chapter 9), Roth, Sandberg, and Svensson (insider action researcher: Chapter 7), or one of the many other approaches reviewed by Shani, David, and Willson (Chapter 5), what is important is that we eventually migrate toward a model that is not yet described anywhere but better reflects the urgent and pressing interests and needs of the three parties in the triangle. From start to finish (or from the beginning of one cycle to the beginning of the next), the needs of all three parties must be kept in dynamic balance. Each must be motivated to continue and to contribute its best to the partnership. As soon as the method becomes rigid, the questions become irrelevant, or the application becomes unimportant, the life force behind collaborative research begins to die. What we learn from the chapters in Part II is not that there is a best way in which to create and preserve this life force but rather that collaborative research is a living and changing system of relationships that requires nurturing through improvisation. Although there will be many who challenge the validity of collaborative research when judging it against criteria for traditional scientific rigor, it is hoped that there will be as many or more who view collaborative research as an important step forward in linking the interests of science, business, and society.

Executive Commentary on Part II

Per-Olof Nyquist

Vice President, Head of Ericsson University

The perceived pace in business forces us to act quickly and often intuitively. We believe that we must achieve speed, efficiency, and effectiveness simultaneously to beat the competition. Is this really the case? Or, do we just lack the methods and tools that will enable us to make use of existing knowledge by combining it with new knowledge. This might allow us to create frameworks, mind-sets, and business logic that can handle speed, efficiency, and effectiveness, beating the competition without killing entire organizations due to exhaustion. I believe that *collaborative research* may be one important vehicle for the development of the necessary methods and tools. However, collaborative research, as depicted by the authors in Chapters 5 through 9, necessitates a different approach to knowledge and knowledge creation in the context of the business environment. Most important, a more open understanding between the very different cultures in the business and academic environments must be established.

To structure, formulate, and generate knowledge requires time for reflection—often achieved in splendid isolation, detached from the very phenomena for which knowledge is supposed to be created. Hence, more fundamental structuring, formulation, and generation of new knowledge are often seen as activities for academics in theoretical environments far from the battlefield of business and competition. Reality is studied by bringing it into the study chambers of academics, depicted as answers on questionnaires, taped interviews, descriptions, and/or case studies and knowledge that is derived from historic and "dead" information. The structured reflections are then published in prestigious journals, usually years after the actions actually happened. The business environment regards the results with some respect but finds them hard to apply because the business realities have changed since the studies were conducted and reported. Executives learn from action and reality in the same way as did the ancient kings and generals. Models that guide action are most often built by individuals' own experiences. The kings and generals of today fight new battles that come with new scenarios and new situations with even less time for reflection. To them the recent published knowledge means little if anything.

However, the need to introduce tools and methods to facilitate the continuous reflection and learning on managerial challenges is yet to be addressed. There are some who spend a rather large part of their professional lives developing their own competencies and new knowledge in their areas of work. This applies, for example, to professionals in medicine. Would we trust a brain surgeon if we did not believe that he or she would spend considerable time developing himself or herself and developing methods and knowledge to be used by other colleagues in the same area of the profession? Still, we believe in executives of global companies without really asking ourselves how much time they spend developing their own competencies or the knowledge about business as such. Learning by doing is often the only method. Does the work situation for an executive allow for this kind of development of competence and knowledge? Or, perhaps we should ask the following questions: Can we afford not to build this competence in a structured way? How can we build an arena where theories and practice meet? Is there an arena where we can formulate the most urgent problems and even find solutions to the very same problems?

Companies in very technological industries acknowledge the need for research and intense competence development in technology. The tradition of building new knowledge does exist in these fields. Consequently, contacts with university faculties are quite deep and widespread in these fields of knowledge. But is this enough? In today's environment, more and more of a competitive advantage is to be found in the areas of how we run our organizations and businesses. Still, we do not treat knowledge and competence in these areas with the same form of focus and structured approach. I believe that we need a new way of viewing how knowledge is created in the business environment but that we must also change our common view of how and when individuals learn from this new knowledge.

Historically, the units for training and education at Ericsson University have been built and managed locally or regionally. No central coordination has been applied. Training and education have not been seen as a core business, and consequently, local needs have been handled locally in the multinational structure. All effort has been put into individual development, launching courses based on perceived needs but with very little direct top management attention. The only exception has been the development of executives and managers. In this case, deep and extensive cooperation has been developed with academia globally, but mainly in the area of applying already formulated knowledge rather than in the area of research. These efforts have been structured and managed from the top of the company in a very strategic and comprehensive way. As business has become more and more global, the need for a global approach to all education and training has become a more important issue.

When launching Ericsson University, the goal was to align training and education to Ericsson's business challenges and formulated strategies. At the same time, it was important to create effectiveness and efficiency in the training and educational units, assemble them under one formal name ("Ericsson University"), and safeguard that the organization avoids duplication of resources for the same purpose globally. This task included all training and education—everything from executive development to language training, advanced technology, and fairly straightforward education for operational and managerial skills needed at the factories. Learning is still regarded by many as a separate part of the business and is not integrated in the actual business. The general perception is that learning takes time and consumes money. However, there are parts of the organization where this perception is changing rapidly. Education and training are no longer the first areas to eliminate by default during difficult times; however, costs and effects are often challenged.

It is evident that a global company must focus efforts on strategies and business, avoid duplication of resources, and focus on effects and results. But how do we get an entire organization to understand the very fundamental difference between training and education as opposed to learning? How can we handle the task when the prevailing conception of learning is still not a part of everyday business? We must focus more on in-depth analysis of learning needs in close contact with management in the operational organizations. Activities must be designed for entire organizations with strong support from management for both planning and execution. At Ericsson University, we have competence in the areas of Ericsson strategies in understanding how people learn, how organizations change, and how to manage and control learning opportunities from facts, methodology, and financial points of view. We do not develop and deliver courses ourselves unless it is of fundamental importance that all steps in the process are owned internally. This strategy means that we work closely with external partners. This gives us access to knowledge from other businesses and academia, and this in turn enables us to share our knowledge with others. However, the biggest challenge is to acquire access to accurate knowledge externally and to structure and formulate the knowledge we already have in the company. This can be achieved only by working with partners, universities, and other knowledge providers that are skilled in the structuring and formulation of knowledge. Therefore, collaborative research can be a useful tool for accomplishing our goals.

During the mid-1900s, Bell Labs was the shining star of technological research in different areas of telecommunications. It was the arena where researchers from many different organizations, businesses, and academia met and interacted, creating innovative products and applications. This organization focused on research in very strong collaboration with business and academia. The results were astonishing, and the reputation was undisputed worldwide. The Bell Labs of the past needs to be reinvented, but in a broader sense to encompass areas of business development, organizational development, and technology. This new organization must be built on a wide range of partners and peripheral links with both academia and other knowledge providers. The organization and its partners must develop and learn from different collaborative research approaches.

The old way of creating knowledge was based on separate arenas for business and academia. Interventions or exchanges of information were handled in a formal way, and the roles and perceptions of each other were very strong—and in some cases were wrong. The roles of business and academia will continue to be different. It is even necessary to protect this difference, but we must create arenas where we can meet and formulate common processes and discussions on knowledge creation. Thus, academia can continue to formulate the more fundamental parts for new knowledge, whereas business can arrive at immediate results and conclusions to leapfrog the competition. The goals of speed, efficiency, and effectiveness can be achieved based on collective reflection together with academia in a very structured manner. These new arenas must be created in real time with real-time access from both sides. Results must be produced with mutual access, but they will probably be formulated very differently due to the fundamental difference in demands for stringency and structure.

Today, links between academia and business are often built on personal contacts. When people move or change the focus of their work, these links are broken. To multiply the positive results from cooperation between business and academia, the cooperation must be institutionalized. It is possible that the true challenge for a corporate university is to be not just a tool for business strategies within the company, or just another name for the education department, but rather a true tool for strategy implementation, business development, and competitive development built on the amalgamated knowledge from the company, partners in academia, and other knowledge providers. This kind of an arena can provide for individual development and, at the same time, facilitate business and organizational development.

Cultures work together very well when they understand each other's preconditions, limitations, and potential. With an open and collaborative mode, this dialogue can be achieved. We must try to combine the various cultures, both business and academic. The business culture is known for speed and PowerPoint presentations as the only means of documentation, a "steel with pride" culture, and a demand for simplification. The academic culture demands meticulous research, lengthy reports, endless lists of references, and ongoing debate. In the business environment, executives are used to buying knowledge from consultant companies because they understand the need for timeliness. When executives meet representatives from academia, they often expect the same performance as they would from any consultant. On presentation of academic reports and documentation, frustration and mistrust can develop on both sides. It is a real challenge to overcome this cultural difference. This can be achieved in an environment of a corporate university applying collaborative research approaches. In a worldwide company, this can be accomplished at both the local and global levels. However, it can be achieved only if we spend the time and effort to understand the various cultures and goals. We must ensure that this collaborative arena enables people to move in and out of it without disrupting the process.

Knowledge is created when humans have time for reflection anywhere and at any time. If this is done in a structured way and kept close to immediate needs, the results can be put into practice or trial immediately. This can benefit both the shortsighted and fast-paced business environment and the more formalized academic environment. When every person in an organization is fully aware of the basic concepts of knowledge creation and documentation, we will be able to handle speed, efficiency, and effectiveness without pushing the entire organization toward exhaustion and will still be able to beat the competition by a wide margin. The future for any organization in a competitive environment lies in the process of creating knowledge and learning how to master this process. In this context, the business environment welcomes initiatives such as collaborative research endeavors, but it is imperative that we get to know each other a lot more before we can benefit from these ventures.

PART III

Illustrations

Realizing Academy-Industry Partnerships

Part I of this volume articulated some of the challenges for management practice and management research. In Part II, the emerging schools of thought, arenas, roles, and mechanisms in collaborative research approaches were presented and examined. In Part III, we aim to present a number of case studies undertaken in collaborative research settings. The studies presented in this third part have been conducted within FENIX, a collaborative research program at the Stockholm School of Economics and Chalmers University of Technology in Göteborg, Sweden, or by researchers associated with FENIX. The studies represent a variety of research and organizational issues, theoretical perspectives, organizations, companies, and parts of companies. The common denominators are the use of a collaborative research approach in conducting the studies and the parallel ambition to both contribute to theoretical development in the field and guide decisions and actions in the organizations. Thus, considering the diversity of the empirical studies, collaborative research activities appear to be applicable to a great variety of organizational and management research issues, organizations and industries, and research settings and arenas.

In Chapter 10, Mikaelsson and Shani examine how a collaborative research approach has been used in the transformation of product development at the Volvo Car Corporation. The authors show that collaborative research efforts could make a fruitful contribution to how practicing managers jointly produce new images of organization change processes that makes sense out of complex processes. The collaborative sensemaking and sensetaking processes fostered the creation of new understanding of managerial actions and the creation of new scientific knowledge.

In Chapter 11, Roth, Berg, and Styhre present a knowledge management model that is anchored in action research methodology, called knowledge facilitation, that has been developed and applied within an organization learning and knowledge-sharing project at AstraZeneca. The authors put into question the prevailing emphasis on technical- and codification-oriented solutions in knowledge management theory and practice. They suggest that knowledge is a "social accomplishment" that is shared and distributed in communication within and between communities of practice.

In Chapter 12, Magnusson presents an experimental collaborative research approach in new product development. The author argues that experimental methods represent a domain of methods that, to date, have been rather unexplored and unexploited in both new product development research and collaborative research approaches. The chapter presents a collaborative research design where academics and practitioners jointly performed collaborative experiments that, according to the author, produced usable knowledge for both scholars and practitioners.

In Chapter 13, Sundgren and Styhre, collaborating with AstraZeneca, address theoretical and practical aspects of organizational creativity. While using collaborative research methodology, the study focuses on the supporting mechanisms for the creative processes and capabilities in pharmaceutical companies. The authors show that although organizational creativity remains a rather elusive concept from a theoretical perspective, it is a useful construct from a practical viewpoint. Hence, organizational creativity deserves careful managerial attention.

In Chapter 14, Engwall and Svensson focus on project management challenges during crisis situations. Through the use of action research, they study the use of small, time-limited organizational units to address upcoming problems in product development projects. In these units, relevant experts are gathered on a full-time basis to focus on one urgent unforeseen problem. This kind of group is typically initiated *during* the execution of a project to attack and solve an unpredicted problem before its consequences becomes too severe. The authors label these extremely temporary and ad hoc organizations *cheetah teams*.

In Chapter 15, Björkman presents a collaborative study of how a trade union is redefining its function and purpose for its members and seeks to develop new service offerings so as to remain a competitive and legitimate partner in the labor market and a policymaker in the Swedish society. The author shows how collaborative research can be used as a vehicle in service development and as an approach for improving interaction among members.

In Chapter 16, Kylén and colleagues discuss how a leadership development initiative at AstraZeneca was supported, developed, and reinforced by a collaborative research project. The authors describe the possible use of collaborative research in leader development and illustrate an alternative leader development approach as a result.

In Chapter 17, Sandberg and Werr present a collaborative research study of a consultancy firm that actively seeks to expand its number of services offered. Working in accordance with the insider action researcher model suggested by Roth, Sandberg, and Svensson (see Chapter 7 in Part II), Sandberg and Werr offer insights into how a collaborative research method may be applicable in knowledge-intensive service organizations such as consultancy firms and into how internal consulting firms can be used to leverage organizational learning.

Finally, in Chapter 18, Mohrman and Mohrman focus on a collaborative research project involving a large oil and chemicals company. The project had the dual purpose of yielding greater academic understanding of performance management systems and transforming the performance management practices of the firm to better support business performance during a period of fundamental change in the industry. The authors capture the hybrid nature of the collaborative research, focusing on both the collaborative processes and the knowledge outcomes to advance theory and practice.

Taken together, the chapters in Part III present a broad variety of empirical studies that, in various ways, draw on the challenges of management practice and management research as well as on collaborative research practices and methods discussed in Parts I and II of the volume. The various illustrations not only are intended to serve as cases that document the use of different collaborative research orientations and practices but also are aimed at making simultaneous contributions to managerial and organizational practice and the scientific body of knowledge in various areas of management and organizational studies. Thus, collaborative research approaches are by no means self-contained and shortsighted but rather are supposed to be used to help further develop managerial theory and practices. In that respect, collaborative research methods are a means to achieve a better understanding of practical puzzles and concerns in organizations.

10 Rethinking and Transforming Product Development

Jon Mikaelsson and A. B. (Rami) Shani

Increasing attention has been given during the past decade to the design of product development organizations. The notion of building alternatives to the functional organization and using different ways of organizing projects is being explored and reported continuously in the literature (Mikaelsson, 2002). Recent research suggests that the use of groups and teams as entities for producing knowledge and processing information in the context of product development seems to be on the rise (Mohrman, Cohen, & Mohrman, 1995; Shani & Sena, 2002). Yet as the pressures for more efficient product development and more innovative products increase, organizations are facing the challenge of continuous search for design- and change-oriented processes.

Most of the literature either explicitly excludes how the process dimension of change affects the design of the organization or assume that a well-designed organization is implemented according to a rational plan (Stacey, 1996). The literature seems to focus either on the design-oriented organization solutions (Hatchuel, Masson, & Weil, 2002) or the change-oriented solutions (Beer & Eisenstat, 2000). The current chapter argues that either focus by itself is limited. The complex nature of the phenomenon requires the integration of the two orientations such that our knowledge of the design and of the change processes will result in the creation of useful learning for practice and generalizable knowledge for management science.

The case involved is the renewal of the Volvo Car Corporation (VCC) product development organization. The change effort has been regarded within Volvo as a successful case in terms of contributing to increased

AUTHORS' NOTE: Susanne Ollila wittingly contributed in planning, data collection, and analysis activities. We also thank Hans Gustavsson, Agneta Lundqvist, Stefan Jutback, and Peter Palmqvist at Volvo Car Corporation for making a significant difference.

181

effectiveness—developing more car models faster and with relatively few resources. The case is of more general interest, however, because it deals simultaneously with changing both the design of the knowledge creation organization and the change process used. As such, this chapter is about exploring the change process that resulted from a deliberate attempt to integrate design-oriented change with principles of self-organizing change processes in the radical transformation of the product development process. Specifically, the focus is on the collaboration inquiry among critical actors (e.g., stakeholders). The aims are twofold: (a) to gain a better understanding of the complex dynamics during a complex change process in a product development organization and (b) to capture and reflect on the collaborative research methodology used in conducting the study. The next section focuses on our guiding and broad theoretical framework. The chapter then provides descriptions of the methodology and results before concluding with a discussion.

Product Development and the Need for Reflexivity _____

The design- and change-focused traditions of sociotechnical system theory advocated, since its inception more than 50 years ago, the use of experimentation and a variety of participative mechanisms during organizational change efforts (Bushe & Shani, 1991; Pasmore, 1988; Taylor & Felton, 1993). More recently, the need for increased involvement of organizational members in the change process has been suggested (Beer & Eisenstat, 2000; van Eijnatten, 2001; Norrgren, Ollila, Olsson, & Schaller, 1997; Shani & Docherty, 2003). In a recent set of studies, it was argued that design-oriented organizations are favorable to collective learning cycles, which are conducive to simultaneous regeneration of objects, skills, and occupations (Hatchuel & Weil, 1999; Hatchuel et al., 2002). There seem to be evidence that active involvement of organizational members in experiments with the design and implementation of change efforts produces better results in terms of successful implementations and improved performance (Adler & Shani, 2001; Beer, Eisenstat, & Spector, 1990; Ingelgård, 1998; Roth, 2002). However, relatively few studies can be found in the literature that report on the study of change in the specific context of large product development organizations.

Product development organizations are viewed as nonroutine knowledge-intensive systems (Mikaelsson, 2002). Reflection-in-action is argued to be important in sensemaking and learning in such environments (Olilla, 2000; Schön, 1991). Boland and Tenkasi (1995) claim that knowledge-intensive companies are composed of various microcommunities of specialized expertise and are often characterized by lateral rather than hierarchical organizational forms. To create knowledge in such companies requires the ability to make strong perspectives within a community and to take the perspectives of others into account. According to Boland and Tenkasi, *perspective taking* is the process whereby diverse individuals appreciate and synergistically use their distinctive knowledge. For this to happen, the diverse knowledge held by individuals in the organization must be presented in its uniqueness and made available for others to incorporate into a perspective-taking process. *Perspective making,* on the other hand, is the process whereby a community develops and strengthens its own knowledge domain and practices, enriching and refining its distinctive perspective complexities as a knowing community. Boland and Tenkasi argue that reflection on one's own perspective is difficult and often not attempted. They discuss reflexivity as the ability to periodically suspend one's natural attitude and notice the taken-for-granted (Holland, 1999). Making the implicit reasonable to another person is the critically important first step in achieving perspective taking, also serving as perspective making for those who create perspectives.

A critical component of the current study is the collaboration around the exchange of perspectives and knowledge among three groups of stakeholders in the change process: the top management (top-down process), the module teams (cross-functional entities—mainly various disciplines of engineers—for understanding the bottom-up process), and the change support team (a temporary team of change agents intermediating in the top-down/bottom-up process). The collaborative inquiry process facilitated perspective taking within and among the various groups of stakeholders. Continuous interactions and reflections played a critical role during the implementation of the restructuring process and in achieving a new equilibrium. Furthermore, it created the organizational capability and built in competencies for continuous collaborative redesign.

Collaborative Research in a New Product Development Setting

A collaborative research orientation that is embedded in a hybrid among action research, action learning, reflective inquiry, and qualitative methodologies was developed and used. At the most basic level, the collaborative research orientation is viewed as a partnership between two or more parties that is created for the purpose of a common goal or a shared purpose. Thus, a collaborative research partnership between management science researchers and organizational members refers to the values, actions, processes, and consequences of sharing and/or creating actionable knowledge (Shani & Docherty, 2003). A collaborative research partnership process that emphasizes action learning and reflective inquiry is likely to increase knowledge and actionable knowledge about the complexities of knowledge creation in a product development setting (see Chapter 5 of this volume). This approach, based on an iterative and collaborative interaction cycle, was used to capture and jointly interpret people's perceptions of key elements in the change effort.

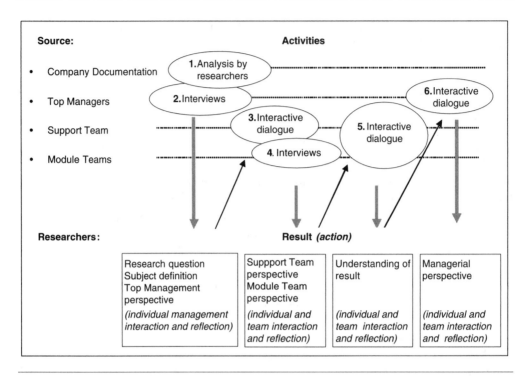

Figure 10.1 The Collaborative Reflective Inquiry Process and Outcomes

The first aim was to capture personal experiences of the three stakeholders (microcommunities) that were involved in the change process: management, the support team, and the module teams. In this regard, the aim was to pinpoint contradictions and dynamics of the actors' experiences rather than consensus, equilibrium, and stability in the various perspectives on the change process. The second aim was to create meetings among groups of stakeholders where collaborative reflection-in-action could facilitate perspective taking.

To accomplish these aims, a six-phase collaborative research process was developed and used. The essence of collaborative reflective inquiry processes is captured in Figure 10.1. Following initial analysis of company documents about the change program, sets of collaborative co-inquiry with top management were conducted via interviews to begin the systematic reflection and sensemaking of the process.

The top managers covered the perspectives of executive managers, change managers, functional line managers, and platform project managers. Four persons from top management—the manager of product and process development, the change project leader, a functional line manager, and the platform project manager—participated. First, the change project leader was interviewed (Activity 2 in Figure 10.1). Next, the support team and module team members were approached separately to capture their individual perspectives (Activities 3 and 4). An interactive dialogue with the support team, as a group, was conducted. The *support team* consisted of engineers, information technology (IT) experts, change consultants, human resources personnel, and an architect. Five persons from the support team took part. This group covered the perspectives of engineering, IT, and the working environment. The *module teams* are 12 cross-functional co-located engineering groups, with 60 to 100 people in every group, each person being responsible for various parts (i.e., modules) of the product. Two of these module teams were included in the study. The choice of which module teams to study was made by listing various kinds of characteristics of all 11 module teams (e.g., supplier dependency, first or second wave of module team implementation, degree of modularization). Two teams—the door team and the interior team—were chosen because they diverged at many of the listed points. Seven members from each of the two teams participated in the study. Four of these persons volunteered for being interviewed, and the others took part after being asked.

In the next step, a collaborative reflection-in-action was conducted with the module team managers and members of the support team. In this session, the two stakeholders' perspectives were used as a base for the interaction (Activity 5 in Figure 10.1). Finally, a session in which top managers reflected and interacted around all three of the perspectives was held (Activity 6).

Rethinking Product Development
at Volvo Car Corporation

Volvo Car Corporation

Many of the car business companies have recently reorganized their product development processes around product platforms and simultaneous engineering. VCC recently made the fifth market introduction of a new car based on a platform. This platform was an important part of VCC's strategic direction developed in 1994, when the merger with Renault was canceled and VCC had to face a new business scenario where, instead of being part of an alliance, it was an independent car manufacturer again. The new strategic direction was based on development of the product portfolio, and this meant a broadening of the product offerings (i.e., more variants). As a consequence, several new cars should be developed within a very limited time. From a product development point of view, this meant the need for an instant increase in product development performance, from one new car every 4 years to at least one new car every year, a challenge that called for a major change.

VCC wanted to find a way in which to take advantage of the available concepts of product development, such as platforms and simultaneous engineering, but also to build on cross-functional teamwork, which was considered a core company capability. The following concept definition was adopted:

All cars based on a platform shall be developed as part of a common module structure, characterized by a high level of common systems and components. This shall be carried out in the context of a long-term partnership with suppliers exercising their own development responsibilities. Production shall take the form of a common and flexible assembly process, and a common engineering procedure shall be established for the purpose of development.

The time limitation and the magnitude of the change meant that nearly all people involved in product development had to take part in the change parallel with their already ongoing product development work. To be able to shorten the time between creation and implementation of change, the decision was made to work with a top-down and bottom-up change model. A number of people were assigned as change agents with the role of supporting both management and the engineers in the module teams.

A co-located pilot engineering team, composed of 35 people, was established to create, in real time, the definition of a new working method when executing its development work during the pilot project. These individuals were assigned to this team in addition to their ordinary assignment of developing the body area of the first car to be introduced with the new platform. The pilot team, acting on the results from the internal study on platform organizing, developed and proposed the implementation of the "module team" concept. It was decided that the module team concept should be adopted by 800 people directly engaged in the parallel development of the cars on the platform.

The Images of the Change Process

Following are examples of the images of the three stakeholder groups' perspectives of the change process. The images are syntheses of the opinions of the people who participated in the study around issues of changing/reorganizing the product development work.

The Top Management Perspective. The manager of product and process development put together a cross-functional management steering committee to manage the implementation of the module team concept. The concept was based on the following three main principles: modularization, co-located and cross-functional teamwork, and coordinated project management of the cars to be developed.

The module team concept was implemented in two waves (steps). The first wave was the establishment of the first five module teams and a platform management team. The second wave was the establishment of the last seven module teams and a complete vehicle team. From a management point of view, whether the implementation could be carried out was never questioned. The module team concept was considered to be a solution to the business challenge as well as an example of a state-of-the-art product development process. Because the pilot team had created its own solutions from a principal framework with continuous backing from a support team, it was considered to be a successful change method to be chosen for the broader implementation as well. This was communicated as follows: "Everyone has two jobs: one to develop the products according to specification and targets and one to increase the efficiency by developing the way in which to work." The expected increase in efficiency was to be a result of increased internal efficiency in each of the module teams as well as a result of a flexible manning of the teams. The module teams were expected to always have an optimal competence and resource level.

The top management believed that there was a resistance to change. There were several efforts to reduce the resistance such as broad communication of the guiding principles, assignment of leaders with a positive attitude toward change, and investment in a complete new office environment with state-of-the-art IT equipment. Another challenge was to spread the findings from the pilot.

The steering committee had weekly meetings with the support team to discuss and solve problems, and committee members sometimes participated in task force work groups together with members from the support team, platform project management, and the module teams. When the support team was withdrawn, the manager of product and process development organized rolling meetings with the platform project manager, the module team leaders, and their line managers.

The Support Team Perspective. The support team started by introducing the module team concept through dialogues with each of the appointed module team leaders. Using documentation from the pilot and the experiences of support team members who had taken part in the pilot, the implementation of the full-scale change process got under way.

Each module team leader formed a group of people with whom the support team interacted. The support team members organized themselves so that each had responsibility for supporting the work of a few of the module teams. In the beginning, a lot of effort was put into the layout of the office environment to support the new way of working. The new office was under construction at the same time as the module teams were formed.

It was difficult to communicate the target of the change. The support team found that understanding the concept was not enough. Triggered by the expectation that was established by management, every module team had to reach an acceptable level of efficiency by a specific date. The support team created the educational and training material that helped people to acquire the knowledge and understanding of the new basic guiding principles, framework, and performance targets. This material was then communicated to the top management and the module team leaders.

The support team found it very difficult to communicate the possibilities without being able to work directly with each group of people. When the support team could have direct contact with individuals, it could create a relationship and find an acceptable solution through the use of dialogue. The support team members themselves used the same office concept as the module teams to "walk the talk." One major part of the concept was access to all information within the module team. This meant, for instance, that the conference room of each team was placed in the middle of the landscape and that it had large openings without doors. Because some of the teams were responsible for several different development areas, it was difficult to make them understand the positive side of overhearing others, and it became a disturbance instead. Another example was the old layout, which had thin mobile screen walls (similar to cubicle walls). In the new layout these screen walls were removed to facilitate easy communication. Some people, however, insisted that they needed privacy to work efficiently. The support team demonstrated some solutions to this, for example, using the so-called silent rooms and moving the mobile drawer pedestals to another spot. Far from everyone accepted the openness, and there was continuous arguing about the screen walls. Some people even made nightly raids to get more screens. There was never a clear decision made as to whether the screen walls were allowed or not.

In general, the understanding of the purpose of co-location was more common. In the beginning, the discussion was focused on the conflict of co-locating people from the purchase department into the module teams. Problems also emerged regarding whether people from testing, production, and styling should move to the module teams. The support team used the top management to get a decision but succeeded only in getting support for co-location at the module team level.

Another issue that was raised for discussion was the substructure of the module teams. In the thinking of the management and support team, it was assumed that the module teams would take care of their needs for structuring and coordination by continuous self-organizing, as had been the case with the pilot team. The pilot team members had organized themselves in a cross-functional core surrounded by supporting competencies, a logic they kept when they became a module team. This was not how it turned out within many of the other module teams. Team members created substructures within the module teams, reflecting the way in which they used to work, with co-location in more functional oriented subteams. Also, it became evident that there was confusion concerning the managerial roles needed within the module teams. For instance, the support team members were surprised when they noted that the old role of design responsibility still dominated in the module team substructure. They thought that aspects other than being a senior designer (e.g., subteam leadership skills) were required to deal with the coordination of subteam activities. It became obvious to the support team that the existing management structure was not strong enough to cope with these issues. Support team members realized that they had concentrated on the system level (the whole module team), and they turned to management to get decisions on how to react to the substructure and the managerial roles created in different ways in various module teams. Despite several discussions with top management, no agreement was reached.

The support team members also believed that the managerial roles were unclear with respect to their own interaction with the module teams. At times, they believed that they were becoming a substitute for management, taking over responsibility from the module teams regarding the change process. At the same time, they believed that the top management group never fully understood the complexities of managing the change process.

The Module Team Perspective. Many issues in the concept were built on the prerequisites of the forgoing pilot. The layout and technical tools were focused in the beginning. On the whole, the technical equipment level was high, but it seemed to be easier for the support team to use expensive IT solutions than to procure simple technical solutions, such as an inexpensive fax machine, on its own.

Openness in the physical environment was a big question; nothing that prevented sight was accepted. However, some of the members thought that walls were of vast importance and thus were allowed to build partitions of thin mobile screen walls. Today, there are not many of these screen walls left; some of them have been taken away by the support team, and others have been removed due to individuals realizing the positive aspects of openness.

The common team room in the pilot did not have a door, and it was meant to be the same in the rest of the module teams. However, some team members claimed a need for secrecy; therefore, they thought that having no door was inappropriate because others could take part in everything discussed in the room. Whether or not to have a door on the team room became an issue. Several discussions later, the support team agreed on letting two or three of the teams try out the "team room with a door" suggestion. The module teams saw this issue as being a matter of principle for the support team, and the module team members could not understand why they had to fight to get a door.

Before the move to the new premises was made, the considered layout was demonstrated in the support team's own workplace. It was criticized by members from the module teams. This criticism was not taken into account, and the module teams were told to understand that this layout was a good solution even for them. According to the module teams, there seemed to be a gap between what they claimed to need and the support team's opinion about their needs.

The module team concept also implied the functions of purchase, supply, and production being co-located within the team. The module teams were expecting the support team to make decisions on this matter given that the support team was, in some sense, thought of as part of the top management. However, this was not the case. Individuals from the purchase department had to be integrated into the module teams in three different steps. First, they moved from their old building to the one where the development people were sitting. Then, they progressed to the module team site and sat together in their own group, that is, not integrated with the rest. Finally, they were dispersed within the team.

Working in cross-functional teams meant that members began to question other members' areas of knowledge and competence. This was not seen as something solely positive given that team members were accustomed to everybody minding his or her own business. The cross-functional work also enabled some people to grab more work than they could handle or was appropriate. Therefore, the roles of various actors within each module team had to be defined. In the beginning, no one really knew what assignments and tasks each team member had or ought to have. This was experienced as a real mess. For example, the module team consisted of subteams, and these teams also came to have leaders, but the role of these leaders was not explicitly pronounced. In some cases, individuals did not even know they were subteam leaders. Finally, the support team created descriptions of the various team roles, but the problem still existed. Some of the team members went to their line managers to clarify the role confusion. The result of all the chaos was that some roles became "all and nothing" simultaneously despite the fact that descriptions existed. Accordingly, it was very difficult for the module team members to feel sure about who expected something from them and about the specific nature of their work.

Integration of the Perspectives

The various stakeholders were not asked explicitly to give their opinions about any certain issues; rather, they were asked to talk freely about the process of developing the module team concept. Yet some common issues were raised. The support team and the module team narratives show that there was lots of interaction between the support team and the module teams around the areas of communication, cross-functional teamwork, and management. Figure 10.2 presents the integration of the various perspectives.

As Figure 10.2 indicates, the discussion about communication in the support team was focused on information access and overhearing, whereas in the module teams it meant debating about whether or not to have a door on the team room, mobile screen walls, and common fax machines. The top management's documentation indicates that the module team concept is a structure for effective communication. According to the support team, cross-functional teamwork was created by focusing on the teamwork at the module team level. The module team members argued that the major issue was the co-location of team members. The top management documentation indicates that the cross-functional teamwork was about solving problems efficiently. The support team emphasized problems due to weak management structure, whereas the module teams thought that the various roles within the teams were unclear because the management of the teams was not clarified. According to the top management documentation, the leaders

Stakeholder Perspective	Common Issues		
	Communication	Cross-Functional Teamwork	Management
Top Management	Structure for effective communication	Problem-solving efficiency	Parallel development of products and work methods
Support Team	Information access and overhearing	Focus on teamwork at module team level	Weak management structure
Module Teams	Team room door, portable screens, and fax	Co-location	Unclear roles

Figure 10.2 A Comparative Synopsis of the Three Perspectives

of the module teams had a new role: to develop products and work methods in parallel.

The Reflection of Top Management on the Various Perspectives

As part of the inquiry process, top management was asked to reflect on the various perspectives and their meaning. Figure 10.2 served as the starting point, and top management was asked to explore the meaning of the data that were collected and to generate ideas for action. As reflection was taking place and confirmation of the results was established, top management also expressed its disappointment at the disparity among the perspectives. Furthermore, there were some individual differences in the reactions and reflections. Some of the persons criticized their own contributions to the change process. They thought that with help from management, some of the disparities, such as the different perceptions about management roles, could be clarified. They also thought that individuals needed support when taking on the new leader responsibility.

Individuals in top management also had opinions regarding the absence of initiative among the module team members, given that they thought that the module team members expected and wanted top management to define their roles and assignments. The whole group of four individuals found it strange that both the module teams and the support team seemed to miss the fact that top management had tried to tear down the hierarchy.

During the discussions, some reflections about the consequences of the various perspectives were made. Also, the meaning of "being agreed" was debated. For quite a long time, the group members tried to understand the various perspectives and then started to talk about future actions, both so as to do something about the problem, as they called it, and to prohibit it from happening in the future:

> I think getting different perspectives is inevitable. Thoughts that have matured in a group for months are often transferred to others in just a few hours. The module teams are in the middle of creating their own understanding of the concept. We could speed up this process by getting those with information to meet and interact with those who don't have the information.

> We should, as soon as possible, gather the managers in the module teams to talk about the situations in the teams today as the workload has increased. Maybe we could use some of these findings [pointing at unclear roles and focus on teamwork at module team level in Figure 10.2] in our discussion.

> I think we should learn from the methods of this study and more specifically from the joint reflection session. To meet others, and to listen to how they understand things, is very important when working together.

Discussion

The Need for Alternative Actionable Knowledge-Based Methodologies

The success of knowledge-intensive organizations is dependent on their ability to link in a meaningful way the microcommunities that exist within them. The ultimate success of product development depends on how these microcommunities and other organizational members relate throughout the knowledge creation process (von Krogh, Ichijo, & Nonaka, 2000). A research methodology is viewed as an enabler of knowledge creation because it provides a platform, the mechanisms, and the processes for interactions between the microcommunities and others in and around the organization (Adler & Shani, 2001).

For management science to become more relevant, research needs to produce actionable knowledge (Starkey & Madan, 2001). Yet in scanning the management science literature, one finds a large variety of research methodologies with little or no considerations to actionable knowledge. Most of the reported studies tend to focus on the generation of knowledge regardless of its actionability. The purpose of the study reported in this chapter was to generate actionable knowledge from the start. The intent was to study an issue/phenomenon that was viewed as having high relevance for both the company and the research community while using a collaborative research methodology that is embedded in true partnership among organizational members and between organizational members and researchers—from both within the company and outside of the company.

The Merit of the Collaborative Research Projects

The study reported in this chapter used a collaborative methodology that is somewhat of a hybrid of action research, action learning, and reflective inquiry. As can be seen from the results section, the conclusion can be drawn that a change effort that deliberately focuses on the interactions among various stakeholders seems to produce some of the intended consequences of the change but does not meet all expectations. The data are presented in terms of how the issues are viewed from the various perspectives. But at the same time, the analysis reveals some important differences in terms of how these issues are interpreted, and that might have hampered the change effort. As stated earlier in the chapter, the inquiry process also allowed for the exploration of the possible exploitation of the differences rather than just focusing on the differences themselves.

The differences of perspectives lead to clashes in the implementation of the change because there are difficulties in taking one another's perspectives and coming to a joint understanding (not necessarily a joint solution). This could be due to failure in making one's diverse knowledge available to others to incorporate, and this is substantial in perspective making, according to Boland and Tenkasi (1995). In Argyris's (1990) terms, this could be seen as an example where no mutual learning occurs because both parties are advocating their own positions rather than trying to understand and reflect on one another's positions.

Our understanding of the case is that although interaction in the change process did produce enough coinciding perspectives to make the change happen, it is doubtful that it achieved the goal of creating a continuous capacity for innovation. The explanation for this could be found in the change strategy applied, which can be seen as limiting the possibilities for collaborative reflection-in-action and knowledge creation. Even if the deliberate ambitions of top management and the support team were to empower the module teams to participate in the design and leave room for self-organizing, all were still caught in their experience from creating and implementing the pilot concept. The pilot team was, in a way, a mirror of the complete product development organization, but it did not take the context of the other teams into account. By using collaborative reflection-in-action with encouragement of perspective taking instead of only perspective making, the emergence of several diverse constructions, which are not able to understand and cooperate with each other sufficiently, could be avoided.

Systematic Reflection-in-Action

Greater emphasis on more reflection-in-action, enabling various stake-holders to understand and accept each other's positions, would facilitate learning (Argyris, Putnam, & McLain, 1985). Therefore, in this case, the goal of achieving an innovative organization capable of sustaining self-organization would have become more likely.

This study leads us to the conclusion that to achieve organizational knowledge creation, it is important to understand how various individuals construct their view of the world. To construct meaning or sensemaking (Weick, 1995), interacting is not enough; systematic reflective inquiry is a key component. However, the purpose of sensemaking through the capturing of experiences by various actors is not to reach consensus or compromise. The strength of continuous systematic reflection-in-action is in revealing and accepting various perspectives so as to surface and combine various types of knowledge in an innovative way. Using contradictory perspectives also provides an arena for knowledge creation in the "double loop" sense and hence constitutes one basis for self-organizing and action to occur.

Our learning from using the collaborative research model, with reflection-in-action, is that revealing various perspectives does not necessarily create conflicts. The use of individual perceptions in the process of perspective taking and perspective making made it possible to enlarge and reveal the diverse knowledge and experience held by various stakeholders. The collaborative reflection-in-action used enlightened the various consequences of the change and facilitated mutual understanding without an immediate demand for consensus.

Conclusion

Designing and managing change of any large product development organization implies a mental business model in which human interactions and performance are embedded. The nonroutine nature of product development organizations seems to compound the complexity and management of change. This study explored the nature of the change process—while it was occurring—as it was perceived by various actors. An alternative collaborative inquiry methodology—a hybrid of action research, action learning, and reflection-in-action—was developed and used in this study. The inquiry approach used generated new insights (knowledge) and led to organizational actions (actionable knowledge).

In the context of product development organizations, the development of collaborative methodologies for ongoing organizational dialogue around the creation of a shared understanding of change, its context, and its complexity is critical. As we have seen in this study, the nonroutine nature of such organizations lends itself to such an approach. At the same time, using such an orientation requires an organizational commitment and a willingness on the part of top management to accept the merit of having different perspective-taking and perspective-making realities. The synergy, challenges, knowledge, and actions generated in this project are evidence that more experimentation is needed with a variety of alternative collaborative inquiry approaches that center on the creation of actionable knowledge.

References

Adler, N., & Shani, A. B. (Rami). (2001). In search of an alternative framework for the creation of actionable knowledge: Table-tennis research at Ericsson. In W. Pasmore & R. Woodman (Eds.), *Research in organizational change and development* (pp. 43–79). Amsterdam: Elsevier Science.

Argyris, C. (1990). *Overcoming organizational defenses.* Boston: Allyn & Bacon.

Argyris, C., Putnam, R., & McLain S. (1985). *Action science.* San Francisco: Jossey-Bass.

Beer, M., & Eisenstat, R. A. (2000). The silent killers of strategy implementation and learning. *Sloan Management Review, 41*(4), 29–40.

Beer, M., Eisenstat, R. A., & Spector, B. (1990). *The critical path to corporate renewal.* Boston: Harvard Business School Press.

Boland, R. J., Jr., & Tenkasi, R. V. (1995). Perspective making and perspective taking in communities of knowing. *Organization Science, 6,* 350–372.

Bushe, G., & Shani, A. B. (Rami). (1991). *Parallel learning structures.* Reading, MA: Addison-Wesley.

Hatchuel, A., Masson, P. L., & Weil, B. (2002). From knowledge management to design-oriented organizations. *International Social Science Journal, 171,* 25–37.

Hatchuel, A., & Weil, B. (1999, July). *Design-oriented organizations: Towards a unified theory of design activities.* Paper presented at the Sixth International Product Development Management Conference, Churchill College, Cambridge, UK.

Holland, R. (1999). Reflexivity. *Human Relations, 52,* 519–556.

Ingelgård, A. (1998). *On macroergonomics and learning strategies in improving working conditions.* Unpublished manuscript, Department of Psychology, Göteborg University, Sweden.

Mikaelsson, J. (2002). Managing change in product development organization: Learning from Volvo Car Corporation. *Leadership and Organization Development Journal, 6,* 301–313.

Mohrman, S. A., Cohen, S. G., & Mohrman, A. M. (1995). *Designing team-based organizations: New forms for knowledge work.* San Francisco: Jossey-Bass.

Norrgren, F., Ollila, S., Olsson, M., & Schaller, J. (1997). *Industriell FoU: Vad utmärker Best Practice-projekt?* (Industrial R&D: What are the characteristics of best practice projects?). Göteborg, Sweden: Institute for Management of Information and Technology.

Ollila, S. (2000). Creativity and innovativeness through reflective project leadership. *Creativity and Innovation Management, 9,* 195–200.

Pasmore, W. A. (1988). *Designing effective organizations: The sociotechnical systems perspective.* New York: John Wiley.

Roth, J. (2002). *Knowledge unplugged: An action research approach to enhancing knowing in R&D organizations*. Doctoral thesis, Chalmers University of Technology, Gothenburg, Sweden.

Schön, D. (1991). *The reflective practitioner: How professionals think in action*. Aldershot, UK: Ashgate Publishing.

Shani, A. B. (Rami), & Docherty, P. (2003). *Learning by design: Building sustainable organizations*. London: Blackwell.

Shani, A. B. (Rami), & Sena, J. (2002). Integrating product and personal development. In P. Docherty, J. Forslin, & A. B. (Rami) Shani (Eds.), *Creating sustainable work systems: Emerging perspectives and practice* (pp. 89–100). London: Routledge.

Stacey, R. D. (1996). *Complexity and creativity in organizations*. San Francisco: Berrett-Koehler.

Starkey, K., & Madan, P. (2001). Bridging the relevancy gap: Aligning stakeholders in the future of management research. *British Journal of Management, 12*, 3–26. (Special issue)

Taylor, J. C., & Felton, D. F. (1993). *Performance by design: Sociotechnical systems in North America*. Englewood Cliffs, NJ: Prentice Hall.

van Eijnatten, F. M. (2001). Chaordic systems thinking for holonic organizational renewal. In R. W. Woodman, & W. A. Pasmore (Eds.), *Research in organizational change and development* (pp. 213–252). Amsterdam: Elsevier Science.

von Krogh, G., Ichijo, K., & Nonaka, I. (2000). *Enabling knowledge creation*. New York: Oxford University Press.

Weick, K. E. (1995). *Sensemaking in organizations*. Thousand Oaks, CA: Sage.

11

Knowledge Facilitation in Action

Jonas Roth, Lena Berg, and Alexander Styhre

I t is commonplace today to make claims that we are living in a knowledge-based, postindustrial society (Teece, 2000). In the knowledge society, the ability to make good use of abstract, codified, and symbol-based information serves as a major production factor. Such ability to make use of information is generally referred to as *knowledge* (Boisot, 1998). In the field of organization theory, knowledge management has emerged as a recent theoretical perspective aiming at depicting the firm as an aggregate of knowledge resources (Grant, 1996; Spender, 1996). In this view, the firm is seen as a social system capable of making use of and creating various forms of knowledge in its day-to-day activities (Leonard-Barton, 1995; Little, Quintas, & Ray, 2002). Making knowledge the smallest entity of analysis in organization studies does, however, imply that the very notion of knowledge is becoming problematic.

Knowledge is a concept relying on a number of ontological and epistemological assumptions (Alvesson & Kärreman, 2001; Blackler, 1995). Knowledge can be personal, tacit, propositional, distributed, codified, and so forth. Therefore, knowledge is best seen as an umbrella term denoting a number of various skills and capabilities aimed at making use of available data and information. One particular field of interest in the knowledge management discourse is how firms actually make use of their knowledge resources (Pfeffer & Sutton, 1999). Because knowledge is deeply ingrained with various culturally and socially embedded beliefs and assumptions, knowledge cannot be simply applied to cases in a tool-like manner. There is a difference between *knowledge-as-resource* and *knowledge-in-action* (Choo, 1998). The capabilities of making use of knowledge resources remain one of the key areas of knowledge management theory. To date, knowledge management theorists have been determined to categorize various types of knowledge rather than to offer detailed accounts on how knowledge can be used in action.

This chapter presents one attempt to turn knowledge resources into action through the use of what we refer to as *knowledge facilitators*. Knowledge facilitators are experienced managers within the firm who help a community of practice (e.g., a new product development team) to codify, decodify, articulate, express, and/or tell stories about their skills, experiences, know-how, and capabilities—in essence, their knowledge of certain areas. The knowledge facilitator's role is to be a person who is capable of making the members of a particular community of practice share their learning and experiences with other members of the community and other organizational members. In this chapter, the knowledge facilitator is seen as the mechanism that bridges the "knowing-doing gap," the rift between knowledge conceptualization and knowledge application that Pfeffer and Sutton (1999) describe as a major impediment to successful knowledge management practices within firms.

The study reported in this chapter was undertaken within the pharmaceutical industry, more specifically in AstraZeneca. AstraZeneca is a major multinational pharmaceutical company operating in the fields of cardiovascular, gastrointestinal, and cancer medicine. The research and development (R&D) centers are located in Europe and in the United States, with more than 10,000 R&D employees and a $2.6 billion (U.S.) R&D investment in 2001. Today, following a merger, the company has more than 50,000 employees worldwide. The pharmaceutical industry is renowned for its R&D intensity and its costly new product development activities. Therefore, it may be characterized as a knowledge-intensive industry. The case presented in this chapter is an outcome from an *action research* project undertaken within the FENIX research and executive Ph.D. program. In the study, what Bartunek and Louis (1996) call an insider/outsider team was formed to create opportunities for critical reflection on existing practices while the insider's insights into the local culture and routines were actively used. The insider/outsider team research activities were, therefore, fruitful in terms of understanding how knowledge can be turned into action.

This chapter is structured as follows. First, the idea of knowledge as an organizational resource is discussed. Second, the methodology of the study is examined. Third, the experiences from the knowledge facilitation activities are outlined. Finally, some implications for practice, as well as for academic research, are put forward.

Turning Knowledge Into Action

Knowledge management theorists are eager to depict knowledge as the single most important resource in organizations. Knowledge is generally defined as the capability of making use of data and information in terms of creating competitive advantage for the local firm. Such capabilities can be individual, community based, or organization or firm based. We can, therefore, speak of the knowledge of the individual, the community or group, or the firm. In much normative, mainstream knowledge literature, knowledge is depicted as a stock of skills and know-how that can be applied in a tool-like manner. Alvesson (2001) writes,

> Knowledge—at least in the context of the business world and of management studies—is normally treated as a functional resource, representing a "truth" or at least something instrumentally useful on a subject matter and/or a set of principles or techniques for dealing with material or social phenomena. (p. 865)

Other knowledge management theorists, in opposition to this functionalist view, conceive of knowledge as being a shared system of beliefs and assumptions that serve to create know-how and skills. For instance, Tsoukas (1996) writes, "Firms are distributed knowledge systems in a strong sense; they are decentered systems. A firm's knowledge cannot be surveyed as a whole; it is not self-contained; it is inherently indeterminate and continually reconfiguring" (p. 13). Here, knowledge is socially embedded, decentered, and continuously evolving. Knowledge is not seen as a tool-like "thing" that is passed around but rather becomes the capability of sharing a particular view of the world. Knowledge is, therefore, based on socialization of individuals in the organization.

Tsoukas and Vladimirou (2001) criticize mainstream knowledge management theory for, to use Collins's (1998) concept, *undersocializing* the use of knowledge in organizations: "Managing organizational knowledge does not narrowly imply efficiently managing hard bits of information but, more subtly, sustaining and strengthening social practice. In knowledge management, digitalization cannot be substituted for socialization" (Tsoukas & Vladimirou, 2001, p. 991). Instead, knowledge management is, Tsoukas and Vladimirou (2001) suggest, a matter of establishing mechanisms for reflection and learning:

> Knowledge management then is primarily the dynamic process of turning an unreflected practice into a reflective one by elucidating the rules guiding the activities of the practice, by helping give a particular shape to collective understandings, and by facilitating the emergence of heuristic knowledge. (p. 990)

As opposed to the view of knowledge as being something that can be simply applied to cases, Tsoukas and Vladimirou argue that organizational knowledge is always embedded in the collective understanding of knowledge. Knowledge is social in nature and, therefore, is entangled with communication.

Another important facet of knowledge is that it is, unlike other resources, not consumed as it is used. Adler (2001) writes, "Knowledge is a remarkable substance. Unlike other resources, most forms of knowledge grow rather than diminish with use" (p. 216). Neo-classic economics dealt with natural resources demonstrating diminishing returns (Burton-Jones, 1999). In the knowledge economy, the production factors are no longer subject to such limitations. As knowledge is being distributed and shared, it is used more efficiently, and as it is better used, it supports its own reproduction. Knowledge, paradoxically, grows as it is consumed. To give away knowledge is to make your own knowledge increase.

In this chapter, the knowledge facilitator role is explicitly aimed at orchestrating the distribution of knowledge within the firm. Drawing on the criticism formulated by, inter alia, Tsoukas (1996) and Alvesson (2001), knowledge is seen here as being not a tool but rather a shared and socially embedded capability or skill. The knowledge facilitator's role is, as will be seen, to create arenas and opportunities (in brief *space* or, as Nonaka and Konno [1998] call it with a Japanese concept, a *Ba*) for sharing knowledge. Thus, the knowledge facilitator does recognize that knowledge in organizations is always entangled with the standard operation procedures and routines of the firm. In a time-compressed and highly competitive market situation, the sharing of knowledge might not occur as a self-organizing process but rather might need some instituted arenas. Therefore, it is important to actively intervene in terms of bridging the knowledge-doing gap. Knowledge is not passed around freely without attention, hence the importance of knowledge facilitators in knowledge-intensive industries.

The Knowledge Facilitation Method

The characteristics of action research, the foreseeable embedded potential in using the action research process to create actionable knowledge (Argyris, 1993), and the contextual or situational characteristics led to the joint decision to use action research in the study. The initial dialogue between the researchers and the organizational members generated the shared belief that the only way in which to gain relevant knowledge and propose and accomplish change is through dialogue, reflective thinking, and action by all participants (Weick, 1989). Weick (1989) makes the point, quite persuasively, that greater heterogeneity among conjectures or "thought trials" supports more robust theorizing. He further notes that teams of researchers are more likely to generate a greater number of diverse conjectures than are researchers working alone. There is an underlying assumption, in this chapter, that this type of research process has the possibility of creating useful actionable and scientifically relevant knowledge at the same time (Adler, 1999; Adler & Norrgren, 1995). Actionable knowledge means knowledge for action that is meaningful for action and that can be translated into action (Adler & Shani, 2001). The emphases are on working with groups of company employees as co-researchers and developing the kind of self-reflexive critical awareness that triggers action based on the knowledge created (Eden & Huxham, 1996). To be able to reach these objectives, an insider/outsider team consisting of two knowledge facilitators from AstraZeneca and two senior researchers from academia was created.

Data collection was built into the knowledge-facilitating process. In most cases, all stages of the process were facilitated by two knowledge-facilitators. The results were analyzed immediately by the facilitators and with the insider/outsider research team on a regular basis. Both facilitators in this case are former project leaders within the company and have lengthy experience in the clinical R&D unit of the company. The research and intervention processes for the knowledge management experiment are not clearly separated in this initiative. Before each step of the knowledge-facilitating process (i.e., each meeting with organizational members), the facilitators planned the intervention by fine-tuning the questions prepared for each step and discussed what intervention method to use based on experience gleaned from previous experiences, the size of the group, and at what stage of the process this particular group was. After each intervention, the results were documented in a mind-map format, the course of events was recapitulated, and the knowledge gained was analyzed. The results were categorized and then presented and reassessed together with the project members at the next brainstorming session. In addition, the progress of the experiment and the results were discussed and analyzed together with research colleagues not directly involved in the knowledge-facilitating process.

Bringing the Knowledge Facilitator Into Action

The intention of the knowledge facilitator initiative was to create a process with tools that could increase knowledge sharing between, for example, clinical project groups in the organization. A few key prerequisites were jointly identified with the management of the clinical unit to make the facilitating action effective. Taking into consideration the focus on effectiveness in the R&D organization, the knowledge management initiative had to be time- and cost-effective. Above all, the project members' time spent in the facilitating process should not jeopardize the chance to meet their project objectives. To legitimize the knowledge facilitator initiative, it was assured of having the full support of management. Moreover, the facilitators had much experience with the organization being studied, had lengthy experience in the clinical R&D unit, and had an extensive personal network. The profile of the facilitators was important to increase trust when approaching the various projects initially. The facilitating process includes two knowledge facilitators who work as a pair during all of the facilitating steps and who are described in three major steps in the following sections and as set out in Table 11.1.

Step 1: Legitimize and familiarize. The first step is to interview the project leader within the project. This step will familiarize the knowledge facilitators with the project and provide an idea of which activities the project leader thinks are important as well as what things are positive or problematic. It

Table 11.1   The Emerging Knowledge-Facilitating Initiative at AstraZeneca

	Meeting With the Team Leader	**Meeting With the Team Group (two to four meetings)**	**Interactive Seminar With Other Team Members**
Content	A structured interview/dialogue	Brainstorming sessions Structuring content Dummy run of seminar	Interactive seminar Directed meeting with target group
Time used	1.5 to 2 hours	2 hours per meeting	Approximately 2 hours
Facilitator role	Lead the discussion Document Schedule meeting with the team	Facilitate the meeting Use methods to build an open climate Structure experiences Provide focus	Introduce and close the session Facilitate the dialogue Document
Output	Facilitator gets insight into the team Team leader obtains time for reflection Mutual sharing of network Legitimacy to continue	Articulation of tacit knowledge Creation of collective knowledge Production of knowledge in a shareable form	Sharing of experience across team boundaries Creation of new knowledge Building of dynamic micro-communities Creation of personal networks

may help the project leader to put words to what he or she already knows. In addition, the facilitators can give the project leader some feedback from other projects and, in so doing, transfer knowledge or point to a person having the knowledge needed. The interview is documented and takes 1½ to 2 hours. At this initial meeting, the facilitators come to an agreement with the project leader regarding how to continue and whom to contact within the project.

Step 2: Unlock the tacit knowledge—Structure explicit knowledge. The second step usually consists of more than one session. The core group of the project gathers in the same room for a 2-hour brainstorming session. The outcome is "knowledge on every wall," as one project member put it, referring to what was captured from the meeting on flip charts and whiteboards (similar to blackboards but with white surfaces). Usually, an additional session is needed after the information from the first brainstorming session has been structured. The time between the sessions gives the project members a chance to reflect on the material, and this often leads to more experiences from the first session being added. The facilitators lead the sessions and structure the information, whereas the project members hold an interactive dialogue. This results in a mind map, with the common knowledge gained from all of the sessions and a draft set of slides jointly produced for the final seminar. The facilitators document all sessions, and the total time spent together with the project members is approximately 6 hours. The facilitators continuously switch roles during the brainstorming sessions. One poses questions, facilitates the dialogue, and directs attention to common interests in the group. The other facilitator listens, captures the process in writing, and prepares to switch roles with his or her colleague.

Step 3: Share with the organization. Step 3 is when the experiences are shared with other members of the organization. It could be a seminar or any other preferred alternative for sharing experience and knowledge. The seminar is interactive, with the attendees asking questions and commenting on what is being said based on their own experiences. It could also be an open dialogue between two groups with the aim of developing a collective understanding of a phenomenon. Depending on the project experience and the results, different methods were used within the process. One practiced way was to have two different project teams experiencing all steps of the facilitating process as separate teams. The teams then met up in a seminar and shared common experiences from earlier collective actions, resulting in a high absorptive capacity in both teams (Cohen & Levinthal, 1990). Using Nonaka and Takeuchi's (1995) terminology, both teams had externalized their tacit knowledge and were, through combination and socialization, sharing what was jointly of interest in an interactive seminar. Furthermore, new knowledge was created when the two teams collectively visualized their tacit and explicit knowledge in the interactive social process that took place. This process is illustrated in Figure 11.1. The seminar usually lasts about 2 hours. The facilitators play a relatively minor role, simply coordinating the meeting and facilitating the dialogue.

Outcomes of the Facilitating Action

"Good luck, but as far as I know, nobody will come and attend those seminars," one executive manager argued before the initiation of the knowledge facilitation activities at AstraZeneca. Another former manager at the company claimed, "Nobody will tell you what went wrong; you will only hear success stories." Despite these words, eight leaders from various projects at the clinical R&D unit have been interviewed, and 14 action learning workshops—leading to five seminars so far—have been held. More than 50 people have been involved in the workshops, and more than 100 (out of 450 in the clinical unit) have attended the interactive seminars.

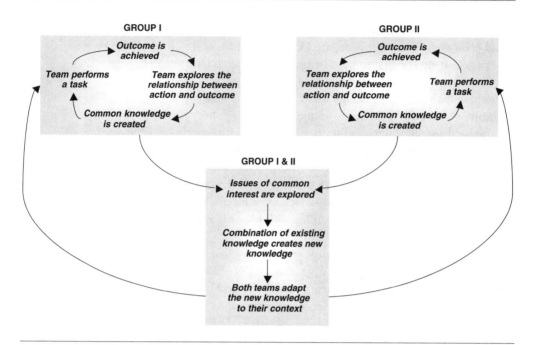

Figure 11.1   Knowledge Creation Based on Visualization of Tacit and Explicit Knowledge in an Interactive Social Process

Contrary to the senior manager's initial perception, the project leaders and members were positive in regard to the knowledge management initiative. Among the quotes from the interviews and workshops was the following: "It is crucial for us to be able to improve the innovative climate, our working routines, and the flexibility within our organization." There were a few ideas and suggestions on how to execute knowledge sharing, but many concerns and obstacles were expressed, including the following. "We do not have the time." "How could anybody be interested in what I [we] know?" "It is hard to assemble the group at this late stage of the project; they [group members] are already occupied with new tasks." "It is so much work structuring what we know."

The outcomes of the facilitating action are tied to the various steps of the process.

Step 1. During the interview with the project leaders, they expressed appreciation for the time to reflect on what had really happened in their projects. One project leader said after the interview, "It is nice to talk to someone who is so interested. It gives me the time to articulate my thoughts—sometimes new thoughts for me as well." The interview gave the project leaders a chance to focus on what was important in their projects when questions such as "What is most crucial in your project now?" and "What experiences do you think other project leaders want your project to share with them?" were raised.

Step 2. At the initial meeting with the project members, a typical brainstorming session started with very stressed and half-interested, albeit slightly curious, individuals. At one of the sessions, a project member said in a very tense manner, "I have to leave for the dentist in 45 minutes, so maybe there's no point in being here." A colleague of hers argued, "I will not present anything to anybody after today, I have so many other things to do in the coming weeks. But I can sit here and listen." After 45 minutes of intensive work with a good dialogue under way and a whiteboard full of "knowledge," we had to remind the person going to the dentist not to miss her appointment. Her colleague, who was only there to listen, was deeply involved in the discussions and was making plans for the next step, that is, presenting their work to colleagues in the organization.

Once the initial tension had lifted, the groups were usually positive about the sessions. "This is very interesting. It gives us time to reflect on what is central in the work we have done," one project assistant reflected. Another member of the project expressed surprise: "Look at how much we have produced in 2 hours. I am impressed." They also saw new things that they had not seen before. For example, the members of one project group jointly drew a very complex map over their lines of communication between various collaborators and outsourcing partners, with dependencies that included their technical organization. One subproject leader said, "This picture is something that we have always needed but have never drawn." The same person came a few weeks later and told us, "The common picture that we drew of the project organization gave us a boost in our current reorganization within the project." The picture was later used in the seminar when explaining to colleagues how communication was organized within the project.

Regarding the facilitator's role and the method used, the participants mentioned the importance of "having a facilitator from outside who knows the clinical process." It was also a way in which to see collectively what they had actually done and to structure that information and knowledge. "You made us see this together," a project member claimed after one session.

Step 3. The interactive seminars have sometimes been of the more traditional type where the project members take turns in telling their colleagues their stories, either one by one or as a panel essentially discussing what they came up with during the brainstorming sessions. Sometimes, they turned into an active dialogue where groups met around a commonly interesting issue and shared experiences on equal terms. One group talked about how important it is to choose the right people for the different external expert committees working with the project group. After the seminar, it was clear to everyone that choosing members for these committees was, in fact, a form of knowledge that this group had gained from working with various committees for a long time. "I am very glad that I went to this [seminar]. Now I know who to contact when it comes to committees," said one person from the audience.

One of the project groups held a dialogue about how it was to work in the clinical R&D organization today compared with prior to the merger and its reorganizations. This discussion led to further discussions in another project group. A "closed" seminar with two project groups and a management group in clinical R&D was held. The management of the unit, which attends most of the seminars, especially appreciated this seminar. One manager said, "This was a great opportunity for myself and my management team to discuss the positive parts from our old organization and how to enable them in the new [organization]."

Discussion

Despite the fact that the enabling of knowledge creation across organizational boundaries provides key potential for sustainable competitive advantage, just how to make this happen is a big challenge for many companies. There is a lack of knowledge management tools that takes the complex and dynamic nature of knowledge into consideration, and the assessment techniques for knowledge creation and transfer are not fully developed. This section explores three issues, building on the results of the study at AstraZeneca: (a) the methodological challenges of the knowledge-facilitating role, (b) the possibilities with the knowledge-facilitating process, and (c) a discussion of how management experiments can get actionable knowledge. The chapter concludes with a section discussing implications management when using the facilitating initiative.

The Knowledge Facilitator in Action

The knowledge facilitator role at AstraZeneca resembles what von Krogh, Ichijo, and Nonaka (2000) call a knowledge activist. In their description, the knowledge activist plays three roles in the knowledge creation process: as a catalyst, as a coordinator of knowledge creation, and as the one who provides the general direction of knowledge creation. In the knowledge management initiative at AstraZeneca, the knowledge facilitator played five roles, three of which closely resembled those of the knowledge activist.

First, the knowledge facilitator serves as a catalyst of knowledge creation. As described in this chapter, knowledge creation across boundaries is a complex process, often subject to strong barriers and requiring a catalyst. In the AstraZeneca case, where there was no formal system for knowledge sharing between projects and where the project leaders expressed their frustration over a lack of time and incentives to spread what they knew, the knowledge facilitators served as catalysts for the action.

Second, the knowledge facilitator serves as a coordinator of knowledge creation initiatives. As such, the knowledge facilitators at Astra-Zeneca connected various knowledge domains within the company, directly through personal contacts but also indirectly through networks as a consequence of the various steps in the knowledge-facilitating process. This process continuously builds relationships among people and enables the ongoing creation of communities of practice in a dynamic way, some temporary and some more stable. The ultimate success of actionable knowledge creation depends on how these groups and other organizational members relate throughout the knowledge creation process. The knowledge facilitators at AstraZeneca make people meet in different constellations, finding the incentives for people to share what they know and create common knowledge.

Third, the knowledge facilitator serves as a guide toward the company's knowledge vision. As such, the knowledge facilitators at AstraZeneca provided the overall direction for knowledge creation in different communities of practice. They had much experience in working within the company and had met with many different project members and project leaders. In addition, they were in continuous dialogue with the management of the unit. As a result, it was possible to maintain the microcommunity perspective while, at the same time, changing the scale to encompass the larger vision of the company, thereby connecting the microcommunities' contribution to the knowledge vision of the company (von Krogh et al., 2000).

Fourth, the knowledge facilitator serves by raising the level of trust among members of the organization. The knowledge facilitators at AstraZeneca were builders of a caring climate. They listened to people's experiences without passing judgment, and everything that was said was documented for those in the room to see. The brainstorming sessions, as well as the interactive seminars, were characterized by a caring climate that invited people to talk about good experiences as well as bad ones.

Fifth, the knowledge facilitator serves as an enabler of a sharing culture. What comes first, the sharing culture or the activities leading to the exchange of knowledge? This and earlier research at the studied site shows that there is consensus within the company that the development of a sharing culture is vital to company success (Ingelgård, Roth, Shani, & Styhre, 2002; Styhre, Ingelgård, & Roth, 2000). The research also shows that there were very few actions that enabled this to happen. Drawing on the experiences from the knowledge management initiative at AstraZeneca, signs of a sharing culture were seen; for example, project members were approaching the knowledge facilitators instead of vice versa. This indicates that if organizational members begin sharing ideas about issues they see as really important, the sharing itself will create a learning culture (Dixon, 2000).

Drawing on the various roles of the knowledge facilitator, important aspects of the knowledge management initiative at AstraZeneca can be derived. One aspect is that the knowledge facilitators at the company are not the major carriers of knowledge. They function as facilitators of the action, whereas the project members are the owners of the knowledge and the main players in the creation and sharing of knowledge. Moreover, the knowledge facilitators are essential for cross-leveling knowledge in that they energize and connect knowledge creation initiatives within the company, thereby establishing the right enabling context. In addition, the knowledge-facilitating process involves all individuals (both the sending and receiving teams) in the sharing of knowledge on equal terms. Both parties have experiences to share, and both parties are interested in new knowledge, thereby enabling both a sharing and a caring arena for knowledge creation. Thus, the knowledge management initiative at AstraZeneca is a combination of a personal role and an actionable process that provides dynamic tools for managing knowledge.

An Actionable Process for Knowledge Creation and Transfer

Having the knowledge facilitator come from the "outside" triggers the knowledge-sharing process and facilitates three important practices to take into consideration when enabling knowledge sharing and creating an affirmative team culture: (a) active reflection, (b) an open dialogue, and (c) the building of heedful relations.

In an organization with a bias for action, the time for reflection may be hard to come by. Throughout the research work, members of the organization expressed the lack of time to reflect as a group, that is, to share and make sense of organizational realities. The emergence of a knowledge facilitator role had implications for how a team reflects on its actions and how those new insights were shared with other teams. As builders of a caring climate, the facilitators listened to people's experiences without judgment, and most of what was said was documented for those in the room to see. The various steps in the knowledge-facilitating process were characterized by a caring climate that invited people to talk about good experiences as well as bad ones. Reflection is the process of stepping back from an experience to process what the experience means, with a view to planning further action (Rigano & Edwards, 1998). It is the critical link among the concrete experience, the interpretation, and the taking of new action. Hedlund (1994) writes of the importance of reflection when making use of tacit knowledge and claims that "the interplay of tacit and articulated knowledge is termed reflection. Genuine knowledge creation usually requires such interplay" (p. 77).

A project-driven organization does not, of necessity, support knowledge transfer between projects because goal orientation, time lines, and cost control direct focus on activities within the project rather than on learning between projects. Thus, the project leader, as compared with the functional manager, has a more narrow and short-term interest that guides project action rather than knowledge transfer for the betterment of the organization. The functional manager, on the other hand, has the responsibility for organizational resources, the working life balance of the employees, and the long-term expertise development of individuals. Therefore, it would be practical and logical for the functional manager to have the responsibility for managing knowledge sharing in a wider sense, for example, across project boundaries. So, why is it still a problem? We saw in our research that a few key aspects of the knowledge-facilitating process and role helped to overcome many of the obstacles that were seen in the organization. These were *time* for reflection and to organize such activities, *authority* and *legitimacy* from both functional management and project management to initiate knowledge activities, *incentive* for the organizational members, and *structure* that was explicit and so could be repeated. The formal power independency of the knowledge facilitator (compared with the functional manager's influence on individual salary and career movements) may be seen as necessary for legitimacy in the project teams. Being an outsider, functioning outside the formal hierarchical structure, enhanced the reflective and open approach of the members involved in reflecting on both successes and failures. The way in which the knowledge-facilitating process is constructed allows a time-efficient structure for the project members to reflect and rapidly produce results that motivate toward continuing the process. Another incentive is that the project members—not the facilitators or any other persons outside the project—are the owners of the knowledge. There is a slight risk associated with introducing a third party into the matrix structure that could lead to unintended consequences for the political system in the organization and a blurred view of who is responsible for what. Experience with the knowledge-facilitating process indicates that close collaboration and an open dialogue among the three parties—the functional management, the project management, and the knowledge facilitator—take care of these risks. The knowledge-facilitating process is, therefore, a powerful tool for managing knowledge creation and sharing.

The knowledge-facilitating process used in this case fits well with the theory of the distributed model of knowledge in an organization in that all individuals in the projects were involved in the process. The process also takes all forms of knowledge into consideration, for example, by having individuals show examples or role-play when their experiences are difficult to verbalize. Having experienced the knowledge-facilitating process, we would argue that people with similar previous experiences with the process could interpret knowledge in a similar way. Through the knowledge-facilitating process, they could, quite straightforwardly and with lots of energy, jointly create knowledge. In addition, the process could be a link between functional managers and project managers by enhancing the capabilities of knowledge sharing, thereby becoming a potential tool for multiproject management (cf. Svensson & Engwall, 2001).

The main product in the pharmaceutical industry is knowledge. When the active substance has been identified, most new product development activities aim at producing knowledge about the drug, its effect, possible side effects, market possibilities, and so forth. Being competitive in the pharmaceutical industry means being better and faster than other pharmaceutical companies at creating and disseminating product-related knowledge within the firm's knowledge network and building those activities into the normal routines and practices of the new product development process.

It is a challenge for all organizations to enhance effective knowledge creation within and among various knowledge domains. It is as important in the deep expert knowledge domain as in the cross-functional team domain or other communities of practice. This challenge is taken seriously by the management of AstraZeneca, but it seems to be problematic to increase the knowledge flow and levels of learning in and among various communities within the company. Brown and Duguid (1991) write, "Experience at work creates its own knowledge, and as most work is a collective, cooperative venture, so most depositional knowledge is intriguingly collective—less held by individuals than shared by workgroups." Action research involves unlocking knowledge that is trapped in the minds of organizational members, creating new knowledge, and applying it effectively toward organizational action (Shani & Pasmore, 1985). As such, the action research approach with the joint inquiry at every facilitating step used in this initiative provided the platform and the links among communities of practice in the knowledge creation process. The shared interest and the caring environment created a sustainable participation in the process, and this in itself—together with the joint inquiry—created new insights and dynamic communities of practice.

Nonaka and Takeuchi's (1995) four modes of knowledge creation constitute a very attractive theory on how knowledge is transformed, transferred, and created in working groups. Although there are many examples and case narratives, they do not provide clear suggestions regarding how to create a sustainable model from the theory. The knowledge-facilitating tool developed at AstraZeneca is one example of making the theory actionable and is, therefore, a step toward a sustainable actionable model for knowledge creation and transfer.

Experimenting to Get Actionable Knowledge

The concept of knowledge management began to show up in the literature during the early 1990s and has virtually exploded since then (Swan & Scarbrough, 2001). To this point, the knowledge management tradition has little experience with experimental research methods given that most of the research knowledge is deductive. As a consequence, most of the literature is either descriptive (e.g., Nonaka & Takeuchi's [1995] four knowledge creation modes) or derived from "best practice" cases and often normative (e.g., Dixon's [2000] modes for sharing knowledge among groups). The research in this chapter has been characterized by experimentation with research methods coupled with existing knowledge management theory and change initiatives in the organizational setting. Experiments are often associated with natural sciences. What may come to mind here is the laboratory experiment, with its clearly defined conditions aiming to reduce interference by other parties. The laboratory experiment has been seen for a long time as the ideal model for knowledge production. Another type of experiment used in both the natural and social sciences is the field experiment, which involves observing objects or systems with or without manipulating them. A third and often forgotten type is the design of artifacts and models of action, such as intervention research (Hatchuel & Molet, 1986), where action is essential for knowledge production. "The essence of management research is in understanding, inventing, and criticizing 'models of collective action' " (Hatchuel, 2001, p. 36).

Hatchuel (2001) claims that in traditional experiments (e.g., laboratory experiments), the knowledge production and action processes were set apart as two different processes in time, but that "this distinction no longer holds for the sciences which create artifacts or collective action processes, like management sciences" (p. 37). This managerial historical fact is neglected in most knowledge management literature (cf. Davenport, De Long, & Beers, 1998; Dougherty, 1999; Pfeffer & Sutton, 1999) and could be one reason why the knowledge management literature is perceived as theoretically dispersed and hard to put into practice (Beer, 2000; De Long & Fahey, 2000).

Experimenting with the knowledge facilitator and process is an assessment technique for collective action that enhances knowledge creation across organizational boundaries. The way in which the knowledge-facilitating process is used provides the situation with flexibility and paves the way for collective activities. The situational adaptability of the knowledge-facilitating process is of importance because "behavior is characterized by improvisation and creativity rather than by detailed preplanning" (Blackler, 1995, p. 875). Because "know-how is not just a feature of individuals, but is distributed within a community" (p. 875), the collective action in the process makes it possible for experiences to be shared.

In summary, this research has used the experimentation in the field of knowledge management, where it has been ignored in most cases. Using experiments as a method of research has added knowledge to knowledge management theory as well as to action research theory. In addition, the experiments have enhanced practices in the studied organization. Thus, experimentation could be one of the carriers of knowledge on the bridge between industry and academy that simultaneously enhances knowledge in both.

Implications for Managers

This chapter has argued that knowledge sharing today is one of the biggest challenges for companies with regard to remaining competitive. An emerging initiative used at the pharmaceutical company AstraZeneca, with the aim of enhancing knowledge creation and dissemination across organizational boundaries, has been described. The initiative developed knowledge management tools that encourage groups in the organizations to meet in different constellations and create common knowledge. The results indicate that the role of the knowledge facilitator is pertinent to knowledge creation and sharing across project boundaries at the clinical R&D unit at AstraZeneca. The initiative embodies important aspects of knowledge sharing across boundaries (i.e., taking different forms and levels of knowledge into consideration) as well as concerning the relational and contextual factors of knowledge. In addition, the knowledge that is created and shared is actionable in the way in which the various steps are used. Using the knowledge management initiative has the following attractive attributes:

- It is relatively simple to use.
- It takes little time away from the day-to-day organizational activities.
- It generates results for the organization.
- It combines knowledge creation and knowledge sharing.
- It enables a caring and sharing culture in the organization.
- It continuously builds relationships and dynamic communities of practice.
- It is a possible tool for multiproject management.

There are a few challenges to using the facilitating model put forward in this chapter. One of the major challenges is to select the right facilitators who are capable of creating an attractive arena for teams to meet, reflect, and learn. It is critical that the facilitators understand the core business, have legitimacy in the organization, and have project management capabilities. The initiative draws some resources from the core activities, where approximately 20% of the facilitators' working time needs to be devoted for the facilitating process to be effective. As the process is outlined, it could hardly be upgraded to a large scale without making the facilitator role one that nearly all team leaders can take on now and then. In addition, most knowledge created and shared in the process is not possible to document in a way that is sustainable over time given that it is contextually bounded and dependent on the social interaction at the different steps. The best way in which to disseminate the shared learning on a wider scale would probably be to incorporate it into the training of employees as live examples and up-to-date cases. When implementing this process in the organization, management must be interested in creating a sharing culture by allowing the time for the knowledge-facilitating process and the emergence of knowledge facilitators. The process should be incorporated into the product development process and thereby built into the day-to-day activities. Management should show its support by being present at seminars and taking the initiative, together with the facilitators, regarding where to start in the organization and on what to focus. The knowledge-facilitating process described could then help to create the organization that sees it as natural to share experiences and, in so doing, to thrive on its most competitive asset.

References

Adler, N. (1999). *Managing complex product development*. Stockholm, Sweden: Stockholm School of Economics, Economic Research Institute.

Adler, N., & Norrgren, F. (1995). *Leverages and mechanisms for learning in complex organizational systems.* Göteborg, Sweden: Chalmers University of Technology, Center for Research on Organizational Renewal.

Adler, N., & Shani, R. (2001). *In search of alternative framework for the creation of actionable knowledge: Table-tennis research at Ericsson.* In W. Pasmore & D. Woodman (Eds.), *Research in organization change and development* (Vol. 13, pp. 43–79). Amsterdam: Elsevier Science.

Adler, P. S. (2001). Market, hierarchy, and trust: The knowledge economy and the future of capitalism. *Organization Science, 12,* 215–234.

Alvesson, M. (2001). Knowledge work: Ambiguity, image, and identity. *Human Relations, 54,* 863–886.

Alvesson, M., & Kärreman, D. (2001). Odd couple: Making sense of the curious concept of knowledge management. *Journal of Management Studies, 38,* 996–1018.

Argyris, C. (1993). *Knowledge for action: A guide to overcoming barriers to organizational change.* San Francisco: Jossey-Bass.

Bartunek, J. M., & Louis, M. R. (1996). *Insider/Outsider team research.* Thousand Oaks, CA: Sage.

Beer, M. (2000). Research that will break the code of change: The role of useful normal science and usable action science. In M. Beer & N. Nohria (Eds.), *Breaking the code of change* (pp. 429–446). Boston: Harvard Business School Press.

Blackler, F. (1995). Knowledge, knowledge work, and organizations: An overview and interpretation. *Organizational Studies, 16,* 1021–1046.

Boisot, M. H. (1998). *Knowledge assets: Securing competitive advantage in the information economy.* Oxford, UK: Oxford University Press.

Brown, J. S., & Duguid, P. (1991). Organizational learning and communities-of-practice: Toward a unified view of working, learning, and innovation. *Organization Science, 2,* 40–57.

Burton-Jones, A. (1999). *Knowledge capitalism: Business, work, and learning in the new economy.* Oxford, UK: Oxford University Press.

Choo, C. W. (1998). *The knowing organisation.* Oxford, UK: Oxford University Press.

Cohen, W. M., & Levinthal, D. A. (1990). Absorptive capacity: A new perspective on learning and innovation. *Administrative Science Quarterly, 35,* 128–152.

Collins, D. (1998). *Organisational change.* London: Routledge.

Davenport, T. H., De Long, D. W., & Beers, M. C. (1998, Winter). Successful knowledge management projects. *Sloan Management Review,* pp. 43–57.

De Long, D. W., & Fahey, L. (2000). Diagnosing cultural barriers to knowledge management. *Academy of Management Executive, 14*(4), 113–127.

Dixon, N. M. (2000). *Common knowledge: How companies thrive by sharing what they know.* Boston: Harvard Business School Press.

Dougherty, D. (1999). *Organizing the organization's knowledge for sustained product innovation: A sensemaking approach* (No. 44). Newark, NJ: Rutgers University, Faculty of Management.

Eden, C., & Huxham, C. (1996). Action research for the study of organizations. In S. R. Clegg, C. Hardy, & W. R. Nord (Eds.), *Handbook of organization studies.* Thousand Oaks, CA: Sage.

Grant, R. M. (1996). Prospering in dynamically-competitive environments: Organizational capability as knowledge integration. *Organizational Science, 20,* 375–387.

Hatchuel, A. (2001). The two pillars of new management research. *British Journal of Management, 12,* 33–39. (Special issue)

Hatchuel, A., & Molet, H. (1986). Rational modeling in understanding and aiding human decision-making: About two case studies. *European Journal of Operational Research, 24,* 178–186.

Hedlund, G. (1994). A model of knowledge management and the N-form corporation. *Strategic Management Journal, 15,* 73–90.

Ingelgård, A., Roth, J., Shani, A. B. R., & Styhre, A. (2002). Dynamic learning capability and actionable knowledge creation: Clinical R&D in a pharmaceutical company. *The Learning Organization, 9*(2), 65–77.

Leonard-Barton, D. (1995). *Wellsprings of knowledge: Building and sustaining the sources of innovation.* Boston: Harvard Business School Press.

Little, S., Quintas, P., & Ray, T. (2002). *Managing knowledge: An essential reader.* London: Sage.

Nonaka, I., & Konno, N. (1998). The concept of "Ba": Building a foundation for knowledge creation. *California Management Review, 40*(3), 40–54. (Special issue)

Nonaka, I., & Takeuchi, H. (1995). *The knowledge creating company.* New York: Oxford University Press.

Pfeffer, J., & Sutton, R. I. (1999). *The knowing-doing gap: How smart companies turn knowledge into action.* Cambridge, MA: Harvard University Press.

Rigano, D., & Edwards, J. (1998). Incorporating reflection into work practice: A case study. *Management Learning, 29,* 431–446.

Shani, A. B. (Rami), & Pasmore, W. A. (1985). Organization inquiry: Towards a new model of the action research process. In D. D. Warrick (Ed.), *Contemporary organization development* (pp. 438–448). Glenview, IL: Scott, Foresman.

Spender, J. C. (1996). Making knowledge the basis of a dynamic theory of the firm. *Strategic Management Journal, 17,* 45–62. (Special issue)

Styhre, A., Ingelgård, A., & Roth, J. (2000). A nonreductionist view of knowledge: Product development in the pharmaceutical industry. *Emergence, 2*(3), 51–67.

Svensson, C., & Engwall, M. (2001, June). *Multi-project management methods applied in new product development: An in-depth study of the application of critical chain.* Paper presented at the European Institute for Advanced Studies in Management Eighth International Product Development Management Conference, Enschede, Netherlands.

Swan, J., & Scarbrough, H. (2001). Knowledge management: Concepts and controversies [editorial]. *Journal of Management Studies, 38,* 913–921. (Special issue)

Teece, D. J. (2000). *Managing intellectual capital: Organizational strategic and policy dimensions.* Oxford, UK: Oxford University Press.

Tsoukas, H. (1996). The firm as a distributed knowledge system: A constructionist approach. *Strategic Management Journal, 17,* 11–25. (Special issue)

Tsoukas, H., & Vladimirou, E. (2001). What is organizational knowledge? *Journal of Management Studies, 38,* 973–993.

von Krogh, G., Ichijo, K., & Nonaka, I. (2000). *Enabling knowledge creation.* New York: Oxford University Press.

Weick, K. E. (1989). Theory construction as disciplined imagination. *Academy of Management Review, 14,* 516–531.

12

User Involvement and Experimentation in Collaborative Research

Peter R. Magnusson

U ser involvement in product innovation has been a research issue for at least 25 years that has produced many findings. Nevertheless, most of these findings *do not offer practicing managers any actionable knowledge*, that is, knowledge that can be used as a basis for their actions. Research has, for instance, shown that user involvement can result in novel ideas and innovations from lead users (Shaw, 1985; von Hippel, 1977, 1986, 1988), may generate more accurate knowledge regarding users' needs and wishes (Hennestad, 1999) and reveal their latent needs (Veryzer, 1998), can work as a mutual learning process for both users and companies (Anderson & Crocca, 1993; Sinkula, 1994), can shorten development times (Gupta & Wilemon, 1990; Iansiti & MacCormack, 1997), and may enable the collaborative creation of business and user value (Prahalad & Ramaswamy, 2000). Unfortunately, managers wanting to involve users in their product involvement get little practical guidance from the literature regarding what to expect from such endeavors. For instance, just learning that users have been the source of a vast majority of innovations is not enough for practitioners. They need to know whether the result is applicable to their businesses. Because user involvement is not without cost, they need to know the extra benefit achieved with user involvement. It is unlikely that the answers to these questions can be found in the literature. Accordingly, for managers not satisfied with just adopting the contemporary hypes and using the right buzzwords, there are a lot of uncertainties that need to be resolved before involving users in their product innovation processes.

Why, after more than 25 years, has it not been established whether users are useful in the innovation process? A plausible explanation can be found in the *research methods* used for studying user involvement. Table 12.1

(Text continues on page 221)

Table 12.1 Sample of Previous Research Regarding User and Customer Involvement, Sorted by Method

Study	Method	Contribution to Understanding User Involvement	Empirical Base	Main Purpose of Study
Athaide et al. (1996)	Questionnaire survey (mail), $N = 242$ ($N_0 = 1,500$, response rate = 22.49%)	It is important for sellers of technological process innovations to know their customers as well as their customers' environments.	B2B; 242 successful companies in process innovation systems or components	To develop a comprehensive inventory of relationship activities undertaken by successful sellers of technological process innovations
Campbell & Cooper (1999)	Questionnaire survey, $N = 88$ ($N_0 = 250$, response rate = 35%); hypothesis building and testing	There was no unanimous support for the positive effect of customer partnership. Only two of five hypotheses were supported.	B2B; chemical (58%), electronic (19%), industrial products (12%)	To investigate whether customer partnership improves the market performance of new products or enhances product or internal factors that drive new product success
Gales & Mansour-Cole (1995)	Questionnaire survey (handed out directly and submitted by mail), $N = 44$; hypothesis building and testing	UI has a positive influence on project success. UI might be costly and time-consuming when confidence is high.	B2B; 44 project managers of toxic waste treatment projects	To develop an information processing model of user involvement in innovation projects
Gupta & Wilemon (1990)	Questionnaire survey (mail), $N = 80$, and interviews, $N = 38$	Continuous customer acceptance testing leads to shorter development times, described as an "as-you-go" process.	B2B; key participants (research and development, marketing, engineering, and manufacturing) from 12 large firms in 5 industries	Exploratory study to examine why product development delays occur, the nature of these delays, and what can be done to avoid them
Martin & Horne (1995)	Questionnaire survey (mail), $N = 88$ ($N_0 = 475$, response rate = 18.5%); hypothesis testing	Increasing direct customer participation in the process in general and in the use of information about the customer at specific stages will likely increase the potential for success.	B2B; single informants from 88 different unspecified companies; assessment of most and least successful innovation (criteria = sales volume and profitability)	To examine the use of internal/external inputs and customer information in most and least successful service innovations

(Continued)

216

Table 12.1 Continued

Study	Method	Contribution to Understanding User Involvement	Empirical Base	Main Purpose of Study
Morrison et al. (2000)	Questionnaire survey (mail), $N = 122$ ($N_0 = 167$, response rate = 73%), and interview (telephone), $N = 26$	Technical capability was an important user characteristic, giving a valuable contribution to the idea generation process.	B2C; online public access systems in Australian libraries (informants = library employees)	To explore the characteristics of innovation, innovators, and innovation sharing by library users of online public access systems in Australia
van Schaik (1999)	Questionnaire survey (mail), $N = 21$ ($N_0 = 105$, response rate = 20%)	Ordinary users could be involved for evaluating different smart card applications.	B2C; smart card services; respondents were university students at a Dutch university	To investigate how users can become involved in guiding system design at an early stage (e.g., can users specify and/or evaluate system functionality?)
Alam (2002)	Interviews with key informants, $N = 34$ (12 cases, 3 interviews per case [2 managers and 1 user])	This was exploratory. It describes 4 key elements of UI; objectives, stages, intensity, and modes of UI.	B2B; financial services; 12 cases	To investigate the process of UI in new B2B service development in the financial services industry
Christensen & Bower (1996)	Interviews, $N = 70$; informants were executives associated with the disk drive industry; also, other public statistical data from the disk drive industry were used	Listening to the customers can mislead the company. Users do not have sufficient knowledge regarding the technological state-of-the-art and so have insufficient knowledge to produce innovations.	B2B; 21 disk drive manufacturing companies	To present an explanatory model linking the demands from a firm's customers and the allocation of resources in technological innovation
Mullins & Sutherland (1998)	Interviews, in-depth retrospective, $N = 16$; informants had been personally and directly involved with managing introduction of new products	Involvement of prospective customers in idea generation and in the use of prototypes early in the new product development process helps the firm to uncover	B2C; one service firm in telecommunications; comparing the introduction of two products per informant (one successful and one not-so-successful product) (success = meeting	To explore how a service firm copes with the uncertainty of rapidly changing markets and to discuss implications for marketing and operating strategies

(Continued)

217

Table 12.1 Continued

Study	Method	Contribution to Understanding User Involvement	Empirical Base	Main Purpose of Study
		customer needs and market opportunities.	or exceeding sales and contribution targets)	
Shaw (1985)	Interviews with key informants	This was descriptive. Fully 26 of 34 projects were developed through multiple and continuous interaction with users, and 22 of these projects were successful.	B2B; 34 projects at 11 companies in medical equipment	To examine how innovating firms achieve "understanding of user needs" and "good internal and external communications" by user interaction
Veryzer (1998)	Interviews, in-depth; case study, multiple case comparison	Indications are that customers ought to be involved early on, even for discontinuous developments. Customer studies (e.g., ethnographical) may reveal latent user needs.	B2C and B2B; 7 new product development projects of various types (industries = electronics, advanced materials and chemicals, and equipment/mechanical systems)	To gain insight into customer research input for discontinuous new product development and the critical factors that influence customers' evaluation of really new products
Gustavsson & Hellgren (1984)	Experimental, 12 groups with 4 to 6 participants	It was discovered that the reviewers came up with suggestions of design improvements that are not currently used.	B2B; retailing; the reviewers were regional safety representatives ($N = 28$) and local safety representatives ($N = 31$)	To investigate whether the customer's audit of building blueprints could be held earlier and thereby increase the customer's influence on the final design
Norling (1993)	Experimental, field experiment, $N = 5$ (duration = 5 weeks)	The participants came up with a number of suggestions for improving the equipment and the services.	A group of 5 public care attendants	To evaluate how a specific user group could enhance the value when using mobile telephony
Urban & von Hippel (1988)	Experimental; 5 "lead users" created a new PC CAD concept that was evaluated in comparison with 3 commercial systems by users	The evaluators prefer the lead users' design in most aspects.	B2B; 5 lead user companies of CAD systems for design of printed circuit boards; evaluators were other users of CAD systems	To validate the "lead user method"

(Continued)

Table 12.1 Continued

Study	Method	Contribution to Understanding User Involvement	Empirical Base	Main Purpose of Study
	in a mail survey, $N = 71$ ($N_0 = 173$, response rate $= 41\%$)			
Anderson & Crocca (1993)	Observation, ethnography, and longitudinal, describing a "co-development" project; single case study	It is a mutual learning process for both users and engineers. Users learn the technology, and engineers learn the social context.	B2B; 2 organizations; electronic databases	To gain knowledge about co-development in general and about its social effects in particular
Hennestad (1999)	Observation, ethnography, and grounded theory; single case study	Interacting with customers generates more accurate knowledge concerning their needs and wishes.	B2C; one sales and servicing company of copying machines and related office equipment	To learn how to mobilize a company for customer orientation
Rothwell (1992)	Review of literature	One should advocate active customer participation and the use of leading-edge customers; they are early adopters on the diffusion curve.	No direct-indirect via literature	To pinpoint the critical factors for successful industrial innovation
Sinkula (1994)	Review of literature	Collaboration with customers contributes to the mutual and iterative learning about applications for new technologies. The knowledge can also play an important role in the sensemaking process.	None; purely theoretical	To elaborate on how market information can be used for organizational learning
Iansiti & MacCormack (1997)	Not specified	Beta testing and prototyping with users captures a rich understanding of needs and alternative technical solutions during project	B2C; no explicit, but conceptual illustrations (e.g., Netscape, Yahoo, Fiat [Punto], NetDynamic, Microsoft, Silicon Graphics)	To illustrate a new approach to product development, from traditional (sequential) to flexible (parallel), and to illustrate how the Web can

(Continued)

Table 12.1 Continued

Study	Method	Contribution to Understanding User Involvement	Empirical Base	Main Purpose of Study
		progression. This leads to shorter project times and better adapted products.		be used to capture user preferences
Prahalad & Ramaswamy (2000)	Not specified	Customers should be seen as a resource for the company. They co-create business value and serve as collaborators, co-developers, and competitors.	B2C and B2B; no explicit, but conceptual illustrations (e.g., Procter & Gamble, Microsoft, Cisco, Netscape, Yahoo, Philips)	To illustrate that customers play, and will continue to play, an active role in the creation of user value

NOTE: UI = user involvement; B2B = business-to-business; B2C = business-to-consumers.

summarizes some of the findings in user involvement. A closer look at the research literature reveals that the assertion of the benefit of user involvement is based mainly on the expression of positive attitudes by respondents from firms that have tried to involve customers in the development of new products. There seems to be a lack of evidence showing exactly how the individual user contributes to product innovation and whether the contribution is of value. Few studies have pinpointed the comparative advantage of involving users. An experimental research approach would offer this. In this chapter, the use of experiments in the area of product innovation research is explored within the context of user involvement. It is shown that experiments can be used to achieve actionable knowledge for both scholars and practitioners.

One goal of the chapter is to account for an experimental research design, the collaborative experimental design (CED), to study user involvement that has been empirically proven to produce useful knowledge for both scholars and practitioners. Another goal is to propose actions to be taken if scholars and managers succeed in bridging the academy-industry gap by using collaborative experiments.

In the remainder of the chapter, the concept of experiments is discussed. We discover that if experiments are to be useful (actionable) for practitioners, they must fulfill additional criteria. Accordingly, there is an academy-industry gap that must be bridged if collaborative experiments are to produce actionable knowledge. The research design, CED, is introduced as one such method that can bridge academy and industry. Then, experiences from a recent application of CED are provided. Finally, actions that should be taken to succeed with collaborative experiments are proposed for scholars and managers.

Experiments as a Means for Actionable Knowledge

The Concept of Experiment

People have used experiments to unveil new knowledge since ancient times. Children acquire much of their knowledge by trial and error. For scientific purposes, experimentation has been used in a more systematic form since the 13th century. During the 16th and 17th centuries, it was thought that the experimental method had a vital impact on the progress of science, for example, Isaac Newton's findings based on experiments (Lewis-Beck, 1993). The title of "father of *modern* experimentation" is often credited to Sir Ronald A. Fisher with his publication, *The Design of Experiments* (Fisher, 1935). In many scholarly disciplines, such as natural science and psychology, the experiment has a natural place in the researchers' assortment of methods. Yet in product innovation, research experiments seem to be limited. A review of the *Journal of Product Innovation Management,* one of the main scientific journals in product innovation research, reveals that the use of experiments has been very limited. In Volumes 16 to 18 (1999–2001), a total of 79 articles were published, of which 63 were based on empirical studies, and only 4 (6.3%) of these articles used an experimental method.[1] For comparison purposes, in the 2001 volume (Volume 86) of the *Journal of Applied Psychology,* 37 of 110 (33.6%) of the empirical studies published used an experimental method.

The basics of experiments are the manipulation (treatment) of one or more independent variables, where their effect (outcome) on one or more dependent variables is examined. In true (laboratory) experiments, it is possible to control the relationship between independent and dependent variables by controlling the experimental environment. Often, it is problematic or even impossible to apply real experiments in social science because the research is performed in the field and involves real people. Field researchers are normally guests at the sites where they work and, accordingly, are not in control of the environment. Therefore, the strict definition of experiments has been loosened up, and the concept of "quasi-experimentation" has been introduced (Campbell & Stanley, 1963; Cook & Campbell, 1979). Quasi-experiments are closely related to laboratory experiments in that both examine the relationship between *treatment* and *outcome.* Quasi-experiments, however, do not aspire to describe the complete causal system to achieve perfect prediction and understanding of the behaviors that occur within the system. The actual explanation of the causality may have several plausible alternatives, hence the importance of exploring alternative interpretations (Cook & Campbell, 1979, pp. 30–32). It is often necessary to do a triangulation (i.e., to complement the experiment with data from direct behavioral observations, face-to-face interviews, etc.) so that the most probable explanation can be captured (Cook, 1983, p. 84).

It should be noted that there are various categories of experiments described in the literature that can be "from the outside" or "from the inside." Outside/Inside alludes to the concept of dual inquiries introduced by Evered and Louis (1981). Experiments from the outside are here referred to as laboratory experiments or quasi-experiments, that is, controlled experimentation with a priori analytic categories. Several of the collaborative research inquiry approaches claim that experimental approaches are being used as well. These are experiments from the inside (e.g., action research), where the effect of an intervention is studied without any prior theory. In this chapter, "an experiment" refers to the traditional experiment from the outside.

Experiments and Actionable Knowledge

Practitioners need a different type of knowledge from that needed by academic researchers. Researchers are satisfied with just gaining "unique knowledge" that will advance the research frontier. Practitioners do not care much whether the knowledge gained is "new to the world" so long as it can be used for implementing successful actions in their companies. What, then, are the criteria for making research results usable as a basis for management action? The literature provides little guidance; therefore, we have to define them ourselves by envisioning the manager's situation. The deduction is made based on the context of user involvement and especially where users are involved to create and propose new product or service ideas.

First, the manager must be able to decide *whether* user involvement provides a positive contribution to the innovation process. It must be possible to compare user involvement in relation to non-user involvement. If user involvement makes a difference, some defined characteristics of the outcome should be significantly different when the users are involved relative to when they are not. Second, the research must explain the causality—*what, how,* and *why* user involvement contributes, that is, what the underlying factors and mechanisms are that decide whether user involvement is a failure or a success. Two "levels" of causality can be identified. The first is to establish *what* the contribution (outcome) is and *how* it comes about (treatment), for example, Treatment A will cause B. Knowing this can actually be "good enough" for the practitioners, but sometimes the underlying reasons need to be established, for example, *why* Treatment A causes B. This is essential to determining whether the findings should be generalized for other contexts.

In summary, to produce actionable knowledge regarding user involvement, the research should meet the following criteria. First, it needs to be established *whether* user involvement gives a positive contribution. Second, the research must also explain *what* the contribution is and *how* it can be achieved. The third criterion, which is desirable but not always necessary, is to explain *why* the user involvement contributes.

In the next section, a research design that fulfills the criteria for being actionable, CED, is described. It has been developed within the CuDIT[2] research project, where overall research questions have asked (a) *what* user involvement, during the early phases of new service innovation, can contribute from a business perspective and (b) *how* it should be done in an auspicious way.

CED: An Experimental Design for Actionable Knowledge

The research design, CED, emulates a realistic way of involving users in the innovation process. The basic design is constituted by experimental trials complemented with *observations* and *interviews*. Due primarily to the lack of total control, it cannot be classified as a true experiment; an adequate designation would be a *quasi-experiment*. As described by Cook and Campbell (1979), a quasi-experiment can be manifested in many ways, spanning from laboratory settings to passive observations. CED is,

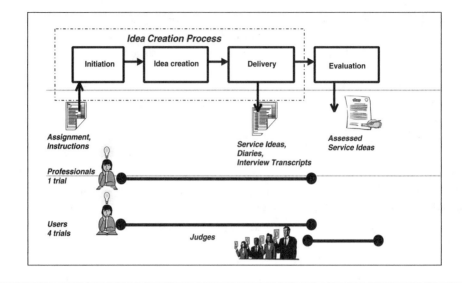

Figure 12.1   Outline of Research Design: The CuDIT Study—An Example of Collaborative Experimental Design

however, more of the true laboratory form, categorized as a "multiple-group posttest design" (Spector, 1993, p. 38). The user involvement is varied in the trials by using different types of users and different procedures for involvement. One of the trials is a reference (control) trial where no user involvement takes place. By comparing the various trials, the effect of user involvement can be determined. Process data are captured during the trials in participants' diaries and afterward in face-to-face interviews.

The design is described in detail by accounting for its implementation in the CuDIT project. The empirical base in CuDIT was the idea generation process of new mobile services based on SMS[3] using five different trials. University students—one of the most common SMS user groups—constituted the users. The research design consists of four stages—*initiation, idea creation, delivery,* and *evaluation*—as outlined in Figure 12.1.

Initiation

At the initiation meeting, the trial groups were gathered and the study was introduced. A common yet individual assignment was given to each participant. The assignment for the user groups was to create service ideas that would provide an added value. The professionals, on the other hand, were instructed to come up with ideas for services that they thought would add value for the user groups. By these various formulations, all groups tried to satisfy the same target group, thereby making the outcome (service ideas) comparable. The services were intended to use an application platform,

Unified Services, which was a converter between SMS messages in GSM and http calls on the Internet. The mobile phone could access information on the Internet by sending and receiving SMS messages.

Giving out instructions for experiments with humans is a vital yet difficult part. Holt (1995) argues that many experimental results lack validity due to poor instructions. He emphasizes that much care needs to be taken when formulating the instructions for an experiment. Therefore, the instructions and assignment for the experiment were given in both verbal and written forms. A diary was handed out to the participants to document the ideas, as well as the activities, that triggered the idea creation. The diary (process) data could be used not only for gaining a deeper understanding of the individual idea creation process but also for triangulation. Following are excerpts (translated from Swedish) of the assignment and instructions given to the users:

[*Assignment*]

Your assignment is to create—using the knowledge you have gained of Unified Services along with a mobile phone—services that produce an added value for you. Put simply, you are going to create one or more services that you perceive as important. You must be able to describe how your solution creates an added value for you. The solution can, for instance, facilitate information retrieval or create a beneficial experience of some kind. Because you are the one who decides, there is no right or wrong here.

[*Instruction*]

It is important that you make notes in the diary of *how your ideas emerged*. That is, where did you get the idea? Was it from someone you have worked with or been in discussion with? Did the idea arise through association when you saw or heard something? The purpose of the narrative is to enable us to understand the originating process of your ideas.

To provide the participants with a sense of how these services might work, they were given access to approximately 10 implemented services. To use and test these, the participants were equipped with a mobile telephone (Ericsson 1018S), a chat board,[4] and a prepaid phone card (Telia GSM Refill) with a value of approximately 25 Euros ($29).[5] All participants received hands-on training on how to use the equipment by testing the preimplemented services. To stimulate the submission of ideas, the ideas remained the intellectual property of the "creators," and an award of 80 Euros was to be given for the best service idea in each trial. The participants could choose to work alone or collaborate with others. If a participant chose to collaborate, it was to be noted in his or her diary. Each individual was expected to produce at least one service idea.

The professional service developers underwent the same initiation procedure except that their submitted ideas became the intellectual property of the company. The standard policy for job-related ideas created by the employees of the company was upheld. However, the company had a regulated payment system for ideas falling under the protection of patent laws. If an idea was patented by the company, the employee would be rewarded with approximately 2,400 Euros or more. So, there was incentive for the professionals to create valuable ideas.

To obtain individual background data, the participants completed a form requiring personal data such as age, experience with mobile telephony, and experience using SMS. In addition, each participant underwent three tests to obtain specific personality characteristics. These were used to detect interaction effects due to personal propensity of the participants.

Idea Creation

The *idea creation period* of the study lasted for 12 days. The communication between trial management and the participants was kept to a minimum. Technical support was available via e-mail or phone. Only questions regarding technical problems or practical use of the telephones and services were addressed. Approximately 20 support questions were received from the four user groups.

The user trials were set up to emulate various ways of involving users. One trial was a "reference" where no user involvement took place. The various setups used are described briefly here.

Setup A (12 persons), "Professionals," consisted of professional service developers who were randomly recruited from Telia Mobile, a Swedish mobile telephony operator. All of them came from an R&D unit responsible for developing new nonvoice mobile services, that is, services based on SMS, WAP, and GPRS.[6] Their professional experience in the field varied from 1 to 10 years. The professionals were instructed not to interact with any of the students in the target group so as to emulate a real work setting where experts try to imagine the users' wants and needs without interacting.

Setup B (16 persons), "Technically Skilled Users," was composed of students in the second through fourth grades at the computer science program. Because the group possessed skills in computer programming (Java language), it was possible to emulate the employment of user toolkits for innovation, promoted by von Hippel and Thomke (Thomke & von Hippel, 2002; von Hippel, 2001). A professional service developer gave a practical introduction to the toolkit (approximately 2 hours). Following the introduction, six computers were available for testing and consultation of the service developer. The training also included a basic refresher course (approximately 3 hours) in Java. The output from this group was expected to be of the same format as that from the other groups. The difference was that these group members had the opportunity to test their ideas by implementing them into working prototypes.

Setup C (19 persons), "Ordinary Users," meant that the participants were supposed to represent nontechnical skilled people. The group was represented by university students in nontechnical study programs such as social science, teacher training, and business administration.

Setup D (20 persons), "Consulting Ordinary Users," came from the same sample of students as did Group C; the persons were randomly assigned to either Group C or Group D. In Trial D, the participants (in groups of 4 or 5 persons), on two occasions, met a professional service designer for consultation during 1- to 2-hour sessions. To emulate a situation where the ownership of the ideas is not in the hands of the company, the professionals were instructed to take a rather passive role and not to reveal any ideas that might come up unless they would have done so in a real-life situation. The information given by the professionals was, therefore, usually limited to informing the users whether their ideas were technically feasible or not or whether their proposed ideas already existed. This approach gave the participating users the opportunity for more individualized learning of the technical possibilities of the system during the innovation process. The discussions with experts could also be expected to facilitate the users' ability to articulate their ideas.

Setup E (17 persons), "Creativity Trained Ordinary Users," consisted of the same type of people as did Setups C and D. There was, however, an important difference: This group had been educated, before entry into the experiment, in different creativity techniques such as brainstorming, slip writing, random input, and "six thinking hats."

Delivery

Following the 12-day idea creation period, a meeting was held at which the *service ideas* and *diaries* were submitted. The service ideas were written descriptions in a predefined format, hence a first conceptualization of the service. The format included the date of idea creation, the developer's name, the name of the service idea, a short functional description, and the intended user value of the service. The five groups produced a total of 429 ideas for new services, with 55 coming from the 12 professional developers and 374 coming from the 72 users. All participants were also interviewed within the subsequent 2 weeks. These interviews were semistructured in nature.

Evaluation

After all trials were concluded, the service ideas were collected and assessed using the conceptual assessment technique (CAT) proposed by Amabile (1996). CAT uses a panel of independent judges to evaluate various dimensions of different "designs" (p. 45). The dependent variable assessed was *quality of the produced ideas,* which for the CuDIT project could be divided into three dimensions: *originality, user value,* and *producibility.* A total of 13 judges, representing both users and experts, were used for the assessment of ideas. One dimension was evaluated at a time. The judges made their assessments independently of each other, not knowing who the inventor of each idea was. Each idea was classified on a scale from 1 to 10. For the three dimensions (originality, user value, and producibility), a score of 1 represented the least original, least valuable, and hardest to produce; a score of 10 corresponded to the most original, most valuable, and easiest to produce.

Summary of the Design Principles

CED emulates, or in fact could be, a "real user involvement." Two or more trials are used, of which one should constitute no user involvement, thereby enabling the determination of *whether* user involvement produces a different outcome. An assessment procedure yields a relative ranking of the generated proposals. By using different setups for the user involvement trials, conclusions can be drawn regarding *what* the contribution is and *how* different ways of involving users affect the outcome. The experimental design is supplemented with diaries and semistructured interviews to enable deeper insights into the contribution of user involvement. The criteria for producing actionable knowledge are, therefore, theoretically fulfilled. This was also the case when applying the method in practice, as demonstrated in the next section.

Experiences From Applying CED_____

The aim of this chapter is to discuss research design. Some of the findings are discussed briefly to illustrate that CED created actionable knowledge. For the interested reader, there are more detailed accountings of the results available (e.g., Kristensson, Magnusson, & Matthing, 2002; Magnusson, 2003, in press).

Producing Actionable Knowledge

The research design has, within the CuDIT project, proven its ability to create actionable knowledge regarding the contribution of user involvement. From the trial comparisons, it was found that the users' ideas were deemed to be more innovative and to have a higher estimated user value than the professional developers' ideas (Kristensson Magnusson, & Matthing, 2002; Magnusson, in press). However, the users' proposals were harder to realize into commercial services (Magnusson, in press). The trial with user toolkits (Setup B) showed that the availability of toolkits had a negative effect on the outcome (Magnusson, 2003).

These findings fulfill the criteria of deciding *whether* user involvement provides a contribution. They also address *what* the contributions are and *how* they can be achieved. The data from the diaries and interviews can enhance the understanding of *why* users do or do not contribute. For instance, the negative effect in the originality of the ideas when letting the users consult the professionals was explained at least partially in the process data. At one of the consultation meetings, a user told the expert that he had come up with an excellent idea that he thought would be very useful for the expert. Nevertheless, the user had dropped the idea because, as he said, "Although it was a superb idea for me as a user, I could not imagine how you [the company] would be able to capitalize on it, so I dropped it." The face-to-face meetings seemed to change the focus of the generated ideas from creating added value for the user to creating profitability for the company, thereby explaining the drop in originality.

Some Unanticipated Findings

The CuDIT study also produced unanticipated yet valuable findings. For instance, a discrepancy was discovered between the company's and the users' comprehension of what a service is. Many users did not differentiate between the telecommunications service itself and the equipment (the mobile telephone) used to access the service. This was manifested in proposals to equip the phone with extra tools such as a bottle opener, an alcohol meter, a radio, and so forth (Magnusson, in press). A practical implication could be that mobile service providers ought to cooperate with mobile telephony equipment manufacturers to design user-adapted offerings.

Another discovery was the limitations of written service idea proposals. The posttrial interviews showed that many of the written ideas ought to be reinterpreted given that a written description is not always sufficient for understanding the true intention of the creator.

A mutual learning process that is difficult to estimate occurred among the participants. The users involved had the opportunity to enhance their competence concerning mobile telephony services, thereby enabling them to better use these services in the future. Several of the user participants expressed their gratitude that a company was interested in how to create better services for them—a goodwill effect for the participating company. The professional service developers gained new unexpected knowledge regarding the users, especially those who participated in Setup D (Consulting Ordinary Users) with direct user interaction. Also, reading and reviewing the users' service idea proposals and diaries provided a new understanding of the targeted users' needs and wishes.

Discussion and Implications for Practice

Using Experiments in Collaborative Research

Although the basics of experiments appear to be relatively simple on the surface, they are quite complex to accomplish in practice. An essential ingredient for successful experiments is systematic planning, which leads to a thorough design. It is very hard to go back and repair mistakes made in the research design. Holt (1995) uses computer programming as a metaphor for describing the problem: "A seemingly small error can render the data useless or difficult to interpret" (p. 355).

The fact that experiments have rarely been used can itself be an impediment; if no one else is using experimental studies, it is hard to develop competence regarding how to design them. In fact, it was by coincidence that I came in contact with experimental studies. The experiments were triggered by meeting another researcher with experimental psychology research expertise.

Experiments may be critiqued for not being "real," so that it is hard to draw general conclusions from them (Mullins, Forlani, & Walker, 1999). This can be a problem for laboratory experiments because they are isolated from the external world. CED is, however, not a laboratory experiment. From a practitioner's point of view, it does not need to be distinguished from the "ordinary work." A problem occurs, however, because researchers are not normally invited to the companies. Researchers are accepted at "arm's length"—interviewing, sending questionnaires, and even passively "sneaking" around in the company doing ethnography. However, allowing a researcher inside the company to work actively with its personnel and/or customers is not yet commonly accepted. The same reluctance is probably true for many researchers.

CED and Collaborative Research

CED differs in many aspects from the mainstream research designs normally used in the area. The dominating research methods for investigating user involvement have been mail surveys and interviews (see Table 12.1). In these, data are collected based on reflections and so capture something (normally successful) from the past that gets interpreted and reported by one or several informants. The researcher analyzes the data into conclusions and findings and then reports back to the surveyed companies either directly or by publishing scientific articles. If the study is based on a limited number of cases, the results might be directly applicable for practitioners. However, many of the studies are based on large samples of companies and even from varying industries, thereby creating aggregated results that are likely harder to use as a basis for action. Another impediment is the large time lag between the study of the event and the publication of the results, and this can make the results irrelevant.

CED collects data from episodes in *real time* without intermediaries. This implies active participation from both academics and practitioners; their actions are performed concurrently and are virtually inseparable. From the researchers' viewpoint, CED is a semicontrolled scientific experiment for collecting data. On the other hand, the practitioners can see the experiment as a pilot study trying different forms of user involvement, that is, something that should—or at least could—be done without researchers' interference. Thus, practitioners can attain usable experiences *during* the trials in real time.

An obvious benefit for practitioners is the *directly applicable* results. For instance, the CuDIT study produced and assessed 429 new service ideas, of which 374 came from users. The company could test various ways of involving users and then draw conclusions regarding their goodness. Knowledge about the studied user groups' needs and wishes was gained.

CED addresses *particular* problems, thereby generating answers that are readily applicable, at least for the participating company. In addition, because the results are grounded in a particular empirical reality, it probably makes it easier for nonparticipant practitioners to interpret and transfer the results into other contexts.

This chapter also suggests that academics' interaction with practitioners will likely generate a better understanding of the practical problems in the studied companies when using CED, thereby facilitating the identification of potential future research questions relevant for practitioners. CED opens up avenues for getting access to a new kind of data. It generates real-time empirical data in an area where much of the literature is founded on anecdotal evidence and normative reasoning relying on retrospective sensemaking (Brown & Eisenhardt, 1995, p. 353). CED complies with the recommendation of Evered and Louis (1981) by simultaneously using the approaches of research from the outside (experiments and interviews) and research from the inside (interaction and process diaries) (p. 392). Experiments can test a priori theories and manifest casual predictions. The process data collected in CED can be used to discover novel, not-yet-theorized knowledge as well as to deepen the understanding of *why* the results occurred in the experiments, thereby giving a causal explanation. Table 12.2 compares CED with some alternative research methods.

Conclusion

This chapter has illustrated the use of CED for investigating user involvement in innovation. It can, of course, also be used in other contexts where the performance of various alternative processes should be compared.

The aggregated "inside and outside" nature of CED gives it unique features. Not only does CED bridge the academy-industry gap, but the two parties are even *integrated*. Researchers and practitioners are together experimenting in a systematic manner, trying out various ways of involving users but from two different perspectives. From the researchers' perspective, it produces knowledge for *understanding* and *explaining* the contribution from users when involving them in service innovation. From the practitioners' perspective, it produces *knowledge for action*. Even more interesting, it *induces action*. The actual research method implies that "real" actions must be taken to conduct the research.

Table 12.2 Collaborative Experimental Design Versus Other Research

	Collaborative Experimental Design	Questionnaires	Interviews	Laboratory Experiments	Observation (passive)	Researcher Intervention Methods
A. Scope of research	Particular	General	Particular or general	Particular	Particular	Particular
B. Time for data acquisition	Live and in retrospect	In retrospect	In retrospect	Live	Live	Live
C. Mode of data acquisition	Direct and intermediate	Intermediate	Intermediate	Direct	Direct	Direct
D. Researcher's position	Outside and inside	Outside	Outside	Outside	Inside	Inside
E. Comparing alternatives	●	◉	◉	●	○	○
F. Causal prediction	●	○	○	●	○	◉
G. Causal explanation	◉	○	◉	○	●	●
H. Theory testing	●	◉	○	●	○	○
I. Theory building	◉	○	◉	○	●	◉
J. Process accounts	◉	—	◉	○	●	●
K. Control of process studied	◉	—	—	●	○	◉
L. Collaboration (academics and practitioners)	●	○	◉	○	◉	●

— = Normally not
○ = To a limited extent
◉ = To a moderate extent
● = To a major extent

A. Is the studied process a particular one or on a more general level?
B, C. Are data collected directly live or in retrospect using intermediates?
D. Is the researcher inside or outside the process studied?
E. Does the method enable comparisons of different variants of the process (e.g., different types of user involvement)?
F. Can the method establish a causal prediction (if A, then B)?
G. Does the method generate an underlying causal explanation (why B when A)?
H, I. To what degree can the method support theory testing and theory building?
J. Are process accounts collected during the research?
K. Can the researcher control the process during the study?
L. To what degree must academics and practitioners collaborate to use the method?

232

Although CED can produce actionable knowledge, this does not imply that it is automatically transformed into actions. It is recommended that the experimental trials be linked to "real" processes in the company. For example, if user involvement in product innovation is explored, the resulting ideas should be taken care of directly when the trial is ended. This was not the case in the CuDIT project described in this chapter, and so it delayed the use of the results. Another important issue is clarifying the intellectual property rights among the participating parties; that is, who owns what?

CED is definitely outside the mainstream not only in the area of product innovation management research but also in the area of traditional collaborative research. Nevertheless, researchers aiming for bridging the academy-industry gap must dare to try new ways of conducting research. It is hoped that endeavors such as the CuDIT project will pave the way for others to try collaborative experimental approaches.

Epilogue

A fortunate incident occurred during the writing of this chapter. On October 9, 2002, the Royal Swedish Academy of Sciences announced that the Bank of Sweden Prize in Economic Sciences in Memory of Alfred Nobel for the year 2002 was to be shared between Daniel Kahneman (Princeton University) and Vernon L. Smith (George Mason University). Smith's award stemmed from his "having established laboratory experiments as a tool in empirical economic analysis, especially in the study of alternative market mechanisms." This acknowledgment helps to establish experimental research methods as a legitimate and respectable discovery process in economics. It is hoped that the same will happen for product innovation research as well.

Notes

1. These were Mullins, Forlani, and Walker (1999); Dahan and Srinivasan (2000); Boone, Lemon, and Staelin (2001); and Kim and Chhajed (2001).

2. CuDIT is an acronym for customer-driven IT (information technology) development. I have conducted the project in cooperation with a doctoral candidate in psychology, Per Kristensson, and a doctoral candidate in business administration, Jonas Matthing, both from the Service Research Center at Karlstad University in Sweden.

3. SMS is an abbreviation for short message service, a technology for sending and receiving text messages using mobile phones. SMS is defined within the GSM specification. GSM is a pan-European standard for mobile telephony. The system was introduced in Europe in 1992 but is today found all over the world.

4. A chat board is a little keyboard that can be plugged into a mobile phone to simplify the input of text messages.

5. The cost of sending an SMS was 0.15 Euros ($.17).

6. WAP (wireless application protocol) is an industry de facto standard. It is a protocol that defines how to access Internet pages directly from a mobile phone. GPRS (general packet radio service) is a standard for nonvoice communications across a mobile telephone network. The maximum speed is 171.2 kilobits per second.

References

Alam, I. (2002). An exploratory investigation of user involvement in new service development. *Journal of the Academy of Marketing Science, 30,* 250–261.

Amabile, T. M. (1996). *Creativity in context.* Boulder, CO: Westview.

Anderson, W. L., & Crocca, W. T. (1993). Engineering practice and co-development of product prototypes. *Communications of the ACM, 36*(4), 49–56.

Athaide, G. A., Meyers, P. W., & Wilemon, D. L. (1996). Seller-buyer interaction during the commercialization of technological process innovations. *Journal of Product Innovation Management, 13,* 406–421.

Boone, D. S., Lemon, K. N., & Staelin, R. (2001). The impact of firm introductory strategies on consumers' perceptions of future product introductions and purchase decisions. *Journal of Product Innovation Management, 18*(2), 96–109.

Brown, S. L., & Eisenhardt, K. M. (1995). Product development: Past research, present findings, and future directions. *Academy of Management Review, 20,* 343–378.

Campbell, A. J., & Cooper, R. G. (1999). Do customer partnerships improve new product success rates? *Industrial Marketing Management, 28,* 507–519.

Campbell, D. T., & Stanley, J. C. (1963). *Experimental and quasi-experimental designs for research.* Boston: Houghton Mifflin.

Christensen, C. M., & Bower, J. (1996). Customer power, strategic investment, and the failure of leading firms. *Strategic Management Journal, 17,* 197–218.

Cook, T. D. (1983). Quasi-experimentation: Its ontology, epistemology, and methodology. In G. Morgan (Ed.), *Beyond method: Strategies for social research* (pp. 79–94). Beverly Hills, CA: Sage.

Cook, T. D., & Campbell, D. T. (1979). *Quasi-experimentation: Design and analysis issues for field settings.* Chicago: Rand McNally.

Dahan, E., & Srinivasan, V. (2000). The predictive power of Internet-based product concept testing using visual depiction and animation. *Journal of Product Innovation Management, 17*(2), 99–109.

Evered, R., & Louis, M. R. (1981). Alternative perspectives in the organizational sciences: "Inquiry from the inside" and "inquiry from the outside." *Academy of Management Review, 6,* 385–395.

Fisher, R. A. (1935). *The design of experiments.* London: Oliver & Boyd.

Gales, L., & Mansour-Cole, D. (1995). User involvement in innovation projects. *Journal of Engineering and Technology Management, 12*(1–2), 77–109.

Gupta, A. K., & Wilemon, D. L. (1990). Accelerating the development of technology-based new products. *California Management Review, 32*(2), 24–44.

Gustavsson, P., & Hellgren, B. (1984). *Beslut och påverkan: En studie av de komplexa beslutsprocesser som bestämmer detaljhandelsanställdas arbetsmiljö i ett stadsdelscentrum* (Decision and influence: A study of complex decision processes determining the work environment in stores in a city center). Ph.D. thesis, University of Linköping, Sweden.

Hennestad, B. W. (1999). Infusing the organisation with customer knowledge. *Scandinavian Journal of Management, 15*(1), 17–41.

Holt, C. A. (1995). Industrial organization: A survey of laboratory research. In J. H. Kagel & A. E. Roth (Eds.), *The handbook of experimental economics* (pp. 349–443). Princeton, NJ: Princeton University Press.

Iansiti, M., & MacCormack, A. (1997). Developing products on Internet time. *Harvard Business Review, 75*(5), 108–117.

Kim, K., & Chhajed, D. (2001). An experimental investigation of valuation change due to commonality in vertical product line extension. *Journal of Product Innovation Management, 18*, 219–230.

Kristensson, P., Magnusson, P. R., & Matthing, J. (2002). Users as a hidden resource for creativity: Findings from an experimental study of user involvement. *Creativity and Innovation Management, 11*(1), 55–61.

Lewis-Beck, M. S. (Ed.). (1993). *Experimental design and methods.* Newbury Park, CA: Sage.

Magnusson, P. (2003). *Using users for innovation: The impact of involving users in service innovation.* Ph.D. thesis, Stockholm School of Economics, Sweden.

Magnusson, P. R. (in press). Benefits of involving users in service innovation. *European Journal of Innovation Management.*

Martin, C. R., & Horne, D. A. (1995). Level of success inputs for service innovations in the same firm. *International Journal of Service Industry Management, 6*(4), 40–56.

Morrison, P. D., Roberts, J. H., & von Hippel, E. (2000). Determinants of user innovation and innovation sharing in a local market. *Management Science, 46*, 1513–1527.

Mullins, J. W., Forlani, D., & Walker, O. C., Jr. (1999). Effects of organizational and decision-maker factors on new product risk taking. *Journal of Product Innovation Management, 16*, 282–294.

Mullins, J. W., & Sutherland, D. J. (1998). New product development in rapidly changing markets: An exploratory study. *Journal of Product Innovation Management, 15*, 224–236.

Norling, P. (1993). *Tjänstekonstruktion* (Service design). Ph.D. thesis, University of Stockholm, Sweden.

Prahalad, C. K., & Ramaswamy, V. (2000). Co-opting customer competence. *Harvard Business Review, 78*(1), 79–87.

Rothwell, R. (1992). Successful industrial innovation: Critical factors for the 1990s. *R&D Management, 22*, 221–239.

Shaw, B. (1985). The role of the interaction between the user and the manufacturer in medical equipment innovation. *R&D Management, 15*, 283–292.

Sinkula, J. M. (1994). Market information process and organizational learning. *Journal of Marketing, 58*(1), 35–45.

Spector, P. E. (1993). Research designs. In M. S. Lewis-Beck (Ed.), *Experimental design and methods* (pp. 1-74). Newbury Park, CA: Sage.

Thomke, S., & von Hippel, E. (2002). Customers as innovators. *Harvard Business Review, 80*(4), 74–81.

Urban, G. L., & von Hippel, E. (1988). Lead user analyses for the development of new industrial products. *Management Science, 34*, 569–582.

van Schaik, P. (1999). Involving users in the specification of functionality using scenarios and model-based evaluation. *Behaviour & Information Technology, 18*, 455–466.

Veryzer, R. W. J. (1998). Key factors affecting customer evaluation of discontinuous new products. *Journal of Product Innovation Management, 15*(2), 136–150.

von Hippel, E. (1977). Has a customer already developed your next product? *Sloan Management Review, 18*(2), 63–74.

von Hippel, E. (1986). Lead users: A source of novel product concepts. *Management Science, 32*, 791–805.

von Hippel, E. (1988). *The sources of innovation.* New York: Oxford University Press.

von Hippel, E. (2001). User toolkits for innovation. *Journal of Product Innovation Management, 18*, 247–257.

13

Managing Organizational Creativity

Mats Sundgren and Alexander Styhre

A n organization's capability for innovation is an important competitive advantage (Brown & Eisenhardt, 1995; Dougherty, 1999; Leonard-Barton, 1995). Underlying innovation is, among other things, *organizational creativity*, that is, the ability to create ideas that can result in new products. To some extent, the development of new products is based on organizational creativity. In contemporary society, often called a postindustrial, knowledge-intensive society (Bell, 1973), it is often recommended that organizations pay greater attention to their capability for innovation. Because knowledge and resources are distributed among a great number of institutions, organizations, and actors in industries, organizational creativity draws on a diversity of sources both internal and external to the firm. In a postindustrial society, knowledge is created through a number of novel associations among corporations, institutions, universities, and research centers (Gibbons et al., 1994). Thus, organizational creativity is a complex matter; to some extent, it breaks down boundaries between inside the firm and outside the firm (cf. Ashkenas, Ulrich, Jick, & Kerr, 1995), and it emerges from a number of sources.

This chapter discusses organizational creativity in a major, multinational pharmaceutical company, AstraZeneca. The pharmaceutical industry is renowned for its intense research and development (R&D), discovery operations, and new product development. In general, the pharmaceutical

AUTHORS' NOTE: We express our gratitude to AstraZeneca, which made our research on organizational creativity possible. The research projects and findings presented in this chapter are the results of a truly collaborative effort involving interactions with many colleagues, researchers, and managers at AstraZeneca, and we are grateful to them. In particular, we thank Sverker Ljunghall, Elof Dimenäs, and Barry Furr, not only for support but also for challenging and interesting discussions.

industry invests considerable amounts in R&D, and the potential gains from a new registered drug are also substantial (Powell, 1998; Yeoh & Roth, 1999). Blockbuster drugs, such as Losec and Prozac, will generate billions of U.S. dollars for their mother companies (Koretz & Lee, 1998). The capacity to think creatively is a key success factor in the pharmaceutical industry (Henderson, 1994). Without the capacity to continuously select and develop new compounds and *candidate drugs*[1], pharmaceutical companies will gradually lose their competitive advantages. Thus, the management of discovery and organizational creativity is of great importance to the pharmaceutical industry.

The development of a pharmaceutical product can be divided into three major research and development processes: discovery, development, and product support and life cycle management. The actual R&D process is an extended task, often running for more than 10 years, that is complex and costly. An additional level of complexity can sometimes be added to this, as many pharmaceutical companies have merged and formed large global R&D organizations with multiple research sites in various locations. Furthermore, there is a demand to be effective and innovative. In the context of pharmaceutical R&D at AstraZeneca, we define organizational creativity as "acts in which new ideas and new ways of solving problems emerge through a motivation-driven collaborative effort by promoting dialogue involving multiple domains of scientific knowledge in order to produce value for the organization's mission and market."

This definition of creativity can be seen as a synthesis of aspects taken from the academician's and practitioner's perspectives. The practitioner's perspective has a more specific customer- and market-driven focus, emphasizing the dimensions of the actual work and value. The academician's perspective emphasizes the aspects of novelty, diversity, and motivation, generally treating creativity as an unbounded enterprise. The two perspectives also reflect the idea that creativity in organizations involves both divergent and convergent thought and action before it becomes effective. At its best, this type of organizational creativity should be interpreted as a normal part of organizational life. Finally, it emphasizes that creativity is not solely about delivering new candidate drugs, but it includes all of the activities in the pharmaceutical industry, new drug development activities, strategic management decisions, and human resource management practices. The definition of creativity is, therefore, aimed at serving as a holistic concept composed of a multiplicity of activities.

The study at AstraZeneca was done between the fall of 2000 and the spring of 2002. Its aim was to examine the company's capacity to manage organizational creativity and provide insight into, know-how on, and models for how organizational creativity can be managed successfully at AstraZeneca. From a methodological point of view, the study was based on the use of an insider/outsider research team (Bartunek & Louis, 1996), where one executive Ph.D. candidate at AstraZeneca served as an insider and three academic researchers served as outside experts. In addition to this research team, executives at AstraZeneca were involved as discussion partners in project formation, research design, analysis, and validation of emerging patterns. As a whole, the research efforts were strongly tied to the interests and concerns of the company, making it possible to explicitly relate the very elusive and epistemologically complex notion of creativity to concrete problems and opportunities in the company. This chapter suggests that it is possible to manage creativity in the organization as an organizational resource because creativity is an outcome of socially embedded processes that can be positively affected by managerial decisions and leadership practices. Rather than seeing creativity as some extraordinary talent or haphazard event, organizational creativity is conceived of as an integrated system of capabilities aimed at producing new ideas that, in the current case, can become candidate drugs and eventually registered drugs.

The Notion of Organizational Creativity

The terms *creative* and *innovative* often tend to overlap in much of the research and management literature. A distinction can be made between them by treating creativity as the generation of ideas for new and improved ways of doing things and treating innovation as the implementation of those ideas in practice (West & Richards, 1999). In general, creativity is perceived in highly individual terms and as something that expresses itself fully only in nonwork areas. It is seen as a process that can be facilitated by ways of working and thinking (Williamson, 2001). Innovation, on the other hand, is often associated and sometimes confused with the related concept of creativity (Ford, 1996). Woodman, Sawyer, and Griffin (1993) refer to creativity as a subset of innovation. Amabile (1988) views creativity as a necessary *precursor* to innovation, defining creativity as the production of novel and useful ideas by an individual or a small group of individuals working together. Creativity can be defined as the ability to produce work that is both novel (e.g., original, unexpected) and, in some sense, valuable or appropriate (e.g., useful, adaptive as concerns task constraints) (Sternberg, 1999). According to Cropley (1999), creativity can be defined as the production of relevant and effective novelty. Innovation can then be seen more as the process of the implementation of creative ideas (Shani & Lau, 2000; West & Richards, 1999).

The research on creativity has emerged from many academic disciplines, including psychology, organizational behavior, education, history, and sociology. The vast research literature on creativity is often either person centered or focused primarily on specific aspects of creativity. These specific aspects have been thoroughly researched and have included primarily four distinct aspects. First, the *creative person* includes personal properties, traits, and behavior in terms of the ability to generate new ideas. Second, the *creative process* includes cognitive variables such as thinking styles, skills, and problem-solving techniques. Third, the *creative product* deals with aspects of evaluating what defines creative output (e.g., originality, relevance, usefulness, complexity, how pleasing the output is). Fourth, the *creative place* investigates various aspects of cultural, environmental, and/ or working climate factors in the organizational context (e.g., Amabile, 1999; Boden, 1996; Ekvall, 1987; Eysenck, 1996). Much research has been influenced by the "romance of creativity" and may oversimplify explanations of events and attribute great creative achievements to single individuals. This fascination is not well suited to understanding and promoting creativity in organizations. Another aspect of "traditional" creativity research is that the various distinct foci of creativity do not provide an understanding of how creativity works in an organizational context. According to Ford (1995a), creativity is not an inherent quality of a person, process, product, or place; rather, it is a domain-specific social construction that is legitimized by judges serving as gatekeepers to a particular domain. Furthermore, most of the research on creativity pays no attention to organizational or professional concerns (Ford, 1995a). Thus, an important step in understanding creativity in an organizational context is to take a more holistic approach and use the concept of *organizational creativity*.

A useful definition of organizational creativity is offered by Woodman and colleagues (1993): "the creation of a valuable, useful new product, service, idea, procedure, or process by individuals working together in a complex social system" (p. 295). Organizational creativity can also refer to the extent to which the organization has instituted formal approaches and tools and has provided resources to encourage meaningful behavior in the organization (Bharadwaj & Menon, 2000). Thus, organizational creativity can be seen as a phenomenon that is structurally embedded in the organization rather than as some innate quality of a few extraordinary individuals, as Jacob (1998) insists, emphasizing that organizational creativity is something more than a collection of creative individuals. To be able to acknowledge the context-specific aspects of creativity in organizations, creativity must be articulated in terms of the organization's mission and cannot represent only novel acts. It must produce value relative to an organization's mission and market, meaning that creativity in an organization is valuable only if it is implemented in such a way that it is adapted to the organization's culture, values, and processes (Gioia, 1995). When seen from a practitioner's perspective, these aspects fall into a definition of organizational creativity in which it includes acts of envisioning, demonstrating, and applying cost-effective methods for the purpose of eliminating technological problems and providing significant and profitable technology-based opportunities in target areas of business activity (Jones, 1995). This notion of organizational creativity is distinctive enough to merit separate research, but it is also sufficiently related to the notion of creativity at the level of the individual to be enriched by studies undertaken to that end.

An important aspect of creative action in organizations deals with the likelihood of its acceptance and with evaluation, decision making, and the realization of new ideas. Ford (1995b) refers to this as the *competitive advantage principle of creativity,* which implies that creative actions are not likely to emerge unless they hold a competitive advantage over old familiar actions. This principle addresses not only the challenge and risk taking of engaging creativity in organizations but also the task of circumventing existing behavior patterns. We believe that the concept of organizational creativity deals specifically with three important aspects in an organization. First, it is not difficult to see that organizational creativity is an important factor for strategic competition in the future. Second, organizational creativity in the organization involves a flexibility and openness toward new ideas, attitudes, and thoughts. This flexibility in the organization is a core aspect of promoting some "creative state of mind" to reduce conformism and imitative and mechanistic behavior in the organizational culture. That the effects of conformism are especially important in scientific research is noted by David Bohm, a physicist who emphasizes the importance of scientific research as "being aware of the ease with which the mind slips comfortably back into this age-old pattern. The act of seeing this deeply and not merely verbally or intellectually is also the act in which originality and creativity can be born" (Bohm, 2000, p. 26). Third, organizational creativity is dependent on motivation.

Organizational Creativity and Motivation

Several studies suggest that motivation is an important component of organizational creativity. This notion derives from the *intrinsic motivation principle* of creativity, which suggests that people will be most creative when they are intrinsically motivated by the interest, enjoyment, satisfaction, and challenge of the work itself (Amabile, 1986; Amabile, Conti, Coon, Lazenby, & Herron, 1996). Extrinsic motivation, on the other hand, relates to factors in work driven by the desire to attain some goal outside of the specific work tasks such as achieving a promised reward, achieving a desired position, and meeting a deadline. Research has shown that high intrinsic motivation and relatively low extrinsic motivation induce creative individuals to be more independent of the domain of knowledge and less susceptible to the pressure to conform (Amabile, 1997; Amabile & Conti, 1999). Intrinsic motivation is also offered as an explanation for why creative people show great involvement and energy in their tasks. Some types of extrinsic motivation can be detrimental to creativity if they involve controlling factors and are incompatible with intrinsic motives (Amabile, 1986). This view of motivation as a fundamental driving force for creative action in organizations requires a more flexible view of attention and support. Another way in which to look at the importance of motivation in organizational creativity lies in the strong traditional belief in the organization as being reliable in its support of creative techniques and its close focus on domain-relevant knowledge and cognitive abilities. Thus, as Sternberg (1999) points out, "Creativity may not only require motivation, but also generate it" (p. 9).

An alternative theoretical framework, defining creativity as being dependent on persons, processes, products, or places, is the systems model of creativity developed by Csikszentmihalyi (1990, 1996, 1999). This framework is useful for understanding organizational creativity. The basic argument is that "creativity" should be defined as a socially constructed label used to describe actions embedded in particular contexts (Ford & Gioia, 2000). According to Csikszentmihalyi's systems model, creativity must be defined with respect to a system that includes individual, social, and cultural factors that influence the creative process and help to bring about a creative outcome. The systems approach describes three interrelated subsystems: the *domain,* the *field,* and the *person.*

The domain can be seen as a symbolic system of rules and procedures that defines a system of its own set of symbolic elements, knowledge, rules, and notations. One important general characteristic of the domain is that every domain has its own internal logic—its pattern of development—and those who operate within it must respond to this logic. For instance, the scientific discipline of biochemistry can be seen as a specific domain constituted by various axioms, practices, rules, and so forth. The domains in organizations are presented as "given knowledge"—the basic factors of the profession—which, in most cases in practice, involves creativity in identifying areas that can be improved both intelligently and cost-effectively (Csikszentmihalyi & Sawyer, 1995).

The second subsystem, the field, can be seen as the gatekeepers, managers, experts, and/or stakeholders who personify and affect the structure of a domain and who are entitled to select a novel idea, service, or product for consideration. In many organizations, the various management teams play this role.

The third subsystem, the person, is the individual or group that produces the novel idea. All three subsystems jointly bring about the occurrence of a "creative" act. The primary role of the person is to introduce variations in a field. The gatekeepers or managers, who comprise and represent the domain, select from among these variations (novel acts). Thus, according to the systems approach, creativity always takes place within specific configurations of knowledge. There can never be any creativity *as such;* creativity is always creativity with others. The strength of this theoretical approach is that it gives opportunities for a better understanding of new product development activities such as those in the pharmaceutical research process—including the discovery process—and views the various development stages of pharmaceutical research as creative processes. Furthermore, the model also emphasizes the importance of the role of management in the creative process. The notion that creativity in an organizational context, as an inter-action between individuals within a domain and gatekeepers (managers, peers, or experts) who reject or retain creative action for future or further implementation, should not be restricted to only one domain (e.g., a depart-ment, a function, a scientific discipline). The result is that creative actions in organizations often face overlapping multiple domains rather than single domains (Ford, 1995b; Ford & Gioia, 2000). Thus, this view of creativity in organizations includes the importance of the interaction of many domains in organizations where various informal social networks play an important role (Bras, 1995).

Research Design and Methodology

The research project discussed here is based on an *action research method-ology* (cf. Babüroglo & Ravn, 1992; Coghlan, 2001; Eden & Huxham, 1996; McNiff, 2000; Reason 1994; for an overview, see Chapter 5 of this volume). It is beyond the scope of this chapter to give a broad discussion of action research methodology. In brief, employees of AstraZeneca have been actively involved in the research process as critical discussion members and interested interviewees, and the research project has been an important vehicle for key persons in the company to reflect on organizational creativ-ity. In addition, other academic researchers have been involved in various stages of the project. Thus, the insider/outsider model suggested by Bartunek and Louis (1996) has served as a platform for the research approach that has been developed to contribute to the theoretical discourse and to guide decisions and actions in the organization.

The ideas and questions behind the project of studying creativity in phar-maceutical research derive primarily from three concerns. First, leading phar-maceutical companies value and pursue innovation, but creativity either is a phenomenon taken for granted and embedded in innovation or is a neglected facet of innovation. The rationale for this seems to be that creativity can be perceived as an individual phenomenon that it is very complicated to study. Second, the question of what is creativity should be replaced by a process- or practice-based definition of creativity; that is, creativity must be examined as an innate quality in practical undertakings. If innovation is important for an organization, creativity should be studied as a collaborative effort. This is an absolute and necessary practical prelude to innovative action. Third, in the scientific research process, which applies well to pharmaceutical R&D, creativity plays an important role as a catalyst for ideas in which existing knowledge can be reformulated into new knowledge.

Part of the current thought on creativity deals with the fact that it cannot have boundaries and that it is difficult or impossible to manage. To chal-lenge this, and to help make sense of it and add value to organizations, a different view must be taken that creativity is professional creativity in which the collaborative effort is emphasized and consideration is given to its context-specific nature with its various subjective judgments. Furthermore, creative products must be thought of in a broader sense. These thoughts lead to some general questions about how to study organizational creativity:

- What organizational aspects are important for improving the understanding of organizational creativity in pharmaceutical R&D?
- What proposals can be formulated to manage organizational creativity at AstraZeneca R&D?

Our discussion is based on an empirical study at AstraZeneca. The findings derive from a retrospective study of seven highly successful and creative pharmaceutical projects in the areas of cancer, gastrointestinal, and cardiovascular therapy during a successful period in the former Zeneca (ICI Pharmaceuticals, Alderley, United Kingdom) and the former Astra (Hässle AB, Mölndal, Sweden). The purpose of the study was to explore how and whether different organizational aspects were able to provide a better understanding of organizational creativity, whether they influenced these projects, and what common features could be identified in the projects. The empirical data came from recent interviews with the most influential researchers, including project leaders and line managers, during the period from 1975 to 1985. This time period is very interesting because of the new drugs that were developed during those years. The study aims at investigating the development activities during this period and focuses on seven projects in the two companies. The projects chosen for study later became successful products that today represent total sales of more than $9 billion (U.S.). The interviews were recorded and later transcribed. Two researchers examined the transcripts independently and suggested various analytical categories from which the material could be examined. Later, a first draft of the results was distributed among some of the interviewees to get feedback.

Perceptions on Organizational Creativity at AstraZeneca

Creativity: An Ambiguous Concept

The interviewees were asked to define creativity. Their views on creativity were derived from a number of different perspectives. One of the researchers saw creativity as a storytelling skill:

First, creativity means the ability to tell a story, and by that I mean the ability to pull together all the information into a form that other people can understand. Second, it is not accepting the status quo. If someone did a clinical trial in a certain way, [it is] not to just repeat what people did yesterday. (employee in development)

By telling stories, the researcher is able to give an understanding of complex processes in new product development. For another researcher, creativity is the ability to make use of existing knowledge to create new chemical compounds, a basic component of a new candidate drug:

> Creativity in the context of the pharmaceutical industry means the ability to put together the available knowledge in order to understand or to propose things that other people have not done before. It must always be based on the accurate knowledge of the specific domain of science or therapy. (employee in discovery)

This most scientific view—knowledge has to be "accurate" and "specific"—derives from the demands on researchers to deliver new candidate drugs. Creativity becomes the capability of mastering a particular field of expertise. Yet another researcher argued that creativity is the capacity for holistic thinking, enabling an overview of an area:

> Creativity is the ability to see the overall view, and being innovative is to identify and find solutions to important problems. A metaphor is if you have a flood in the house, an innovative approach would be to change to broader pipes. A creative approach would be to reconstruct the plan of the house. (employee in discovery)

In this view, creativity is the ability to align identified problems and market opportunities with existing knowledge. Creativity is, therefore, context-based thinking that broadens the scope through a radical rethinking of what is at hand. Finally, one of the researchers referred to creativity as a cultural quality:

> It's quite easy to say we want to be creative, but it is very difficult to generate the culture that can foster creativity. It is not an easy thing. People usually use the term *innovation* rather than *creativity* because they think that innovation can be managed. In general, creativity cannot be managed. Only high-quality managers who understand creativity can manage it. (employee in development)

Individuals can always be creative, but making it possible for there to be creativity in communities or departments is more complicated. Creativity is, therefore, primarily of interest when it is managed in departments or work teams. Taken together, the notion of creativity was examined and discussed from many different perspectives. Creativity was aligned with a number of different qualities and organizational processes and was never given a specific meaning by the interviewees.

Organizational Slack and Creativity

Organizational slack can be defined as resources "in excess of what is required to maintain the organization" (Cyert & March, 1963, p. 36). Many successful firms that have achieved significant technological improvements show substantial slack that makes it possible to find creative solutions to problems. According to Cyert and March (1963), resources are more likely to be allocated if they are actively sought by single subunits. In this scenario, slack is available for projects that would not necessarily be approved with a tight budget. There may, however, be a U-shaped relationship between slack and its effective exploitation in innovation projects (West & Richards, 1999). This means that there is a certain optimum between the amount of slack and maximum efficiency. An absence of slack is believed to inhibit innovation (West & Richards, 1999).

The study of research projects in the former Hässle AB and ICI Pharmaceuticals (the two companies that merged to become AstraZeneca) shows that the flexibility of project plans allowed a relatively high acceptance for the testing of new ideas simply because the project plans were not very detailed. Resource allocation was made easier in some cases because the line management often played the role of the project management. In addition, projects were handled with a certain degree of organizational slack so that the resources that were not already appropriated or claimed for organizational activities could be used to support invention. One conclusion from the results of the study is that the context of which the projects were a part did have some ways in which to facilitate managing slack such as smaller organizations and mixed roles. However, the management of those projects realized the importance of slack resources that are critical in handling the emerging possibilities and threats that appeared during the different phases of the projects.

Informal Networks and Transdisciplinary Cooperation in the Research Process

The vast research literature on creativity has put much effort into describing what creativity is. More important, but less explored, is the question of *where* creativity is. The results of the study of the seven successful projects at Hässle AB and ICI Pharmaceuticals demonstrate that many breakthroughs in solving problems or generating new ideas took place in various informal network activities. These networks became important sites of knowledge transfer and improved interactions among various researchers. *Informal networks* in this context are different types of social communication, interaction, and information exchange. The informal nature of this kind of networking lies in the fact that they often (or always) took place outside the line and project organization. In addition, the networks were driven by motivation and research interests, and they sometimes were very ad hoc and short-lived. Previous research has shown the importance of social networks in promoting creativity, especially the form of networks called "weak ties" (Granovetter, 1982). A weak tie, in contrast to a strong tie, is an infrequently occurring interaction containing little or no contact among individuals. The weak ties are similar to the interactions that take place in the informal networks described previously in that the interaction is often among different groups and not within the same group. The networking activities that took place in the projects were more or less based on weak ties, similar to the kind of networks proposed by Granovetter. However, they were different in the sense that they were based to a greater extent on long-standing relations with different actors within or outside the company.

An example taken from the study illustrates not only the informality of the networks but also that decisions, often concerning critical problems in the projects, were made very quickly. A very pragmatic approach was taken by gathering the most appropriate skills for the problem without reference to project or organizational belonging:

It [the project] was very much based on ad hoc meetings—for better or for worse, I think. It resulted in swift and well thought out decisions, but it was not the structured leadership that is aimed at today. (employee in development)

The ability of the organization to distribute information and make quick decisions was also emphasized by another interviewee, who argued that organizational hierarchies had destructive effects on information and, consequently, on creativity:

Hierarchy is destructive for information. Information is the backbone of a creative environment. If that prerequisite—the access to information—is absent, then there will be very little creativity. Unless you have a good way of distributing information, then only a few persons at the top will be able to present new ideas. All this is reinforced by that damn reward system. There is nothing but a "dog eat dog" mentality where you just care for yourself. It's all very destructive. Unfortunately, top management does not recognize the problem because they are not aware of the basic mechanisms of scientific activities. (employee in discovery)

That different informal networks also improved the structure of accessing and managing information-facilitated decisions is illustrated in the following example:

Because the routes of accessing information were short, you were able to take decisions and go on without going through groups of hierarchies; it was possible to work in "fast-forward." It was very informal, of course, and many decisions were made in the corridors, which is probably disturbing for some people. Yet I think it was an effective way to work, at least for that organization. (employee in development)

In a sense, the result of the informal networking activities was a very pragmatic and rapid decision-making procedure in many of the projects. Furthermore, it was clear that intuition played an important role in the decision-making process in several of the projects, and this may be an indication of a relatively high ability to take risks.

Creativity, Tenacity, and Commitment

Most of the interviewees argued that the key quality of creative researchers is the ability to maintain and nourish interest in one particular substance for a considerable period of time. As researchers, they became spokespersons for particular projects. Because the development period for new pharmaceutical products is very long, it is of great importance that researchers are able to maintain their interest. One researcher pointed out the importance of being passionate about research:

> I always enjoyed doing research. I wouldn't have done it if I didn't enjoy it. I was doing research in an area that I found fascinating and wanted to work in. (employee in discovery)

One important component of organizational creativity was the ability to maintain a critical yet open-minded discussion on research issues:

> It was a climate in which you could question things to a high degree. In the research management team, we tried to question each other's ideas, actually without anybody getting angry or embarrassed. (employee in development)

One researcher described his somewhat heated relations with his superior as an important component of the creative process:

> I could argue and scream until I was blue in the face at the R&D director—it's rather amazing—and he actually tolerated that. Then he gave it some thought—did this person say something sensible? (employee in development)

Because pharmaceutical research goes on in areas that are not fully explored, there is always a risk of failure. As a consequence, it is necessary for creative researchers to be dedicated to their ideas even when they are criticized by others. As one interviewee put it, researchers had to nourish a certain "arrogance":

> The people in discovery had a strong belief that they were right. They had courage in spite of threats to their careers. It was the thin line between arrogance, belief, and courage. (employee in discovery)

Creative work always takes place "in between" known domains—new discovery and uncertain impact of what was discovered. Qualities such as full commitment, tenacity, and long-term perspective make it possible to find creative organizational solutions to problems. Because creative individuals and creative communities of practice must maintain their belief in certain ideas, it is often very challenging to manage these individuals.

Implications for Managing Organizational Creativity in Pharmaceutical R&D

Besides supporting the rather obvious and abstract strategic concerns of finding new chemical entities and developing competitive pharmaceutical products, organizational creativity has to do with the more profound underlying aspect of paying attention to various phenomena and structures of creativity in a complex research organization. The large modern pharmaceutical R&D organization is more dependent on different internal and external stakeholders than were the former Astra and Zeneca (Hässle AB and ICI Pharmaceuticals). Moreover, the research process in the pharmaceutical industry is now a heavily regulated business. In the pursuit of greater efficiency, and to be able to deal with complex risk taking during the long development times, new business processes are created that are not completely harmonious with aspects of organizational creativity. In this environment, the notion of creativity as a capability in the organization might be taken for granted or, worse, might not be accepted in practice because of different mind-sets and assumptions. However, it is also important to point out that regulations should not always be perceived only as impediments to creativity; regulations may at times enable creative thinking in terms of imposing standard operations and shared worldviews. Still, creativity in the pharmaceutical industry is creativity under the influence of regulations.

Given the most pertinent characteristics of the pharmaceutical industry, perhaps the most important aspect of organizational creativity has to do with understanding and improving the complex and nonlinear dynamics between intrinsic and extrinsic motivation and the creation of new ideas. An understanding of these dynamics can constitute a sustainable ability to change ways of thinking and find alternative ways of venturing into other scientific domains of knowledge that will lead to innovative ways of conducting scientific work. One concrete example of how to promote organizational creativity at AstraZeneca is to address the need to create a common platform by establishing an understandable language, images, models, and aspects of creativity as an organizational capability. This platform can lead to greater interest in and awareness of various aspects of creativity in the organization, and this can subsequently promote a dialogue in the organization that will change attitudes toward organizational creativity. This platform should be promoted and established at all levels of the organization.

With a common foundation that allows discussion of the phenomena among all levels of the company, an organizational momentum can begin to build—a momentum that would support organizational creativity, further leading to intelligent ideas and concrete actions. However, this momentum cannot begin without management. The true concern and active involvement of management in handling creativity in organizations is a neglected area. A lack of interest in examining it may lead to only halfhearted initiatives. This area, if any, is where organizational creativity must be pursued.

The research done on organizational creativity at AstraZeneca prompted a number of immediate and indirect effects in the company. Besides general attention to the topic, several activities were started to integrate what was learned from the research into AstraZeneca's practices. The findings were reported at different seminars and meetings in the company during the period, raising interest in the notion of organizational creativity. It may be said that the research project helped to put the concept of creativity on the organization's strategic agenda. The idea of organizational creativity was also analyzed using the global company employee survey, where it was addressed in a number of questions. One of AstraZeneca's Informatics projects, aimed at making information and knowledge on drug discovery and drug development more easily accessible, has integrated the notion of organizational creativity into its statement of aims. The company's Diversity Program, making use of all the various skills and know-how in the company, was informed of the research. Because creativity is based on the capacity to think in new ways and conceive new combinations of ideas, diversity can be closely related to organizational creativity. A strategic group formed in the company to deal with the long-term competitiveness of the firm was informed of the research findings. In addition to the interest in the research project at AstraZeneca, the research project was given attention in an extensive review article in the leading French weekly business magazine, *Les Echos*. All in all, the research on organizational creativity at AstraZeneca delivered insight, applicable models, and vocabularies and also had other, more tangible effects on the company.

Implications for Further Research

An organization's capability for innovation is of key importance for maintaining a long-term, sustainable competitive advantage. Because creativity is the ability to conceive new ideas and combinations of ideas, it precedes innovation. In the study presented in this chapter, based on the case of AstraZeneca, the notion of organizational creativity is used to capture the capacity of the firm to deliver new candidate drugs and products as well as new ways of operating and working. Although much research into the phenomenon of creativity depicts it as being either some extraordinary talent or a serendipitous process, we argue that creativity can and should be managed as an organizational resource. Organizational creativity is an outcome of leadership practices, an awareness of the need for creativity, the symbolic and linguistic capabilities of the firm to discuss creativity, the ability to make a connection among key actors in the discovery process, and so forth. Organizational creativity is not only something that happens as an effect of extraordinarily favorable conditions but is also something that can be influenced by managerial decisions, resource allocations, and ways in which to spur motivation. Organizational creativity is by no means immune to managerial influence. We further suggest that insider/outsider research can be used to align academic organizational research and organizational and managerial concerns and interests. The insider/outsider efforts gave new insight that was beneficial to both practitioners and academic researchers. We hope that the findings generated by the project have made a contribution to the study of management and organizations as well as to AstraZeneca.

Note

1. Drugs proven to offer desirable health effects in laboratory settings will proceed to clinical trials and will hopefully become registered drugs in the future.

References

Amabile, T. A. (1999). *Creativity in context: Update to the social psychology of creativity*. Boulder, CO: Westview.

Amabile, T. A., & Conti, R. (1999). Changes in the work environment for creativity during downsizing. *Academy of Management Journal, 42*, 630–640.

Amabile, T. M. (1986). The social psychology of creativity: A componential conceptualization. *Journal of Personality and Social Psychology, 45*, 357–377.

Amabile, T. M. (1988). A model of creativity and innovation in organizations. *Research in Organizational Behavior, 10*, 123–167.

Amabile, T. M. (1997). Motivating creativity in organizations: On doing what you love and loving what you do. *California Management Review, 40*(1), 39–59.

Amabile, T. M., Conti, R., Coon, H., Lazenby, J., & Herron, M. (1996). Assessing the work environment for creativity. *Academy of Management Journal, 39*, 1154–1184.

Ashkenas, R., Ulrich, D., Jick, T., & Kerr, S. (1995). *The boundaryless organization: Breaking the chains of the organizational structure*. San Francisco: Jossey-Bass.

Babüroglo, O. N., & Ravn, I. (1992). Normative action research. *Organization Studies, 13*(1), 19–34.

Bartunek, J. M., & Louis, M. R. (1996). *Insider/Outsider team research*. Thousand Oaks, CA: Sage.

Bell, D. (1973). *The coming post-industrial society*. New York: Basic Books.

Bharadwaj, S., & Menon, A. (2000). Making innovation happen in organizations: Individual creativity mechanisms, organizational creativity mechanisms, or both? *Journal of Product Innovation Management, 17*, 424–434.

Boden, M. (1996). *Dimensions of creativity*. London: Bradford Book.

Bohm, D. (2000). *On creativity* (L. Nichol, Ed.). London: Routledge.

Bras, D. J. (1995). Creativity: It's all in your social network. In C. M. Ford & D. A. Gioia (Eds.), *Creative action in organizations: Ivory tower visions and real world voices* (pp. 94–99). Thousand Oaks, CA: Sage.

Brown, S. L., & Eisenhardt, K. M. (1995). Product development: Past research, present findings, and future directions. *Academy of Management Review, 20,* 343–378.

Coghlan, D. (2001). Insider action research projects: Implications for practicing managers. *Management Learning, 32*(1), 49–60.

Cropley, A. J. (1999). Definitions of creativity. In *Encyclopaedia of creativity* (Vol. 1, pp. 511–524). London: Academic Press.

Csikszentmihalyi, M. (1990). The domain of creativity. In M. A. Runco & R. S. Albert (Eds.), *Theories of creativity* (pp. 190–212). Newbury Park, CA: Sage.

Csikszentmihalyi, M. (1996). *Creativity: Flow and the psychology of discovery and invention*. New York: HarperCollins.

Csikszentmihalyi, M. (1999). Implications of a systems perspective for the study of creativity. In R. J. Sternberg (Ed.), *Handbook of creativity* (pp. 313–333). Cambridge, UK: Cambridge University Press.

Csikszentmihalyi, M., & Sawyer, K. (1995). Shifting the focus from individual to organizational creativity. In C. M. Ford & D. A. Gioia (Eds.), *Creative action in organizations: Ivory tower visions and real world voices* (pp. 167–172). Thousand Oaks, CA: Sage.

Cyert, R. M., & March, J. G. (1963). *A behavioral theory of the firm*. New York: Prentice Hall.

Dougherty, D. (1999). Organizing for innovation. In S. R. Clegg, C. Hardy, & W. R. Nord (Eds.), *Managing organizations*. London: Sage.

Eden, C., & Huxham, C. (1996). Action research for the study of organizations. In S. R. Clegg, C. Hardy, & W. R. Nord (Eds.), *Handbook of organization studies* (pp. 525–542). London: Sage.

Ekvall, G. (1987). The climate metaphor in organizational theory. In I. B. M. Bass & P. J. D. Drent (Eds.), *Advances in organizational psychology: An international review* (pp. 177–190). Newbury Park, CA: Sage.

Eysenck, H. J. (1996). The measurement of creativity. In M. A. Boden (Ed.), *Dimensions of creativity* (pp. 199–242). London: Bradford Book.

Ford, C. M. (1995a). Creativity is a mystery. In C. M. Ford & D. A. Gioia (Eds.), *Creative action in organizations: Ivory tower visions and real world voices* (pp. 12–53). Thousand Oaks, CA: Sage.

Ford, C. M. (1995b). A multi-domain model of creative action taking. In C. M. Ford & D. A. Gioia (Eds.), *Creative action in organizations: Ivory tower visions and real world voices* (pp. 330–353). Thousand Oaks, CA: Sage.

Ford, C. M. (1996). A theory of individual creative action in multiple social domains. *Academy of Management Review, 21,* 1112–1142.

Ford, C. M., & Gioia, D. A. (2000). Factors influencing creativity in the domain of managerial decision making. *Journal of Management, 26,* 705–732.

Gibbons, M., Limoges, C., Nowotny, H., Schartzman, S., Scott, P., & Trow, M. (Eds.). (1994). *The new production of knowledge*. London: Sage.

Gioia, D. A. (1995). Contrasts and convergences in creativity: Themes in academic and practitioner views. In C. M. Ford & D. A. Gioia (Eds.), *Creative action in organizations: Ivory tower visions and real world voices* (pp. 317–329). Thousand Oaks, CA: Sage.

Granovetter, M. S. (1982). The strength of weak ties: A network theory revisited. In P. V. Marsden & N. Lin (Eds.), *Social structure and network analysis* (pp. 105–130). Beverly Hills, CA: Sage.

Henderson, R. (1994). The evolution of integrative capability: Innovation in cardiovascular drug discovery. *Industrial and Corporate Change, 3,* 607–626.

Jacob, N. (1998). *Creativity in organisations.* New Delhi: Wheeler Publishing.

Jones, F. B. (1995). The changing face of creativity. In C. M. Ford & D. A. Gioia (Eds.), *Creative action in organizations: Ivory tower visions and real world voices* (pp. 195–240). Thousand Oaks, CA: Sage.

Koretz, S., & Lee, G. (1998). Knowledge management and drug development. *Journal of Knowledge Management, 2*(2), 53–58.

Leonard-Barton, D. (1995). *Wellspring of knowledge: Building and sustaining the sources of innovation.* Boston: Harvard Business School Press.

McNiff, J. (2000). *Action research in organizations.* London: Routledge.

Powell, W. (1998). Learning from collaboration: Knowledge and networks in the biotechnology and pharmaceutical industries. *California Management Review, 40*(3), 228–240.

Reason P. (1994). Three approaches to participative inquiry. In N. K. Denzin & Y. S. Lincoln (Eds.), *Handbook of qualitative research* (pp. 324–339). Thousand Oaks, CA: Sage.

Shani, A. B. (Rami), & Lau, J. B. (2000). *Behavior in organizations: An experimental approach.* New York: McGraw-Hill.

Sternberg, R. J. (1999). The concept of creativity: Prospects and paradigms. In R. J. Sternberg (Ed.), *Handbook of creativity* (pp. 9–10). Cambridge, UK: Cambridge University Press.

West, M. A., & Richards T. (1999). Innovation. In *Encyclopaedia of creativity* (Vol. 2, pp. 45–56). London: Academic Press.

Williamson, B. (2001). Creativity, the corporate curriculum, and the future: A case study. *Futures, 33,* 541–555.

Woodman, R. W., Sawyer, J. E., & Griffin, R. W. (1993). Towards a theory of organizational creativity. *Academy of Management Review, 18,* 293–321.

Yeoh, P-L., & Roth, K. (1999). An empirical analysis of sustained advantage in the U.S. pharmaceutical industry: Impact of firm resources and capabilities. *Strategic Management Journal, 20,* 637–653.

14

The Cheetah Strategy

Saving Projects in Crises

Mats Engwall and Charlotta Svensson

Development projects are dynamic endeavors. The process of creating a new product, or developing a new business, cannot be planned in all of its details (Kreiner, 1995; Spender & Kessler, 1995). During the execution of development projects, the environmental conditions usually change over time (Kreiner, 1995). Prerequisites are modified, new market windows are opened, old market windows are closed, serendipitous knowledge is developed (Lindkvist, Söderlund, & Tell, 1998), preferences are adjusted (Baier, March, & Saetren, 1986), objectives are reinterpreted, possibilities emerge, and unpredicted problems are discovered (Dalton, 1959).

In general, theories on organizations and product development are dominated by a static paradigm (Brown & Eisenhardt, 1995; Krishnan & Ulrich, 2001), with a strong emphasis on planned and intended long-term patterns and structures. Little attention has been paid to how unpredicted, but urgent, problems that emerge during a development project are attacked. Instead, research has emphasized the effectiveness of autonomous project teams (Clark & Wheelwright, 1992b), cross-functional structures (Brown & Eisenhardt, 1995; Dougherty, 1992), powerful project managers (Ancona & Caldwell, 1990; Clark & Fujimoto, 1991; Karlsson & Nellore, 1998), the design of development processes (Cooper, 1993; Eisenhardt & Tabrizi, 1995), and multi-project portfolio strategies (Cusumano & Nobeoka, 1998; Wheelwright & Clark, 1992). The lesson taught is that a project that has a senior project manager with significant authority and a tight project team, consisting of specialists from all functional disciplines involved, has a much higher probability of succeeding than do projects that lack one or both of these features.

This chapter discusses the implicit strategy of meeting critical upcoming problems in product development projects by initiating small, time-limited organizational units where relevant experts are gathered on a full-time basis to focus on one urgent unforeseen problem. This kind of group is typically initiated *during* the execution of a project to attack and solve an unpredicted problem before its consequences become too severe. By initiating such a time-limited, small "appendix organization" of dedicated experts, the problem is given full attention by a small part of the project organization but is decoupled from the other issues on the project's agenda. We label these extremely temporary and unplanned organizations *cheetah teams* (Engwall & Svensson, 2001).

This kind of ad hoc problem-solving behavior—an implicit strategy "in use"—is used frequently today in the management of product development projects. Anchored in a qualitative case study of a cheetah team in action, this chapter addresses the following issues:

- Is the implicit strategy to use cheetah teams good or bad?
- Does the existence of cheetah teams constitute a best practice, or is it a symptom of management failure?

Initiating a cheetah team is usually very effective, at least in the short term, at solving the problem in question quickly. However, initiating a cheetah team also means reprioritizing and reallocating resources. The extra people, equipment, money, and attention allocated to the cheetah team has to be taken from somewhere. Usually, other actions have to be postponed and/or other problems have to remain unsolved.

By putting the use of the ad hoc, but formal, organizing in focus, we hope to contribute to the understanding of an important organizational construct in modern organizations. It enables us to include some of the dynamic features of product development projects that current theories do not fully comprehend. By pursuing a collaborative research approach, we also hope that our contribution to the understanding will contribute to the theoretical discourse as well as to decisions and actions in organizations.

The chapter is structured as follows. In the next section, the cheetah team concept is outlined. Thereafter, the research methodology is described briefly, followed by an empirical example from a study of a cheetah team in action. Then, the advantages and risks of a cheetah team strategy are discussed. Finally, the chapter concludes by reflecting on why cheetah teams exist. Is initiating cheetah teams a best practice, management failure, or something else?

The Cheetah Team Concept

A cheetah team is an organizational ideal type. The concept denotes a frequent empirical phenomenon, which in organizations can be identified under several different labels. "Task force," "emergency team," "SWAT team," "hot group," and "red team" are labels that sometimes are used with similar connotations (but sometimes also with other connotations).

There are five structural characteristics of a cheetah team:

1. It is explicitly sanctioned by a parent organization.

2. It is issued to accomplish a specified mission as soon as possible.

3. Its explicit intention is to be dissolved when the mission is accomplished.

4. Its members are committed on a full-time basis.

5. It is not planned in advance.

Taken one at a time, none of these characteristics is exclusive; most of them are shared with other kinds of temporary organizations such as project organizations (cf. Engwall, 1995; Lindkvist et al., 1998). Taken together, however, the features constitute a special kind of formalized ad hoc organization formed within projects and with an extremely limited duration (Table 14.1). The metaphor of the cheetah has two references. First, it refers to the tiger team project organization defined by Clark and Wheelwright (1992a). However, whereas a tiger team is a planned autonomous project team, a cheetah team is always unplanned and initiated ad hoc. Second, the cheetah metaphor refers to the significant quality of the animal itself. The cheetah is the fastest of all land animals, but only over short distances. Over an extended distance, the horse can outrun the cheetah. But nothing surpasses this cheetah in short sprints. It accelerates from 0 to 45 miles per hour (0 to 72 kilometers per hour) in 2 seconds.

Cheetah teams constitute an extreme form of formalized temporary organizations (Lundin & Söderholm, 1995). They are elite units that consist of a group of individuals selected especially and mobilized quickly for the mission. The teams are small, have a short life cycle, and are extremely focused. They are typically organized as instant responses to crucial problems. They are not planned for in advance. Usually, they also have permission to break rules within the organization that other teams and projects have to follow. (For a more in-depth analysis of the cheetah team concept, see Engwall & Svensson, 2000.)

Research Approach

The ideas presented in this chapter derive from serendipitous findings from a collaborative research effort on product development. For 3 years, we have collaborated in a broad and explorative research project within a product development division of a telecommunications company. The division manifests a dynamic, fast-moving, and highly competitive technological

Table 14.1   Cheetah Teams Versus Other Temporary Organizations

	Projects/Temporary Organizations	Tiger Teams/Pure Project Organizations	Cheetah Teams
Explicitly sanctioned	•	•	•
To accomplish a specific mission	•	•	•
To be dissolved	•	•	•
Members committed on a full-time basis		•	•
Not planned in advance			•

environment where an extensive amount of complex development projects are carried out simultaneously.

The research project was designed with an insider/outsider approach (cf. Bartunek & Louis, 1996). Whereas one of the authors (the "outsider") was an independent academic scholar, the second author (the "insider") had a deep personal experience of working in the division under study and had central role in the formation of the studied organization. Because the second author still held a position at the division, she could be described as a self-ethnographer, that is, an ethnographer studying her own organization (Alvesson, 1999). However, there was also an important action dimension in her research work (see Chapter 7 of this volume).

The findings are serendipitous in respect to how the phenomenon became part of a research study. The ad hoc problem-solving approach during the execution of a development project was a way of working that was taken for granted by the insider author ("This is how urgent problems are solved!"). During a lunch at the studied premises, the two authors discussed why projects almost always are seen as being behind schedule or forced to reduce their scope. The insider author remarked that the most successful way of working seemed to be when small teams were gathered to solve one specific problem within a project. This strategy was almost always successful. But how could this be achieved in an environment with multiple large projects executed in parallel, where many people have to share their time among projects, thereby making it hard to focus on one thing at a time? And what would happen if this way of working were to be used more extensively?

Research Design and Data Gathering

A qualitative case study approach was chosen, based on detailed analysis of one lead case (Yin, 1994). The purpose was to generate new concepts and, in so doing, challenge and contribute to existing theories (Eisenhardt, 1989; Emory & Cooper, 1991).

The empirical data were mainly collected from a lead case from which the second author had deep personal experiences. She had been the project manager of the project described. This case was chosen because of the closeness and easy access to data (Alvesson, 1999; Coghlan & Brannick, 2001). Like most qualitative case studies, the study combined various data collection methods such as archives, interviews, (self-) ethnography, and direct observations (Eisenhardt, 1989). The initial step was to reconstruct the course of events of the lead case. The "insider author" (the former project manager) started this process by bringing back memories of the events and common experiences from the case in dialogue with the leader of the cheetah team in question. Thereafter, the outcomes from this dialogue were complemented and checked by a thorough analysis of written material from the project such as e-mail communications, meeting minutes, personal notes, and formal progress reports. In the next step, the whole case was reconstructed during an extensive in-depth interview. The "outsider author," who did not have any personal connection to the case, interviewed the project manager for more than 6 hours. This interview resulted in a written "within-case analysis" (Eisenhardt, 1989), that is, a written description of the case, including a rough outline of its characteristics.

In the next step, data from two additional cases (not presented here [see Engwall & Svensson, 2000]) were gathered by open-ended interviews with the project managers and cheetah team leaders in question. These cases were primarily supplementary examples to the lead case and were used to develop and sharpen the analysis. Through the iterative process of adding each of these two cases to the analysis, the cross-case search for patterns resulted in significant similarities and differences between cases being identified (Eisenhardt, 1989). Thereafter, tentative stories of the cases were written.

Validation

A central activity was to generate a description that captured vital aspects of the phenomenon under study. The goal was for the developed categories to be close to the empirical material in the sense that they would be recognizable and meaningful for the individuals involved in the practice under study (cf. Werr, 1999). Consequently, each of the case descriptions was sent back to the involved persons at the companies for comments and remarks, even though the two researchers decided on final adjustments. Over this long iterative process of interpretation, the various concepts and descriptions have been successively tested, reformulated, and chiseled out.

Cheetah Teams in Action: An Empirical Example

The lead case is an example taken from a product development unit within a Swedish telecommunications company. The unit was organized as a multiproject matrix (Engwall & Sjögren Källqvist, 2001) with several parallel development projects. The projects had to negotiate resource allocation from common functional departments, and it was not unusual for personnel to be shared among many projects.

The Situation

The studied project was a product development project composed of both hardware and software products to be used within a product system. The project life cycle was approximately 2 years and involved up to 220 persons. The following illustration is presented in the present tense.

It is November 1996, and the project is in its final phase, close to the start of volume production. Only a few external tests remain, and these tests are expected to be nonproblematic. The tests are being performed by an external certified testing organization. To ensure that no faults are found, the project previously performed all of the tests in-house, in accordance with the test specifications known to be used by the external test site. It is essential that no faults be found because the availability of time slots at the test site is a scant resource. Thus, a failure during testing will have a direct impact on the promised delivery dates.

Despite precautions, the project manager gets a call late one afternoon in mid-November from the subproject manager responsible for all of the remaining system tests. The project has failed in one test case. This is totally unexpected, and the cause is unclear. Can it be due to a production fault? Can it be due to transport damages? The in-house pretests passed without any problems, so it cannot be due to any design problems.

Team Life Cycle

Half an hour later, representatives of the project are gathered in the project manager's office for an immediate crisis meeting. The engineer at the test site is on the speakerphone. The first thing to sort out is whether this is a real fault. Before any major actions are taken, it has to be ascertained whether a trivial mistake is responsible for the test failure. The meeting concludes with a determination that no trivial reason is likely to be found for the failure. A new meeting is scheduled for early the next morning to gather the necessary technical expertise. The failure analysis team has to be augmented by experts external to the project organization.

When it becomes clear that there are no immediate remedies to the problem, management officially sanctions a temporary team to focus on solving this specific problem. A subproject manager, renowned for her coordinating and technical skills, is appointed as team leader. The team is responsible for identifying the source of the problem and implementing a solution in time for the next time slot at the test site. The team members gather each morning to monitor progress and identify new actions that need to be taken. This troubleshooting is given the highest priority within the organization.

The first week's meetings are attended by up to 10 persons, and approximately 15 persons are involved in fault finding. After the first week, the source of the problem has been localized and the core of the team is cut to 5 persons. The fault is localized to an old component. The external test site has changed its test specifications, which is why the fault was not seen during pretesting. The team continues to carry out fault finding to ensure a rapid solution and an immediate implementation. The team is being managed within the project, but two key experts are from outside the main project organization.

Consequences

A new test slot is available in mid-December, and the tests are rerun after redesigning the component. After further revisions, the tests are passed by a broad margin in early January. Simultaneously, a parallel project is encountering the same problem and fails during the same test case. This project can also make use of the solution developed by the team. The dedicated team members specify technical improvements that later prevent two subsequent projects from encountering the same kind of trouble. In mid-January, the team is dismissed and its members return to their former duties, whether inside or outside the project.

Meanwhile, the other project members have been able to attend to their planned duties within the project. Whereas the team members immediately dropped their ongoing duties when the failure occurred, they worked as a buffer to the rest of the project organization that could continue with other project activities. Because the tests had to be rerun, expenditures increased for booking of the test site and test personnel. The duties relinquished by the team members were delayed, canceled, or performed by less experienced personnel.

Advantages and Risks With a Cheetah Team Strategy

As shown in the case, a cheetah team might be an effective tool for fast problem solving in the management of a project portfolio. The project in crisis was successfully rescued from costly delays, broken customer commitments, and catastrophic dips in the project members' morale. Therefore, launching cheetah teams in troublesome situations might be a strategy with some obvious advantages.

Advantages With Cheetah Teams

First, a cheetah team constructs a buffer between the problem and the rest of the organization (Thompson, 1967). As in the case described, the cheetah team absorbs the uncertainties of the unsolved problem (Spender & Kessler, 1995) before they propagate and affect the rest of the project or even the entire organization. In other words, initiating a cheetah team means that a specified problem (or set of coupled problems) and a specified set of personnel are deliberately decoupled from the structures and procedures of their parent organization for a short period of time (Lundin & Söderholm, 1995). Because the cheetah team is assigned with highly competent people who are fully concentrated on solving the problem, the rest of the project members can continue with their planned activities and rest assured that the problem is being taken care of as efficiently as possible.

Second, a cheetah team explicitly allocates attention to the problem in question. Because time and capabilities for attention is limited in organizations, everything cannot be attended to at once (Baier et al., 1986; Cohen, March, & Olsen, 1972/1988). Consequently, one way of paying attention to one issue is to take attention away from competing issues. Thus, the decoupling of the cheetah team not only works as a buffer toward the rest of the organization but also protects the selected experts from disturbances. In the case described, for instance, the cheetah team members were ordered to leave everything they had at hand immediately. Simultaneously, the priority of the team gives the problem precedence over competing issues in the project. Thus, the core of the crisis is sealed off from the plans and priorities of the ordinary agenda (Bohn, 2000).

Third, a cheetah team creates extraordinary commitment. The very initiation of a cheetah team symbolizes that the situation is regarded as extraordinary. It induces a sense of urgency, and this legitimizes extraordinary actions. It manifests "a moral equivalent of war" (James, 1911) in the organization. The mission of the team is a heroic undertaking, and if the team succeeds, its members will probably be regarded as heroes. Thus, the high commitment level helps the team members to make sense of the situation. It brings in value and logic from which the actions can be understood (Weick, 1995).

Applying the Cheetah Team Strategy:
Some Significant Risks

What starts as an effective strategy for attacking the causes of crucial organizational problems can easily be transformed into a situation of continuous firefighting ("putting out fires") and reoccurring attempts at attacking the symptoms (Bohn, 2000), with the consequences of productivity losses and performance drops. Although this was not included in the study, it is easy to hypothesize how the seductive strengths of cheetah teams can turn the organization into chaos if they become the standard solution for every problem in projects.

First, there is a risk of domino effects (Sjögren Källqvist, 2002). When a cheetah team is initiated to save a problematic project, other ongoing projects and activities suffer from having to give away their resources (Eskeröd, 1998).

There is an obvious risk that while the cheetah team is solving problems in one project, it indirectly is creating new problems in other projects because these are delayed due to lack of resources. At worst, some of these projects are so endangered that new cheetah teams are needed to save them, which means that still other projects have to give their resources away. These projects become endangered and new cheetah teams are needed, and so forth. Thus, a cheetah team strategy might easily be reduced to a never-ending loop of resource redistribution among ongoing projects.

Second, there is a risk of cascade effects. Because the cheetah team is allowed to sidestep organizational routines, it could be tempting to provide "quick and dirty" patch solutions (Bohn, 2000). This might save time in the short term, but even if the symptoms at hand are solved, there is a strong possibility that either the problem will show up again or the patchwork will create new problems. "The new problems that patching has created, and the old ones that it has failed to solve, act up more and more, until a large fraction of the incoming problems are actually old ones returning" (Bohn, 2000, p. 88). Thus, the focus on extraordinary action can become a weakness. There is an emphasis on getting things done "here and now" rather than on analyzing the long-term consequences of these actions.

The third risk is overuse. Because there usually are more problems in organizations than there is time to deal with them (Bohn, 2000), issuing a cheetah team every time an unforeseen problem occurs increases the risk of domino and cascade effects and takes out the extraordinary symbolism in the strategy. In addition, because the cheetah team members are instantly drawn out from ongoing activities, frequent cheetah team initiations disrupt the rhythm of the ordinary work and make planning and scheduling extremely difficult (Gersick, 1994). Finally, because cheetah teams emphasize fast results, an overuse means that the organization easily becomes shortsighted and loses its adaptation ability (Weick, 1995). Old successful solutions tend to be repeated with new problems, signals from the environment tend to be interpreted to fit with current actions taken (Weick, 1995), and possibilities for experimenting (March, 1988) and long-term learning tend to be excluded from the organization's agenda (Ekstedt, Lundin, Söderholm, & Wirdenius, 1999).

Cheetah Teams: Good or Bad?

The cheetah is an animal that is extremely fast in short distances, with an extraordinary ability to accelerate from rest to full speed. But after the effort spent to capture its prey, the cheetah is exhausted and needs to recover. The metaphor of a cheetah team suggests that this is a team that is formed instantaneously with highly competent people who immediately start to solve the problem at hand. After the problem is solved, the team members need to recover and return to their ordinary duties.

How should the need for a cheetah team be regarded in the first place? Is it a symbol of organizational failure in terms of bad project planning, continuous overallocated resources, or overoptimism? This could, of course, be the answer, but the studied cases suggest not. In the case described in this chapter, the initiation of the cheetah team was a response to the unforeseen, and this in turn might be perceived as a consequence of the changing nature of contemporary business. In a changing environment, it is not possible to predict all possible future scenarios. Furthermore, it is probably not even desirable to try to do so given that this would require such great amounts of time spent on planning that the intended project result would be obsolete before it was finished (cf. Kreiner, 1995).

Even though it is impossible to make detailed plans in advance for how to manage an unforeseen problem, it might be possible to prepare for it. One way would be to set up cheetah team-like "fire brigade" teams to save projects on request. The significant positive effects would be direct availability of resources and the possibility for advance training to gain efficient teamwork in action. The major problem would be how to ensure that these teams are equipped with the right competencies to match the upcoming unforeseen problems.

As suggested in the previous section, there is an obvious risk when cheetah teams are used as firefighting units, fixing the immediately visible symptoms of the fire rather than the cause of the fire. Also, with an overuse of cheetah teams, the power of "extraordinary" fades away and the implicit strategy may eventually lose its effectiveness. Thus, an institutionalization of this approach to problem solving, from an implicit strategy to an explicit one, might be hazardous and prove to be counterproductive.

To summarize, when applied judiciously, an *implicit* strategy to issue cheetah teams seems to be effective in managing upcoming crucial problems. But the frequent use of several parallel cheetah teams might be an indication that the organization is starting to lose control over its projects and resource use.

Epilogue

As early as 30 years ago, leading organizational thinkers such as Bennis (see Bennis & Slater, 1968) and Toffler (1970) proclaimed that many of the permanent structures of the bureaucracy would soon be replaced by short-term, temporary adaptive systems, with each one being specifically designed to handle a specific task. Cheetah teams are examples of such temporary systems, even though their unplanned and ad hoc character makes them extreme. Today, many contemporary organizations are competing in uncertain contexts with a high pace of innovation, change, and development. By studying cheetah teams, as well as similar ad hoc processes in organizations, new significant features of the everyday life in organizations of the "real world" are brought into the academic discussion.

References

Alvesson, M. (1999). *Methodology for close up studies: Struggling with closeness and closure* (Working Paper 1994/4). Lund, Sweden: Lund University, School of Economics and Management.

Ancona, D. G., & Caldwell, D. (1990). Beyond boundary spanning: Managing external dependence in product development teams. *Journal of High Technology Management, 1,* 119–135.

Baier, V. E., March, J. G., & Saetren, H. (1986). Implementation and ambiguity. *Scandinavian Journal of Management, 2*(3–4), 197–212.

Bartunek, J. M., & Louis, M. R. (1996). *Insider/Outsider team research.* Thousand Oaks, CA: Sage.

Bennis, W. G., & Slater, P. E. (1968). *The temporary society.* New York: Harper & Row.

Bohn, R. (2000). Stop fighting fires. *Harvard Business Review, 78*(4), 82–91.

Brown, S. L., & Eisenhardt, K. M. (1995). Product development: Past research, present findings, and future directions. *Academy of Management Review, 20,* 343–378.

Clark, K. B., & Fujimoto, T. (1991). *Product development performance.* Boston: Harvard Business School Press.

Clark, K. B., & Wheelwright, S. C. (1992a). Organizing and leading "heavyweight" development teams. *California Management Review, 34*(3), 9–28.

Clark, K. B., & Wheelwright, S. (1992b). *Revolutionizing product development: Quantum leaps in speed, efficiency, and quality.* New York: Free Press.

Coghlan, D., & Brannick, T. (2001). *Doing action research in your own organization.* London: Sage.

Cohen, M., March, J. G., & Olsen, J. P. (1988). A garbage can model of organizational choice. In J. G. March (Ed.), *Decisions and organizations.* Cambridge, UK: Basil Blackwell. (Original work published 1972)

Cooper, R. G. (1993). *Winning at new products: Accelerating the process from idea to launch* (2nd ed.). Reading, MA: Perseus Books.

Cusumano, M., & Nobeoka, K. (1998). *Thinking beyond lean: How multi-project management is transforming product development at Toyota and other companies.* New York: Free Press.

Dalton, M. (1959). *Men who manage.* New York: John Wiley.

Dougherty, D. (1992). A practice-centered model of organizational renewal through product innovation. *Strategic Management Journal, 13,* 77–92.

Eisenhardt, K. M. (1989). Building theories from case study research. *Academy of Management Review, 14,* 532–550.

Eisenhardt, K. M., & Tabrizi, B. N. (1995). Accelerating adaptive processes: Product innovation in the global computer industry. *Administrative Science Quarterly, 40,* 84–110.

Ekstedt, E., Lundin, R. A., Söderholm, A., & Wirdenius, H. (1999). *Neo-industrial organising: Renewal by action and knowledge formation in a project-intensive economy.* London: Routledge.

Emory, C. W., & Cooper, D. R. (1991). *Business research methods* (4th ed.). Homewood, IL: Irwin.

Engwall, M. (1995). *Jakten på det effektiva projektet* (In search of the effective project). Stockholm, Sweden: Nerenius & Santérus Förlag.

Engwall, M., & Sjögren Källqvist, A. (2001). *Dynamics of a multi-project matrix: Conflicts and coordination* (FENIX Working Paper No. 7). Stockholm, Sweden: Stockholm School of Economics. Retrieved March 15 from www.fenix.chalmers.se

Engwall, M., & Svensson, C. (2000, August). *How cheetahs run: Cheetah teams in product development projects—The most extreme form of temporary organizations?* Paper presented at the meeting of the Academy of Management, Toronto.

Engwall, M., & Svensson, C. (2001). Cheetah teams. *Harvard Business Review, 79*(2), 20–21.

Eskeröd, P. (1998). The human resource allocation process when organizing by projects. In R. Lundin & C. Midler (Eds.), *Projects as arenas for renewal and learning processes* (pp. 125–131). Norwell, MA: Kluwer Academic.

Gersick, C. (1994). Pacing strategic change: The case of a new venture. *Academy of Management Journal, 37*, 9–45.

James, W. (1911). *Memories and studies.* London: Longmans, Green.

Karlsson, C., & Nellore, R. (1998). The superweight project team and manager. *International Journal of Innovation Management, 2*, 309–338.

Kreiner, K. (1995). In search of relevance: Project management in drifting environments. *Scandinavian Journal of Management, 11*, 335–346.

Krishnan, V., & Ulrich, K. T. (2001). Product development decisions: A review of the literature. *Management Science, 47*, 1–21.

Lindkvist, L., Söderlund, J., & Tell, F. (1998). Managing product development projects: On the significance of fountains and deadlines. *Organization Studies, 19*, 931–951.

Lundin, R. A., & Söderholm, A. (1995). A theory of the temporary organization. *Scandinavian Journal of Management, 11*, 437–455.

March, J. (1988). The technology of foolishness. In J. March (Ed.), *Decisions and organizations* (pp. 253–265). Cambridge, UK: Basil Blackwell.

Sjögren Källqvist, A. (2002). *Projektledning från ovan: Beroenden och kopplingar i en industriell multi-projektverksamhet* (Project management from above: Dependencies and couplings in an industial multiproject environment). Licentiate thesis, Department of Industrial Economics and Management, Royal Institute of Technology, Stockholm, Sweden.

Spender, J. C., & Kessler, E. H. (1995). Managing the uncertainties of innovation: Extending Thompson (1967). *Human Relations, 48*, 35–56.

Thompson, J. D. (1967). *Organizations in action.* New York: McGraw-Hill.

Toffler, A. (1970). *Future shock.* London: Pan Books.

Weick, K. E. (1995). *Sensemaking in organizations.* Thousand Oaks, CA: Sage.

Werr, A. (1999). *The language of change: The roles of methods in the work of management consultants.* Ph.D. dissertation, Stockholm School of Economics, Stockholm, Sweden.

Wheelwright, S. C., & Clark, K. B. (1992). Creating project plans to focus product development. *Harvard Business Review, 70*(2), 70–82.

Yin, R. K. (1994). *Case study research, design, and methods* (2nd ed.). Thousand Oaks, CA: Sage.

15

Service Innovation

A Collaborative Approach

Hans Björkman

This chapter is a story about the development and use of a new service innovation tool at SIF, the Swedish trade union for white-collar workers in industry, following a collaborative research endeavor. SIF is a politically independent trade union that organizes white-collar employees in the manufacturing, construction, computer, and consulting industries. Maybe this story could have taken place in many different kinds of organizations. However, the specific background and context are important. SIF is the major industrial white-collar trade union in Sweden. The organization, with a growing number of members and strong financial resources, is among the leading unions in Sweden. However, the traditional trade union role—basically, to represent its members—is not sufficient anymore. The challenge is not to substitute the representative role but rather to combine representation with provision of advice and tools to individuals. These multiple roles may have been an important factor behind the professionalization of the unions given that highly specialized services need to be developed (and sometimes even provided) by experts. Because the membership fee level cannot be changed dramatically, trade unions basically meet the same challenges as do private companies in terms of efficiency and effectiveness.

In theory, democratic organizations that are membership led should have no problem in "doing the right thing." All members are considered equal and

AUTHOR'S NOTE: I am very thankful for being employed by SIF, an organization signified by its openness and curiosity. Many colleagues and members of the organization participated in this study. I express my gratitude to all contributors. In particular, I thank my SIF colleagues, Jeanette Sandelius and Lars Sköld, but also my research supervisor, Horst Hart, for enthusiasm, advice, and practical help.

have equal opportunities to participate in decision making. In reality, there are considerable differences around the decision-making process. Some members are able to establish exchange relations and benefit from their membership, whereas others are not. Some members are highly satisfied with the services provided through the union, whereas others just pay their membership fees without benefiting from these services. Trade unions are organized around traditional issues such as wage formation, employment and job security, and member recruitment. Collective actions have been the "trademark" for many of them, yet they have always provided individual services to their members. Today, union members tend to become more empowered and develop resources of their own, enabling them to take greater individual responsibility. Hence, a modern trade union must combine its collective tasks with the development of services designed to meet individual needs and must also acknowledge members as "empowering partners." A transformed membership may include members in a design process, resulting in services, developed *with* or *by* members, not just *for* them (Kaulio, 1998). Such a different service innovation process not only may provide new and more attractive services but also may provide new opportunities to participate in trade union work.

This chapter starts from the fact that the organization has made the strategic decision to transform itself from a traditional union into a modern, attractive, service-oriented, competitive organization. This decision has been supported by a substantial allocation of economic resources for organizational renewal. A number of measures have been initiated to learn about individual preferences and opinions among members (customer satisfaction surveys) and to establish permanent or situational information technology-based networks with members. There is widespread consensus that organizational renewal has to be conducted in close and deep dialogue between the organization and its members.

Collaborative Research Endeavors and the Tradition for Service Development in Unions

The Scandinavian tradition of service development and the role of unions has a documented and impressive list of research insights that resulted in major organizational actions. From the famous experiments by Curt Lewin, the Tavistock Institute and the sociotechnical school inherited the idea of research participation in development or improvement activities within organizations. Action science developed a stronghold in Norway and later in Sweden. Action research became an instrument for organizational development (Pasmore, 2001). Central in this notion of action research was the role of the experiment. Yet although these experiments were often quite successful, they led to a limited diffusion (Gustavsen, 2001; Herbst, 1974).

From this *one company–one researcher–one problem* action research design during the past 20 years, an alternative research strategy has emerged.

The experimental design has been replaced by open dialogue involving actors engaged in participative self-designing activities (Mohrman & Cummings, 1989). In Scandinavia, designs based on *broad network- and participation-oriented action research* have been employed successfully since at least the 1970s (Naschold, Cole, Gustavsen, & van Beinum, 1993; Shotter & Gustavsen, 1999). Thus, experimental approaches and their emphasis of rigor and control have been substituted with openness, pluralism, and theoretical pragmatism. Openness and broad participation are assumed to be a leverage to improve knowledge diffusion. Many actors who are part of the design also feel motivated to participate in diffusion processes. Within this action science school, networks with other actors in similar situations are assumed to be important. Networks provide experience and alternatives to an organization (Shotter, 1993). Most people engaged are aware that success from renewal efforts depends on how well members are involved in change processes already in their initial design-oriented phases (Beer, Eisenstat, & Spector, 1990; Beer & Nohria, 2000; Gustavsen, 1992; Naschold et al., 1993; van Einatten, 1993). These researchers have a common argument explaining the desirability of broad participation of organizational stakeholders regardless of whether they are employees, customers, or clients. Participation generates diversity (alternatives) as well as consensus.

There are numerous examples of successful research projects in both traditions. However, they seem to suffer from a common difficulty: The results have limited consequences for actors other than those who participated directly in projects. Knowledge transfer from projects to others does not occur.

Contrary to the standpoint taken by the labor movement in other countries, Swedish unions traditionally are active in design and implementation of action research-based change programs in the labor market. Unions have been active organizers of both company-based and national programs. However, participation is restricted to activities outside the organizations. Unions have seldom offered their own organizations as arenas for action research activities.

Our study at SIF is one part of a large-scale modernization project. This project highlights that a modern union needs to develop services that correspond to a variety of individual needs. In a trade union context, services could consist of new methods for advice concerning wage levels, career planning advice service, and so forth. This chapter describes and evaluates a method used in a subproject with the objective of developing a basis for an attractive trade union membership for managers and project managers. The method has been designed to enhance organizational learning. The chapter discusses a pilot version of a model for user involvement in service innovation derived from this theoretical tradition. Is it possible to combine assumptions from the two action research paradigms and use them as design principles for a different action research project? If this is possible, does it make any difference in outcome? Or, to be more precise, is the project *efficient,* and does it contribute to the solution of an observed organizational problem? In addition, is the project *effective* in terms of knowledge diffusion, are recommendations from the pilot used in other contexts, and does the organization learn from pilot experiences?

Contemporary Discourse on Service, Innovation, and Service Innovation

Service research emerged from the mid-1970s as a multidisciplinary research area, influenced by sociology, psychology, business administration, and other disciplines (Pettersson, 2000). The specific properties of a service have been described in an array of definitions. Cagan and Vogel (2002) state, "A service is an activity that enhances experience; it requires an array of products to deliver its core activity" (p. 7). The given definition indicates the obvious interconnectedness between services and products. The specific nature of services compared with goods may be referred to as intangibility, perishability, simultaneity, and heterogeneity of services (Edvardsson & Gustafsson, 1999). That the production and consumption of the service takes place simultaneously makes the customer involved in the production and consumption process (Grönroos, 1992; Johne & Storey, 1998; Normann, 2000). Thus, the understanding of the resources, activities, and processes that create value for different users or user groups is crucial (Edvardsson, 1996). Service research may be divided into several subdisciplines such as service quality, service construction, and service development (Pettersson, 2000). This study is mainly related to service development and is foremost to user involvement during early innovative stages of the development process.

The importance of involving customers in product innovation is emphasized by many (e.g., Gupta & Wilemon, 1990; Kaulio, 1997; von Hippel, 1988). But how may customers be involved in service innovation? Hatchuel and Weil (1999) argue that the increase in the innovation rhythm needs to be met by new organizational models. Organizations facing "intensive innovation" are confronted by continuous and dynamic change in the development of their products or services. Organizing for intensive innovation becomes a challenge.

Product and service development models are genealogically related to project management, thereby having similar pros and cons. Still, there are significant differences as well. Service development models often exclude the initial innovation/invention phase. From our perspective—service development in an organization built on individual members and characterized by democracy and participation—they provide very little for user participation in innovation activities.

Project-oriented approaches can improve the consistency of the project, reduce costs and delays, and improve the coordination between experts inside and outside the organization. But it is unclear whether project management fosters innovation and learning (Hatchuel & Weil, 1999) given that the major role of project models is to reduce risks. Another problem is that project management seldom tells us *how* innovation takes place. A number of service development process models have been proposed (Edvardsson & Gustafsson, 1999), but they seldom show *how* or *when* the customers or users are involved. Scheuing and Johnson (1989) propose a comprehensive model in which user involvement is postulated. Even though this model captures the innovation phase, users are not involved until later. The sequential shape of the model emphasizes the risk-reducing function. But does it enhance innovation?

The assumptions behind this study are that service innovation does not have to be organized as a strictly sequential process and that users may be involved in earlier conceptual phases than in the model proposed by Scheuing and Johnson (1989). This chapter proposes and evaluates a "design dialogue platform" as a model for conceptual and knowledge development through user involvement. The design dialogue platform model focuses on the initial phases of service development as they are used both to contribute to the environmental analysis and to create service ideas/concepts. In comparison with the Scheuing–Johnson model, the platform model does not postulate a sequential relation between early stages in the development process, and it involves users earlier. Some of the background concepts are derived from research and theory development by the CGS group at Ecoles des Mines in Paris (Hatchuel, Le Masson, & Weil, 2001; Hatchuel & Weil, 1999).

A concept may be defined as "something conceived in the mind: thought, notion, an abstract or generic idea generalized from particular instances" (Merriam-Webster, 1998, p. 238). Hatchuel and colleagues (2001) define the role and origins of concepts as both a result and a departure point of knowledge dynamics. Because knowledge is needed to define a concept, the concept development process must take place simultaneously with the knowledge development process. Design could be defined as the process that links concepts and knowledge. Hatchuel and colleagues propose that a design is innovative if, and only if, there is a new link between values and competencies.

Thus, innovative design is the art of linking concepts, knowledge, value, and competencies. The target of an innovation process is not a well-specified goal but rather what has been called "a field of innovation," that is, an area for innovative design.

The design and development of new services originating from the knowledge side of an organization tend to create results that resemble already existing versions. They become upgraded versions, they use existing technologies or operations, and they transfer solutions from one service area to another. In short, they tend to lack the creative elements that make them radical. The knowledge base needs to be confronted with and provoked by an alternative approach articulated by individuals with a different concept of reality. Hatchuel and colleagues (2001) discuss the theoretical implications of the discrepancies between concepts and knowledge (Figure 15.1).

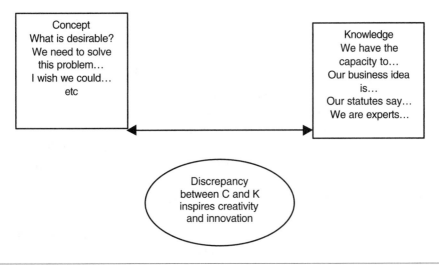

Figure 15.1. Concept and Knowledge

Their examples show the importance of a dialogue between spokespersons from these two realities. They provide examples of groups and teams that fulfill the role of translating between the concept and knowledge worlds as well as activities that bridge the gap between them. However, these authors seem to take the nature of the mediating activities for granted.

Redefined in this context, the study reported in this chapter is an attempt to establish a platform (the *design dialogue platform*), opening up and bridging the discrepancies between the concept and knowledge worlds. It is considered to be a platform because of the experiences. If positive, they are subsequently used on a larger scale within the organization. As a platform, intermediating arrangements need to be stable, repetitive, and well codified to be used without the continuous involvement of the research team.

There are a number of alternative principles that can be linked up when designing the platform. At one extreme, the platform can be developed as an expert-oriented *interpreting* organization (close to the knowledge system), gathering opinions from membership, translating them into service ideas, and presenting them to the administrative parts of the organization. At the other extreme, broad-based interaction with the membership can be organized, mirroring the "true" priorities and needs of members.

One way in which to integrate a common problem to be solved with different and even conflicting knowledge systems is to formulate common design principles in the shape of a vision-led and value-driven design-oriented strategy that is specific to innovation. These principles focus on the gap between the knowledge systems within the organization and the content of services and activities preferred by its members. These design principles are similar to those proposed by Gustavsen (2001, pp. 18–19) in his concept of "democratic dialogue," as described in the following boxed text.

The dialogue is a process of exchange; ideas and arguments move to and from, as well as among, the participants.

- Everybody should be active. Consequently, each participant has an obligation not only to put forward his or her own ideas but also to help others contribute their ideas.
  - All participants are equal.
  - Work experience is the basis for participation. This is the only type of experience that, by definition, all participants have.
  - At least some of the experience that each participant has when joining the dialogue must be considered legitimate.
  - It must be possible for everybody to develop an understanding of the issues at stake.

- All arguments that pertain to the issues under discussion are legitimate.
  - Each participant must accept that other participants can have better arguments.
  - The work role, authority, etc., of all the participants can be made subject to discussion.
  - The participants should be able to tolerate an increasing degree of difference of opinion.

The design dialogue platform that is proposed and evaluated in this chapter is developed to unify values and concepts derived from the members to promote organizational concept creation and learning.

The purpose of the study in this chapter was to evaluate a platform for development of concepts and knowledge (Figure 15.2). The platform consists of two parts:

1. Concept and knowledge development undertaken by members

2. Organizational learning through participation in and evaluation of the concept and knowledge development accomplished by the members

Research Approach

Intervention research is a process by which an organization and researchers establish a joint research program on clearly specified issues. The research goal is not only to understand established behavior, structures, and processes but also to identify potential new models that can better fit new

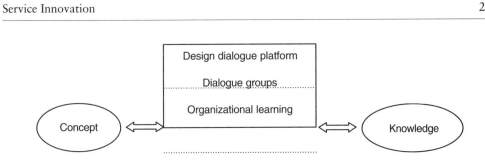

Figure 15.2. A Platform for Development and Integration of Concepts and Knowledge

strategies or contexts. Thus, the research goals are both analytic and exploratory. The researcher can, in agreement with the organization, do experimental studies to identify new principles and their differences from established well-known principles, participate in the implementation of experiments, and reformulate and validate new principles and abstract theoretical values in the field (cf. Hatchuel & Weil, 1998; for an overview, see Chapter 5 of this volume).

The study has a pronounced intervention component. It is directly connected to strategic decision making, and results are reported to and examined by the union's management team on a regular basis. It is intended to bring impulsivity and new ideas to executive staff as an inspiration in the overall modernization process. The purpose of this project was to analyze how the union could develop a more attractive membership package for managers. Multiple methods were used: media analysis, analysis of competitors, internal evaluation of existing service offers to managers, and scenario techniques. To obtain knowledge of values, attitudes, and needs among managers, and to gather new service ideas/concepts, dialogue groups were used. One "insider researcher" (employed by the union) and one "outsider researcher" (the supervisor of the inside researcher) participated in the project group. The insider researcher's familiarity with the organization and internal credibility, in combination with the academic knowledge and challenging perspectives brought into the project group by the outsider researcher, were of significant importance in the planning, execution, and evaluation of the project.

The Dialogue Groups

Various configurations of the groups (project managers/managers, major city/regional center, and members/nonmembers) were used to increase the variety of arguments and results. Four groups were organized, each with a specified kind of participants:

1. Project managers: members (major city)

2. Managers: members (regional center)

3. Managers: members and nonmembers (regional center)

4. Managers: nonmembers (major city)

Each group consisted of four to seven participants during the first meetings. Because of the small number of participants, it is not possible to attain any reliable conclusions concerning various group results. Even though the similarities among the groups turned out to be more obvious than the differences, it was clear that different perspectives developed in the project managers group.

The initial dialogue group meetings were held as 2-hour sessions mediated by the insider researcher. The discussions focused on three topics:

- To be a manager—situation, role, opportunities, threats
- How managers could be strengthened in their roles and what kind of knowledge and skills they may need to acquire
- How "external parties" (e.g., trade unions) may contribute to enhancing managers' situation

Each of these aspects was described by each participant. After a short time allotted for individual reflection, each aspect was then discussed in the group. At the end of each meeting, the participants were asked whether they wanted to participate in one more meeting with the group. Of the four initial groups, three met a second time, with these second meetings attended by three or four persons. The final dialogue group meetings were organized in a similar fashion as the initial meetings except that one internal service developer (from the project group) and the outsider researcher participated—as discussion partners, not as idea creators. The discussion focused on the same aspects as did the discussion during the initial dialogue group meetings, but the later discussion placed more emphasis on the creation of clear service ideas. All of the dialogue group meetings were videotaped, and the project group followed the initial meetings on a television screen. Documentation made by the dialogue groups and analysis of the videotapes were used to produce a list of service ideas that had been discussed. This service idea list was then used in the evaluation process.

Evaluation of the Emerging Patterns

The following criteria and methods were used in the evaluation process.

Process Capabilities. Is it possible, from existing knowledge of member needs and satisfaction, to identify members/users who have the capabilities and motivation to participate in the design of a new generation of services to members and potential members? This was evaluated through statistical data on the group recruitment process.

Process Evaluation Conducted by Participants. Do members/potential members in innovative groups find it useful and interesting to participate? This was measured through a questionnaire.

Development of New Knowledge/Concepts and Organizational Learning. What kind of knowledge or innovative ideas can be generated from innovative groups consisting mainly of members/potential members? How does the use of the model contribute to organizational learning? This was evaluated by the researchers, the project group, and managers employed by SIF.

An Overall Assessment of the Design Dialogue Platform Model. Is the model useful as a regular method for concept and knowledge creation? Can it enhance member participation? This was evaluated by the project group.

One evaluation perspective in this study is that of focusing on creative products and services; the output from the dialogue groups will be assessed, thereby giving measures for the results of the creative process. Amabile (1996) has developed the Conceptual Assessment Technique (CAT), a methodology in which researchers ask experts to rate products' creativity with little additional guidance. The used definition of creativity ("a product or response is creative insofar as appropriate observers independently agree it is creative") avoids reliance on provided definitions ("people know creativity when they see it") (Amabile, 1982). This study has been influenced by the CAT methodology but does not follow it strictly. Because of the strong focus on organizational learning and the need to evaluate the design dialogue platform from multiple perspectives, we have not used independent experts. The innovation assessment was made by the project group, including the two researchers, whereas the usability assessment was made by department managers and regional managers at SIF.

Contributions From the Project

The pilot project has been evaluated from several perspectives, including a preassessment of the opportunities to use the design dialogue group model as a regular innovation tool in the organization. The pilot project assessment is principally related to the model's efficiency, that is, whether or not the model worked. It is followed by a brief description and analysis of the model's diffusion that provides information concerning the model's effectiveness, that is, whether or not it is usable.

Table 15.1   Evaluation Made by Group Members

1. It is not easy to find the time to participate in this kind of meeting.	7.7
2. It has been easy to understand how to work in the group.	7.1
3. The work in the group has not been too strongly moderated.	7.6
4. It has been easy to make oneself heard in the group.	9.4
5. The group has been engaged in its task.	9.2
6. The group has been creative.	9.0
7. I have been engaged in the group.	8.7
8. I have been creative in the group.	8.4
9. I have participated in an interesting exchange of ideas and experiences.	8.7
10. It was worth the time to participate in the group.	8.7
11. The group has contributed important ideas to SIF.	7.7

NOTE: The results displayed in the table are average scores from participants in the three groups that met twice. The scores are measured on a 10-point scale where 1 = *disagree* and 10 = *agree completely.*

The Efficiency of the Model

The process capabilities were evaluated through statistical data on the group recruitment process. During the initial phase, the project administrator made telephone calls to managers selected from the membership register. When 46 persons had been contacted, only one had responded that he wanted to participate in a dialogue group. Hence, a professional market interview firm was used to recruit people to the dialogue groups. The firm's resources and its members' skills made this process more effective; approximately 1 of 10 people agreed to participate. Of the 40 individuals recruited to the groups, 21 actually participated in the initial meetings.

At the end of the initial meetings, the participants were asked whether they would join for another discussion with the same group (completed with one service developer and one researcher). Three of the four groups met again; the biggest group was the only one that failed. Of the 21 persons participating in the initial meetings, 10 participated in the second meetings.

After the second meeting with the dialogue groups, a short evaluation was made. The participants individually assessed the method by considering various proposals. The results were measured on a 10-point scale where 1 = *disagree* and 10 = *agree completely* (Table 15.1).

During the sessions, a large number of suggestions for new service initiatives or improvement of existing services were made. They were discussed in the group and were also videotaped. In addition, the participants were asked to take notes on inventions and improvements. Each suggestion was registered together with a short description.

The results then were evaluated from five perspectives:

1. Innovation

2. Service idea level (clearly defined services/ideas on a systems level)

3. Service users' interaction (SIF as a provider of services/platforms for relations)

4. Usability

5. Cultural knowledge

Innovation

The project group evaluated the ideas generated from the dialogue groups. Every project group participant rated the service ideas on a 5-point scale where 5 = *very innovative idea*. The average innovation score was 2.75, indicating that the majority of the obtained service ideas generated concerned traditional services and activities. Together, the project group did not find the ideas generated to be very innovative. As is discussed later, the group gained other kinds of knowledge by using the dialogue groups.

Service Idea Level

The researchers made a rough assessment to find out whether the generated service ideas contributed on a specific service level or on an architectural/systems level. The results showed that approximately two thirds of the ideas were not defined very clearly and so could be seen as formulated on an architectural/systems level. Even though this evaluation was hard to make with precision, it provided information concerning the service idea level.

Service Users' Interaction

The researchers studied the anticipated user roles if the proposed services were to be developed. Although a majority of the service ideas related to services that would be distributed by the union and consumed by individual members, one third of the service ideas were built on relations among members such as "networks for managers" and "mentoring programs." Thus, the preferred role of the union seems to be both as a service provider and as a provider of relational platforms.

Usability

A list of the developed 65 service ideas was sent to all 35 departments/managers in the SIF organization. The task was to evaluate the ideas on a 100-point scale—the more interesting and important the idea, the more points that were awarded. Each evaluator was instructed to use 100 points total. A low response rate of less than 25% (8 of 35) makes the results problematic to evaluate. The most interesting perspective for the evaluation has been the analysis of the relations between the usability scores

Table 15.2   Innovation/Usability Matrix: Service Ideas Highly Ranked on Innovation
or Usability

	Low Innovation Score	**High Innovation Score**
High Usability Points	Negotiating help, advice on legal matters, and agreements Advice on salaries for managers and project managers Contracts for managers, preprinting forms, and preassessments	To be visible for managers Mentoring programs
Low Usability Points		Emerge as the union for project managers "Case discussions"—difficult cases Participants' initiated networks Individualized Web portals "Knowledge warehouse"—information about education and training for managers

and innovation scores. Among the five ideas with the highest usability scores, only two obtained higher than average innovation scores—and their scores were just slightly higher than average.

Put in a matrix where high innovation scores are defined as higher than the average score (i.e., higher than 2.75) and high usability points are defined as higher than the average (i.e., higher than 12), Table 15.2 shows the service ideas ranked with high innovation scores or high usability points.

A matrix consisting of the total number of obtained service ideas shows a clear pattern: A majority of the high usability ideas have not been assessed as highly innovative, and a majority of the high innovation ideas have obtained low usability points (Table 15.3).

Cultural Knowledge

The service ideas were not the only results from the work with the design dialogue platform. The discussions in the groups contributed cultural knowledge as an important part of organizational learning. This aspect has been evaluated by the project group as the group members have created a list of what they learned.

Effectiveness of the Design Dialogue Group Model

The effectiveness of the model relates to the possible diffusion of the methodology within the organization. The project group evaluated the

Table 15.3   Innovation/Usability Matrix: All Service Ideas

	Low Innovation Score	High Innovation Score
High Usability Points	12	6
Low Usability Points	22	25

model from a diffusion perspective. Since then, a modified model has been used in the organization.

The evaluation of the dialogue platform model has been made as a SWOT (strengths, weaknesses, opportunities, and threats) analysis concerning the prospects of implementing the design dialogue process as a regular user interface/development method. This analysis has been conducted by the project group.

Strengths

The participants found the discussions to be interesting and important; they were mobilized and became more interested in SIF as a union. The model enables the union to get close to the members and yield a deeper understanding. The close meeting between members and internal experts is of benefit to all parties. The participants are active, and the discussions become creative and stimulating. Another advantage is that participants do not have to represent others, making this kind of contact with members different from many other meetings in an organization based on representative democracy. The discussions result in a picture of important issues for the group and provide a new kind of framework for the development of action plans. The method also gives better precision in our service innovation and development processes. This is a structured dialogue with our members.

Weaknesses

A more extended use of the model will require a strong organization for the recruitment of participants as well as considerable resources for analysis and transformation of the results into action. Will there be a sufficient number of employees who have the interest, opportunities, and competencies to participate? Training, writing manuals, and creating a strong organization will require vast resources. The results are dependent on how the selection of participants is made. A few people may acquire a high degree of influence over the union activities and services, and it is not known whether the participants are representative of the members (and potential members). And what about the quality of the output? To date, we have not found a single service idea that could be defined as a real "breakthrough." Will the method be accepted as a legitimate form of trade union participation? Is it possible to develop this as one of the major methods for participation in a hierarchical democracy, or does it call for a union with more lateral communication?

Opportunities

Once the organization is appropriately equipped, it is a quick and inexpensive method that provides opportunities for listening to potential members, evaluating new ideas, and helping to track new trends. We can easily organize dialogue with various groups such as women/men, more/less qualified employees, and people in specific occupations. We can also design the dialogue to focus on more specific issues such as salaries and benefits. We get to know many members and may use the group participants as a basis for networking. This is a new way in which to enhance "the sense of unity" and to gain a higher level of recognition of member situations and needs.

Possible Threats

The method, as such, may cause misinterpretations of member needs and ideas because the selection of participants may be manipulated and the moderators' own points of view may bias the group discussions. The method is also time-consuming, and it is not known whether it is possible to keep the enthusiasm within the organization when the method has become common practice. It could be dangerous if the method is recognized as the one and only way in which to involve members in idea creation. From a democratic point of view, the method may be seen as problematic. Nonmembers may gain influence over SIF activities and services. The democratic structure, based on representation, may be threatened. Dialogue groups may substitute company club activities and workplace visits. Elected members and SIF staff may react with hostility.

Since the pilot study, a modified version of the dialogue group methodology has been used at SIF. This version has the following characteristics:

- The groups meet in one 2-hour session.
- The session is led by an SIF employee and held in an SIF office.
- Discussion guidelines are designed to facilitate the processing of gathered information. Normally, the results from the design group discussions are presented and distributed the day after the session.
- Staff have followed the discussions on television monitors.
- All participants have individually assessed the method by considering the same proposals as in the pilot project.

When a project was started, to map needs concerning development of competency and skills among members in the construction consultant industry, the project members were trained in the dialogue group methodology and took the role as group moderators.

During the preparation stages of SIF's information technology sector negotiations, national negotiating officers used the methodology to enhance the understanding of attitudes and needs among members. Ideas concerning important issues from a member perspective were collected and could be evaluated through a Web-based survey with some 2,500 respondents (of the 25,000 members in the information technology sector). The methodology also had a strong impact on the meetings held with members on a regional level. There is a direct connection between the discussions held in the design dialogue groups and the proposals that SIF brought into the negotiations.

Furthermore, 12 SIF employees were trained in the methodology during an internal seminar. In the near future, dialogue groups will be used in the preparations for the next rounds of collective bargaining involving approximately 250,000 members. The use of the dialogue groups will be similar to that in the information technology negotiations, but the approach will be a bit more ambitious. Dialogue groups will also be used when Web-based virtual communities for managers, students, and local union representatives in the information technology sector are developed. The preparations for the next SIF congress, to be held in November 2004, started early in 2003. An important issue that could be investigated through the use of dialogue groups concerns the development of the members' democratic participation in the congress discussions. The challenge is to let the members tell their union how they want to influence the organization.

A Reflection on the Project and Its Results

As researchers, we often have an idea about the outcome of the research when our projects are set up. Intervention researchers are not exceptional in this respect. The purpose of intervention research to produce actionable knowledge may, during the preparation phase, have a greater impact on anticipated results. On the other hand, the importance and possible usefulness of the results we attain generate both opportunities and interest in the project.

The pilot study showed that it was more difficult to find participants for the dialogue groups than we had expected. Those who participated in the dialogue groups found the discussions to be very interesting and useful. The service ideas obtained were less clearly defined than expected and were not as innovative as expected. The group members not only wanted individual services from the union but also recognized the union as a possible builder of relational platforms. Service ideas defined as innovative by the project group were not seen as very usable by the organization. In addition, the participants in the project group learned a great deal about the situation for managers and project managers. Considering the effectiveness of the model, the project group assessment of the design dialogue platform as a model for service development and organizational learning concludes that the model could be further developed and used as a major model in the organization.

The use of the methodology, after the pilot study was conducted, shows evidence that the method could be used successfully.

One set of results from the pilot study is surprising and unanticipated. The experiment aimed at a dialogue focusing on ideas for concrete new services related to union membership. Most of the service ideas that pertain to this goal score low on innovativeness; they are incremental improvements or extensions of existing elements in the service portfolio. In addition, it is possible for the organization to consider these for further development and so have a value in use. The other set of suggestions considered to be innovative, but difficult to implement, are different in nature. They propose lateral networks for dialogue among members and propose a different focus of the union where it would enable and facilitate knowledge creation and learning.

Broadening our perspective, this is an interesting finding that addresses the general problem of how ordinary members can influence the priorities of the union. When provided with the opportunity, members tend to put forward ideas that improve opportunities for dialogue and knowledge exchange. The existing organization, however, tends to reject such ideas, but not because they are impossible to implement; indeed, arranging dialogue processes is not necessarily difficult to accomplish. A traditional union is based on shared technological dependencies. Available resources are shared for many purposes and services that are successfully coordinated through the standardization of procedures. The suggestions thrown up by the model can be interpreted as threats to basic technologies. They assume a different shape of the union's technological core, pushing it more in the direction of shared dependencies. When the union's administrative organization is confronted by the suggestions, the administrators evaluate the suggestions as impossible or too complicated to implement.

Implications for the
Management of Service Innovation

It has been possible to develop a design dialogue model within the organization studied. This may also be a suitable solution for other organizations wishing to create a concept- and knowledge-building interface with their customers/users. Today, we can make some predictions about the usability of the model in the studied organization. Is the model usable in other settings? It might be, but it has to be adapted due to context, culture, and other factors. Nevertheless, some important findings could be helpful for organizations aiming at using customers/users as a source of business/product/service development and organizational learning.

The assessment made by the users involved showed clearly that the *process* was seen as creative, whereas the project group did not find the *results* to be innovative. However, it may be possible to generate more innovative ideas if the group discussions are more focused on specific objects/areas. In addition, the kind of cultural knowledge that the design dialogue groups provided may be a strong enough argument for using the model.

The next step in this research and development project will be to use a design dialogue platform as a regular customer interface and learning method. The managerial implications need to be discussed within the organization. Service innovation and development within the organization will call for new skills and expertise from the staff to act more as process consultants and observers.

References

Amabile, T. M. (1982). Social psychology of creativity: A consensual assessment technique. *Journal of Personality and Social Psychology, 43,* 997–1013.

Amabile, T. M. (1996). *Creativity in context.* Boulder, CO: Westview.

Beer, M., Eisenstat, R. A., & Spector, B. (1990). *The critical past to corporate renewal.* Boston: Harvard Business School Press.

Beer, M., & Nohria, N. (Eds.). (2000). *Breaking the code of change.* Boston: Harvard Business School Press.

Cagan, J., & Vogel, C. M. (2002). *What drives new product development?* Upper Saddle River, NJ: Prentice Hall.

Edvardsson, B. (1996). *Tjänsteutveckling med inbyggd kvalitet* (Qualitative service development). Working paper, Karlstad University, Sweden.

Edvardsson, B., & Gustafsson, A. (1999). Quality in the development of new products and services. In B. Edvardsson & A. Gustafsson (Eds.), *The Nordic School of Quality Management* (pp. 191–193). Lund, Sweden: Studentlitteratur.

Grönroos, C. (1992). *Service management, Ledning, strategi och marknadsföring i Servicekonkurrens* (Service management, leadership, strategy, and marketing in competition). Göteborg, Sweden: ISL Förlag.

Gupta, A. K., & Wilemon, D. L. (1990). Accelerating the development of technology-based new products. *Californian Management Review, 32*(2), 24–44.

Gustavsen, B. (1992). *Dialogue and development.* Assen, Netherlands: Van Gorkum.

Gustavsen, B. (2001). Theory and practice: The mediating discourse. In P. B. Reason & H. Bradbury (Eds.), *Handbook of action research* (pp. 17–26). London: Sage.

Hatchuel, A., Lemasson, P., & Weil, B. (2001). From R&D to RID: Design strategies and the management of innovation fields. In *Proceedings of the Eighth International Product Development Management Conference* (pp. 415–430). Enschede, Netherlands: EIASM.

Hatchuel, A., & Weil, B. (1999, July). *Design-oriented organizations: Towards a unified theory of design activities.* Paper presented at the Sixth International Product Development Management Conference, Churchill College, Cambridge, UK.

Herbst, P. G. (1974). *Socio-technical design: Strategies in multi-disciplinary research.* London: Tavistock.

Johne, A., & Storey, C. (1998). New service development: A review of the literature and annotated biography. *European Journal of Marketing, 32*(3/4), 184–251.

Kaulio, M. A. (1997). *Customer-focused product development: A practice-centered perspective.* Ph.D. thesis, Chalmers University of Technology, Göteborg, Sweden.

Kaulio, M. A. (1998). Customer, consumer, and user involvement in product development: A framework and a review of selected methods. *Total Quality Management, 9*(1), 141–149.

Merriam-Webster. (1998). *Merriam-Webster's collegiate dictionary.* Springfield, MA: Author.

Mohrman, S. A., & Cummings, T. G. (1989). *Self-designing organizations.* Reading, MA: Addison-Wesley.

Naschold, F., Cole, R. E., Gustavsen, B., & van Beinum, H. (1993). *Constructing the industrial society.* Assen, Netherlands: Van Gorkum.

Normann, R. (2000). *Service management: Strategy and leadership in service business.* Chichester, UK: Wiley.

Pasmore, W. (2001). Action research in the workplace: The socio-technical perspective. In P. B. Reason & H. Bradbury (Eds.), *Handbook of action research* (pp. 38–47). London: Sage.

Pettersson, P. (2000). *Kvalitet i livslånga tjänsterelationer: Svenska kyrkan ur tjänsteteoretiskt och religionssociologiskt perspektiv* (Quality in lifelong service relationships: The Church of Sweden in service, theoretical, and sociology of religion perspective). Ph.D. thesis, Karlstad University, Sweden.

Scheuing, E. E., & Johnson, E. (1989). A proposed model for new service development. *Journal of Services Marketing, 3,* 25–34.

Shotter, J. (1993). *Conversational realities.* London: Sage.

Shotter, J., & Gustavsen, B. (1999). *The role of "dialogue conferences" in the development of "learning regions": Doing "from within" our lives together what we cannot do apart.* Stockholm, Sweden: Center for Advanced Studies of Leadership.

van Einatten, F. M. (1993). *The paradigm that changed the workplace.* Assen, Netherlands: Van Gorkum.

von Hippel, E. (1988). *The sources of innovation.* New York: Oxford University Press.

16 The Collaborative Development of Leader@site

Sven F. Kylén, Kina Mulec, Jan Wickenberg,
Jonas Roth, and Mats Sundgren

How can the leadership of scientists be improved in pharmaceutical research and development (R&D) in a new company and still retain the characteristics and success factors at the site level? This became an important strategic issue following the merger between Astra and Zeneca in 1999 that made AstraZeneca one of the largest pharmaceutical companies in the world. The new company not only became bigger but also became a truly global multinational company. Therefore, leadership matters became a key challenge for the company after the merger. The issue of leadership became a strategic one because the new R&D organization demanded greater coordination to ensure both effectiveness in operations and a capacity for innovation. The previous semi-independent R&D sites, with different idiosyncratic cultures and leadership styles, now had to be integrated within one global organization.

One of the Swedish R&D sites of AstraZeneca decided to pursue an action following the strategic decision around leadership development. After attending a FENIX seminar on "The Human Resource Management Role in Leadership Development in Learning Organizations," management of the R&D site took the opportunity to discuss how to improve the leadership development activities at the site level. FENIX researchers were invited to develop and change the site's leadership activities, often organized in a rather ad hoc manner, and turn them into an integrated and up-to-date program. Two perspectives were taken into account: (a) the perspective of scientific

AUTHORS' NOTE: We thank Hans Glise, Kerstin Kylberg-Hansen, Elisabet Wistrand, and Marie Olsson for supporting Leader@site as a research project. We also thank all of the leaders at the research and development site in Mölndal, Sweden, for allowing us to challenge them on leadership/management issues in interviews and experiments.

generic accumulated knowledge and (b) nurturing local success factors that could be deeply embedded in the sociocultural context in the way leaders were acting at the site.

The human resources (HR) department was well motivated to change the leadership development activities because there had been some criticism of its generic standardized way of working with leadership development. The view held by site management was that a site-based and site-adapted program could optimize program design according to the requirements given by the corporate level and the specific needs at the site. It was a clearly stated HR demand from the start that researchers were supposed to take part in delivering the first pilot of the new program while giving advice and providing expert knowledge. This initiative included both an action research methodology and insider/outsider (I/O) participation. The possibility of taking an active part in the leadership development program (LDP) led to discussions about FENIX internal research methodology. The active part of delivering the pilot of the LDP was discussed (e.g., pure consultancy vs. research project types of issues). Concerns were raised that tension between consultancy and research would result in a "messy" research project in which scientific objectivity would be at risk. On the other hand, several opportunities were recognized, and the challenge was generally regarded as an experiment in which FENIX ought to participate. In addition, at the R&D site, most employees and the target group (the leaders) knew very well what research would make an extraordinary arena for experimentation. Furthermore, discussion of finding new and alternative ways in which to engage collectively in research problems close to their emerging research interest was viewed as critical. The result of the discussions led to the engagement of FENIX in the R&D project.

A Joint Definition of Purpose

The purpose of the project was to develop a generic Leadership Development Program (LDP) called Leader@site. In addition, the intent was to investigate and further develop a research method that allowed the insider view of culture competence to meet the outsider view of academic knowledge about leadership development programs. This was supposed to be done by collective action based on the two objectives. The purpose of this chapter is to show how the I/O team research method (Bartunek & Louis, 1996) was applied to enable collective scientific-based action and, through this, to implement adequate knowledge in the LDP from the academic community blended with company culture and traditions (Figure 16.1).

The I/O team research method focuses on the meeting between outside academic field-workers and company insiders. Data are to be analyzed by the I/O team both before and after various experiments/interventions have

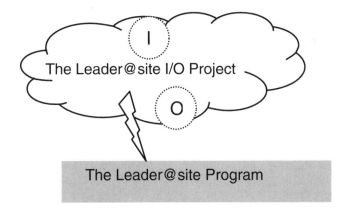

Figure 16.1 The Project With Its Main Deliverable: The Program

been tried out. It was a demand from both the company and FENIX to work collaboratively. The choice of method was driven by the desire to maintain a balance among a mix of local (implicit) practitioner theories (Elden & Levin, 1991; Heider, 1958), general (externalized knowledge) scientifically based theories (Kylén, 1999), and free and validated choice (Argyris & Schön, 1974).

The Context of the Research Project and the R&D Site

Research was conducted at one of the Swedish R&D sites of AstraZeneca. AstraZeneca has an R&D organization employing more than 10,000 researchers, divided into a handful of R&D sites. Research is conducted within various therapeutic areas such as gastrointestinal, cardiovascular, and cancer medicine. The R&D site in which the project took place has been one of the most successful sites in the pharmaceutical industry. It has been the innovator of new chemical entities (original chemical molecules), some of which became mega-brand products (i.e., products yielding more than $1 billion [U.S.] annually in sales). Thus, the site has a very good track record in terms of being a significant return on investment. In addition, the R&D site represents an exceptionally high academic education level, with 30% of the employees having postgraduate degrees. In addition, the R&D site has a tradition of close collaboration with academia and university hospitals. It is being organized as a matrix to create an innovative organizational climate (Ekvall, 1996) and strong knowledge creation interaction patterns (Kylén, 1999; Kylén & Shani, 2002) well suited for R&D work.

Framing the Need for Developing Methods That Enable Collective Action _____

Modern organizations are dependent on continual innovation. The importance of localness, uniqueness, and the involvement of many employees is often stressed as parameters for organizational capacities for innovation (Shani & Pasmore, 1985; see also Chapter 7 of this volume). At AstraZeneca, there are expectations on organizational members to take responsibility for developing effective solutions and creating knowledge for practice. This brings up questions about methodological choices on how social scientists, management, and organizational researchers could and preferably should work when being involved in organization change programs and interventions.

There is a discussion in the field of management studies on how methodological choices affect knowledge creation. Gibbons and colleagues (1994) argue for "Mode 2" knowledge creation, focusing on practice and context where multidisciplinary knowledge is needed and constantly validated by practitioners. "Mode 1" focuses on a generic intradisciplinary theory where researchers are in charge of the validating process. Adler and Norrgren (see Chapter 4 of this volume) discuss the need for further developing partnerships between industry/practitioners and academia/researchers and see them as transdisciplinary collaborative partnerships. The capacity of transforming academic knowledge into practical applications to address practitioners' problems and simultaneously initiate research activities is a critical capability for collaborative researchers. These partnerships need more of the Mode 2-type knowledge production competencies. Gibbons and colleagues' (1994) Mode 2 research has some similarities with Argyris and Schön's (1974, 1978) Model II–reasoning, where valid information, free choice, and shared control enable a higher quality of learning and development than does Model I (unilateral control and defensiveness).

A Team's Ability to Make a Difference_____

A team's capacity for effective learning and knowledge creation is dependent on the innovative climate in the workplace (Ekvall, 1996) and nondefensive action routines (Kylén, 1999). Shani and Lau (2000) argue that creating conditions that allow teams to achieve synergy is likely to produce superior solutions. However, synergy, learning, and innovation are not common denominators. Hackman (1990) describes the phenomenon as "trip wires," meaning that we often have an unrealistic view of what teams can accomplish if time and resources are not invested in developing the appropriate human interaction. In Hackman's formulation, "The unstated assumption is that there is some magic in group interaction, and by working together, members will evolve any structures that the team actually needs. It is a false hope; there is no such magic" (p. 498).

Hambrick (1995) identifies a number of factors that seem to harm interaction in, development of, and change in teams: harmful rivalry, "groupthink," and fragmentation. He claims that these factors are symptoms of "non-team behavior." Katzenbach (1997) argues that many groups are not "real teams." Hambrick's (1995) factors could be seen as defensive approaches, with their roots in interactions riddled by distorted communication, rigid mental models, and organizational political behavior. These examples of defensive action, consciously using mechanisms that work against creative interaction, learning, change, and development in the team, suggest that individuals act on the basis of their beliefs, for their own sake, or in the interest of their home bases (Frost & Egri, 1991).

Edmondson, Bohmer, and Pisano (2001) argue that teams that are good at learning do so using "in-action" rather than "after-action" analyses, trying new ideas as they go along. The question then becomes the following: How can an in-action learning capability be achieved? Organizational learning and development competence have been identified in the literature as important components of both effectiveness and creativity (Argyris, 1993; Senge, 1990). It is often the existing mental models and standard actions that need to be challenged to enable knowledge and behavior to develop (Kylén, 1999). The development process, when using a team approach, includes the need to continuously invest in the development of the research team to secure optimal functioning.

_____The Development of an I/O Team

Bartunek and Moch (1987) recognize various patterns in how change occurs during an action research process. _First-order change_ is where a specific change is identified and implemented within an existing way of thinking. _Second-order change_ is where a change requires altering the core assumptions that underlie the situation. _Third-order change_ is where the members of an organization learn to question their own assumptions and points of view as well as to develop and implement new ones. Various phases can be seen when it is time for the implementation of change. Although this is one of the most difficult steps in an action research effort, it is not a recognized problem in traditional research because the researchers are not usually involved at this stage. Shani and Pasmore (1985) argue, "It is here [during the implementation phase] where relationships are most important in overcoming the natural roadblocks to change" (p. 446). The relationships between the insiders and the outsiders (the researchers) are, of course, crucial in conducting good research. Even more important for action research is that the insiders and outsiders have good reputations and networks within the organization when the changes are to be implemented. Shani and Pasmore identified four critical components of the action research process: (a) the _contextual factors,_ which involve both the individual and the organizational factors; (b) the _quality of relationships,_ where trust, concern for others, equality of influence, and a common language are of importance; (c) the *quality of the action research process,* where key steps in the inquiry process are developed and implemented; and (d) the *outcomes* of the action research effort, where the organizational improvement and creation of new knowledge are generated. Perhaps no other methodology is so well suited to studying the process of change in organizations, given that change itself is a continuous and unpredictable happening. However, if there are significant value differences between insiders and outsiders, the I/O team research might not be a suitable method.

Experiences From the Collaborative Research Activities

The Organization of the Research Project

The company financed the research project, and there were resources to cover one senior researcher for 8 hours per week and one research project coordinator for 40 hours per week. The HR department put in 30 hours a week of project leadership. The site also had three researchers who were working half-time at FENIX and half-time at the site as part of their doctoral program. As a group, they were supposed to put in approximately 15 hours per week (5 hours each) of their company time, focusing mainly on I/O team meetings but also on important interventions. Hard data showed that the input of hours deviated individually due to the candidates' research questions. The project started on a 1-year basis and was later prolonged to a second year. At the time of the writing of this chapter, there were discussions about a possible third year for exporting thoughts and findings to other sites of the corporation.

The LDP was manned by a project leader (an *insider* from the HR function), a project coordinator (starting as an *outsider* but soon becoming an *outsider/insider* after working full-time in HR), a senior researcher from FENIX (an *outsider* as well as the research leader), and three executive Ph.D. candidates (*insiders/outsiders*) (Figure 16.2).

Apart from the six persons constituting the inner core of the I/O action research team, there was an active network around each individual that was used to make other persons temporary members of the team. The team members were assigned tasks to run as part of the research project between meetings, sometimes together but mostly on their own. The team members all were involved in activities where stakeholders, such as managers, project leaders, union leaders, employees, and researchers, constantly discussed the topic with the involved team members.

Meeting "Energy Dependencies"

The project meetings were subject to an interesting effect. The team carried through 25 project meetings under which the perceived level of

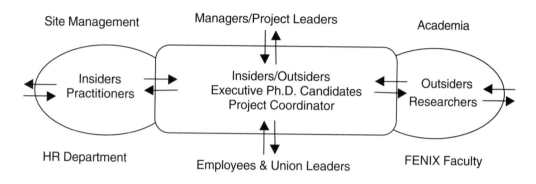

Figure 16.2 The Insider/Outsider Team Working With the Leader@site Research Project

engagement (the "energy level") fluctuated considerably. Also, the attendance at the meetings varied; sometimes the project manager was absent, but more often one or more team members were away. A strong covariation was observed between the energy level and the level of attendance during the various meetings; whenever the meetings where fully manned, creativity and innovation would color discussions of problem solving, whereas whenever the meetings were only partly manned, solutions would be colored by innovative solutions to a lesser extent. A plausible explanation is that if there was not an adequate balance of players, this would lead to a decrease of energy and less productive reasoning and innovative ideas.

An Outsider Becoming an Insider: The Emergence of the I/O Role

The project coordinator started as an outsider in the role of research assistant. After a few months, the first parts of the LDP commenced and the administration of the leadership courses was included in her assignment. She also took responsibility for the design and development of the program Web site, and in this work she needed to coordinate with a few information technology (IT) related functions at AstraZeneca. She also collected and interpreted research data. After 6 months, she observed that she had "gone partly native"—to use a term from anthropology—becoming an I/O.

The FENIX training of the executive Ph.D. candidates is designed to bridge the gap between academy and industry. During their education, the executive Ph.D. candidates experienced a similar kind of frustration of there being one too many sets of directives and cultures to be rationally and emotionally manageable. The executive Ph.D. candidates were to bridge a gap of two cultures, and initially their mind-sets were to find one best way by rationally breaking down one strategy rather than two (see Chapter 7 of this volume). Eventually, the executive Ph.D. candidates felt more comfortable when participating in the two cultures simultaneously. Thus, they had gained experience in this "double logic" before starting to work in this research project.

Product Innovations by the I/O Team

The I/O team had a wide range of ideas, concepts, implemented lectures, and tools for experimental learning. The most quality-adding parts and important pitfalls of the team are discussed here.

Communication and Strategy

The team recognized that the focus of the company was not on leadership development. The future customers of the Leader@site program, the leaders, might have developed an attitude toward LDPs that would bias their perception of it. To override such a bias, a communication strategy was developed based on the following values:

1. *New and different:* Examples include using natural language on the Web site and avoiding the reuse of clichés from former development programs.

2. *Challenging:* Examples include asking participants to explain their positions on what they do in their work and asking them to reflect on work in a critical way.

3. *Recognizing the informal side of organization:* It is okay to discuss what we *really* do.

4. *Reciprocal participation:* Participants are just that—participants— and not bystanders.

5. *Low contact threshold:* Make it simple for people to get in contact with us rather than holding people at arm's length by instructions and rules on the intranet.

Product branding of the LDP was done by inventing a name, Leader@site, and a logo. The program had to spell out clearly how different it is from previous programs. At the same time, the name of the new program was aimed at creating a collective arena for leadership development for managers and project leaders at the site. Furthermore, the name needed to reflect that it was a site-specific leadership program based on the needs of the leaders at the local site.

An intranet Web site was developed by the project coordinator with support from AstraZeneca's IT function. The Web site was designed to host information on activities, guidelines, links, and literature about leadership and leadership development. To reduce turnover time, much of the

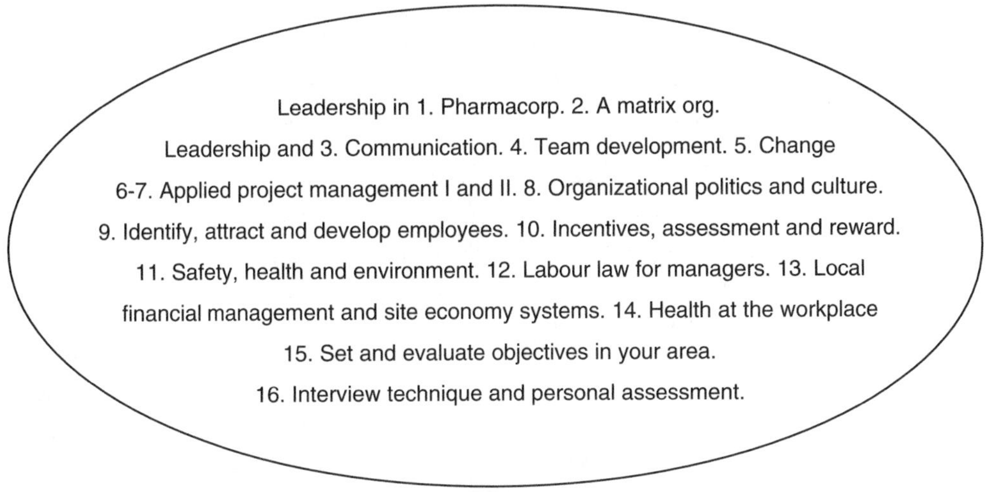

Leadership in 1. Pharmacorp. 2. A matrix org.

Leadership and 3. Communication. 4. Team development. 5. Change

6-7. Applied project management I and II. 8. Organizational politics and culture.

9. Identify, attract and develop employees. 10. Incentives, assessment and reward.

11. Safety, health and environment. 12. Labour law for managers. 13. Local

financial management and site economy systems. 14. Health at the workplace

15. Set and evaluate objectives in your area.

16. Interview technique and personal assessment.

Figure 16.3 The Smorgasbord of Activities

communication with leaders was done through the use of e-mail. A permanent link that allowed for simple use of the communication tool was established. This communication tool resulted in active dialogue that led to the development of the five strategic site values.

LDP Design and Feedback

The new LDP was supposed to be flexible enough to make sure that the participants could compose their own development program based on their own responsibilities and needs. The solution was envisaged as a smorgasbord of activities where participants were invited to attain the managerial knowledge and leadership skills they lacked. Courses and the first eight workshops focused on leadership issues, whereas the next eight workshops were oriented toward the training of various management "tools and techniques" (Figure 16.3).

The participants in the workshops were also given opportunities to reflect on leadership and their own experiences as leaders. The reflection was done mainly in an activity called *coach group,* where five or six leaders and an external coach met on 11 occasions during an 18-month period. During these occasions, they jointly discussed and reflected on practical problems from the leaders' daily activities.

Interviews with the first cohort (17 participants in three coach groups) were conducted to find out more about the needs and motivation of the participants as well as what a successful R&D site and its leaders needed in terms of leadership and leadership skills development. The result from the first few interviews showed that people did not engage in ongoing reflection of their leadership role and that divergent views and perspectives on leadership were not very common. The I/O team came to the conclusion that it would be interesting to see what happened when the participants were confronted with this finding. The result was long interviews with diverse views and insights about the needs, functions, and skills that are required of leaders at the local R&D site. These interviews also showed that energy, engagement, and motivation were created when the respondents were being challenged by the two interviewers' questions (e.g., "How do you know that? Couldn't it be [like this] instead?"). Questions such as "Do you have time to exercise leadership?" and "What difference does leadership make?" were supposed to clarify whether the leaders had a vocabulary of leadership and whether they were knowledgeable about robust theories of leadership. Although the interview study showed that most leaders lacked an extensive leadership vocabulary and often made use of unreflected theories of action, an interesting finding was that some interviewees picked up vocabulary and made quick but precise improvements to their theories of leadership during the interviews. The interviewees showed little or no resistance to change and showed great interest in learning.

The course modules were evaluated by questionnaires and interviews. The evaluation painted the same picture as did the interviews just described. That is, the participants expressed a wish for the trainers to be more challenging and also wanted to be questioned about their values and views.

The team proposed numerous incremental changes after each course evaluation. The project manager and the project coordinator took care of these suggestions by providing feedback to the internal and external trainers. The interviews had also shown that there was a lack of activities around two topics with which the I/O team decided to experiment. One was line project work, which became a workshop called the "Matrix Dilemma," where line managers and project leaders could bring concrete problems to be discussed and mirrored to theories around matrix organizations. Another topic was problems with handling change associated with culture. This became a small group seminar on organizational politics, culture, and leadership.

The low degree of awareness in leadership and findings for challenging assumptions about leadership brought about the need for an individual counseling session at the focal site. The session was given at the start of the program. Leaders received feedback on measurement instruments showing what leadership abilities the individuals needed to develop but also giving the individuals a chance to step back and not enter the program. The individual counseling sessions proved to be very successful and provided a deeper understanding in the I/O team of the need to maintain a holistic view of the leaders' development, that is, where they are when starting the program, where they are supposed to be after the program, and how they will get there. The result created an "ideal model" (Figure 16.4) that showed the gaps and inconsistencies in the program, offering opportunities to make clear choices on where to focus and improve.

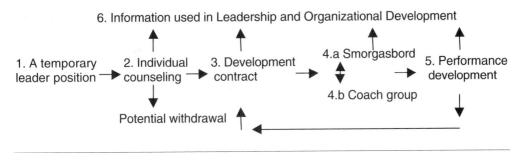

Figure 16.4 The "Ideal Model"

The model starts with individual counseling (Step 2 in Figure 16.4) for a manager or leader who has had a temporary leadership position (at least 1 year of experience) (Step 1) and who has been recommended for the program. The counseling builds on development instruments and an interview. As a consequence of these first two steps, the leader could decide to withdraw from the program due to a lack of interest, wrong timing, or some other reason. The counseling is also supposed to give the leader fuel for discussions with the participant's manager and with HR about what to develop during the 18-month program.

A competence development contract (Step 3) among the leader, the participant's manager, and the HR staff, using the 360-degree technique (in which feedback on performance is sought out from all those who work directly with the individual such as his or her supervisor, peers, and subordinates) and other assessments, should be the basis for what activities to choose from among the smorgasbord (Step 4a) of leadership knowledge and management tools. It should also assess whether the coach group (Step 4b) activities ought to be part of the portfolio. Thereafter, a 360-degree postmeasurement was supposed to show whether any behavioral changes could be seen 2 years from the starting point. This performance development (Step 5) could, of course, be useful at the aggregated level for developmental activities (Step 6) in improving this leadership program and other leadership development activities, and it could be used in organizational development as well.

The trust in FENIX was reinforced after the first year, and the I/O team was regarded as an increasingly important resource in ensuring quality of the program. Incremental changes to the existing program deepened as the local theories were spelled out in the interviews. The I/O team worked a lot with the delving interviews, which had much important information as to what to develop in leaders, as well as how to develop leaders, at this particular site. The information about and insights into the energy and engagement that could be created from challenging questions made it easier to adapt the scientifically based management knowledge. The arguments for a stronger focus on a business perspective, cultural issues, organizational political impact on the cross-site projects, and creativity became easier to understand among the leaders after working through the interviews.

However, it is noteworthy that after the first year, the I/O team still lacked an opportunity to properly investigate the coaching part of the program. There was more openness, but restrictions still existed around full insight into some parts of the program. It was not until the middle of the second year that the three coaches decided to have learning sessions together with the I/O team. These meetings were very fruitful, making it possible to evaluate and develop the coach groups. The information provided by coaches initiated discussions of new improvements and changes in the program. But the fact that the research project was coming to an end made it harder to get energized again. One consequence was that the overall design of the LDP was implemented, but the evaluation and contracting were not. Another is that the coach groups were running, but it was unknown to what degree the coaches followed the design principles.

Pitfalls of the I/O Team

There were, of course, pitfalls of the I/O team. One of the aspects that was "not good enough," from our perspective, was that it took a long time before the coaching part of the program came up for discussion. Therefore, this prolonged the time before we were able to evaluate and improve. Members of the I/O team and leaders participating in the LDP posed questions and doubts regarding the choice of coaches, coaching method and initialization, coach group composition, and weak connection to the content of the smorgasbord of courses. In the latter part of the LDP, the coaches and coaching process were open to research and evaluation.

Early course evaluation interviews showed that many participants did not understand why the smorgasbord of modules was not obligatory. This suggests that the managerial influence on the developmental contracts, as well as the leaders' ability to take responsibility for their own leadership development and learning, was not sufficiently developed and communicated. It also became clear that the participants viewed the choices given as a major weakness of the program. The I/O team had difficulty in arriving at a decision on how to address this issue.

The I/O team offered other parts of the company the chance to share data on an aggregated level (i.e., unit level) to facilitate leadership and organizational development activities. The interest level in the workshop session was high as the management team recognized findings and developed activities to further develop and maintain. However, interest faded when there was no response to the research teams' suggestions of how to continue and improve the LDP. Thus, there seemed to be little interest, outside of the research team, in creating constant change and experimenting with what was discussed at the workshop and developed in the research project and LDP. This came as a big surprise to the I/O team.

Reflecting on the Use of the Method

FENIX researchers experimented with the I/O team methodology through the creation of a team of insiders (HR practitioners) and outsiders (senior researchers in academia) together with insiders/outsiders (executive Ph.D. candidates and the project coordinator). The issue was to develop a new program based on science without violating traditions. It was to combine local implicit practitioner theories (Elden & Levin, 1991) with external validated knowledge (Kylén, 1999) to secure future success.

The I/O team method made it possible to run a research project that created knowledge on practical realities for the benefit of the leaders' development. The project influenced the relations between FENIX and AstraZeneca in a positive way and became, perhaps because of the method, an important bridge between the company and academic researchers, thereby widening academic contacts to social and management science. A collaborative effort can be very fruitful, and this research program is an example of the power of strengthening relations (Shani & Pasmore, 1985). In addition, the I/O team methodology was a major force in creating an innovative dialogue and collective actions as well as a tool for implementing results.

The I/O team agreed that when new ways of thinking emerged, it was a fun project and produced valuable results. The "think tank" culture that evolved made it possible to facilitate leadership development that could not have occurred without the I/O action research team methodology. The innovative climate and creative interaction patterns (Kylén, 1999) made it possible to attain a high quality of inquiry and implementation (Shani & Pasmore, 1985). There were, however, signs of trip wires (Hackman, 1990) that caused pitfalls and inhibited the research project from achieving its full potential. This affected the outcome of the LDP. It may be that there are limitations of what can be handled in an I/O team. We believe that more time to build the team spirit and define teamwork procedures would have been beneficial for the collaborative research project.

The I/O team method served as an important experiment in which the FENIX executive Ph.D. candidates could engage in a collective intervention. One of the most important experiences was that the executive Ph.D. candidates could easily support and manage the method and process. They demonstrated that they had the competence to do so. As an example, they combined external ideas with internal practitioner theories. Many of the ideas came from the outsider (senior researcher) and the knowledge in the academic network. These ideas seemingly were rejected by the insiders' network if they were not transformed into the local terminology and context by the insiders/outsiders (executive Ph.D. candidates) team. The insiders/outsiders functioned as interpreters who could connect the scientifically based ideas with the local theories of practice that were nurtured by the practitioners. The quality of this research project, using the I/O team method, was actually dependent on the executive Ph.D. candidates' capacity to combine local practitioner theory with general scientific theory. The skill of rapidly evaluating from both professional and organizational-political standpoints made the project reach first-, second-, and third-order changes (Bartunek & Moch, 1987) without harming interaction (Hambrick, 1995) between team members of the company and academia. Instead, conditions were created that made the team reach a synergy that sometimes led to superior solutions (Shani & Lau, 2000) such as the concepts of the smorgasbord, individual counseling, and the ideal model.

Conclusion

This study can be seen as an example of how a collaborative research project can be conducted and managed. The actual development of the pilot project of the LDP, Leader@site, demanded a collaborative approach from FENIX senior researchers and executive Ph.D. candidates. In this collaboration, the researchers had to combine the deliverance of general management science and R&D leadership with the local unit traditions to secure the success factors of the environment. This process required a close collaboration with practitioners to gain insight into their company culture, competence, and local theories. The approach enabled an experimental method with the I/O action team research methodology, building on the FENIX executive Ph.D. candidates' special role and emerging competencies. The study demonstrates that several new insights were gained in how the method could support the development of leaders in an R&D environment. The study shows an interesting deviation from the predominant model of I/O teams in action research, which more or less pays sole attention to two roles: insiders and outsiders. However, this study illustrates the importance of an I/O team to also consist of another type of actor, namely the I/O team members, in this case represented by the Ph.D. candidates and the project coordinator. Thus, the main conclusion is to demonstrate the potential of this new role. The I/O actor can be described as a critical two-way link as well as a mediator in the I/O team who has a deep understanding and capacity to interpret and translate among multiple worlds.

References

Argyris, C. (1993). *Knowledge for action: A guide to overcoming barriers to organizational change.* San Francisco: Jossey-Bass.

Argyris, C., & Schön, D. A. (1974). *Theory in practice: Increasing professional effectiveness.* San Francisco: Jossey-Bass.

Argyris, C., & Schön, D. A. (1978). *Organizational learning: Theory, method, and practice.* Reading, MA: Addison-Wesley.

Bartunek, J. M., & Louis, M. R. (1996). *Insider/Outsider team research*. Thousand Oaks, CA: Sage.

Bartunek, J. M., & Moch, M. K. (1987). First order, second order, and third order change and organization development interventions: A cognitive approach. *Journal of Applied Behavioral Science, 23*, 483–500.

Edmondson, A., Bohmer, R., & Pisano, G. (2001). Speeding up team learning. *Harvard Business Review, 79*(9), 125–132.

Ekvall, G. (1996). Organizational climate for creativity and creation. *European Journal of Work and Organisational Psychology, 5*(1), 105–123.

Elden, M., & Levin, M. (1991). Cogenerative learning: Bringing participation into action research. In W. F. Whyte (Ed.), *Participatory action research* (pp. 127–142). Newbury Park, CA: Sage.

Frost, P. J., & Egri, C. P. (1991). The political process of innovation. *Research in Organizational Behavior, 13*, 229–295.

Gibbons, M., Limoges, H., Nowotny, H., Schwartzman, S., Scott, P., & Trow, M. (1994). *The new production of knowledge: The dynamics of science and research in contemporary societies*. London: Sage.

Hackman, J. R. (1990). *Teams that work*. San Francisco: Jossey-Bass.

Hambrick, D. C. (1995). Fragmentation and the other problems CEOs have with their top management teams. *California Management Review, 30*(1), 110–128.

Heider, F. (1958). *The psychology of interpersonal relations*. New York: John Wiley.

Katzenbach, J. R. (1997). The myth of the top management team. *Harvard Business Review, 85*(6), 83–93.

Kylén, S. (1999). *Interaktionsmönster i arbetsgrupper, offensiva och defensiva handlingsrutiner* (Patterns of interaction, change, and defensive action routines). Göteborg, Sweden: University of Göteborg, Department of Psychology.

Kylén, S. F., & Shani, A. B. (Rami). (2002). Triggering creativity in teams: An exploratory investigation. *Creativity and Innovation Management, 11*(1), 17–30.

Senge, P. (1990). *The fifth discipline: The art and practice of the learning organisation*. London: Random House.

Shani, A. B. (Rami), & Lau, J. B. (2000). *Behavior in organizations: An experimental approach*. New York: McGraw-Hill.

Shani, A. B. (Rami), & Pasmore, W. A. (1985). Organization inquiry: Towards a new model of the action research process. In D. Warrick (Ed.), *Contemporary organization development: Current thinking and applications* (pp. 438–448). Glenview, IL: Scott, Foresman.

17

Product Innovation in a Solutions Business

Robert Sandberg and Andreas Werr

"We offer customer solutions, not just products" is a common formulation in mission statements of many organizations today. The growing interest in a customer solutions strategy is based on the increasing service content in many organizations' offerings (Normann, 2001); increased business complexity, privatization, and outsourcing (Davies et al., 2001); and means of moving the business focus from the products to the customers (Hax & Wilde, 1999; Vandermerwe, 2000).

In the business-to-business segment, the customer-centric logic of a solutions business is often represented in a stand-alone consulting business. Based on Good (1985), we use the term *corporate consulting* to designate this type of consulting unit. IBM is often cited as an illustration of a firm that has successfully transformed itself from a provider of hardware-based products to more software-based services (see, e.g., Normann, 2001; Vandermerwe, 2000). The "new" IBM is built around the service organization IBM Global Services, a corporate consultancy in part, which accounts for approximately 40% of IBM's total revenues. More important, the services provided, such as business consulting, information technology (IT) consulting, and outsourcing, are seen as a central mechanism for leveraging the technological capabilities of the parent organization.

The customer-centric characteristic of a solutions business changes the conditions and strategies for managing innovation from product innovation to customer-sourced innovation (Hax & Wilde, 1999). It is typically characterized by co-creation and customization (Cornet et al., 2000). However, the traditional offerings still have to be renewed and sold as stand-alone products. The solutions business should, therefore, offer exceptional possibilities for customer-driven product innovation by enabling the application

AUTHORS' NOTE: This chapter is based on Sandberg and Werr (2003).

of innovation processes with anthropological characteristics (Berggren & Nacher, 2001). These methods provide a deep understanding of unarticulated user needs to be applied in the product innovation processes.

As organizational front-end units working with direct market relations and profit/loss responsibility, many corporate consulting units have a boundary-spanning organizational position (Foote, Galbraith, Hope, & Miller, 2001; Sawhney & Parikh, 2001). This gives them the potential to build an essential stock of customer-centric market knowledge and enables them to develop a deep understanding of the parent organization's products and core capabilities they incorporate. Market knowledge and knowledge about the parent organization's products, services, and incorporated core capabilities could be exchanged between the market and the product business through a mix of internal and external assignments. This "cross-pollination" (Bessant & Rush, 1995) gives the corporate consulting unit great potential to contribute to the new product development (NPD) in the parent organization.

Growing academic interest in customer solutions businesses has focused mainly on strategic aspects. Apart from consulting reports (e.g., Cornet et al., 2000; Foote et al., 2001), studies on the internal consequences of moving toward a solutions business are lacking, not least from an innovation management perspective. This is a topic of practical importance, especially for corporations that, like IBM, embark on a path of mixed business—with solutions and stand-alone products. The purpose of this chapter is to study the consultative component of a solutions business and its interaction with the product business's innovation processes. More specifically, our aim is to identify the key factors that hinder knowledge generated in the consulting operations from being applied in the product business. This application of knowledge is analyzed in the context of an IT consulting business, Telia Promotor, owned by the Swedish telecommunications operator Telia.

Methodology

The study is part of a 4-year research project on the role and management of corporate consultancies. It was formulated against the background of one of the authors' practical experiences as a marketing director of Telia Promotor. In this position, he experienced frustrations connected to the role of the corporate consultancy as well as the strategic potential of this kind of organization in a solutions business.

The author has remained a part-time employee of the organization throughout the research project. This enabled the generation of rich empirical longitudinal data from a number of data sources, including ethnographic observations. He could be described as a "complete participant" (Gold, 1958) with a "complete membership role" (Adler & Adler, 1987) expected to last permanently. Consequently, part of the data collection followed a "self-ethnographic" approach (Alvesson, 1999; Hayano, 1979; Nielsen & Repstad, 1993; Riemer, 1977).

The participant observations of the self-ethnographer were important in that they contributed to a broad and deep understanding of Telia Promotor and its relation with the parent organization. However, the closeness of one of the authors also had some drawbacks, including difficulty in seeing beyond what was taken for granted and a tendency toward subjectivity (Adler & Adler, 1987; Alvesson, 1999). The second author and other participants in the research project facilitated the self-ethnographer's distancing from the empirical setting.

The senior researcher carried out some of the interviews but primarily participated in the later stages of the study. His distanced role was important for interpreting the data and writing up the findings. He helped the insider to distance himself from the action and contributed new perspectives based on his earlier research on management consulting. The insider/outsider characteristic (Bartunek & Louis, 1996) of the study was, therefore, important for designing a robust study with high practical relevance. Furthermore, it was an important input to a subsequent insider action research study, focusing on Telia Promotor's mission and identity, as part of a companywide change program (for a description, see Chapter 11 of this volume).

The information gained, through the observations and experiences of the insider, was complemented by a series of 13 semistructured interviews. They were partly conducted by the outsider with personnel from both the consulting unit and the parent organization, Telia. The focus of the interviews was the corporate role of Telia Promotor and its relations with other parts of Telia. Special attention was given to knowledge creation and extension in the innovation processes in general and in NPD activities in particular. Quotations presented in the case description are drawn directly from these interviews.

The Case of Telia Promotor

The case of Telia Promotor focuses on the second half of the 1990s. The unit's organizational position in Telia can be described as semi-integrated, with half of the turnover coming from internal clients within the traditional Telia product business and the other half coming from clients outside of Telia. At that time, Telia Promotor had approximately 300 employees, of which a majority acted as IT and business consultants. The consulting unit's external home market included Telia's largest customers.

NPD at Telia

Telia's product business was divided among several different units of which three types are especially important for this study: market units, product management units, and product development units. The *market units* were divided on the basis of market segment. Each market unit was responsible for marketing and sales for its particular segment. The *product management units* were responsible for overall planning, with a product manager in charge of each product group. NPD work was purchased from the *product development units,* which used their own resources as well as internal and external consultants.

After decades of developing the infrastructure for telecommunications and data communications, Telia's NPD process was rigorous. NPD procedures were bureaucratized through a stage-gate process with extensive guiding principles regarding toll gates and documentation.

The Services Offered by Telia Promotor

Telia Promotor's mission was to act as Telia's consulting firm on the external market, offering business consulting and systems integration. Most projects were delivered as customer-specific turnkey solutions and included software-intensive elements such as computer telephony integration and Internet/intranet applications. Telia's product business provided parts of these solutions in the form of communications services.

Telia Promotor's assignments normally spanned several stages, covering strategic analysis, functional specifications, software development, and systems integration. Implementation projects were sometimes followed by additional management support services to help the client start using the installed functionality.

Acquiring Knowledge of the Customers

In delivering these services, Telia Promotor had to expand the parent organization's contacts with its customers. Traditionally, Telia had maintained relations with the customer's IT and telecommunications support functions. The consulting unit, however, needed access to management representatives from the client's business because the solutions included applications that were highly customized and integrated into the client's processes and IT systems. This enabled project managers to build broad and deep personal networks with people in the client organizations, giving the consultants access to valuable market knowledge (Table 17.1). The knowledge gained about the client was combined with technological knowledge to create new knowledge:

> Our ability to integrate solutions is important. First, we have the knowledge of the products and services. Then, we have a lot of contact with the customer, which forces us to be creative. In this way, we can see the synergies. (project manager at Telia Promotor)

Table 17.1   Knowledge Created Within Telia Promotor

Market Knowledge	Technical Knowledge

• Extension of networks with the client organization
• Increased understanding of the client:
   ➢ The client's business and strategy
   ➢ The client's industry
   ➢ The client's customers
• Knowledge of the role of Telia's products
• Gaps in functionality of Telia's products
	• Early use of new technology (within computer telephony integration, Internet/intranet, etc.)
	• Knowledge of external technical platforms
	• Understanding of limitations in product business platforms and development tools
	• Understanding of the customer's technical systems
	• Possibilities of bundling and systems integration

Examples of such synergistic effects include the development of the first Internet banking solutions in Sweden during the second half of the 1990s and, more recently, the development of a new type of call center solution enabling speech recognition and control. Table 17.1 summarizes the knowledge created within Telia Promotor.

Extending Knowledge to the Product Business

The consultants were regarded as the troubleshooters of Telia and were continuously engaged in internal assignments for various units and functions. Three important groups of internal clients for Telia Promotor were the market units, the product management units, and the product development units—that is, core actors in the innovation process at Telia.

The focus of Telia Promotor assignments in the *market units,* based on their combined knowledge of markets and technology, was generally that of supporting sales activities. Such assignments were, however, relatively rare given that the consultants were regarded by the salespeople with some skepticism. This skepticism can be traced back to three factors. First, Telia Promotor's direct contact with customers was often disliked by the salespeople because it threatened the single point of contact strategy maintained by the market units. Second, the consultants were regarded as costly, so involving Telia Promotor was often avoided. There was a general feeling among the salespeople that the consultants' main objective was to maximize consulting hours rather than to maximize Telia sales. Third, account managers sometimes expressed fears that the advice of consultants could disrupt projected sales by enhancing the performance of clients' existing products, thereby making the purchase of new equipment unnecessary.

The second group of clients was the *product development units*. Telia Promotor was often given the assignment of supporting internal development projects in these units. These assignments included mainly technical specification and implementation of new products and services where the market knowledge of the consulting unit was appreciated:

Their close relationships with external clients are very important for us using them. Of course, they could have been 100% external, but the internal assignments are crucial for us in order to get feedback from the market. (manager at Telia research and development [R&D])

Telia Promotor also possessed critical technical knowledge derived from an early adoption strategy for new technologies. This knowledge, however, was seldom regarded as relevant by the product development units because it did not fit the large-scale telecommunications systems that were the focus of these units. The focus on products for a mass market, where stability and quality were regarded as central, also led to the application of an elaborate NPD process resulting in lead times that were considerably longer than those at Telia Promotor. Consequently, Telia Promotor and the product development units had very different views of the NPD process, causing somewhat negative attitudes toward one another's ways of working. In relation to the product development units' NPD process, the consultants' pragmatic, customer-focused approach was often regarded as "quick and dirty."

The third main group of internal clients was the *product management units*. Product managers repeatedly used the consultants for customer-driven development. With the support of Telia Promotor, external clients were invited in as pilot customers in the development of new products and services. Through these pilot projects, market knowledge and technology knowledge were created, linked, and evaluated. The product managers were pleased with the knowledge provided by the consulting unit in such projects. However, they also reported feeling abandoned when these projects were over.

On a more emotional level, the feelings between the consultants and the various representatives of the product business were strained. This is due to the role and power position of the consulting unit being perceived as a threat by the larger product business at Telia's core:

It's hard not to be perceived as a threat by other units given our role and mission. We take their people, their technology, and their customers. Then we come back as consultants and charge them. (former division manager at Telia Promotor)

Thus, knowledge creation within the consulting unit was intensive, but the diffusion of this knowledge to the rest of the organization was neither conscious nor systematic.

Understanding the Barriers to Knowledge Extension

The preceding case illustrates the potential of a corporate consulting unit to act as a source for generating knowledge vital to the innovation processes

Table 17.2 Differences in Business Logic

	Consulting Business	Product Business
Time frame for planning	Short	Long
Perception of market	Unique clients	Homogeneous market
Operational focus	Flexibility, effectiveness, one off	Productivity, efficiency, repetition
Character of expertise	Integrative, generalist	Specialized, technical

of the product business. However, the various units of the product business showed limited interest in the activities and knowledge of the consulting unit. Suspicion and ignorance of one another's competence and motives governed the relationship between the consulting unit and the product business. The impediments to knowledge extension are the focus of this section.

Conflicting Business Logics

A central source of strain in relationships between the consultants and the different parts of the product business was the differences that existed between the product-driven dominant logic (Normann, 1977; Prahalad & Bettis, 1986) and the consulting logic of the consulting unit (Table 17.2).

The respective organizational logic that underlies the consulting unit and the product business differs largely in both the perceived missions and type of knowledge deemed necessary to achieve these missions. These differences are both beneficial and problematic. Such organizational differences, and how they can hinder innovation, are described by Dougherty (1992) as "interpretive barriers between different thought worlds." However, Dougherty deliberately limits her discussion to the cognitive aspects of the differences between the thought worlds of organizational units. The preceding case indicates a broader range of aspects, and this leads us to introduce the concept of *knowledge filters*. This concept covers three aspects of knowledge extension: knowledge search, cognition, and politics.

Hindering Knowledge Filters

Based on Ansoff (1984), we argue that there are three types of knowledge filters that can impede the flow of knowledge between organizations: the surveillance filter, the mentality filter, and the power filter. The *surveillance filter* determines the direction and scope of the organization's information search behavior and, thereby, determines what knowledge is perceived as relevant and worthwhile to acquire. The *mentality filter* acts in favor of knowledge that matches the existing basic assumptions of the individual because this knowledge is more readily accepted than knowledge that points in other directions. The *power filter* tends to filter out information that constitutes a threat to existing power structures and works in favor of knowledge that strengthens one's own position. In what follows, these knowledge filters are applied as an analytical framework to help us understand the observed impediments to the application of Telia Promotor's knowledge in Telia's innovation processes. In so doing, we discuss Telia Promotor's relations with Telia's market units, product development units, and product management units.

Market Units and Customer Relationships

The flow of knowledge and expertise from the consulting unit to the market units was hampered by a number of factors relating to all three knowledge filters. Many people in the market units were not aware of Telia Promotor's knowledge, indicating a strong surveillance filter. Normally, salespeople found information on the products and services they sold in catalogs and databases on the intranet. These sources covered the standardized products and services of Telia. The more abstract services of Telia Promotor, however, were seldom visible in these systems. Furthermore, the salespeople's incentives to engage in further investigation were limited because the consulting services were regarded as time-consuming to sell and rendered fewer sales commissions than did the standard products.

The mentality filter was also strong, owing to the differences in logic marketed as an essential part of Telia's offer by managers in the market units. People on the sales end still saw Telia as a provider of communications capacity and the necessary hardware that went with it. Consequently, customer needs and problems were often treated by adding capacity rather than by providing advisory services that could increase the utility of the client's existing technical solutions.

The market units' resistance to the knowledge created in the corporate consulting unit could be further understood in terms of power filters. For the people in the market units, Telia Promotor's close customer contact and market knowledge were perceived as a threat to their own official responsibility as the customer's sole contact point at Telia. Furthermore, as a typical project-based front-end unit (Davies & Brady, 2000), Telia Promotor had developed strong capabilities in tendering and bidding that included presale marketing activities. The market units' position as the single point of contact for the customer required them to mediate in these activities. However, the market units' limited experience in selling customer-specific solutions rather than products was a constant source of misunderstanding and conflict between the market units and Telia Promotor. The conflicts had a strong political dimension in that they concerned access to the critical resource—the customers.

The NPD Process and Knowledge Extension

The knowledge flow between Telia Promotor and the product development units was also impeded by all three knowledge filters. The surveillance filter often caused the product business to regard the knowledge produced at Telia Promotor as irrelevant. Telia focused on large-scale development of standardized telecommunications services, making technical platforms the ultimate *goal* of the NPD process. For the customer, solutions developed by the consulting unit and the technical platforms purchased from external suppliers were a *means* of solving the customer's specific needs. These external platforms were often hard to integrate with the technical systems of Telia. Consequently, Telia Promotor was not always viewed as a potential source of technical knowledge by the people in the product development units.

The typical logic of the technical people (Dougherty, 1992) also meant that those in product development focused on a structured NPD process and technical policies. For them, the direct customer access of the consulting unit was not always seen as a resource. It often generated a continuous flow of new and changing requirements on the product, something that hindered the product development units from meeting their internal targets.

The differences in logic further activated the power filter. People in product development saw the technical knowledge of Telia Promotor, based on new platforms and technologies developed outside of Telia, as a threat rather than a resource. This advanced knowledge was not compatible with the knowledge and expertise on which their current power position was based. As one manager in product development at Telia expressed it, "Telia Promotor might see ways to make our business their own."

An Important Resource for Product Managers

The relationship between the consulting unit and the product managers was more positive. In this relation, only the surveillance filter was activated because the established processes of innovation at Telia did not recognize Telia Promotor as a potential source of customer knowledge or as an access point to deeper customer contacts, for example, for lead user development (von Hippel, 1986).

When product managers found consultants and/or assignments that matched the needs of the product business, the consulting services became highly valued. As typical planners, the product managers thought conceptually in terms of linking market and technology (Dougherty, 1992). With the support of the consulting unit, their abstract ideas could be turned into real projects because of the consultants' closeness to the market and integrative abilities. Neither the market knowledge nor the technological knowledge threatened the established knowledge of the product managers but rather complemented it.

The consultants also supported product managers in generating ideas. In the consultants' external assignments, new functionality based on new high-technology components and platforms was often introduced. Through these customer-specific solutions, the product managers gained new ideas for future commoditized services.

Consequently, Telia product managers were frequent internal clients of Telia Promotor. Assignments focused on the front end of innovation. During these early stages of the innovation process, the dominant logic of the consulting unit was not as incompatible with the product logic as it was during the later stages, where a more rigorous NPD process was followed. During the early phases of innovation, the differences in the technical platforms applied by the consultants, as opposed to those applied by the product business, were also less of a problem. During these phases, the conceptual ideas and the functionality perceived by the user were in focus.

Thus, the case of Telia Promotor demonstrates that corporate consultants can act as knowledge brokers in the innovation process even without systematically established mechanisms that support the knowledge flows between the product business and the consulting unit. Hargadon (1998) describes knowledge brokers as either external (acting between firms) or internal (acting between divisions). However, corporate consultancies could be described as a combination of the two, acting between the product business and its external environment.

Conclusions and Implications

Through a collaborative research approach, this chapter has explored the role of a corporate consulting unit in the innovation processes of an organization combining a product-oriented strategy with a customer solutions strategy. The synergies between these two strategies are potentially strong, especially in innovation processes where the customer-oriented consulting business can provide customer knowledge. However, we also found that tapping into this source of knowledge was not without problems. Although the consulting unit supported product and market units through internal consulting assignments, in product and business development, knowledge transfer was strained by a number of knowledge filters: the surveillance filter, the mentality filter, and the power filter (Table 17.3).

The study originated from the practical experience of one of the authors who had remained a member of the studied organization. Consequently, the results and interpretations from the study not only were elaborated in the academic field but also were discussed continuously with people from the organizational setting. Moreover, after completing the study, several seminars were held with Telia Promotor and the parent organization Telia, with a focus on the managerial implications. Simultaneously, the research implications were shared through seminars and conferences in the academic conferences.

Managerial Implications

Corporate consultancies represent a potentially powerful tool for organizations wanting to move from a product-driven logic toward a customer-driven

Table 17.3   Knowledge Filters Observed in the Case

	Surveillance Filter	**Mentality Filter**	**Power Filter**
Market units	Consulting services are perceived as abstract. Limited information is available in salespeople's information sources.	Consultant's focus on selling hours is incompatible with a logic of selling products.	Consultant's closeness to customer threatens the single point-of-contact position.
Product development units	Consultant's technical knowledge is perceived as irrelevant.	Consulting services are viewed as "quick and dirty." Consultant's market knowledge is perceived as a disturbance.	There is fear of a takeover by consulting unit. There is competing technical knowledge within consulting unit.
Product management units	Consulting unit is not formally recognized as a knowledge source in new product development process.	—	—

logic without giving up their existing product business. Through a mixture of external and internal assignments, corporate consulting units in this situation can act as knowledge brokers between the client organization and the innovation processes of the product business. This is a potentially important function, yet it is often neglected because corporate consultancies are largely legitimized as ways of generating extra income and/or protecting the product business's technological core through competitive differentiation (Cornet et al., 2000; Davies et al., 2001). Realizing this potential requires that managers begin to view corporate consulting services as an integral part of the innovation process rather than as a mere extension for customization, which is a common view in many product businesses (Nambisan, 2001).

The realization of the knowledge flow underlying these potential synergies is, however, not trivial. Achieving this synergy is impeded by a number of knowledge filters and so requires active management of the relationship between the corporate consulting unit and the product business.

One approach to managing the surveillance filter might be to clearly identify the corporate consulting unit as a source of knowledge in the product and business development of the product business, especially during the early phases of innovation.

Overcoming the mentality filter requires building a mutual understanding of the other organization's business logic and practice. Dougherty (1992) suggests three intermediary processes for such thought world awareness: (a) building on the unique insight from each thought world, (b) developing collaborative mechanisms, and (c) developing organizational context for collective action.

Tackling the power filter requires designing and adapting organizational governance structures to support rather than impede cooperation. This could be achieved by "success fees" for the corporate consulting unit's participation in NPD projects, a clear statement of the respective units' responsibilities in terms of product responsibility versus consulting, and so forth.

Based on our findings from this case study, we argue that product management units could serve as an effective mediator between the solutions business and the product business and that this role should be more formally recognized. However, closer integration of the consulting unit and the product business carries the risk of eliminating the specific characteristic of the consulting unit that made it valuable in the first place, that is, its ability to create knowledge from and about the market.

Research Implications

This study sheds light on the innovation processes of organizations simultaneously pursuing a customer solutions business and a product-oriented business. The differences between these business logics are identified as one of the main underlying causes of knowledge filters hindering the transfer of consultants' knowledge to the product business. Further investigation of these logics in a large sample of organizations should be motivated by this case study.

Another aspect that should be addressed in further research is the complexity of the products offered by the parent organization. Consulting services are often offered as an extension of high-value, engineering, and software-intensive capital goods—so-called *complex product systems* (CoPS) (Hobday, 1998). We may find that suppliers of CoPS, such as the parent organization of the previously mentioned IBM Global Services, find it less problematic to integrate the consulting business with the product business.

Finally, research should further investigate possible ways in which to handle the knowledge filters identified. This would include research on the structural relations between the consulting business and the product-oriented business as well as the incentive structure and management systems used to steer the corporate consulting operation.

References

Adler, P. A., & Adler, P. (1987). *Membership roles in field research.* Newbury Park, CA: Sage.

Alvesson, M. (1999). *Methodology for close up studies: Struggling with closeness and closure* (Working Paper 1999/4). Lund, Sweden: Lund University, School of Economics and Management.

Ansoff, H. I. (1984). *Implanting strategic management.* Englewood Cliffs, NJ: Prentice Hall.

Bartunek, J., & Louis, M. R. (1996). *Insider/Outsider team research.* Thousand Oaks, CA: Sage.

Berggren, E., & Nacher, T. (2001). Introducing new products can be hazardous to your company: Use the right new-solutions delivery tools. *Academy of Management Executive, 15*(3), 92–101.

Bessant, J., & Rush, H. (1995). Building bridges for innovation: The role of consultants in technology transfer. *Research Policy, 24,* 97–114.

Cornet, E., Katz, R., Molloy, R., Schädler, J., Sharma, D., & Tipping, A. (2000). *Customer solutions: From pilots to profits* [report]. New York: Booz Allen Hamilton.

Davies, A., & Brady, T. (2000). Organisational capabilities and learning in complex product systems: Towards repeatable solutions. *Research Policy, 29,* 931–953.

Davies, A., Tang, P., Brady, T., Hobday, M., Rush, H., & Gann, D. (2001). *Integrated solutions: The new economy between manufacturing and services* [report]. Sussex, UK: University of Sussex, SPRU (Science and Technology Policy Research).

Dougherty, D. (1992). Interpretive barriers to successful product innovation in large firms. *Organization Science, 3*(2), 179–202.

Foote, N., Galbraith, J., Hope, Q., & Miller, D. (2001). Making solutions the answer. *McKinsey Quarterly, 3,* 84–97.

Gold, R. L. (1958). Roles in sociological field observations. *Social Forces, 36,* 217–223.

Good, R. F. (1985). Pros and cons of corporate consulting. *Journal of Management Consulting, 2*(3), 29–34.

Hargadon, A. (1998). Firms as knowledge brokers: Lessons in pursuing continuous innovation. *California Management Review, 40*(3), 209–227.

Hax, A. C., & Wilde, D. L. (1999). The Delta model: Adaptive management for a changing world. *Sloan Management Review, 40*(2), 11–28.

Hayano, D. M. (1979). Auto-ethnography: Paradigms, problems, and prospects. *Human Organization, 38,* 99–104.

Hobday, M. (1998). Product complexity, innovation, and industrial organisation. *Research Policy, 26,* 698–710.

Nambisan, S. (2001). Why service businesses are not product businesses. *Sloan Management Review, 42*(4), 72–80.

Nielsen, J. C. R., & Repstad, P. (1993). *From nearness to distance—and back: On analyzing your own organisation.* Copenhagen, Denmark: Copenhagen Business School, Institute of Organisation and Industrial Sociology.

Normann, R. (1977). *Management for growth.* New York: John Wiley.

Normann, R. (2001). *Reframing business: When the map changes the landscape.* Chichester, UK: Wiley.

Prahalad, C. K., & Bettis, R. A. (1986). The dominant logic: A new linkage between diversity and performance. *Strategic Management Journal, 7,* 485–502.

Riemer, J. W. (1977). Varieties of opportunistic research. *Urban Life, 5,* 467–477.

Sandberg, R., & Werr, A. (2003). Corporate consulting in product innovation: Overcoming the barriers for utilisation. *European Journal of Innovation Management, 6*(2).

Sawhney, M., & Parikh, D. (2001). Where value lives in a networked world. *Harvard Business Review, 79*(1), 79–86.

Vandermerwe, S. (2000). How increasing value to customers improves business results. *Sloan Management Review, 42*(1), 27–37.

von Hippel, E. (1986). Lead users: A source of novel product concepts. *Management Science, 32,* 791–805.

18 Self-Designing a Performance Management System

Allan M. Mohrman, Jr., and Susan A. Mohrman

The systems and practices that an organization uses to manage performance are integrally related to the capacity of the organization to accomplish its business objectives and the capacity of its employees to accomplish their purposes (Mohrman, Resnick-West, & Lawler, 1989). In this chapter, we describe a collaborative research project involving a large oil and chemicals company (referred to with the pseudonym "Oilco") and the authors. The project had the dual purpose of increasing academic understanding of performance management (PM) systems and transforming the PM practices of the firm to support strategic business initiatives and to help drive fundamental change. We describe our research collaboration with Oilco, focusing both on the collaborative processes and the knowledge outcomes. We first describe the two organizational contexts of the partners in the collaboration.

The Organizational Contexts

Oilco is a petroleum and chemicals company that, during the late 1980s, began to shift its corporate strategies and organizational models to become more competitive in its fast-changing global environment. At first, the organizational change strategy was relatively uncoordinated, with pockets of change taking place throughout the company. Various local business units had initiated total quality management projects, team-based reorganizations, culture change activities, and other organizational effectiveness projects.

AUTHORS' NOTE: We acknowledge the collegiality and support of Marty Nyvall and Gerald Mount of "Oilco."

Like many companies, Oilco found itself with an increasing number of "anomalies" (Kuhn, 1970), that is, pockets of emergent practice that did not fit easily within its formal hierarchical organizational model and bureaucratic corporate context. To deal with change from within and outside of the company, management drafted a new corporate mission and vision and also outlined a corporate change strategy. One key initiative was to transform the company's human resource (HR) management practices so that they would fit the emerging ways of doing work and become a strategic business tool. Over time, HR practices had become increasingly out of step with the changes that were cropping up in how work was done. The lead focus in this effort was PM. PM practices were chosen because they were seen as drivers of many other HR practices. Thus, PM was viewed as a catalyst for change that could set the HR context for the new Oilco.

The Center for Effective Organizations (CEO), a research center in the business school at the University of Southern California where the authors were research scientists at the time of the study, was established in 1979 to house collaborative organizational science research between organizations and academic researchers, that is, research to advance academic theory while simultaneously yielding knowledge to inform practice (Cummings, Mohrman, Mohrman, & Ledford, 1985; Mohrman, Mohrman, Lawler, & Ledford, 1999). One underlying premise is that the field of organization research is one of the "sciences of the artificial" (Simon, 1969). Organizations are purposefully created by people and are continually re-created through the self-designing activities of people in the organizations (Weick, 1993) as they work together, encounter performance challenges, and/or see their purposes change. A second premise of our research center is that organizational practice often precedes academic knowledge. Research methodologies that study organizations as dynamic rather than fixed entities with enduring features are required (Huber & Glick, 1993; Lawler, 1985). As noted by Lewin (1951), the best way in which to understand organizations is to study them when they are changing. Finally, because an organizations is created and changed by humans, we believe that the organization can best be understood by a dual focus on the structures and processes that comprise the organization and on the humans whose aspirations and worldviews influence organizational behavior (Mohrman, Mohrman, & Tenkasi, 1997).

CEO holds to the core epistemological principle that developing and testing theories and models of organizations depends fundamentally on research approaches that enable the academic and practitioner communities to learn jointly. This principle of joint learning is also core to the pragmatic institutional arrangements of the center and the organizations with which it works. It is only because of the prospect that organizations are going to learn something of use to them that they are willing to fund and participate in research projects with CEO. Conversely, CEO researchers are interested only in projects that bring the prospect of new knowledge. The research methodology described in this chapter is our own, embedded in the context of our experience and the long-term institutional arrangements between CEO and its corporate sponsors. It is similar to the intervention research approach (Hatchuel & Molet, 1986) described in Chapter 5 of this volume, but it also has similarities to action research and traditional organizational research.

Our collaborative research methodology stresses contextual sensitivity and is based on the belief that processes and systems have to be designed by the organization itself to meet its needs and aspirations. With Oilco, we sought to design management models, tools, and procedures in the context of the corporation's transformation project as well as to produce knowledge that serves action and builds management science theories (Lawler, 1985). Our knowledge of PM and our collaborative design-oriented research methodology both were important factors in Oilco's decision to work with us. Oilco was 1 of 40 corporations that sponsored CEO and its collaborative research agenda. Oilco was attracted to the notion of basing organizational decisions on knowledge gained through rigorous research processes. Our work with Oilco followed similar collaborations with other companies in studying PM processes and more general organizational design issues. These earlier studies had generated several scholarly and practitioner articles and books, some focusing particularly on the design of PM systems (Mohrman et al., 1989).

The Temporary System for Collaboration

We were originally approached by Oilco's HR executives. Together, we designed a collaborative approach that reflected the fact that this was a corporate business initiative and not an administratively driven HR project. Top management appointed a nine-member task force consisting of the heads of seven of the corporation's companies and two heads of corporate functions—all members of the senior management team. These presidents and vice presidents were highly visible managers with large bases of authority and respect. They were selected to represent conservative, command-and-control, oil industry traditionalists as well as more progressive, change-oriented, participative factions of top management. There was also a mix of younger, upwardly mobile managers and those who were more established and seasoned at the top. Three members of corporate HR provided support to the task team. The two authors were collaborative research partners representing our center. The task team's mandate was to conduct a study of performance appraisal at Oilco and recommend appropriate changes to its highest corporate management committee. The task team was to be guided in its deliberations by the recently established corporate vision and was requested not to make changes to the compensation system.

This task force developed a mission statement that included the development, implementation, and assessment of a performance appraisal process that "embodied corporate values and encouraged individual and team performance toward the achievement of company objectives." Key aspects of the mandate given to this team and of the mission it adopted were that it included research and evaluation, thereby opening the door to research collaboration. This senior management task team also decided to be the design team and the assessment team for the new PM system, although it would ultimately appoint an implementation team to handle the logistics of implementation.

Purposes, Contributions, and Roles

Although we were collaborators in the research, Oilco and CEO had different purposes, brought different resources to the collaboration, and played different roles in it. The collaboration's capacity for learning and usefulness depended on this diversity.

Purposes

Oilco's purpose was to design a new way in which to manage performance that fit its changing context and contributed to business performance. Our purposes were to learn more about the important elements of PM and the kinds of PM systems that can work in the Oilco context and, more generally, to understand the potential of PM to lead corporate change. It was critical to the success of this collaboration that the purposes overlapped. Because the company's representatives accepted that there was no solid foundation of knowledge about PM approaches appropriate for new organizational forms, they shared our interest in, and indeed felt an urgency about, conducting a rigorous, contextually sensitive research study. Our ability to validate research-based models of PM depended on Oilco's effectiveness in designing a system based on research learning and successful implementation of that system so that the impact could be evaluated.

Contributions

Company collaborators brought deep expertise about the Oilco context, including its organization and management processes, various settings, organizational technologies, and strengths and weaknesses. They also brought resources to pay for the costs of research collaboration—costs that they hoped would be paid back in increased performance capability. These costs included the time of all employees involved. Although located in a university, our salaries for research activities needed to be covered by grants and research contracts. The project also included the costs of travel and survey administration. The company collaborators contributed their internal legitimacy and authority in obtaining the participation of many company members in the research process and in driving system implementation.

We contributed grounded knowledge of PM systems from previous studies, as well as knowledge of the critical unanswered questions, so that the research in Oilco could extend existing knowledge rather than "reinvent the wheel." In addition, we contributed knowledge of research methodology and the process of self-design. The collaborators depended deeply on one another's contributions. Each of our purposes could be achieved only by combining our contributions. For example, the company could succeed in developing a knowledge-based system only if we brought robust state-of-the-art knowledge and applied our research skills to design research capable of addressing the company's key questions. We, on the other hand, depended on the company's deep knowledge of context to interpret the system interactions inherent in the operation of any set of PM practices. Although we were attributed legitimacy in the research process as a consequence of our academic record, we depended on the organizational legitimacy of our company collaborators to elicit compliance with requests for people's time to respond to interviews and surveys as well as to try out new practices.

Roles in the Self-Design Process

We had been in an advisory role to Oilco management since prior to the decision to form and staff the task force. During the initial meeting of the task team, in which it drafted its mission and decided to act as the design team, we introduced our self-design model (Figure 18.1) to guide the task team's process. This model was based on our systematic examination of our field notes from earlier collaborative research with companies undergoing intentional organization redesign (Mohrman & Cummings, 1987, 1989). It provides a roadmap of the elements of action that were found to be antecedents of successful redesign. The self-design model is inherently a learning model that is highly compatible with a research approach. It stresses the need to *lay a foundation* for strategy-driven redesign through (a) identifying the values that are to guide the design activities and the new organization, (b) learning about what is known in the organizational sciences and from practice that is relevant to the task at hand, and (c) diagnosing the functioning of the current system and identifying the gap between the current and desired states. *Criteria* for the design are generated from the learning that results as the foundation is constructed. Laying the foundation and identifying the criteria establish shared cognitive frameworks to guide the *design* activities. These design activities, as well as the subsequent *implementation and assessment* activities through which the design can be improved and the foundation can be renewed, constitute iterative action learning that can yield contextually specific knowledge as well as contribute to general academic knowledge.

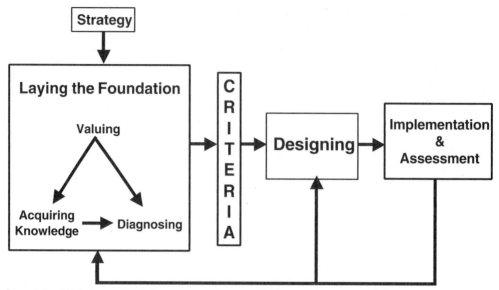

Figure 18.1   The Self-Design Strategy

Table 18.1 describes the roles and tasks carried out by the parties in this collaboration. In what follows, we summarize the key activities and products during the stages of self-design, emphasizing the collaborative elements.

Laying the Foundation

The task team spent its first meetings laying the foundation to design a new PM system to support Oilco's business strategy.

Values

Most members of the task force had participated in senior management's formulation of HR values to support Oilco's new strategic direction. Consequently, they needed only to reiterate these values and discuss them as they pertained to PM: (a) providing respect for individuals and concern for employees to reach their fullest potential; (b) promoting maximum employee understanding of, and contribution to, the business; (c) promoting honesty and ethical action; (d) participating in decision making in each business unit; (e) promoting teamwork, risk taking, and innovation; and (f) recognizing and rewarding contributions.

Table 18.1 Roles in Self-Design of Performance Management System at Oilco

	Company Roles	Academic Roles	Products
Self-design overall	Designed the new practices	Provided frameworks and methods for learning and self-design	New PM system design and a process for learning from action
Laying the foundation:			
Valuing	Determined valued outcomes	Facilitated process	Business and social system values to guide the design
Acquiring knowledge	Read articles Reviewed examples of appraisal systems Visited other companies Discussed frameworks from previous PM research Interpreted and made sense of information Identified relevant research areas	Shared and discussed frameworks from literature and research experiences Interpreted and made sense of information Identified theoretically and practically important research areas	Shared models Questions to frame research and diagnosis Knowledge of various design options
Diagnosing	Generated self-reflective questions to frame diagnosis and research Provided system knowledge to inform research design Interpreted research findings Provided data	Designed research for: • Diagnosing the current system • Testing existing frameworks at Oilco Collected data Analyzed data and discovered new knowledge	Systematic data-based depiction of strengths and weaknesses of current system Contextually determined relevance of various models and frameworks New knowledge
Setting criteria	Set criteria that reflected values, knowledge, and diagnosis	Facilitated sensemaking of values, knowledge, and diagnosis	Key criteria to guide designing
Designing	Chose design specifications that best fit the criteria and political realities at Oilco Generated alternative designs to fit specifications Modified and approved final design	Facilitated designing process Provided consultative input to design	High-level design specifications of PM methods, including process descriptions and instrumentation
Implementing	Determined guidelines for implementation Established implementation team that generated implementation plan and materials Approved implementation plan Resourced implementation activities	Provided consultative input about implementation	Implementation plan Instrumentation and activities: • Communication • Materials • Workshops

(Continued)

Table 18.1 Continued

	Company Roles	Academic Roles	Products
Assessing and iterating	Determined guidelines for an ongoing periodic assessment and learning process Approved and resourced assessment plan Interpreted assessment findings Decided design changes and additions to OPM and additional implementation steps when needed	Advised on methods for assessing the adequacy of the implementation process, the impact of the design, and the validity of the frameworks underlying it Designed assessment research Collected data Analyzed data Provided feedback Participated in joint sensemaking Consulted to redesign and action planning as well as ongoing learning process	Assessment instruments and process Assessment report and interpretation Modifications to OPM Plan for ongoing assessment/learning

NOTE: PM = performance management; OPM = Oilco Performance Management system.

Knowledge Acquisition

The task team developed a library of PM systems from other companies, visited those deemed of highest interest, and read several articles on the topic. We provided a framework for conceptualizing PM (Figure 18.2). It depicts PM as a cycle of activities starting with the definition of the work to be done (e.g., through job descriptions and/or goals) and continuing through the development of needed competencies, including review and feedback about performance. Each stage supports and is supported by contextual systems such as compensation and training (Figure 18.2a). This cycle happens at multiple nested levels of the organizational system (Figure 18.2b). Individual performance is nested within the performance of the team or unit, which in turn is nested within performance of the larger business. The effectiveness of the system's performance is judged against the strategy and goals of the corporation, and the performance of each level of the system needs to be managed in the context of the performance requirements of the larger units of which they are a part. These frameworks (Mohrman, 1990; Mohrman, Cohen, & Mohrman, 1995) were generated in earlier collaborative studies of PM with companies experiencing pressures similar to those that Oilco was facing.

These earlier studies had generated a clear finding that the impact of PM on performance improvement and competency development does not relate to particular rating techniques and forms used; rather, these impacts depended on the nature of the process used, in particular, on the degree to which the process achieved mutuality between employees and their managers. It had become clear in our studies that employees and their managers had different purposes for the PM activities and that they often saw employees'

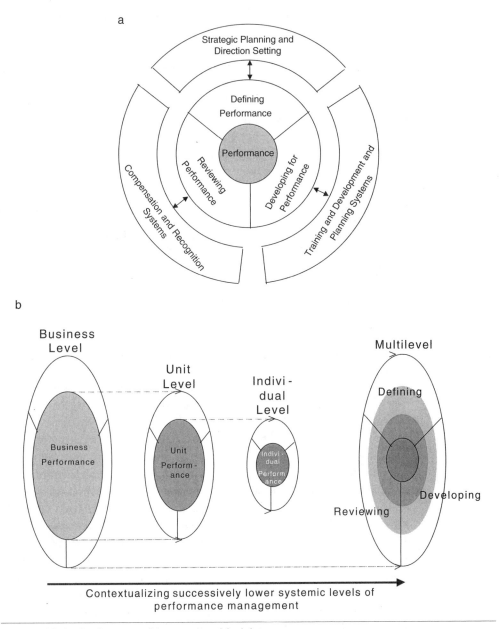

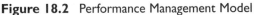

Figure 18.2 Performance Management Model
(a) Performance Management Process and Supportive Organizational Systems
(b) Multilevel Performance Management

performance through very different lenses. Performance improvement ensued if the PM activities resulted in a sharing of perceptions and the development of common understandings between employees and supervisors about the definition of work to be done and how it was to be evaluated as well as its actual appraisal.

These and other findings from the earlier studies, which had also been informed by the broader academic work in the field of PM, were shared with the task team. This additional shared knowledge helped the task team to frame the domain of PM and the diagnostic/research process. The task team members took a broader view of PM than they had started with, viewing it (a) not as a single appraisal event but rather as a cycle of activities, (b) not as occurring only at the individual level but rather as occurring at the levels of larger performing units as well, and (c) not as forms and formal interactions but rather as an ongoing process of two-way communication between employees (individually and in groups) and managers.

Diagnosis/Research

Task team members brought their own concerns that helped to shape the diagnostic activities: (a) that the current systems were no longer working effectively because people had become preoccupied with the salary delivery aspects of PM, (b) that in many cases employees were not receiving feedback at all, and (c) that the processes did not fit with the team-based knowledge settings in the company, where the current processes pitted interdependent employees against each other in competition for a fixed pie of rewards. More broadly, they were concerned that the management of performance was occurring through a set of top-down, bureaucratic processes rather than through meaningful interactions between managers and employees. The task force combined these practical concerns with the frameworks we provided to formulate a series of research questions to investigate through diagnostic interviews and surveys.

The diagnostic activities constituted the first research opportunity. The generation of academic knowledge through collaborative research depends on the systematic gathering, analysis, and interpretation of data (Ledford & Mohrman, 1993). We crafted the interview protocols and surveys to confirm and extend the model that had been grounded in earlier collaborative studies of PM (Lawler, Mohrman, & Resnick, 1984; Mohrman, Mohrman, & Lawler, 1992; Mohrman, Mohrman, & Worley, 1990). The Oilco diagnostic survey was further grounded through the diagnostic interviews (Glaser & Strauss, 1967; Locke, 2000). Linking the survey to the Oilco setting also allowed for the discovery of context-specific knowledge and increased the likelihood of usefulness to Oilco. The survey data provided a baseline for longitudinally assessing the impacts of the eventual new system. The interview sample reflected the diversity of settings in the company and numbered around 300. We were highly dependent on task team members to provide an understanding of the work of the organization and the subpopulations to be sampled. We also depended on them to review the instruments to ensure that the language was appropriate and that their concerns were adequately represented. The survey was administered to a random sample of the corporation's entire management and professional workforce, with more than 2,000 responses and a response rate exceeding 80%.

Among the interesting findings was the high level of importance that employees at all levels in the organization attached to PM—yet they believed that it was being poorly carried out by their managers. Employees felt at risk during this time of transformation. They believed that they had a lot to lose because of the close connection of PM to salary and career opportunities. Survey results showed that employees did not believe that managers gave adequate attention to PM or were rewarded for doing so. Employees believed that their ratings were often changed by higher level managers to fit a predetermined ranking of employees for salary action, that the appraisals were often not related to key job requirements, and that there was little attention given to competency and career development. In addition, employees believed that the system worked against a number of the desired new cultural attributes: teamwork, innovation, and respect.

The diagnosis confirmed that the basic frameworks and main findings from earlier settings applied as well in the Oilco context. For example, closer alignment between manager and employee assessments of performance, higher levels of performance, and greater performance improvement were reported when employees reported higher mutuality between themselves and their managers during the processes of goal setting and performance appraisal. To extend earlier theory, we built into the survey a more sophisticated test of the impact of work interdependency and team structures on the effectiveness of various PM elements, providing a compelling case that individual PM in highly interdependent team settings fails to take into account major antecedents of performance and sources of knowledge about the levels of performance. From an academic perspective, these cross-sectional findings enhanced the model of multilevel PM. From a practical standpoint, they provided evidence that the system must enable team PM where appropriate.

Criteria

Based on the foundation it had laid, the task team generated a list of criteria that became touchstones for the design, implementation, and assessment activities that followed. These criteria stated that the new system should do the following:

1. Promote and motivate both individual and team performance.

2. Build commitment and trust by encouraging mutuality, communication, and employee involvement.

3. Be clear, open, and understandable such as in how PM relates to pay.

4. Be perceived as fair and credible.

5. Be flexible and adaptable to different jobs, different teams, and new work designs.

6. Provide useful input to other practices such as career development and pay.

Design

Keeping the criteria and models of PM in mind, the task team designed a new Oilco Performance Management system (OPM) consisting of three processes that comprise the PM cycle: performance definition, development, and performance review. *Performance definition* includes defining and agreeing on the work expectations and the criteria by which work would be evaluated. This includes goal setting and clarifying roles, tasks, and other accountabilities. Performance definition was to take place as part of the company's business planning cycle. *Development* is based on the performance needed and includes planning for the needs of the performer and the resources required. The developmental and resource plans are to be carried out over the course of the performance cycle. *Performance review* occurs at the end of the cycle according to the agreed-on criteria. To allow for change and adjustments, at least one interim review is prescribed.

Based on the research findings concerning the importance of mutuality, OPM includes participative mechanisms by which supervisors and performers assume more equal two-way roles in all stages. All processes are to be done jointly. Interim reviews can be initiated by either party, when appropriate, so that changing conditions can be incorporated. Recognizing interdependencies in the system, supervisors and performers also jointly select others (e.g., coworkers, customers, other managers) to provide input into the review.

The review is expressed on multiple dimensions and is no longer summarized in a single rating to be plugged into a salary formula, thereby severing the previously automatic connection between appraisal and salary action. Managers' ranking of employees for salary purposes now takes place after the performance reviews are finalized rather than before. Employees subsequently receive feedback about where they fall in the salary ranking and the bases for their ranking. This change is intended to promote understanding that salary action is not based solely on considerations of absolute performance but rather is also based on relative performance, experience, position in grade, and the labor market.

Individual and team goals and performance are explicitly linked to the business plans and corporate goals. Individuals' work definitions and reviews are to take place after the work group and manager get together to set group goals and review group performance.

The new system provided an action learning opportunity to test, through implementation and assessment, whether processes designed based on academic models and contextual understanding actually resulted in improved practice.

Implementation

After top management accepted the new design, the task force formed an implementation team made up of two direct reports to each of the task force members. This group planned and managed the rollout of the new PM system. The new system was carefully set out in documents supplied to all employees. A training and development firm was hired to create the materials and plan the training. Both the design and implementation teams reviewed the materials at several junctures to ensure that they fit with the specifications and intent of the design team. A total of 600 managers received 5 days of training so that they, in turn, could provide 2 days of training to every remaining manager and professional in the organization, that is, approximately 20,000 people. Everyone in the organization had the opportunity to learn the intent and logic of the system as well as its mechanics. The training offered an opportunity to discuss the new system and to "practice" new behaviors through role-playing.

Assessment/Research

Baseline data had been collected during diagnosis. Selected measures were repeated 24 months later, shortly after the first full OPM cycle using the new system, and again 24 months after that. As with diagnosis, a random sample of all management and professional employees was surveyed. Other data were collected from interviews and archival sources. Assessment had two focuses. First, we measured the degree to which the design elements of OPM were actually implemented in practice and reflected in behavior. Second, we analyzed whether the OPM practices resulted in the desired effects. The design team was active in crafting the methods and interpreting the results.

Degree of OPM Implementation

Fully 97% of all employees received the training at implementation. Three years later, 88% of new employees had received some type of PM training. The vast majority of employees and their managers followed the new practices during the first PM cycle, and this was also true 2 years later after three full PM cycles. Some core OPM activities, although practiced by most during the first year, became even more pervasive and established over time. The average number of interim reviews and the percentage of people with development plans both increased significantly over the assessment period as people became accustomed to these OPM elements and convinced of their utility. The degree of mutuality with which PM activities were practiced also showed a significant increase over the assessment period.

Effects of OPM

We compared baseline results on appropriate scales with results on the same scales 2 and 4 years later using t tests. Each survey was administered at approximately the same time of the calendar year and, as such, at the same point in the performance cycle. During the years after OPM implementation, Oilco and its industry ran into business difficulties, necessitating layoffs and performance pressures that led to increases in responsibilities and stresses on remaining employees. Consequently, people's job satisfaction and trust in the organization fell, and people were less likely to report that managers had sufficient time and other resources for PM. Nevertheless employees reported an increase in management encouragement of OPM. Indeed, the ultimate objectives of OPM were being met, thereby confirming its design logic.

In particular, survey results showed that people better understood their organization, the role they played in it, and the contribution their performance made to their business. People reported a higher level of two desired cultural attributes: teamwork and a climate supportive of innovation. Also, people were significantly more satisfied with their career opportunities, reflecting OPM's emphasis on development.

One of the most vexing problems in appraising performance, as we had seen repeatedly in our studies, is that appraisers and appraisees do not agree on the appraisees' level of performance. Indeed, at the time of Oilco's baseline diagnosis, employees at all levels in the organization judged their own performance to be significantly higher than they considered it to be judged by their supervising managers. After just one performance cycle, and continuing for the two cycles thereafter, this gap closed virtually to zero, indicating that employees essentially agreed with and accepted the judgments of their managers. We expected that this would occur because of increased mutuality.

Another vexation was the way in which Oilco's stress on pay for performance had resulted in managers predetermining pay decisions before rating performance to boost the correlation between pay and performance. Our data revealed that, using OPM, people actually began to see less of a connection between their performance and their pay. As intended by the OPM design, they showed an increased understanding that their pay was based on many considerations, only one of which was performance.

We also used correlations and regression analyses to suggest how, and the degree to which, OPM and related processes affected various outcomes. In particular, the degree to which the collective set of OPM processes was carried out was strongly connected to improved performance by an individual. The degree to which the individual's customers and/or clients provided input into the appraisal process was also strongly associated with higher performance.

OPM training and materials stressed that individual PM was best conducted in the context of managing the performance of the work group to which an individual belonged. Indeed, the data showed that the use of OPM practices significantly and directly promoted team and unit performance as well as performance change. OPM practices also had direct significant effects on the effectiveness of team-oriented and lateral work processes, directly encouraged a climate for innovation, and spurred the creation of organizational and process improvements. All of these had positive effects on individual, team, and unit performance.

In short, as interpreted by both academic and company collaborators, the longitudinal assessment found that implementation of the OPM system accomplished the outcomes and fostered the cultural values it was designed to promote. This pattern of findings is consistent with the theory underlying the design.

Further Uses of Assessment Results

Not only did the assessment confirm the logic of OPM and evaluate its impact, but the results also were of further use by both Oilco and academia.

For Ongoing Oilco Self-Design

To increase resource commitment to OPM and make it more visible, Oilco created an Office of Performance Management headed up by a line manager who had chaired the implementation task force. This office shared the assessment results throughout the organization, facilitated discussion and dissemination of best practices, set up ongoing OPM training, and encouraged OPM use and improvement throughout Oilco. A subset of vice presidents from the original design task force served as an OPM executive committee whose role was to recommend corporate policies to strengthen the design of OPM and create a supportive context for it.

During the first cycle of OPM, several parts of the corporation that were operating in teams adapted it for team-level PM by using the entire process at the team level. In other units, the team planning and review practices suggested as part of OPM spurred the implementation of formal teams. As a result of this and the favorable assessment data, the OPM executive committee recommended, and corporate Oilco decided to stress, the use of a team-oriented PM process corporation-wide.

By clearly distinguishing compensation practices from OPM and essentially illuminating their problems, the design team created pressures to redesign the compensation system. As a first step, individual pay decisions were changed from being based on a strict linear ranking of all employees in comparable job levels to placing employees into three or five categories. Subsequently, corporate pay practices were changed to emphasize collective performance by creating two new bonuses for everyone: one based on their local business unit's performance and the other based on the performance of their division as a whole.

The assessment had shown that when customers, co-workers, and others were solicited for input into reviews and they provided it, the results were better on all dimensions than if only the managers and employees contributed to the evaluations. This experience spurred Oilco to adopt 360-degree approaches to management development—yet another shift from the hierarchical worldview.

For Academic Understanding

At Oilco, the PM practices were designed to reflect the organizational worldview to which management wanted to change. These practices implied a different organizational model from the existing top-down hierarchical control model. Because PM is a set of practices that touch every employee and are central to how employees relate to the organization and get a sense of worth, it is clearly an efficient tool for building a community of shared views. In many locations at Oilco, changes in work design to create flat organizations and teams were reinforced by the new PM. Originally viewed as anomalies because they did not fit with Oilco's hierarchical and individual orientation, these work design changes provided an opportunity to see and learn about a new way of doing work. Combined with the changes embodied in OPM, they created a push for even more fundamental changes in PM and the organization of work.

Through this collaboration, we developed an appreciation for the central role that PM can play, either as a key element of change or as a stubborn barrier to change. The latter had previously been the case at Oilco. In some of our prior studies, PM had primarily played a lagging support role for transformation—as part of the context that needed to be changed to allow the "real" elements of change to work. Alternatively, in other studies, the company's desire was to increase the effectiveness of PM as a business tool—not contemplating fundamental change. In those cases, we had come to understand that increasing the effectiveness of PM required making supportive changes to other aspects of the organization's design (e.g., work designs, performance definitions, organizational capacities and competencies, hierarchical relationships, HR practices) and focusing on the performance of units as the context for individual PM. The Oilco collaboration deepened our understanding of how changes in PM can be used to catalyze change in the organization in a purposeful way (Mohrman & Mohrman, 1998).

In many organizations, traditional PM practices have so shaped worldviews that even when faced with anomalies, the companies stay locked into the status quo. Firms often deal with feedback that their hierarchically driven, individual approaches to managing performance are not working by trying to strengthen them. They search for better measures, provide more training, and/or focus on methods to control adherence to prescribed practices, thereby perpetuating the old paradigm. At Oilco, in contrast, the new approaches to PM explicitly and successfully recognized the importance of the anomalies and stimulated changes in worldview and organizational practice.

We captured this new appreciation in new models of change (Mohrman & Mohrman, 1998) in publications aimed at advancing theory and practice. In our continuing research program, we were propelled toward two research focuses building on the findings from this and other collaborations. First, having learned that the PM of individuals was a management tool with very limited potential until one moved up a level of aggregation and simultaneously managed the performance of groups, we flipped our focus and began to study the design of team-based organizations—focusing on the entire organization and all processes, including PM (Mohrman et al., 1995). Second, at Oilco and elsewhere, we observed many indications of the power of practicing PM as a lateral, open, reflective, and systemic process as opposed to one that is hierarchical, closed, defensive, and isolated. Doing the former contributed to innovation, development, and improved performance at all levels and embodied some core attributes of organizational learning. Doing the latter worked against these outcomes. One can make the case that open and reflective PM is a source of continual organizational learning. Since that time, we and our CEO colleagues have pursued studies and generated publications examining organizational processes, including open system PM, that enable an organization to learn to perform more effectively and to continue to redesign itself through time.

Conclusion

Our collaboration with Oilco in their self-design of a new PM system is an example of the combination of academic and practitioner knowledge to yield advances in practice and theory. The success of this collaboration depended fundamentally on Oilco's interest in basing new practices on research-based knowledge and the corporation's openness to new conceptualizations of the domain. It also required that we immerse ourselves in understanding and learning from Oilco's context and that both parties learn together about PM in this context. Each party brought different resources and purposes to the collaboration, and each played different roles. The self-design process provided a change methodology that included the incorporation of existing knowledge, the generation of new knowledge, the translation of knowledge into practical approaches and methodologies, and the testing of these in practice.

References

Cummings, T. G., Mohrman, S. A., Mohrman, A. M., Jr., & Ledford, G. E., Jr. (1985). Organization design for the future: A collaborative research approach. In E. E. Lawler, III, A. M. Mohrman, Jr., S. A. Mohrman, G. E. Ledford, Jr., T. G. Cummings, & Associates (Eds.), *Doing research that is useful for theory and practice* (pp. 275–305). San Francisco: Jossey-Bass.

Glaser, B. G., & Strauss, A. L. (1967). *The discovery of grounded theory.* Hawthorne, NY: Aldine.

Hatchuel, A., & Molet, H. (1986). Rational modelling in understanding and aiding human decision-making: About two case studies. *European Journal of Operational Research, 24,* 178–186.

Huber, G. P., & Glick, W. H. (Eds.). (1993). *Organizational change and redesign: Ideas and insights for improving performance.* New York: Oxford University Press.

Kuhn, T. S. (1970). *The structure of scientific revolutions.* Chicago: University of Chicago Press.

Lawler, E. E., III. (1985). Challenging traditional research assumptions. In E. E. Lawler, III, A. M. Mohrman, Jr., S. A. Mohrman, G. E. Ledford, Jr., T. G. Cummings, & Associates (Eds.), *Doing research that is useful for theory and practice* (pp. 1–17). San Francisco: Jossey-Bass.

Lawler, E. E., III, Mohrman, A. M., Jr., & Resnick, S. (1984). Performance appraisal revisited. *Organizational Dynamics, 13*(1), 20–35.

Ledford, G. E., Jr., & Mohrman, S. A. (1993). Looking backward and forward at action research. *Human Relations, 46,* 1349–1359.

Lewin, K. (1951). *Field theory in the social sciences.* New York: Harper & Row.

Locke, K. (2000). *Grounded theory in management research.* London: Sage.

Mohrman, A. M., Jr. (1990). Deming versus performance appraisal: Is there a resolution? In G. N. McLean, S. R. Damme, & R. A. Swanson (Eds.), *Performance appraisal: Perspectives on a quality management approach* (pp. 3–23). Alexandria, VA: American Society for Training and Development.

Mohrman, A. M., Jr., & Mohrman, S. A. (1998). Catalyzing organizational change and learning: The role of performance management. In S. A. Mohrman, J. R. Galbraith, E. E. Lawler, III, & Associates (Eds.), *Tomorrow's organization: Crafting winning capabilities in a dynamic world* (pp. 362–393). San Francisco: Jossey-Bass.

Mohrman, A. M., Jr., Mohrman, S. A., & Lawler, E. E., III. (1992). The performance management of teams. In W. J. Bruns, Jr. (Ed.), *Performance measurement, evaluation, and incentives,* (pp. 217–241). Boston: Harvard Business School Press.

Mohrman, A. M., Jr., Mohrman, S. A., Lawler, E. E., III, & Ledford, G. E., Jr. (1999). Introduction to the new edition. In E. E. Lawler, III, A. M. Mohrman, Jr., S. A. Mohrman, G. E. Ledford, Jr., T. G. Cummings, & Associates (Eds.), *Doing research that is useful for theory and practice* (2nd ed., pp. ix–xlix). Lanham, MD: Lexington.

Mohrman, A. M., Mohrman, S. A., & Worley, C. (1990). High technology performance management. In M. A. von Glinow & S. A. Mohrman (Eds.), *Managing complexity in high technology organizations.* New York: Oxford University Press.

Mohrman, A. M., Jr., Resnick-West, S., & Lawler, E. E., III. (1989). *Designing performance appraisal systems.* San Francisco: Jossey-Bass.

Mohrman, S. A., & Cummings, T. G. (1987). Self designing organizations. In R. W. Woodman & W. A. Pasmore (Eds.), *Research in organizational change and development* (Vol. 1). Greenwich, CT: JAI.

Mohrman, S. A., & Cummings, T. G. (1989). *Self-designing organizations: Learning how to create high performance.* Reading, MA: Addison-Wesley.

Mohrman, S. A., Cohen, S. G., & Mohrman, A. M., Jr. (1995). *Designing team-based organizations: New applications for knowledge work*. San Francisco: Jossey-Bass.

Mohrman, S. A., Mohrman, A. M., Jr., & Tenkasi, R. (1997). The discipline of organization design. In C. L. Cooper & S. E. Jackson (Eds.), *Creating tomorrow's organisations: A handbook for future research in organizational behavior* (pp. 191–205). West Sussex, UK: Wiley.

Simon, H. A. (1969). *The sciences of the artificial*. Cambridge, MA: MIT Press.

Weick, K. E. (1993). Organizational redesign as improvisation. In G. P. Huber & W. H. Glick (Eds.), *Organizational change and redesign: Ideas and insights for improving performance* (pp. 346–382). New York: Oxford University Press.

Academic Commentary on Part III

Anne Sigismund Huff

ATM, *London Business School*

The chapters in Part III of the volume focus on some of the most important questions facing organizations today: product development, knowledge facilitation, user involvement, organizational creativity, responses to crises, service innovation, leadership, product innovation, and performance management. By reporting on academic-practitioner research in these areas, the section substantially counters David Knights's concern (academic commentary on Part I) that few rewarding collaborations have taken place. Although undesired outcomes are admitted on occasion, the achievements found here should inspire further efforts to take advantage of the inherent differences between practitioners and academics.

Some projects appear to be quite close to classical research in their objectives and outputs. For example, Sundgren and Styhre's piece (Chapter 13) on managing organizational creativity is a study of the most successful discoveries in Astra and Zeneca before their merger. Collaboration between one insider researcher and three outsider academics revolved around the interpretation of retrospective interviews, a process that also drew in the interviewees. This is a FENIX executive Ph.D. project. The researcher from within the company clearly has wonderful access to data and is highly motivated by AstraZeneca's need to discover more blockbuster pharmaceuticals. But other than its collaborative approach to analysis, which is very significant, this project is not much different from Ph.D. projects at many other academic institutions.

Similarly, several chapters in this section use the familiar vocabulary of experimentation to carry out their projects. Magnusson's (Chapter 12) classic design asked users to develop new ideas for mobile phone services. Five different groups (including one professional developer group from within the company sponsoring the research) were given new phones and a 12-day period to create ideas for their use. A total of 13 judges, both experts and other users, concluded that users' proposals were more innovative, with higher estimated user value than the proposals of the professionals. However, users' ideas were also considered to be more difficult to realize. Because the author varied setup conditions, it was possible to systematically assess several different ways in which to involve users. Interestingly, given the purpose of this volume, professional developers gained most when they served as consultants for users developing ideas. Although marketing research might use experimental design, it is unlikely that a marketing department would have come up with this initial condition and insight. Furthermore, the author's academic interest in understanding the contribution of users to service innovation provides a broader background for company partners interested in taking action based on the experiments.

Some projects reported in this section seem to be closer to management consultancy than to academic research. In Kylén and colleagues' piece (Chapter 16), for example, FENIX researchers collaborating on the development of Leader@site say that they worried about the blurred lines between consultancy and research as well as those between experimentation and implementation. However, they decided that as representatives of an academic institution, they needed to understand more about the practical consequences of the leadership development courses they were offering. Therefore, they responded positively to AstraZeneca's human resources department request for help in using research-tested ideas to encourage knowledge creation and learning in teams. The result of the collaboration was a generic platform for leadership development, supported by a Web site.

The distinctions between "classic" academic research design and consultancy—between theoretical interests and knowledge for action—may help readers and potential researchers to connect the work reported in this section to other more familiar projects. But it is very important to recognize that these chapters help us to move beyond these traditional categories. They can and should be read primarily for emerging vocabularies and new recipes for knowledge generated through practitioner-academic partnerships. Thus, in Chapter 10, Mikaelsson and Shani encourage cross-functional engineering teams at Volvo to use the language of experimentation in an iterative six-stage cycle to reflect on their experience of mandated change. Blends and innovations like this occur in nearly every chapter of this section, including the ones already mentioned. They should help others to tailor partnerships to their unique circumstances while anticipating some of the pitfalls experienced by these forerunners.

In commenting on Section I, Knights was concerned, as are many of the authors in this volume, with the inherent difficulties that can counteract the potential benefits of collaboration. Several chapters in Part III of the volume are particularly forthright about the complications of working across inherently different backgrounds, vocabulary, needs, and ways of working in academic-practitioner partnerships. They also show, however, that working across differences is inherent in today's way of working *within* organizations. Mikaelsson and Shani (Chapter 10) catalog significant difficulties encountered by groups trying to work more closely together at Volvo. Sandberg and Werr (Chapter 17) develop a very similar story when trying to understand why different parts of Telia underuse information from Telia Promotor, the company's information technology and business consulting arm. Telia Promotor's potential to serve as the "troubleshooter" was taken up most often by product managers. The authors use the data they collected to show that marketers and new product developers were much less likely to take advantage of inputs from this unit because of three different "filters" stemming from the distinctive mind-set required to do their own work.

Better engagement obviously requires better understanding of the other—a solution that is easy to identify but hard to achieve. The impetus for doing so, in a busy and pressured world, is most likely to be that cooperative effort generates insights that could not be gained by one partner alone. Part III of the volume provides evidence that this can happen and shows, in some cases, that benefits extend beyond initial goals. In Chapter 12, Magnusson describes how product developers get a more innovative and much larger set of ideas for new services than they could generate within their own group, as they might have hoped. They also learn how much users blur the boundary between phone service and the phone itself—suggesting, for example, that a useful phone might come equipped with a bottle opener or an alcoholmeter. In Björkman's piece (Chapter 15), the trade union working to find new forms of dialogue with its members creates a desired platform for further development but also discovers that its members are interested in more dialogue among themselves, not a function traditionally performed by the union.

The final chapter in this volume (Chapter 18), by Allan and Susan Mohrman from the Center for Effective Organizations (CEO) at the University of Southern California, is particularly helpful in understanding how direct benefits and unexpected insights such as these might be gained. Both partners in the work described were driven by the need for knowledge that they could not satisfy within their own or similar organizations. Both parties gained what they had hoped for, according to the authors, but also found over time that they were altered in significant ways that they had not anticipated. This evolutionary report is one of the clearest success stories in the volume, and it is the possibility that practitioner-academic partnerships can become the source of unanticipated growth that fuels my personal interest in facilitating this form of research.

The story in the final chapter is worth outlining in a little detail. Executives at "Oilco," a petroleum and chemicals company, believed that their performance system was one of several areas of bureaucracy that did not fit with a new corporate vision. They asked CEO's researchers to help them understand and alter the current system with several highly visible managers, asking only that the work group not make changes to the compensation system, in part because employees had become preoccupied with salary as a source of feedback.

CEO's guiding philosophy, from its founding in 1979, is to work only on "research to advance academic theory while simultaneously yielding knowledge to inform practice." In this case, the researchers wanted to build on their previous experience to understand more about the potential of performance management to drive organizational change. They were pleased to have a partner that also wanted new knowledge from the collaboration.

The chapter provides interesting detail about how a quite extensive new system was designed and how that system departed from past practice. Performance reviews were further decoupled from salary assessments to help employees understand that salary actions are based on relative factors not included in their own appraisals. The new system was also more explicitly linked to business and corporate goals. Even though economic downturn put the system under pressure, a quite sophisticated evaluation showed that it was being broadly implemented within the company and that it was strongly associated with higher performance. These achievements were based on a new model of performance appraisal that satisfied the needs of both academic and practitioner partners.

Interestingly, both partners also realized unanticipated outcomes. After establishing an Office of Performance Management to increase the visibility of their commitment and then looking at its early results, top managers began to reconsider the compensation system. A first step was to abandon a strict linear ranking of all employees in favor of a limited number of broad categories. They also added bonuses based on collective performance rather than just individual performance.

The academics took a similar step away from their initial assumptions and models. Initially, they assumed that performance appraisal was a tool for change. Through their involvement with the Oilco project, they came to understand the converse as well—that effective performance management required making changes in other aspects of the organization. In short, they developed a more systemic model than they had previously, and they published these findings in academic outlets.

Both of these unanticipated outcomes are strong arguments indeed for partnership. Therefore, Chapter 18 is a useful source of information about what may be required to realize similar benefits in other places. An initial observation is that Oilco has an ongoing relationship with CEO and that several participants in this project had worked on other projects sponsored by the two organizations before the success story outlined. Several other chapters in this volume similarly grew out of long-term relationships, including the several chapters based on projects in the companies that founded FENIX. This depth of experience appears to significantly increase the odds of success from academic-practitioner partnerships. The cautionary tale is that the cost of successful collaboration may be even higher than is realized. The much more positive view is that continuing collaboration is likely to bring increasing gains. And why not? We know that successful entrepreneurs rarely succeed in their first efforts, but they have the stamina to try again and again until they get it right. Collaboration appears to require the same confidence that opportunities for significantly better knowledge creation are worth pursuing.

A second enabling condition found in Chapter 18 is almost certainly that Oilco was highly motivated to undertake an expensive research project by several reinforcing pressures. Not only did Oilco's top managers have considerable evidence that their current evaluation system was not working, they had just initiated a new vision statement for the company that they wanted to be more broadly understood and they were trying to implement a major change effort. The researchers on the team were perhaps less pressured initially, but they became increasingly engaged as it became clear that the project could make more than incremental additions to their current knowledge base.

Ultimate success, in short, typically grows out of strong need. This volume suggests that the need can be found in the topics most pressing managers today—topics that include product development, knowledge facilitation, user involvement, organizational creativity, responses to crises, service innovation, leadership, product innovation, and performance management. It will be interesting to see the further benefits that can be realized around these and other pressing issues. Part III of the volume provides useful information about when, why, and how that might be accomplished.

Executive Commentary on Part III

Björn Frössevi

Vice President, Head of
Business Development, Softronic

Competition in the emerging knowledge-based society has changed significantly over the past two decades. For most companies, it has become necessary to focus on boundary-spanning challenges. Consulting companies are expected to deliver comprehensive business solutions that integrate services and products. Softronic, with its subsidiary Consultus, has struggled with delivering integrated information technology (IT) and management solutions over the past 20 years.

The IT consultancy business has gone through severe changes during recent decades. As a comparatively young industry originated for internal mainframe departments, it has developed through specialized service organizations into a rather mature market. Some of these specialized skills include services and projects based on IT skills and knowledge. However, in the mature market, specialized skills are not enough. Combining these skills with business understanding also applies to management consulting, but here another competitive edge—globalization—has been an even more important factor for developing businesses and market presence.

During the 1990s, global competition was realized in Sweden. International players had almost totally monopolized the market for advanced management consultancy. For the Swedish player, this created a need to build both formal and informal international strategic alliances and partnerships. We are still early in this phase, and most likely this need will increase over time.

Today a knowledge-based firm needs a more balanced portfolio of offerings to cope with the demand from customers and increased competition. New business models and ways of relating to the industry will have to be developed due to changes in company structures following mergers and spin-outs from large companies and universities. Softronic is an international IT and management consultancy company, listed in the Stockholm Stock Exchange, with a focus on leading change processes in three dimensions:

strategic, structural, and human. The main challenge for our business today is to develop new ways of working more closely with both customers and partners, such as research organizations, to solve real organizational problems more rapidly. At the same time, innovative solutions are needed to provide a competitive advantage and to bridge the gap between traditional organizational and business development with leadership and management training. The opportunities to develop new ways of enhancing reflection among managers will contribute to the development process and to managers' own learning and development in parallel.

The chapters in Part III of this volume elaborate on some of the most important questions facing complex organizations today, including how to continuously innovate and deliver new products and services, how to engage the various stakeholders in the process, and what leadership tactics are necessary to facilitate learning and innovation. The described collaborative efforts clearly show the complexity in bridging the corporate and academic agendas. They also show some inspiring results that may convince companies and academics to pursue continued experimentation in building joint research and development (R&D) management.

In Chapter 10, Mikaelsson and Shani encourage cross-functional engineering teams at Volvo to use experiments as a tool in the change process. In Chapter 11, Roth, Berg, and Styhre show the need for new roles and organizational mechanisms in knowledge-based organizations. In Chapter 12, Magnusson shows that in the development of new telephone services, professional developers gained most when they served as consultants for users developing the ideas. Product developers had more innovative ideas for new services, as well as a greater number of them, when they collaborated closely with the end users. In Chapter 13, Sundgren and Styhre elaborate on the experiences of organizing around the discovery process in Astra and Zeneca prior to their merger. In Chapter 14, Engwall and Svensson focus on the necessity for organized task forces to manage emerging challenges in multi-project-based organizations. In Chapter 15, Björkman tells the story of a trade union working to find new forms of dialogue with its members to create a desired platform for further development but also discovering that its members are interested in more dialogue among themselves—not a function traditionally performed by the union. In Chapter 16, Kylén and colleagues describe how a generic platform for leadership development supported by a Web site is developed as a result of a collaborative research project. In Chapter 17, Sandberg and Werr show why various parts of Telia underuse information from Telia Promotor, the company's IT and business consulting arm. This clearly lowers Telia Promotor's potential to serve as a "troubleshooter." In Chapter 18, Mohrman and Mohrman relate the story of how an Office of Performance Management system was created as a result of a collaborative research project. Together, these nine case studies provide a broad spectrum of possible setups for collaborative research projects and different outcomes for both the short run and the long run.

To get a sense of what happens in the various research projects, it is necessary for the process to be co-owned by the members, leaders, managers, and executives—and not only by the management researchers. A better understanding for the different logic of managerial practice and management research will be important given the pressure that the engaged actors are under. The examples in Chapters 10 through 18 provide evidence about the merits of collaborative research. However, the process and format for how the final results are presented still need to be developed to bridge the parallel logic and challenges facing practicing managers and management researchers, respectively. In this interplay, management consultants may find new and interesting roles.

The daily life of an executive does not leave room for extensive reflection or even relevant data collection for most of the issues that are being addressed. The available time for sharpening one's professional skills is extremely small. The expectations from the various stakeholders often point in different directions. Urgent decisions and actions that need to be made clearly outnumber the kinds of elaborate analyses one can make on strategy formation processes, new organizational structures, or leadership models. This reality does not mean that one should not experiment with new ways of working to find a better balance between actions and decisions in real time and a continuous ongoing reflection on future directions for actions and decisions. It is clear that the management technology is important in explaining performance and competitiveness in international and highly competitive industries. Continued joint experimentation in the exploration of alternative ways of developing boundary-spanning collaborations is likely to enhance R&D capacity. We are currently engaged in a large-scale experiment where our management consultants, together with FENIX researchers and managers from various companies, organize laboratories to elaborate on complex managerial challenges. These laboratories provide new perspectives, interpretations, and analyses to guide managers' actions and decisions. They also provide important opportunities for management research to develop the organizations and their leaders. The laboratories are organized as parallel activities to other strategy, organizational, and leadership development programs. The purpose is to experiment with new ideas of strategic relevance and to leverage the participants' input in the experimentations. The activities and initiatives within the laboratories are, in principle, organized as isolated cases and are not there to substitute for existing leadership development activities. Activities in the laboratories are participant driven. Both the choice of issues and the pedagogical approaches used need to reflect that they are not an easily available solution to the "red and hot" issues. The solutions developed are a function of the participants' abilities to experiment and learn from mutual experimentation in real problem-solving situations. Each of the participants is supposed to bring his or her own success stories and failures and to reflect on them. The dialogue around the stories and their meanings serves as a catalyst for ideas that are brought back to the parent companies.

These laboratories are then fed input from organized scouting activities where different *scouts* or observers in companies engage in management research projects. They collect data on a specific issue or problem that could alter the outcome through a thorough analysis of alternatives. The laboratories are also provided with a decision forum—an integration team with the role of collecting ideas and patterns, deciding on surveys and studies, and determining actions resulting from the information gathered. The integration team will consist of influential people from the company (who have rapid decision-making abilities) and a small group of senior management researchers and consultants. The integration team will be in control of resources for activities to be offered to company development and training programs, when and where they are most urgently needed. The team needs the capacity to arrange workshops, seminars, mentor relations, and other arenas for the exchange of information connected to real and difficult management and leadership situations.

Softronic foresees great potential in this boundary-spanning way of working. The transfer of knowledge among various groups of actors turns into the co-creation of new knowledge, which could possibly lead to a competitive advantage for all engaged actors. What is called collaborative research in this volume captures an important approach of how to develop a way of working for knowledge-based organizations.

PART IV

Collaborative Research in Organizations

Lessons and Challenges

In this final part of the volume, we try to integrate the various parts and chapters and attempt to draw some learning about collaborative research in organizations. Because of the nature of the phenomenon and the exploratory nature of our approach, the normal custom for a concluding part to summarize the findings presented and come out with a few solid conclusions is not applicable. The 18 chapters, two forewords, and six commentaries that make up the book, written by 36 practitioners and researchers representing various academic disciplines from 10 academic institutions and 9 companies, cover a great amount of diverse material. The range of collaborative research orientations, illustrations, and topics studied provides a rich point of departure for ongoing learning. Thus, this final part should rather be viewed as a deeper level of reflection on this collective 5-year research journey.

In the first section of this part of the volume, we integrate and discuss the main contributions of Parts II and III by identifying and exploring the patterns that have emerged from the use of the various collaborative research orientations and studies. In the second section, we cluster the variety of criticisms that can be found in the academic literature and attempt to address them based on the learning and reflection on the studies reported in the volume. Finally, in the third section, we discuss the future of collaborative research, advancing the themes that were presented in the volume's framing (Part I) while drawing on the specific contributions in the book.

Facets of Collaborative Research

The principal motives, aims, and framing of this volume were laid out in some detail in the preface and Part I of the book and need only a brief recapturing here. The emerging discourse in the management sciences and the increasing challenges faced by management are likely to benefit from substantial experimentation with collaborative research in organizations. Thus, the stage was set for three central paths of investigation: the exploration of the current discourse and challenges; the identification of some key alternative roadmaps, lenses, and mechanisms; and the illustration of some emerging academy-industry research partnerships.

Although the notions of collaborative research in organizations are not new, and although many scholar-practitioners have developed a variety of collaborative research orientations, they have had relatively limited impact on the emerging discourse, managerial challenges, and scientific knowledge. Part II of the volume used, as a point of departure, the essential works of scholars and practitioners from various disciplines and organizations that developed and advanced our understanding of collaborative research. We have attempted to provide a comprehensive snapshot of the collaborative research field. Coupling the literature with our own set of empirical studies resulted in the identification and exploration of five different facets of collaborative research: the somewhat different roadmaps of the various schools of thought or orientations for collaborative research in organizations (Chapter 5), the role and development process of an executive Ph.D. program that served as a critical bridge in collaborative research (Chapter 6), the dual role of the insider action researcher (Chapter 7), and the jam session (Chapter 8) and structural learning mechanisms (Chapter 9).

Our goal was to advance the scientific knowledge about collaborative research in a comprehensive interdisciplinary and action-oriented approach by integrating practices in the 11 successful projects (described in Chapters 8 through 18) with the existing body of knowledge. As such, the empirical studies present research results from explicit academy-industry joint research efforts and document both the collaborative process of the projects and the specific scientific knowledge and actionable knowledge that were generated. Table IV.1 presents a comparative synopsis of the 11 cases, background about the companies, key issues/primary focus/research questions that emerged as the focus of the studies, the dominant collaborative research orientations used, outcomes in terms of knowledge creation and organizational/managerial actions.

Table IV.I   A Comparative Synopsis of the Illustrations

	Digital Media Newspaper (Chapter 8)	Pharmacy Operation Division of Kaiser Permanente (Chapter 9)	Car Manufacturing (Chapter 10)	Pharmaceuticals (Chapter 11)	Telecommuni-cations (Chapter 12)	Pharmaceutials (Chapter 13)	Telecommuni-cations Manufacturing (Chapter 14)	White-Collar Union Organization (Chapter 15)	Pharmaceuticals (Chapter 16)	Business Consulting (Chapter 17)	Oil and Petroleum (Chapter 18)
The company context	Newspaper company 1,000 employees $0.1 billion (U.S.)	Kaiser Permanente is America's leading health maintenance organization The Pharmacy Operation division has 3,500 employees $1 billion (U.S.)	Volvo Car Corporation Automotive industry 17,500 employees $10.7 billion (U.S.) Premium brand Struggling with positioning in a mature market	AstraZeneca Pharmaceuticals company Leader in cardiovascular, gastrointestinal, and cancer medicine 54,000 employees $17.4 billion (U.S.) Efficiency in drug development in a fusioned company	Telia Telecommuni-cations industry Leading national operator 17,000 employees $5.7 billion (U.S.) Struggling with finding a position where value can be added	AstraZeneca Pharmaceuticals company Leader in cardiovascular, gastrointestinal, and cancer medicine 54,000 employees $17.4 billion (U.S.) Efficiency in drug development	Ericsson Telecommuni-cations Leading system producer 85,000 employees $21 billion (U.S.) Moving upward in value proposition	SIF White-collar union 300,000 members Necessity of new value proposition to the members	AstraZeneca Pharmaceuticals company Leader in cardiovascular, gastrointestinal, and cancer medicine 54,000 employees $17.4 billion (U.S.) Major challenge is to find efficiency in drug development	Telia Telecommuni-cations Leading national operator 17,000 employees $5.7 billion (U.S.) Struggling with finding a position where value can be added	Large oil and petroleum company 54,423 employees $21 billion (U.S.)
Key issue/ Primary focus/ Research question	Experimentation and development of a research methodology that can be employed as a collaborative research method	Identifying and understanding the major organization issues and challenges Developing action and supporting change initiatives	Studying the change process Improving efficiency in research and development	Enhancing knowledge transfer and sharing between clinical trial projects	Integration of customers and users in experimental new service development	How to maintain and reinforce a creative capacity in drug discovery and development	Improving project management in research and development	Understanding the changing needs and expectations of union members	Understanding the nature of leader development and the consequences of collaborative approaches	Understanding how internal management consultants can be leveraged in the organizational learning to improve performance	Improvement of performance management systems

(Continued)

Table IV.1   Continued

	Digital Media Newspaper (Chapter 8)	Pharmacy Operation Division of Kaiser Permanente (Chapter 9)	Car Manufacturing (Chapter 10)	Pharmaceuticals (Chapter 11)	Telecommunications (Chapter 12)	Pharmaceuticals (Chapter 13)	Telecommunications Manufacturing (Chapter 14)	White-Collar Union Organization (Chapter 15)	Pharmaceuticals (Chapter 16)	Business Consulting (Chapter 17)	Oil and Petroleum (Chapter 18)
The collaborative research orientation	Hybrid of intervention research, developmental action inquiry, and table tennis research	Hybrid of clinical inquiry/ research and intervention research	Hybrid of action research, action learning, and reflective inquiry	Hybrid of action research and appreciative inquiry	Participative inquiry with experimental design	Action research	Hybrid of action research with insider/ outsider research teams and action learning	Hybrid of participative inquiry and action research	Hybrid of action science, appreciative inquiry, and action research	Action research	Action research
Outcomes A. Knowledge creation B. Organizational/ Managerial action	Input into the implementation of change initiatives The development of new service programs, new incentive program, and quality of service	Improved dialogue across boundaries Input into the implementation of change initiatives Reflection on and modification of operation and support systems Input into the restructuring of the division	A reflective methodology on change and managerial work The introduction of new mechanisms for change	Learning about knowledge sharing in project team and the multiple roles for knowledge facilitators Intervention methodology and the introduction of new role for knowledge facilitation	Better understanding of how users and customers can be integrated into the development of new services Increased awareness and improved discussions on the need for user involvement	Knowledge about organizational creativity Increased awareness of and improved discussions on the conception of organizational creativity	New insights into the management and use of temporary task forces Redesign of the project management organization	Collaborative research can be used as vehicle in service development Improving dialogue as a process of change Improving dialogue approach in interaction with members	Understanding the use of collaborative approaches in leader development A new approach for leader development at the company	Enhanced understanding of the role of the internal management consultancies and of knowledge diffusion across organizational units A new learning mechanism for the consultancy firm	A new insight into the role of performance management systems in the transformation of organizations Created self-designing performance management systems

Participating Organizations, Collaborative Research, and the Research Focuses

The companies reported on in this volume cover illustrations of collaborative reseach projects in nine different industries: newspaper, health care, auto manufacturing, pharmaceuticals, telecommunications, telecommunications manufacturing, oil and petroleum, business consulting, and white-collar union organization. As can be seen in Table IV.1, the collaborative research projects focused on addressing a large variety of issues and topics: studying the change process, improving efficiency in research and development (R&D), enhancing knowledge transfer and sharing between clinical trial projects, integrating customers and users in experimental new service development, maintaining and reinforcing a creative capacity in drug discovery and development, improving project management in R&D, understanding the changing needs and expectations of union members, understanding the nature of leader development and the consequences of collaborative approaches, understanding how internal management consultants can be leveraged in the organizational learning to improve performance, and improving performance management systems.

The academy-industry collaborative research efforts described in the volume illustrate that the leaders of the efforts and the processes that they chose to follow led to the decisions to focus on a wide range of topics based on their understanding of the challenges that they were facing or were likely to face. Clear choices were made about the "red and hot" topics and the refined research questions that evolved (Adler & Shani, 2000). As we reflected on the cases, it became evident that in the context of collaborative research, one can find the entire gamut of organizational and management research topics.

The Various Collaborative Research Orientations

Chapter 5 presented and briefly discussed eight different collaborative research orientations as alternative roadmaps for action that were developed during the past decade. The argument was made that, although there are some shared trajectories and elements among these orientations, each one seems to have some distinct features. An unexpected finding of this project is the discovery that most of the collaborative research projects illustrated in this volume seem to have used a hybrid of collaborative research orientations. A careful review of Table IV.1 reveals that 4 of the 11 illustrations used one "pure" collaborative research orientation (e.g., action research in a large oil and petroleum company [Chapter 18], participative inquiry with experimental design in a telecommunications company [Chapter 12]). Of the 11 reported illustrations, 7 used a hybrid of two or more collaborative research orientations (e.g., hybrid of action research, action science, and reflective inquiry in a car manufacturing company [Chapter 10], hybrid of clinical inquiry/research and intervention research in a health care provider [Chapter 9]).

The collaborative research cases described in this volume illustrate that the leaders of the efforts adopted collaborative research orientations as they saw fit based on their understanding of the challenges that they were facing or were likely to face, the existing culture and practices, and the input provided by the insider/outsider expertise. Clear choices were made, either at the conscious or unconscious level, about the specific collaborative orientation to follow. As we reflected on the cases, it became evident that in the context of collaborative research, variations do exist, and exploring the various options available and their degrees of fit to the issues at hand and the organizations is likely to serve the efforts well.

Collaborative Research Lenses and Mechanisms

Chapters 6 through 9 attempted to capture some of the distinct mechanisms that drive (or serve as the engine of) collaborative research. Of the 11 illustrations, 9 were an integral part of the collaborative research program that was based on partnerships between two universities and four companies. The collaborative research projects were a critical component in the development of the executive Ph.D. candidates (Chapters 4 and 6). All 11 illustrations used insider/outsider research teams to lead and guide the projects. In 10 of the projects, the members of the teams, who were the insiders, played a critical role The complexity of the role duality in which they found themselves was articulated in Chapter 7. As can be seen in the various projects, managing the dual-role complexity requires the creation of supportive mechanisms.

Chapters 8 and 9 focused on capturing the essence of two such mechanisms: jam session and structural learning mechanisms. At the most basic level, the jam session is viewed as a methodology aimed at data collection and joint data analysis and an arena for dialogue by individuals who have shared concerns and interests. The structural learning mechanism is described as an institutionalized structure and procedural arrangements that get created for the purpose of systematically addressing organizational/research issues (Bushe & Shani, 1991; Shani & Docherty, 2003). Both are viewed as formalized institutionalized results of active decisions by management regarding the company's position as well as current and future challenges.

The cases described in the volume illustrate that the leaders of the efforts developed structural learning mechanisms as they saw fit based on their understanding of the challenges they were likely to face, the existing culture and practices, the firm dynamics, and the insider/outsider degree of comfort with the specific design choice. As we reflected on the cases, it became evident that in the context of collaborative research, variations of structural learning mechanisms are created. Furthermore, they are used and can be used for very different purposes. Yet specific design choices are available and must be explored prior to establishing the specific configuration of the structural learning mechanism (Shani & Docherty, 2003).

Collaborative Research and Outcomes

The 11 collaborative research projects resulted in outcomes that were relevant to both practice and theory. On the practical side, they influenced or triggered actions within the firms. For example, the insights that were generated as a result of the collaborative research conducted via the structural learning mechanism at Kaiser Permanente's Pharmacy Operation division have continuously provided input into the implementation of various change initiatives, the development of new service programs, the development of new incentive programs, the quality of service provided, the response to changing customer needs, and the restructuring of the division (Chapter 9). At Telia, the collaborative research project resulted in a better understanding of how users and customers can be integrated into the development of new telecommunications services, increasing awareness and improving discussions on the need for user involvement (Chapter 17). At Volvo, the collaborative research project provided new mechanisms for change implementation (Chapter 10).

Table IV.1 provides a synopsis of some of the new knowledge that was created as a result of the collaborative research projects. Just like the actionable knowledge creation, many new insights into some of the issues that were investigated were captured in the chapters. For example, in the telecommunications case at Ericsson, new theoretical insights in the management and use of temporary task forces were created (Chapter 14). In the pharmaceuticals case at AstraZeneca, new theoretical knowledge about organizational creativity was created (Chapter 13). The collaborative research project of the white-collar union organization, SIF, resulted in new theoretical insights about the use of dialogue as a process of change in improving and facilitating service development (Chapter 15).

The 11 collaborative research efforts described in the volume illustrate that all resulted in the creation of knowledge of relevance to management practice and new theoretical knowledge of relevance to the scientific community. Regardless of the choices that were made about the specific collaborative orientations or hybrids of orientations, the choices about the specific configurations of the structural learning mechanisms to support the effort, and the choices about the configurations and composition of the insider/outsider research teams, the reported outcomes demonstrated that the efforts both yielded the advancement of theory and influenced managerial decision making and practice. The complexity of managing collaborative research that yields the results described is continuously examined in the literature. The next section identifies some of the main criticisms and attempts to address them in the context of the findings reported in the book.

Collaborative Research: A Critical Dialogue

This book was aimed at advancing and supporting collaborative research in organizations. Collaborative research was defined in Chapter 5 as an *emergent and systematic inquiry process, embedded in a true partnership between researchers and members of a living system for the purpose of generating actionable scientific knowledge.* Although various forms of collaborative research approaches have been used for a significant period of time (see Chapter 5), there are researchers who view collaborative research as marginal and not a legitimate form of management research. A review of the literature reveals that collaborative research has been criticized from a variety of perspectives. This criticism can be separated into four clusters. In this section, we identify each cluster and attempt to address the key issues that were raised.

The Epistemological Critique

The first form of criticism can be referred to as an *epistemological critique* of collaborative research (Babüroglo & Ravn, 1992; Griseri, 2002; McNiff, 2000; Pålshaugen, 2001). This body of text raises the issue of how knowledge is produced and how it is gaining its distinguishing mark as knowledge rather than being just information or opinions. In brief, it addresses how claims are qualified as knowledge. This perspective on knowledge production is basically formulated from two different perspectives. On the one hand, protagonists of positivist research argue that collaborative research efforts fail to address and respond to issues of objectivity—a favored detached position of the researcher—and value neutral observations. In a positivist research ideal, collaborative research efforts are simply to ingrain with practical interests and concerns to fully qualify as scientifically based knowledge. On the other hand, the nonpositivist critique raises the issue of epistemology, but on different foundations. For nonpositivist or postpositivist researchers, collaborative research efforts do not primarily break with positivist doctrines—which, in fact, these critics celebrate rather than denounce—but instead focus too much on methodological issues at the expense of theoretical development (Kilduff & Kelemen, 2001). For nonpositivist and postpositivist researchers, it is theory that makes science durable; therefore, collaborative researchers should pay more attention to theory rather than enable practical effects in organizations. Thus, in the epistemological critique of collaborative research, positivists, nonpositivists, and postpositivists join hands in terms of depicting collaborative research as a research approach that fails to fully adhere to what is regarded as academic standards and good scholarship (Lincoln, 2001).

The Political Critique

The second body of criticism can be grouped under the cluster of a *political critique* of collaborative research. This critique does not primarily concern itself with what is and is not legitimate knowledge because, after all, what is regarded as knowledge and nonknowledge is contingent, situational, and context dependent. Instead, the political critique of collaborative research focuses on the role of the researcher per se. For proponents of a political view of research, the academic research needs to maintain a detached position vis-à-vis the object of study. In a liberal democratic society, the academic researcher needs to safeguard a detached and credible position in relation to what is being studied. Thus, an academic researcher should not be sponsored by employees or employers. The political critique of action research has been especially eloquently formulated by protagonists of the critical management studies program (see, e.g., Fournier & Grey, 2000; Grey, 2001) that clearly assigns the academic researcher as an independent agent in the social fabric. For example, Jones (2000) writes, "Management studies more generally involves a range of practices by which academic and management knowledge are distinguished. Within this range, practices of Critical Management Studies (CMS) involve distinctive anxieties about collaboration" (p. 161).

The Ethical Critique

The third type of criticism addresses a similar topic to the political critique, but from a slightly different angle that can be clustered under the heading of *ethical critique* of collaborative research. This critique advances the argument that collaborative research does not primarily discuss the qualifications of knowledge or the role of the researcher per se but rather discusses the implications from research intervention as such (Heron & Reason, 2001). Collaborative research often praises itself for enabling organizational changes and actionable knowledge. What collaborative researchers regard as a major contribution is exactly what proponents of the ethical critique cluster view as problematic. Instead of assuming that the interventions are good, productive, or useful for the organization, it is claimed that such interventions unfreeze the organization without the collaborative researcher's willingness to be fully accountable for such consequences. The ethical critique emphasizes that when researchers undertake organizational interventions, it is vital that they are able to monitor and handle the process carefully. There is a problem of ethics because not all collaborative research efforts are designed or intended to control all of the effects in the interventions—their emergent processes and consequences.

The Efficiency Critique

Finally, the fourth body of criticism is aimed at discussing the efficiency of collaborative research. The *efficiency critique* of collaborative research is the most pragmatic of the four critique clusters. It focuses, as the name implies, on the costs and efforts involved in conducting organization and management studies. Drawing on a division of labor axiom, collaborative research is regarded as a fairly costly and cumbersome form of empirical research. It is much easier and less costly for researchers to stick to one of their roles rather than trying to wear two hats at the same time or trying to serve as the bridge between the academy and industry. At the most basic level, to collaborate with organization members with limited insights into organization and management theory, and to make practicing managers joint researchers whose input is an important part of the research process, is not the most effective way in which to organize empirical work.

Toward a Dialogue: Initial Reply to the Four Sets of Critiques

The four different critique clusters of collaborative research address various ontological, epistemological, ethical, and methodological issues and concerns that are of great relevance for all types of research. Regarding collaborative research, we believe that the four sets of issues raise important questions that collaborative researchers need to consider and, hopefully, be capable of answering. The epistemological critique formulates ideas on what is and is not legitimate knowledge. Legitimate knowledge is an outcome from negotiations among various social actors who are dependent on prior beliefs and ideologies regarding knowledge. A more pluralistic view of knowledge than that pursued by hardcore positivists does at least not disqualify collaborative research methods from being a legitimate approach to organization and management studies. As suggested in Chapter 1, management theory has, from the outset, been entangled with practical concerns and objectives. In that respect, collaborative research approaches contribute to an old tradition in the field. In summary, we believe that the epistemological critique is based on a rather historical and limited conception of what knowledge is. This does not imply that the critique is irrelevant, but we do not think that such criticism makes collaborative research less useful.

The second perspective, the political critique, also raises several important questions in terms of the politics of knowledge and the role of the researcher in society. Still, we think that there is a tendency in this debate to overrate the possibilities for a detached apolitical role of the researcher. Most research funding is based on political decisions and favored agendas, and researchers have to relate to the politics of knowledge production in society. There is a tendency to turn a complex social reality into a dual structure where, on the one hand, free liberal researchers are capable of examining social processes detached from its practical matters and, on the other, collaborative researchers are paid by companies to pursue their goals by other means. In our experience, academic freedom has never been put into question by management of the companies with whom we have collaborated. Instead, management has been very eager for researchers to maintain their role as individuals who could contribute with reflexive practices in the organizations. In addition, we believe that the political critique overrates the amount of collaborative research in the field. It is not our attempt, as protagonists of collaborative research, to argue that all organization and management research should be organized in a collaborative manner. A large part of the management research is perhaps best organized as it is currently, that is, by public funding. But in an increasingly pluralistic society (Hardy & Clegg, 1997; Spender, 1998; Van Maanen, 2000), we suggest that there may be some space left for more collaborative research efforts because managerial problems may benefit from such a research approach. Thus, we do not want to colonialize the entire field (Van Maanen, 2000); rather, we argue for the legitimacy of collaborative research as an alternative inquiry orientation that yields much-needed outcomes not generated by other research orientations.

The ethical criticism of collaborative research addresses the effects of interventions in organizations. We believe that it is an important issue to keep in mind when participating in any kind of inquiry in and with living social systems. Yet we think that this criticism overestimates the degree of order and stability in organizations. In our experience, organizations are not safe and calm havens where organizational members are sheltered from day-to-day turmoil (see, e.g., Huy, 2002). Instead, organizations are, as suggested by Weick (1979), characterized by a continuous process of organizing complex, confusing, and multifaceted events and occurrences into a coherent and manageable whole (see also Tsoukas & Chia, 2002). Everyday life in organizations is not characterized by lack of ambiguity and puzzles; on the contrary, there is a need for continuous reflection on what is going on in the organizations. Argyris (1973) argues that, in the context of helping relationships, "to intervene is to come in between for the purpose of accomplishing a goal. ... It is an intentional effort to change the status quo of a living system" (p. 21). Thus, any act of discovery, by its very nature, can be viewed as an intervention into a living system. In the context of collaborative research, organizational members involved in the process are likely to have more control and say about the acceptable degree of intervention. In most other research orientations, the participants have no control or influence on the discovery process. Having the insider/outsider research team configuration composed of organizational members and outsiders to guide the inquiry effort may be intimidating for some, but it provides an additional safeguard around the depth of the intervention. Taken together, the ethical consequences of collaborative research need to be examined and addressed continuously. Yet it is an important empirical question to address in future research about the possible negative consequences of research in general and of collaborative research in particular.

Finally, the efficiency critique emphasizes that collaborative research is a cumbersome endeavor. The bottom line is whether organization and management researchers should conduct research that is relatively easy to control and manage or whether research should aim to address problems that are of great practical interest (see Weick, 1999). The issue that needs to be addressed is by what standards we evaluate and judge scientific work. The increased emphasis on performance indicators, when evaluating academic effectiveness, has been addressed by numerous writers (see, e.g., Czarniawska & Genell, 2002). For some, this represents a step toward increased professionalization of the field; for others, it is a troublesome development because it will effectively block the incentives for experimentation and novel thinking. Although debate about the issue is important, it is beyond the scope of this final part of the volume. Nevertheless, in the context of collaborative research (and this book), we would argue that academic performance and good scholarship imply publishing research and continuously striving to develop new ways of working. Thus, the advancement of management practice and theoretical development requires a balance between the two approaches.

Collaborative research needs to be continuously debated and related to other approaches to organizational and management inquiry. Thus, various forms of criticism and dialogue about the creation of new and actionable knowledge will serve as an ongoing catalyst for enabling the development of new ways of thinking that may further enhance collaborative work. This volume can be viewed as one contribution to the debate and as an invitation for continuous dialogue about alternative approaches for the advancement of organizational and management practice and science. The next stage in our dialogue is to identify some directions for future research.

Directions for Collaborative Research and Management Practice

The contributors to this book provided insights into how collaborative research approaches can contribute to change, learning, and actions in organizations as well as to theoretical developments. From the framing of the challenge in Part I and the lenses, mechanisms, and cases presented and discussed in Parts II and III, some important directions for future collaborative research and management practice emerged. These future directions can be separated into four paths that we explore in this final section.

Elaborate and Boundary-Spanning R&D on Management

The first path is to pursue *R&D on management* as a true collaborative endeavor with the purpose of meeting the boundary-spanning nature of the challenges that both management practice and management research face. Hatchuel and Glise (Chapter 1) argued that R&D on management needs to become a functional process in firms—one that is just as important and as elaborate as R&D on the technologies on which firms base their business. In addition, the authors suggested that future performance and competitiveness will be dependent on firms' capacity to handle their R&D on management in a more elaborate way. Thus, they suggested collaborative partnerships with management researchers as a possible way in which to build this necessary competence and tradition. Starkey and Tempest (Chapter 2) argued that management research will be necessary to pursue a more relevant discourse to motivate its future existence and that this pursuit will be based on collaborative endeavors together with informed management practice. Despite these double opportunities and much repeated emphasis on management research to engage more closely with management practice, it is evident that collaborative research approaches do not have sufficient support from the various stakeholders. Stymne (Chapter 3) and Adler and Norrgren (Chapter 4) illustrated some of the specific challenges facing researchers and practitioners in the process of building the foundation for organizational learning and change. These challenges include organizational politics, incumbent beliefs and ideologies, and a gap between espoused theories and theories in use.

A sustainable continuous development and diffusion of collaborative research is dependent on research approaches anchored in empirical work. Such empirical work needs to show how the dual task and challenge of continuously developing theoretical and methodological rigor while also developing practical relevance not only is possible but also opens up new opportunities for various stakeholders. As Starkey and Tempest (Chapter 2) argued, a growing concern is that academic management research conducted at business schools will not be able to maintain its credibility on the basis of solely theoretical contributions. Starkey and Tempest claimed that a significant part of management research has little relevance for management practice, and this in turn may open a debate over whether it is useful to invest financial resources in one such paradigmatic endeavor. Collaborative research has the potential to contribute to managerial reflexivity and learning, to guide complex change initiatives, to renew management research, and to develop new theory. However, stakeholders first need to embrace the boundary-spanning nature of the possible answers to the current challenges and to allow for the necessary learning to pursue collaborative projects enabling these results.

The Development of
Collaborative Research Methodology

The second path is *extensive experimentation and offensive elaboration on collaborative research methodology*. The great opportunity for collaborative researchers is that academic research is based on a couple of hundred years of experience that may be useful when negotiating an adequate trade-off between what may be called academic rigor, on the one hand, and practical relevance, on the other. However, the opportunity exists for more elaborate and rigorous collaborative research approaches guiding and supporting the establishment of R&D on management as functional processes. This is likely to necessitate extensive work by experienced management researchers and leading managers while engaging other stakeholders in the development and experimentation with a new set of methodologies. To continue the collaborative effort and withhold the boundary-spanning engagement, the methodologies and research approach need to pursue the double-purposed road.

To make a difference, these new collaborative methodologies and research approaches will have to be offensive rather than defensive in character, not only compensating for the problems of being close to the organizations that are being studied but also leveraging that closeness in time, space, and (often) personnel to introduce new means of enhancing validity in management research. One dominant assumption—that research aimed at practical relevance will inevitably lead to lower academic (methodological and theoretical) quality of the research—is, among other things, based on the idea that no major theoretical or methodological innovations will follow from the new opportunities that may emerge when collaborative research is conducted. The findings in this volume demonstrated an opposing view. Collaborative research, if conducted well, has the potential of delivering not only valuable empirical results but also new theoretical developments and methodological approaches.

These methodological innovations will require extensive experimentation. Key actors representing various stakeholders need to invest significant effort into such experimental activities. When encountering established structures with new and innovative initiatives, it is easy to argue that reflection and action should be separated in time and space. Another way is to let management consultants serve as vehicles for transferring and transforming academic knowledge into relevant practical solutions for managerial practice and managers. However, such solutions will, at best, further widen the gap between academic research quality and practical relevance and will fail to facilitate the necessary development of these two desirable outcomes. Academic rigor in management research probably follows the prerequisites for the field and the nature of the possible empirical evidence. Hence, management research needs to leverage the emerging opportunities by introducing new methodologies that will result in the holistic capturing of the phenomena under study—as other sciences have done following technological and other developments in laboratories. Relevance for managerial practice and managers probably must follow the actual emerging challenges that they face. Carrying out such tasks requires reflexivity, identifying relevant patterns in complexity, capturing significant opportunities in uncertainty, and introducing strategies, structures, and processes based on various basic assumptions.

Integrating the idea that R&D in management should be organized and treated like any other R&D (Chapter 1) with the notions that co-production of knowledge with the end user and the need for alignment of research, teaching, and practical roles (Chapter 2) and with the view that substantial experimentation on research approaches may create significant methodological renewal (Chapters 3 and 4) calls for an epistemological pluralism. The epistemological pluralism orientation requires a reexamination of some basic assumptions of scientific validity, and this is likely to generate the continuous development of different design alternatives in the formation of management research endeavors. This pluralism on epistemology and methodology, while requiring major advancements in our thinking and experimentation, is likely to enhance actual validity in research rather than limit discussions to different ideologies.

Practice-Driven Innovation and Theoretical Development

The third path is to invite *practice and practitioners to drive innovation in management science and theoretical development*. Despite significant growth in volume and the strong emphasis in the academy on theoretical and methodological rigor, management research as a scientific discipline has not been capable of delivering very many innovations of relevance for management practice. Hatchuel and Glise (Chapter 1) suggested that management practice to date has encountered only three major structural changes, all driven by major changes in the demand for managerial practice and for innovative and reflexive managers. The current ideal of academic research and good scholarship, and the preferences for certain research processes, may serve as an explanation for why most management research efforts produce limited innovative research activities. Thus, collaborative research approaches, when mastering the parallel challenge of scientific rigor and practical relevance (Hodgkinson, Herriot, & Anderson, 2001), may support an alternative view challenging dominant theoretical frameworks. We believe that one emerging opportunity for management research is to recognize the co-evolutionary relationship between scientific rigor and practical relevance. The development of those vital aspects of the research process is likely to create an opening for breakthrough innovations.

Institutionalization of Platforms and Incentives

The fourth path is to *institutionalize necessary platforms and incentives for collaborative research efforts*. Starkey and Tempest (Chapter 2) argued that collaborations between academic researchers and practitioners in the field of management are rare and that in the ones that do exist, academic researchers hold a top-down principal investigator model of research. According to the authors, management researchers tend to adhere to Mode 1 of pure academic research as a source of knowledge creation and as a governing ideal. Adler and Norrgren (Chapter 4) told the story of how prerequisites and incentives for collaborative research at an operational level differ significantly from the espoused ideals and future directions from the various stakeholders.

For researchers to truly pursue collaborative research efforts, the significant time and energy such efforts take must be appreciated by the scientific community and valued from a career perspective. Hence, universities need to fully appreciate contributions to what is called the third assignment-stakeholder interaction, committees need to appreciate the rigor in collaborative methodologies both in defenses of Ph.D. theses and conference presentations and in recruitment of associate and full professors, leading scientific journals must perceive collaborative research approaches as equal to other research approaches, and leading scholars need to pursue collaborative research and not simply prescribe such research as interesting. For practitioners to truly pursue collaborative research endeavors, they need to perceive the significant impact that such endeavors may have in building a long-term and in-house capacity for continuous reflexivity on complex managerial challenges. Hence, boards and top management need to value the long-term investment, key opinion leaders need to appreciate the collaborative and reflexive rational guiding actions and decisions, and collaborative approaches need to be understood as important vehicles for organizational change.

In addition to tradition and incentives, the various stakeholder organizations lack the necessary support systems as administrative systems that support programs spanning over many disciplinary and regional boundaries, employing researchers from various departments, schools, and universities that are temporary and changing in size and content and that are governed by the various stakeholders. Given the proposed and announced importance, the discourse needs to be turned into actual experiments that will help to revisit the conceptions of academic rigor and practical relevance. Industrial R&D practices had to challenge implicit assumptions about linearity and interdependencies to meet new demands and capture new market opportunities. In a similar manner, it would be useful for collaborative management researchers to rethink their assumptions. As Grey (2001) shows, an iterative dialogue around problem construction and solution implementation is not necessarily linear. For Leydesdorff and Etzkowitz (1997), the roles of the various sectors are not clear. This means that pursuing either the path of continued increased scientific rigor or the path of continued increased relevance is not acceptable. Instead, it is necessary for management research to simultaneously meet those two demands and to continuously reflect on, develop, and renew the necessary methodologies that add to the theoretical discourse and inform managers' decisions and actions.

Conclusion

Most books end with a concluding chapter that summarizes the findings presented in the book. At some level, achieving such an objective is not possible. The 11 collaborative research studies that were carried out in various companies and geographical locations provide the essence of the volume and, as we have seen, cover an enormous amount of information. Parts I and II attempted to frame the need and identify the current orientations, lenses, and mechanisms to carry out collaborative research. This final part (Part IV) has attempted to synthesize some of the information across the current set of challenges, collaborative research orientations, reported empirical cases, and the ongoing debate in the scientific literature.

In the first area that was addressed in this final part, we focused on four comparative themes that emerged out of the empirical studies: the participating organizations, collaborative research, and the specific research focuses; the various collaborative research orientations used; the specific collaborative research lenses and mechanisms used; and the collaborative research outcomes (Table IV.1). In the second section of this final part, we focused on identifying and clustering the critiques that can be found in the literature about collaborative research, and we attempted to address each of them. The critiques were clustered under the following headings: epistemological, political, ethical, and efficiency. In the third section of this final part, we attempted to identify future research directions. Four specific paths were advanced and briefly discussed: elaborate and boundary-spanning R&D on management, development of collaborative research methodology, practice-driven innovation and theoretical development, and institutionalization of platforms and incentives.

Collaborative research is aimed at generating new insights that can simultaneously influence both action and the creation of new theoretical development. As we have seen in this volume, collaborative research is not viewed as a substitute for all other research approaches. Rather, it is viewed as a way in which to possibly leverage and sustain the role for management research and, at the same time, increase our theoretical development of complex organizational and management issues. Furthermore, as we have seen, there is no one best way in which to conduct collaborative research. Rather, it is viewed as a framework of inquiry that allows for collaborative exploration on both the process and the content in the research endeavors. In that sense, it may create an opportunity for capturing and managing the continuous emerging nature of the workplace dynamics. However, all collaborative research approaches are time-consuming and energy-demanding, and there are no shortcuts in the process. Critical to the process is the need to examine the various collaborative management orientations, lenses, and mechanisms and to make clear choices about the inquiry path at the front end of the research process. Their true partnership ideal and emergent inquiry process make collaborative management orientations complex and not easy to organize, lead, or manage. Yet, as we have seen, collaborative research might be the way in which to bridge the emerging gap of management research toward the development of sustainable learning, action, and organizational success.

References

Adler, N., & Shani, A. B. (Rami). (2000). In search of an alternative framework for the creation of actionable knowledge: Table-tennis research at Ericsson. In W. Pasmore & R. Woodman (Eds.), *Research in organization change and development* (Vol. 13, pp. 43–79). Greenwich, CT: JAI.

Argyris, C. (1973). *Intervention theory and method*. Reading, MA: Addison-Wesley.

Babüroglo, O. N., & Ravn, I. (1992). Normative action research. *Organization Studies, 13,* 19–34.

Bushe, G. R., & Shani, A. B. (Rami). (1991). *Parallel learning structures: Increasing innovations in bureaucracies*. Reading, MA: Addison-Wesley.

Czarniawska, B., & Genell, K. (2002). Gone shopping? Universities on their way to the market. *Scandinavian Journal of Management, 18,* 455–475.

Fournier, V., & Grey, C., (2000). At the critical moment: Conditions and prospects for critical management studies. *Human Relations, 53,* 7–32.

Grey, C. (2001). Re-imaging relevance: A response to Starkey and Madan. *British Journal of Management, 12,* 27–32. (Special issue)

Griseri, P. (2002). *Management knowledge: A critical view*. Houndmills, UK: Palgrave.

Hardy, C., & Clegg, S. R. (1997). Relativity without relativism: Reflexivity in post-paradigm organization studies. *British Journal of Management, 8,* 5–17. (Special issue)

Heron, J., & Reason, P. (2001). The practice of co-operative inquiry: Research "with" rather than "on" people. In P. Reason & H. Bradbury (Eds.), *Handbook of action research: Participative inquiry and practice* (pp. 179–188). London: Sage.

Hodgkinson, G. P., Herriot, P., & Anderson, N. (2001). Re-aligning the stakeholders in management research: Lessons from industrial, work, and organizational psychology. *British Journal of Management, 12,* 49–54. (Special issue)

Huy, Q. N. (2002). Emotional balancing of organizational continuity and radical change: The contribution of middle managers. *Administrative Science Quarterly, 47,* 31–69.

Jones, D. (2000). Knowledge workers "R" Us: Academics, practitioners, and "specific intellectuals." In C. Pritchard, R. Hull, M. Chumer, & H. Willmott (Eds.), *Managing knowledge: Critical investigations of work and learning*. New York: St. Martin's.

Kilduff, M., & Kelemen, M. (2001). The consolation of organisation theory. *British Journal of Management, 12,* 55–59. (Special issue)

Leydesdorff, L., & Etzkowitz, H. (1997). A triple helix of university-industry-government relations. In H. Etzkowitz & L. Leydesdorff (Eds.), *Universities and the global knowledge economy: A triple helix of university-industry-government relations* (pp. 155–162). London: Pinter.

Lincoln, Y. S. (2001). Engaging sympathies: Relationships between action research and social constructivism. In P. Reason & H. Bradbury (Eds.), *Handbook of action research* (pp. 124–132). London: Sage.

McNiff, J. (2000). *Action research in organisations.* London: Routledge.

Pålshaugen, Ø. (2001). The use of words: Improving enterprises by improving their conversations. In P. Reason & H. Bradbury (Eds.), *Handbook of action research: Participative inquiry and practice* (pp. 209–218). London: Sage.

Shani, A. B. (Rami), & Docherty, P. (2003). *Learning by design: Building sustainable organisations.* London: Blackwell.

Spender, J-C. (1998). Pluralist epistemology and the knowledge-based theory of the firm. *Organisation, 5*(2), 233–256.

Tsoukas, H., & Chia, R. (2002). On organizational becoming: Rethinking organization change. *Organization Science, 13,* 567–582.

Van Maanen, J. (2000). Fear and loathing in organization studies. In P. J. Frost, A. Y. Lewin, & R. L. Daft (Eds.), *Talking about organisation science: Debates and dialogues from Crossroads* (pp. 93–103). London: Sage.

Weick, K. E. (1979). *The social psychology of organizing.* New York: McGraw-Hill.

Weick, K. E. (1999). That's moving: Theories that matter. *Journal of Management Inquiry, 8,* 134–142.

Index

About the Editors

Niclas Adler, Ph.D., is Associate Professor at the Stockholm School of Economics and is Director of the FENIX program in Sweden. He is a former executive director of the Stockholm School of Entrepreneurship and is a board member for seven technology-based and venture capital companies. His most recent work has focused on business creation and renewal in established structures, alternative approaches to organizing complex product development, and collaborative research methodologies in the pursuit of actionable knowledge creation.

A. B. (Rami) Shani, Ph.D., is Professor of Organizational Behavior and Change at California Polytechnic State University and is Visiting Research Professor at the FENIX program in Sweden. His research interests include organization design and change, action research methodologies in the pursuit of actionable knowledge creation, creating sustainable work systems, and learning organizations. He is the co-author of *Behavior in Organizations; Parallel Learning Structures: Creating Innovations in Bureaucracies; Creating Sustainable Work Systems: Emerging Perspectives and Practice;* and *Learning by Design: Building Sustainable Organizations.* He has a Ph.D. in organizational behavior.

Alexander Styhre, Ph.D., is Associate Professor in the Department of Project Management at Chalmers University of Technology and is Research Leader at the FENIX program in Sweden. His research interest is focused on knowledge-intensive organizations and strategic human resource management practices.

About the Contributors

In this volume, our aim is to shed light on an emerging alternative in the creation of new management landscape. Based on a 5-year collaboration by 28 researchers and practitioners from various academic and industrial backgrounds, we have explored a variety of collaborative management research approaches in theory and practice of conducting inquiry. Our goal was to illuminate the existing possibilities and emerging alternatives for inquiry—toward the creation of new management landscapes. We invited 8 colleagues who did not take part in the projects to join us in our reflection and learning. Each of these colleagues is a recognized leader either as an executive or as a scholar. The following author biographies are in alphabetical order:

Lena Berg, M.Sc., is Project Director for AstraZeneca in Sweden. She has been working in the pharmaceuticals industry for more than 20 years and has broad experience in managing clinical projects at various levels, from the early phases of clinical development to the submission of file to the health authorities. She has a master of science in pharmacy.

Hans Björkman, M.Sc., is an executive Ph.D. candidate at the FENIX program in Sweden and is Service Developer at SIF, the Swedish trade union for white-collar workers in industry. His research deals with the development of collaborative scientific approaches for service development that are based on members' interactions. He has a master of science in business and public law.

Sofia Börjesson, Ph.D., is Assistant Professor in the Department of Project Management and is Research Leader at the FENIX program in Sweden. Her research is focused on organizational knowledge and design for continuous change, especially in emerging markets. She also focuses on the development of alternative research designs and methodologies.

Albert David, Ph.D., is Professor of Management and Organization Theory at Evry-Val d'Essonne University and Ecole des Mines de Paris. His research is focused on the steering of change processes within organizations and the organizational role of management techniques. His recent collaborative research projects deal with the evolution of e-organizations and with the management of innovation in biogenetic research programs. He also has written several articles on epistemology and methodologies in collaborative management research.

Mikael Dohlsten, M.D., Ph.D., is Global Vice President and Head of Cardiovascular and Gastrointestinal Discovery at AstraZeneca in Sweden and is Adjunct Professor in Cell and Molecular Biology at Lund University. He has spent nearly 15 years in the pharmaceutical industry and has held various research and development management positions, including head of preclinical research at Pharmacia & Upjohn and head of preclinical research and development at Astra Draco, both in Lund. He is also the author of some 150 international scientific articles and book chapters.

Mats Engwall, Ph.D., is Associate Professor at the Stockholm School of Economics and is Research Leader at the FENIX program in Sweden. His research revolves around project management practices in industry and project organizing in a broad sense. He currently focuses on process dynamics and knowledge creation in product development as well as the logics and management of projectified organizations. He has a Ph.D. in industrial organization.

Tobias Fredberg, M.Sc., is a Ph.D. candidate at the FENIX program in Sweden. His research interest is directed toward strategy and design in the creation of media products on the Internet. He has a master of science in economics.

Björn Frössevi, M.Sc., is Vice President and Head of Business Development at Softronic. He has been working as a strategic consultant in international business development for the past 10 years. He has held various management positions, including head of business development and strategy at Consultus and head of business development at SSES (Stockholm School of Entrepreneurship). He is also a member of several academic and industry boards.

Hans Glise, M.D., Ph.D., is Senior Vice President and Head of Global Development at NovoNordisk A/S in Denmark and is Associate Professor of Surgery in Sahlgrenska Hospital at Göteborg University. He is also chairman of the FENIX program board in Sweden. He has held various research and development management positions in the pharmaceuticals industry, including vice president, head of gastrointestinal therapy area; vice president, clinical research and development; and director of gastrointestinal management and strategies at AstraZeneca. He also has extensive experience as chief of surgery. He is the author of some 100 international scientific articles and book chapters.

Horst Hart, Ph.D., is Associate Professor and Head of Executive Ph.D. Education at the FENIX program in Sweden. He is a former director of the research program on Work Organizations at the National Institute of Working Life in Sweden. His research interests include business development, knowledge management, and organizational renewal. He has a Ph.D. in sociology.

Armand Hatchuel, Ph.D., is Professor of Industrial Design and Management at Ecole des Mines de Paris and Deputy Director of CGS (the Center for Management Science) in France. He is also a visiting professor at the FENIX program in Sweden. His research has been in the area of the theory, history, and development of industrial models of management and design, focusing specifically on the new knowledge dynamics related to that long wave of change.

Anne Sigismund Huff, Ph.D., is Director of the Advanced Institute for Management (AIM), an initiative funded by the ESRC and EPSRC and visiting professor at London Business School. She received an M.A. in Sociology and a Ph.D. in Management from Northwestern University, and has been on the faculty at UCLA, the University of Illinois, and the University of Colorado. Her research interests focus on strategic change, both as a dynamic process of interaction among firms and as a cognitive process affected by the interaction of individuals over time. She is the strategy editor for the book series Foundations in Organization Science (Sage Publications) and serves on the editorial boards of the *Strategic Management Journal, the Journal of Management Studies,* the *British Journal of Management, Management Learning* and the electronic journal, *M@n@gement*. In 1998-1999 she was President of the Academy of Management, an international organization of over 12,000 scholars interested in management issues.

Sven F. Kylén, Ph.D., is Program Director of the Swedish Knowledge Foundation and Research Leader at the FENIX program in Sweden. He is the former director of the FENIX Executive Ph.D. Program. He has a background in the field of individual, group, organization development, and management education. His research interests include organizational development, interventions in groups, creativity, interaction routines, leadership development, and establishment of sustainable research environments. He has a Ph.D. in psychology.

David Knights, Ph.D., is Professor and Head of the School of Management at the University of Keele in Great Britain. He has published 21 books and more than 200 articles. His most recent books are *Management Lives: Power and Identity in Work Organisations* and *The Re-engineering Revolution? Critical Studies of Corporate Change*. He created a collaborative research program with the financial services sector in 1994 and continues to be involved in its management.

Peter R. Magnusson, M.Sc., M.B.A., is an executive Ph.D. candidate at the FENIX program in Sweden. Since 1990, he has worked with service innovation and development within the Telia group. His research deals with involvement of end users in the innovation process of mobile telephony services. He has a master of science in electrical engineering.

Jon Mikaelsson, M.Sc., is an executive Ph.D. candidate at the FENIX program in Sweden. He is a member of the management team of research and development and has been employed by Volvo Car Corporation since 1984. His thesis focuses especially on the development of managerial work, activities, and outcomes in product development organization. The research is built on experiences at Volvo, Ford Motor Company, and Ericsson.

Allan M. Mohrman, Jr., Ph.D., is Co-founder of the Center for Effective Organizations at the University of Southern California. His research interests include performance management, organizational design and change, and research methodology for theory and practice. He is the co-author of *Doing Research That Is Useful for Theory and Practice; Designing Performance Appraisal Systems; Large Scale Organizational Change;* and *Designing Team-Based Organizations: New Forms for Knowledge Work.* He has a Ph.D. in organizational behavior.

Susan A. Mohrman, Ph.D., is Senior Research Scientist at the Center for Effective Organizations at the University of Southern California and is Visiting Professor at the FENIX program in Sweden. She researches organizational design and effectiveness issues, knowledge and technology management, and useful research methodologies. She is the co-author of *Self-Designing Organizations; Doing Research That Is Useful for Theory and Practice; Designing Team-Based Organization;* and *Organizing for High Performance.* She has a Ph.D. in organizational behavior.

Kina Mulec, M.Sc., has been a research and project assistant in several projects at the FENIX program in Sweden. These projects have focused on organizational change strategies, stress prevention in Swedish organizations, and knowledge management. Her main interests focus on coaching and leadership development. She is currently involved in two research projects covering these areas at AstraZeneca in Sweden.

Flemming Norrgren, Ph.D., is Professor of Project Management at Chalmers University of Technology and is Associate Director of the FENIX program in Sweden. He has acted as research director for three large multidisciplinary programs since 1989. His ongoing research deals with leadership of research and development projects, content and effects of change strategies, and "experimental" learning in industry-university collaboration. He has a Ph.D. in psychology.

Per-Olof Nyquist, M.Sc., M.B.A., is Head of Ericsson University and Vice President of Ericsson. During his 18 years at Ericsson, he has held several line and managerial positions in software design of telecommunications systems, systems design and coordination, organizational development, strategic product management, and business management. Prior to forming and launching the global venture of Ericsson University, he was responsible for competence management and recruitment strategies for the Ericsson group.

Hans-Olov Olsson, M.Sc., is president and chief executive officer of Volvo Car Corporation. He has many years of experience in the automotive industry and has previously served as president of Volvo Cars Japan, Europe, and North America.

William A. Pasmore, Ph.D., is Partner at Mercer Delta Consulting, a firm that specializes in consulting to chief executive officers and senior teams on matters of organizational design and transformation. For many years, he served on the faculty of Case Western Reserve University, where he taught courses in organization development and engaged in a number of action research projects with companies. He is the author/editor of more than 15 books in the field, including (most recently) *Relationships That Enable Enterprise Change* (with R. Carucci) and *Research in Organization Change and Development* (Vol. 14 with R. Woodman).

Andrew M. Pettigrew, Ph.D., is Associate Dean Research and Professor of Strategy and Organisation at Warwick Business School, Warwick University. Between 1985 and 1995 he founded and directed the Centre for Corporate Strategy and Change. He has held previous academic positions at Yale University, London Business School, and Harvard Business School, where in the academic year 2001 he was a Visiting Professor.

He is a Fellow of both the Academy of Management and the British Academy of Management. He was the first Chairman of the British Academy of Management (1987-1990) and then President (1990-1993). In 1998 he was elected a Founding Academician of the Academy of the Social Sciences. In 2001 he was elected the Distinguished Scholar of the Academy of Management, the first European scholar to be so honored. His latest books include *The Handbook of Strategy and Management* (co-edited with Howard Thomas and Richard Whittington). London: Sage, and Pettigrew, A. M.., et al. (Eds.), (2003). *Innovative Organizations in International Perspective*, London: Sage.

Jonas Roth, Ph.D., is Knowledge Manager for AstraZeneca in Sweden and is Researcher at the FENIX program in Sweden. He has been working in pharmaceuticals research for more than 10 years, holding project management and functional management positions. More recently, he has been working and doing research on organizational change projects to enhance knowledge creation in the research and development organization of AstraZeneca.

Robert Sandberg, M.Sc., is an executive Ph.D. candidate at the FENIX program in Sweden. His research interest is primarily related to consulting services and customer solutions businesses, focusing on two main issues: knowledge management and organizational identity. He was previously marketing director of the corporate consulting unit Telia Promotor, where he now acts as a business consultant. He has a master of science in mechanical engineering.

Ken Starkey, Ph.D., is Professor of Management and Organizational Learning at Nottingham University, where he is Chair of the Strategy and IT Division. His research interests include strategy and learning, the social philosophy of management, careers and organization development, and management education. He is the former chair of the British Academy of Management Research Committee and is the author of a number of reports on the future of management research and management education.

Michael Stebbins, Ph.D., is Professor of Organization Design at California Polytechnic State University. His research interests include the use of information and communications technology, the design of product development processes, the development of sustainable work systems, and change management. He has a Ph.D. in business administration.

Bengt Stymne, Ph.D., is Professor of Organization Theory at the Stockholm School of Economics and is Research Director at the FENIX program in Sweden. He was a co-founder and managing director of SIAR (Swedish Institute for Administrative Research) and has been managing director of EFI (Economic Research Institute) at the Stockholm School of Economics. He is one of the founders of SSES (Stockholm School of Entrepreneurship). He has published books and articles on organization design and strategy, organizational values, industrial democracy, and information technology and management.

Mats Sundgren, M.Sc., is an executive Ph.D. candidate at the FENIX program in Sweden and is Scientific Adviser for AstraZeneca in Sweden. His research focuses on understanding aspects of organizational creativity in pharmaceuticals research and development. He has been working in the field of pharmaceuticals research for more than 16 years and has broad experience in various positions involving product development, patents, line management, and project management. He has a master of science in chemical engineering.

Charlotta Svensson, M.Sc., is an executive Ph.D. candidate at the FENIX program in Sweden and is a Department Head at Ericsson. Her research focuses on organizing development of complex product systems in multiproject environments. She has several years of experience as a project manager and project office manager at Ericsson. She is currently working in the area of organizational development and multiproject management. She has a master of science in industrial engineering and management.

Sue Tempest, Ph.D., is Lecturer in Strategic Management and Director of the Executive M.B.A. Program at Nottingham University Business School. Her research interests focus on organizational learning, management development in business schools, and strategy and new organizational forms.

Judy L. Valenzuela, Ph.D., is Pharmacy Services Director for Kaiser Permanente's Southern California Region. She has more than 25 years of experience in pharmacy management and is responsible for all outpatient and inpatient services for a patient population of more than 300,000 Kaiser Permanente members.

Andreas Werr, Ph.D., is Assistant Professor at the Stockholm School of Economics and is Research Leader at the FENIX program in Sweden. His main domain of research is the phenomenon of management consulting, which he has studied from a number of theoretical and empirical perspectives. His current research interests focus on the management of professional service firms, interorganizational knowledge transfer and creation, and the use and effects of management consultants in client organizations.

Jan Wickenberg, M.Sc., is an executive Ph.D. candidate at the FENIX program in Sweden and is Management Adviser for AstraZeneca in Sweden. He worked for 10 years as an information technology project manager before joining the FENIX program. His research interest is the informal side of organizational life, especially organizational politics. He has a master of science in computer science.

Cory Willson, M.B.A., is Lecturer at California Polytechnic State University. He lectures in the area of organizational behavior and change. The main domain of his research focuses on collaborative research methodologies and the development of partnerships within and between organizational boundaries.